The American Political Journal

The American Political Journal

An Introductory Reader

Edited by

Clifton McCleskey

1982 THE DORSEY PRESS
Homewood, Illinois   60430

Contents

PART FIVE
Political Processes and Public Policy

Regulatory Politics and Policies

PART SIX
State and Local Government

State Issues

Local Issues

Introduction

This collection of articles is inspired in large part by two important and related trends over the past quarter century of American life. One of those trends involves the way people get their information about the larger world, especially the world of government and politics. Over the past two decades or so, the importance of television as a source of news and information on public affairs has steadily increased, while popular reliance on newspapers and magazines has declined. In my judgment, the consequences have been unfortunate, affecting adversely the processes of opinion formation and lowering the level of citizen information about and understanding of politics.

But, as ill winds are reputed to do, this one has blown benefits to some. At least partly as a result of this shift toward television, American newspapers—at least those with aspirations to status as national publications, such as the *New York Times*, *The Wall Street Journal*, the *Washington Post*, and the *Christian Science Monitor*—began to offer readers longer and more interpretative articles. Freed by television and radio from the need to be first with the bare facts of the news, the better newspapers have taken advantage of the opportunity to provide more analysis and more depth in their coverage of public affairs. This trend shows quite clearly in what is written for editorial pages (especially in the so-called op-ed articles), but it can be seen as well in regular news stories. For those persons who are interested enough to partake of it, our national newspapers today provide very substantial fare.

Regrettably, not enough people take advantage of the opportunities thus provided; too many limit their intake of news and analysis to television and perhaps the local newspaper. This book is in part an attempt to demonstrate to college students the vital role that any of the national newspapers can play in keeping them informed about the political problems and issues of their times. I invite students to compare the meat offered in these articles with the froth provided by even the best television treatment of public affairs. Word for word, idea for idea, there simply is no comparison. Attentive readers of the *Times*, the *Post*, the *Monitor* or *The Wall Street Journal* are regularly exposed to indepth discussion of major issues in American life—defense policy, taxing and spending, discriminatory treatment, educational policy, international relations, and so on. Each of the national newspapers has its own style, coverage, approach to journalism, and political orientation. One may agree or disagree with what is printed in them, but their capacity to stimulate and to inform is beyond doubt.

Unfortunately, most of that material disappears from sight overnight, used to wrap the garbage or at best to feed the recycling process. Though the major newspapers are now well-indexed, and available on microfilm, retrieval of the information and analyses they provide is for most people highly inconvenient and sometimes impossible.

This anthology, then, is designed to broaden students' exposure to and keep in circulation longer some of the best of this political journalism. At the same time, I hope to enable those college students who have become primarily dependent on television for public affairs information to see just how valuable a first-rate newspaper can be as a source of ideas and information. The shortcomings of television's public affairs reporting have been exposed repeatedly; my hope here is to demonstrate concretely the superior quality and value of printed sources.

I also hope that this anthology will serve as a useful supplement to textbooks on American government and politics. Through a quarter century of teaching introductory courses in American politics, I have found that students often need help connecting the broad generalizations necessary in a textbook with specific events in the real, day-to-day world of government. A textbook's general discussion, say, of the role of the White House staff can be assimilated much more readily by students if they are at the same time reading an informed account of the way Edwin Meese, counselor to President Reagan, goes about his duties. It is equally important that students come to appreciate the way the scholarly findings and generalizations embodied in textbooks can help them to make sense of events reported in the daily newspaper. In short, I seek here to demonstrate the symbiotic relationship between political journalism (as reflected in this anthology) and scholarship (as reflected in textbooks and lectures).

What is being offered here are perspectives on American politics and public affairs, twice filtered—once by the writers and editors of *The Wall Street Journal* and again by the present compiler as he selects some items and discards others. The resulting collection is a mixture of editorials, interpretative news stories, and articles by scholars and informed observers. It does not pretend to provide a complete description or profile of American political life and issues; no single work, no single set of works, can do so. What it does offer are viewpoints, ideas, and information, chosen with an eye for intrinsic importance, the quality of argument and writing, and capacity to stimulate thought and discussion. In a good many instances, particularly where the nature of the topic and the alternatives offered by *The Wall Street Journal* permit, I have tried to present opposing points of view (for example, the articles by Arthur Schlesinger, Jr., and Irving Kristol that

open the section on American foreign policy). However, in a good many cases, an insistence on balancing the perspectives offered on particular issues would have resulted in limiting the range of issues covered and the loss of much rich material. Needless to say, I do not always agree with the thrust of particular articles; their inclusion here reflects not my endorsement of their contents but my judgment that they are informative and thought-provoking.

Though an anthology of this sort could be put together from any one of our national newspapers or from a combination of them, two considerations led to the decision to draw solely from *The Wall Street Journal.* One is the fact that the *Journal* is not designed to be a general coverage newspaper; it gives far less space to rapes and robberies, to entertainment and sports, to particular poitical events, than either the *Times* or the *Post.* Instead the *Journal* attempts primarily to reach that segment of the citizenry most interested in commerce and industry. Though its business news is often quite detailed, the *Journal's* public affairs reporting concentrates heavily on providing accurate overviews and general interpretations—precisely what college students

in introductory American government courses need.

My second reason for drawing articles solely from *The Wall Street Journal* is a far more practical one, I must confess. The publisher of this anthology, The Dorsey Press, is a wholly owned subsidiary of the same firm that publishes the *Journal* (Dow Jones, Inc.). Like any good parent, Dow Jones sometimes indulges its offspring, in this case by generous permissions to republish copyrighted material and by valuable assistance in the production process. As any editor of an anthology can testify, permissions to republish can be a monstrous headache, one I am happy to have avoided altogether.

The articles themselves have been organized along lines roughly paralleling those of leading textbooks in American government. Instructors should have little difficulty in adapting these selections to the organization of the textbook being used.

Should my belief in the pedagogical value of the *American Political Journal* be confirmed by classroom instructors, I anticipate that it will be updated at close intervals.

———

Reprinted by permission of the Chicago Tribune–New York News Syndicate, Inc.

We the People

1

The Immigrants

U.S. Policy on Whom To Admit Draws Fire As Outdated and Futile

Law Is a Patchwork, Border A Sieve; Refugee Influx Befuddles the Authorities

Treating Iceland Like India

By ROBERT E. TAYLOR

Staff Reporter of THE WALL STREET JOURNAL

CHULA VISTA, Calif.—By late afternoon, hundreds of them sit silently on an open slope at the Mexican border, watching. On the American side, U.S. Border Patrol agents watch back from a hill a quarter-mile off. "They'll come after dark," one says.

And they do. Two hours after sunset on this strip of border called the War Zone, the dark hills are alive with fleeting shapes as the unequal combat waged here nightly is replayed again.

The agents have vehicles and horses, infrared telescopes that see in the dark, helicopters, searchlights and electronic sensor alarms battle-proved in Vietnam. The Mexicans have persistence, numbers and the night. It is enough.

Agent Robert Hines, tipped off by a sensor alarm, collars 19 people sprinting through the zone for the U.S. border town of San Ysidro. But there are too many running shapes, too many alarms; as he hustles to respond to another alarm, three figures flit past behind him.

He never knows how many escape him, but he does know that many of those caught and dumped back across the border will try again and again until they succeed. "It's frustrating as hell," Mr. Hines says. A colleague adds: "It's like standing with your finger in a dike that has a million holes in it."

What happens nightly here is also a live demonstration of what now is widely viewed as the futility and failure of U.S. immigration policy. A Greek chorus of critics, including many in the immigration bureaucracy itself, denounces the laws governing it as cumbersome, arbitrary and hopelessly outdated; refugee policy in particular is viewed as a mess, with the administration wildly tacking this way and that.

Troubled Agency

The agency charged with enforcing the laws clearly is failing. The Immigration and Naturalization Service (which includes the Border Patrol) is undermanned, mismanaged and plagued by low morale and charges of brutality. While hundreds of thousands of aliens seeking legal entry here are stuck for years in its bureaucratic machinery, it can't stop hundreds of thousands more who just sneak in or overstay visas and melt into the resident population.

The agency, called INS, "is absolutely overwhelmed by the sheer number of people it has to deal with," says Peter Schey, executive director of the National Center for Immigrants' Rights. And a Congress practically paralyzed by conflicting pressures from special interest groups has been unable to do much about either reforming the laws or their enforcement. Instead, it appointed a select commission to recommend an overhaul of the system, but a protracted struggle is likely over the measures that it is expected to suggest.

Meanwhile, even those with sharply divergent views on the benefits of immigration are alarmed at the failure to control it. Roger Conner, head of the Federation for American Immigration Reform, a group that wants to curb the flow sharply, says, "If you don't have control of your immigration, you don't have control of your future." Federal Refugee Coordinator Victor Pal-

mieri, who worries that a backlash against immigrants may lead to harsh and repressive legislation, says of the pell-mell Cuban influx: "The U.S. was denied the fundamental basis for refugee and immigration policy—the ability to screen and process people to see if they meet your criteria."

The Main Problem

Though highly publicized, the Cuban inflow is insignificant compared with the huge steady northward flood of illegal Mexican nationals. To stop them, an undernourished Border Patrol fields only 350 agents at a time along a 1,945-mile span from the Gulf to the Pacific—an impossible job made even more so by spot shortages of vehicles and gasoline.

So the immigrants pour through to the farms of the Southwest, to the garment-industry sweatshops and small plants of Los Angeles, to barrios in a dozen cities where they simply disappear from official view. If the INS raids an employer's plant and scoops them up for deportation, they come back—and often bring friends.

No one knows how many are here. Estimates of foreigners living illegally in the U.S.—mostly Mexicans—range up to 12 million or more; Census Bureau officials say about 3.5 million, but this may be too low. Thin as it is, the Border Patrol catches hundreds of thousands a year and estimates that two slip in for each one apprehended. Some agents think that the ratio is closer to five to one.

The effect of this secret population is a puzzle: Studies disagree on whether the migrants are a drain on the domestic economy or whether they contribute more to it than they take away.

The social effect is equally hard to gauge, but there is mounting concern that the migrants are creating what ambassador-at-large Robert Krueger calls "a permanent underclass." Labor Secretary Ray Marshall adds: "I am convinced that we are sowing the seed of future civil-rights struggles, and we would be better off if we were to confront the issue now."

While the army of illegals slips through

3

the back door to the U.S., many others trying to enter lawfully are stalled outside the front door. This year, more than 700,000 aliens will take up legal residence here, compared with an annual average of about 400,000 during the mid-l970s—while the waiting list has grown to nearly one million from 600,000 or so. Some people have been waiting 10 years. They are victims of a patchwork of laws that immigration attorney Dan Danilov calls "an abysmal mess."

The history of these laws reflects a national schizophrenia about immigration in a country forged by immigrants. For years, the U.S. didn't put any numerical limit at all on inflow; in 1819, it even passed a "steerage law" that improved shipboard conditions for newcomers headed here.

But in 1882, alarmed by an influx of Chinese laborers, it banned Chinese and didn't let them in again for more than 60 years. It opened the golden door to nearly nine million immigrants from 1900 to 1910—and then in the 1920s slammed it on a lot of fingers by imposing national-origin quotas that, in effect, greatly favored Western Europe at the expense of other areas, including nations with predominantly black or Asian populations. By 1965, national-origin quotas were viewed as racist and scrapped.

Legal Tangle

Though current law is a tangle of exemptions, exceptions and special cases, it basically encourages family reunification; spouses, young children and parents of any U.S. citizen, for example, can enter in unlimited numbers.

Other close relatives of citizens, and all close relatives of aliens legally living here, must wait in line under a "preference category" system that provides a fixed number of available slots for each category. The system also provides some protection for the American labor force. There are slots for professionals, people of exceptional ability in the arts and sciences, and workers with skills in short supply here—but foreigners with no close relatives in the U.S. and no needed skill or background generally can't get in unless they qualify as refugees.

In all, 280,000 slots are currently available each year, and Uncle Sam treats each nation the same in doing them out—no more than 20,000 preference visas a year for any one country. The law thus treats Iceland as if it were as populous as India. It also is blind to the vast differences in desire to emigrate among people of different nations.

The result has been an enormous disparity in the time people must wait to join relatives here. The Mexican wife of an alien legally living in the U.S., for example, now must wait about five years to join him. In most other places, the wait isn't more than six months. In teeming Hong Kong, allowed only a few hundred slots as a dependency of the British Crown, some have waited 10 years.

U.S. handling of refugees, a separate and growing class of immigrants, also has been "haphazard, incoherent and often inadequate," according to the House Judiciary Committee. The law governing refugees hasn't been any better, according to other critics.

Until recently, it restricted refugee admission almost exclusively to people fleeing from Communist governments or from the Middle East. Legal roadblocks barred all but a trickle of those trying to escape from oppressive rightist regimes, some with U.S. ties, such as Haiti's, and the small number of refugee preference slots available were totally inadequate to handle waves of escapees from Hungary in the '50s, Cuba in the '60s and Vietnam in the '70s. Congress and various Attorneys General had to whip up solutions on the spot.

The 1979 Refugee Act, which took effect in March, stripped away the anti-communist bias and increased refugee preference slots to some 50,000. The 120,000 Cubans and 15,-000 Haitians descended on Florida. Publicly torn between welcoming them and trying to stop them, the administration finally decided it couldn't send them back to sea—but it also declined to admit them under the Refugee Act, on the ground that that law was intended only to aid immigrants who had been screened and granted visas abroad.

Instead, it waffled; it called the newcomers "entrants," a label that entitled them to fewer federal dollars for resettlement than refugees. This maneuver, private resettlement experts say, has unfairly complicated the Cubans' and Haitians' adjustment here. Government officials explain that the administration was torn between compassion—along with a desire to embarrass the Castro regime — and fear that granting formal refugee status might lure new flotillas of refugees fleeing from Caribbean poverty.

Principal Forum

The select commission appointed by Congress now is the principal forum for debate over what should be done about refugees, illegal aliens and other immigrants. Staff director Lawrence Fuchs says the group seems headed toward agreement on some measures, including:

—A firm ceiling of about 750,000 people a year or a flexible goal for all immigration.

—A revamped, more flexible preference system.

—Amnesty for most illegal aliens who already live and work here, allowing them to stay and become citizens.

—A law against hiring other illegal aliens and sanctions against employers who do. Neither exists now.

—A counterfeit-proof identity card or data-bank system identifying all citizens and legal alien residents permitted to work here.

—A beefed-up INS.

Even if commission members agree on these steps, and there isn't any certainty they will, some of the proposals may never make it through Congress. The administration and labor unions, for example, strongly back sanctions against employers of illegals, and most immigration experts agree that without such penalties the flow northward from the Mexican border can't be checked effectively. But potent Sun Belt agricultural and business interests have defeated in the Senate two sanctions bills that passed the House.

Farmers' Position

Southwestern farmers say they need aliens. "California agriculture can't survive without Mexican laborers," says a grower who has 100 acres of olives at Corning, Calif. He says he and his neighbors lost $1 million or more last year when the Border Patrol scooped up his work force at the height of picking season, and he insists he can't get enough American workers at prevailing piecework rates.

The select commission is considering a temporary program that would phase out Mexican labor over five years—giving farmers time to adjust. But Mr. Fuchs concedes that even that idea faces heavy fire from organized labor, which prefers an immediate ban.

Almost everybody loathes the identity-card proposal. Hispanic groups fear that it would increase police and other official harassment of Hispanics. Civil-liberties groups oppose it as Big Brotherism and unwarranted invasion of privacy. Secretary of Health and Human Services Patricia Harris says the Social Security system would blow a gasket if charged with producing and keeping track of it.

But commission staffers don't see any alternative. "People look at it and say, 'I hate it, I hate it, we need it,'" says one. The Rev. Theodore Hesburgh, president of the University of Notre Dame and commission chairman, pleads: "Give me a better solution, and I'll be for it."

Observers agree, however, that any overhaul of immigration policy requires an overhaul of the INS. Its manual record-keeping system is so overtaxed that it recently lost 50,000 files in New York alone. It has drifted without a permanent head for almost a year, and the Justice Department has left unfilled INS jobs authorized by Congress.

When it tries to act, it is often immobilized by red tape and long legal battles, a deportation can take five years, and one celebrated case has lasted almost 20. Some of its Border Patrol agents have been charged in brutal beatings of immigrants, and morale among others who feel they are carrying water in a sieve is low. "It's a disaster," a congressional staffer says.

If it is and if political leaders are paralyzed and confused, that may be because bureaucrats and lawmakers alike are so divided in their own minds. In them, the historical American schizophrenia about the immigration issue lives on.

Refugee Coordinator Palmieri, for one, expects economic and political turmoil to push ever more people out of Southeast Asia, Latin America and the Caribbean toward the U.S., but he admits he doesn't know what to do about it. He says the U.S. can't accept many more immigrants than it is currently taking in but also can't afford to be seen as "a nation that builds walls around its own affluence." He adds:

"I'm trying to manage what is, in many ways, an unmanageable problem.

---

2 *February 24, 1981*

Hispanic Population Swells to 6.4% of U.S., Census Figures Show

* * *

Spanish-Origin Residents in '80 Totaled 14.6 Million; Tally Method Changed, Though

By a WALL STREET JOURNAL *Staff Reporter*

WASHINGTON—Preliminary 1980 census totals show a significant increase in persons of Spanish origin in the U.S., the Commerce Department said.

Data from the department's Census Bureau show that the 1980 Spanish-origin population was 14.6 million, or 6.4% of the total population, up from 9.1 million, or 4.5%, a decade earlier. The report said the higher count was due, in part, to "the inclusion of a sizable, but unknown, number of persons" in the U.S. illegally.

The bureau also released other racial breakdowns, but said they were complicated by a change in the way people of Spanish origin classify themselves. In 1970 some 93% of Spanish-origin persons were classified as "white" in census reports. Last year, about 56% of Hispanics classified themselves as "white" and 40% classified themselves as "other."

"Because of the changes, the 1980 population totals for 'white' and 'other' aren't comparable to 1970 census figures," the report said. Nampeo McKenney, assistant division chief for ethnic and racial statistics, said that later reports would attempt to reconcile the category differences.

Preliminary totals showed the nation's total population at 226,504,825 last year, up from 203,211,926 in 1970.

Last year, 188.3 million, or 83% of the total, were classified as white, compared with 177.7 million, or 88%, a decade earlier. Blacks in 1980 numbered 26.5 million, or 12%, up from the 1970 total of 22.6 million, or 11%.

The report said that 1.4 million persons, or 0.6% of the total population in 1980, were of American Indian, Eskimo or Aleut descent, up from 827,268 persons, or 0.4%, in 1970. Persons of Asian and Pacific extraction totaled about 3.5 million, or 1.5% of the total, last year, about double the 1970 numbers of 1.5 million persons and 0.8%.

Because of the change in Hispanic reporting, the "other" category swelled to 6.8 million persons, or 3% of the total, last year from 516,673 persons, or 0.3%, a decade earlier.

Some Trends of Our Times

---

3 *September 10, 1980*

School Scandal

Another school year has begun and before it ends another 100,000-plus public school teachers will have been assaulted, by students, parents, school interlopers. Every crime imaginable, including rape and murder, will have been committed in America's halls of learning against students and teachers alike. If the last two years are any guide, the level of violence will rise significantly even as school populations decline. Another crop of children, particularly those in poor inner-city districts, will learn more about fear and trauma than about the three R's, and this will be reflected in declining literacy rates.

The dimensions of this national scandal are huge. All signals point to a steady deterioration in the quality of public education. Teacher fears and frustrations are manifested in a decline in their own respect for the systems they serve, a feeling that would require a superhuman effort to conceal from their students. We are even hearing unashamed proposals that public education be abolished, a thought that would have been unheard of a decade or so ago.

The obvious question is, why do school boards tolerate such conditions? In some places they don't, of course, proving that the best administrators still somehow manage. But the national statistics make it clear that the task has become far more difficult. And there is every reason to believe that this is largely due to the attacks, mainly through the courts, on the authority of local school boards and administrators by powerful forces intent on turning the schools into social laboratories. Their ideas may have been well-intended, for the most part, but the evidence suggests that they have been wrong.

To be fair, we must acknowledge that the social environment in which the schools operate has changed dramatically these last 20 years. Mass migrations, such as the ones from the South and Puerto Rico, have presented the familiar melting pot problems for the cities. Public housing has wrecked the assimilative function that urban neighborhoods once provided. Careless management of city budgets has weakened law enforcement. Public policy has contributed to family breakups. The churches have lost influence.

But there has been more than that, with a direct impact on the schools. One analysis of school dropouts and expulsions detects a rise when busing programs uproot children from comfortable and familiar surroundings and plunk them down in some unfamiliar place. This should come as no surprise to anyone who has ever dealt with children but it seems never to have occurred to busing proponents.

At the high school level, there was also the advent of the "student rights" movement of the early 1970s. This was an outgrowth of efforts, through "public interest" law groups and "alternative" movements, to organize young people into some sort of cohesive, new left political force. The movement didn't particularly succeed in that but it did succeed in putting

laws on the books that give teachers and principals uncertainties about what forms of discipline or punishment might subject them to a lawsuit. It also reinforced the notion among those students who are naturally rebellious that their grievances were justified.

Finally there has been a further erosion of local authority by the engrossing of power by state and federal educational officials. This movement was in large part promoted by the teachers unions, who saw it as a way of installing power where they can influence it most effectively. But it also means that the ideas of remote theorists in Washington or state capitals often supersede the more realistic judgments of local authorities, with the result that the teacher members of the unions are the ones put to risk.

For example, the Juvenile Justice and Delinquency Prevention Act of 1974, sponsored by Indiana Senator Birch Bayh and now coming up for reauthorization in Congress, requires states receiving its funding to adopt

"advanced techniques" for dealing with juvenile delinquency. As spelled out, this has mainly involved attempting to rehabilitate youthful offenders in the schools rather than sending them off to reform schools or exacting some other form of punishment. One of the most frequent horror stories heard from teachers is that of having to confront the same hard-core toughs day after day, even after they have been assaulted by such youths.

It is not necessary to blame all the problems of school crime on bad legislation or bad sociology—or even to claim that all the modern experiments are failures—to say that the record does not speak well of these trends and movements. It would be more encouraging if the social and political liberals who have had their way on so many things were showing some sign of recognition that they might have been wrong. But whether they are or not, a broad public is disturbed by what is happening in the schools.

4

Old-Time Religion

An Evangelical Revival Is Sweeping the Nation But With Little Effect

---

Millions Quit Main Churches For 'Born-Again' Sects That Focus on Inner Self

---

Shunning the Sinful World

By JONATHAN KAUFMAN
Staff Reporter of THE WALL STREET JOURNAL

The spirit of religious awakening is once again moving across the land. But unlike a similar Great Religious Awakening 2½ centuries ago that helped sow the seeds of the American Revolution, the current evangelical revival has so far sowed little except

curiosity among nonbelievers and self-doubt among many faithful.

Evangelicals embrace the literalness and absolute authority of the Bible, emphasize the importance of being "born again" and preach a return to conservative social values.

Some 27 million people, mostly in the South and the Midwest, call themselves evangelicals. Several million of them are Protestants who have grown disenchanted with the teachings of their mainline churches such as the Episcopal and the Presbyterian. A parallel movement among Roman Catholics, the "Charismatic Renewal," has attracted four million followers since its founding, in 1967. Overall, one out of every three Americans says he has been "born again," according to a recent Gallup Poll. And every week television evangelists like Oral Roberts, Pat Robertson and Jerry Falwell reach an estimated 128 million viewers.

Effect Has Been Small

As impressive as those statistics are, the movement has affected American society far less than did the Great Awakening of the mid-1700s, which marked the beginning of "a new era, not merely of American Protes-

tantism but in the evolution of the American mind," according to Perry Miller, the historian.

"I heard on one of those TV evangelism shows the other night that 33% of all Americans are 'born again," says Douglas Gallagher, pastor of the Bloomfield Hills Baptist Church near Detroit and an evangelical. "But if that's true, why is the crime rate still so high? Why is there still so much use of narcotics? Where is our impact?"

Unlike many mainline Protestant churches that in the 1960s preached a "social gospel" of helping the poor, fighting perceived injustice and attempting to reform corporate and political institutions, the evangelical movement of the 1980s emphasizes the importance of personal conversion and salvation—the "me generation" finds religion, some cynics would call it.

Shying From Involvement

Combined with this highly individualized message is a historical tendency for evangelicals to shy away from involvement in the secular, sinful world. "We're not as socially conscious as some other religious groups," says Christopher Lyons, pastor of the Wheaton Bible Church in Wheaton, Ill. "There are probably enough evangelicals here in Wheaton to run the town, but we don't. We don't want to.''

Thus even though evangelicalism has been attracting growing numbers of adherents, Americans in parts of the country where it hasn't caught on remain largely unaware of the movement's scope.

"If you're part of the evangelical subculture, it's your whole life," says Martin Marty, a divinity professor at the University of Chicago, as he draws circles on a map to illustrate evangelical and non-evangelical strongholds. ''You go to church, you buy the religious books, you watch the television programs. But if you're not part of the subculture, you never know it exists.''

Getting Involved in Politics

Some evangelicals would like to change that. Declaring that ''the basic moral issues such as homosexuality, abortion and pornography have become political issues,'' Mr. Falwell, whose ''Old Time Gospel Hour'' reaches 25 million television viewers every Sunday, has established a political-action group known as Moral Majority to get more evangelicals involved in politics. So far, the group has registered two million of them to vote in the fall election. By November it plans to have registered three million more.

But while the entrance of evangelicals into politics may well polarize debate on highly emotional issues like abortion and homosexuality, any attempt to mobilize an ''evangelical vote'' or to unite evangelicals behind a single political candidate is likely to founder on the shoals of apathy and political disunity. The evangelical movement may have the armies, Prof. Marty notes, but many of its followers aren't ''mobilizable.'' A recent study of the nonvoter, for example, found that nonvoters tend to be more religious than the population as a whole, with many attending prayer meeting twice a week—but never voting in local or national elections.

Even more important, when evangelicals do vote they don't all vote the same way: For example, all three leading candidates for President—Jimmy Carter, Ronald Reagan and John Anderson—despite their widely differing political views, claim to be evangelical Christians; President Carter and Rep. Anderson say they have been ''born again.''

Evangelicals do agree, however, on questions of religion—primarily the absolute authority of the Bible and the divinity of Christ—and it is in religion that they have had their greatest effect, especially among the mainline Protestant churches.

Since 1965 the mainline churches—Episcopal, Presbyterian, Methodist and United Church of Christ—have lost three million members, or 15% of their membership. By contrast, membership in evangelical churches has swelled by more than 25% during the same period.

''The rise of the evangelicals has made those of us in the mainline denominations rethink who we are,'' says Paul Sherry, an official with the United Church of Christ. ''Evangelicalism is bringing back into the mainstream the fervor on which the success of any religion depends.''

Mainline-church ministers still debate what has caused the steady emptying of their pews. But the growth in evangelicalism seems linked to its ability to provide churchgoers a feeling of personal relevance.

''The rapid rate of technological change, the high rate of unemployment, the economic uncertainty, these are all things that drive people to religion—and to drink,'' says Dean Kelly, an official with the National Council of Churches and author of an influential study called ''Why Conservative Churches Are Growing.''

The mainline churches, says Mr. Kelly, have failed to minister to the needs that grow out of these phenomena. Too often over the course of the past 20 years, Mr. Kelly and others charge, mainline-church ministers have focused too much attention on the problems of the secular world—poverty, injustice, the war in Vietnam—and too little on the problems of their parishioners.

A Practical Guide

''Two years ago I went on a retreat with the officers from my church, and they all said they wanted more sermons that would give them a practical guide on how to live the Christian life—in their families, in their businesses, in their friendships,'' says William Enright, pastor of the First Presbyterian Church in Glen Ellyn, Ill., a Chicago suburb. ''Too often the church in the past has been esoteric, talking above the people rather than at their level.''

Virginia Adair, a substitute teacher who left the Presbyterian denomination and joined Mr. Lyon's Wheaton Bible Church, says she did so because she ''wanted a sermon that I could go home and remember for the rest of the week.'' At the Presbyterian church she attended in Philadelphia, says Mrs. Adair, extending her arm outward. ''They put God way up here where He wasn't personal to you. He was just someone you worshipped on Sundays.''

Almost without exception, the mainline churches that have gone against the trend of slumping membership have focused on the personal aspects of the Christian mssage and expanded their fellowship groups such as Bible-study classes and community service organizations. An example would be the Southern Baptists, a denomination whose members strive to be ''born again.''

However, this turning inward would seem to conflict with the efforts of preachers like Mr. Falwell to mobilize evangelicals into a strong political force. Indeed, although Moral Majority has registered an impressive number of voters, the group concedes that it often fights a losing battle against apathy and evangelicalism's strong individualistic strain.

On the Side of the Poor

''It's difficult,'' says Robert Billings, Moral Majority's executive director. ''We get all excited about an issue and go out and organize, and then three weeks later we're back inside our four walls singing ''Amazing Grace.''

More liberal evangelicals, popularly known as ''neo-evangelicals,'' face a similar problem. ''The God of the Bible is on the side of the poor,'' says Jim Wallis, editor of Sojourner's Magazine and one of the most influential of the neo-evangelicals. ''The biblical economic vision has to do with the simple life, with the sharing of resources, with the redistribution of income and power.''

But such a messsage, Mr. Wallis concedes, ''isn't going to be very popular,'' especially when it must compete against not only a growing conservative trend in the country but also conservatively inclined TV evangelists like Mr. Falwell who, Mr. Wallis charges, ''tailor the Gospel to economic assumptions that are already popular.''

In the end, however, it may not be appropriate to measure the effect of a religion solely by its political effectiveness.

''When we were living in New Jersey, John Mark, our fourth child, was born brain-damaged,'' says Vicki Howard, a housewife who belongs to the Wheaton Bible Church. ''It was a very difficult and a very questioning time for us. We didn't know it at the time, but across the street from us was another couple whose child had also been brain-damaged in an accident. They saw the way the people in our church came over and helped us and gave us support, and one day they reached out to one of their neighbors who belonged to the church and said, ''We saw something that was very real, that was very out of the ordinary.''

''That couple was born again,'' says Mrs. Howard. ''They joined our church in New Jersey and became very active.'' Mrs. Howard turns her palms upward. ''They were touched by what they saw,'' she says. ''That's impact, but it's not the kind of impact that people talk about. It's not the kind of impact you read about in the newspapers.''

King Leer

Sexual Pitches in Ads Become More Explicit And More Pervasive

---

Shock Value Is Used to Peddle Tea and Traveler's Checks To a Turned-Off Public

---

Providing the Shiverin' Fits

By Gail Bronson

Staff Reporter of The Wall Street Journal

Scene: An artist's skylit studio. A young man lies nude, the bedsheets in disarray. He awakens to find a tender note on his pillow. The phone rings and he gets up to answer it.

Woman's voice: "You snore."

Artist (smiling): "And you always steal the covers."

More cozy patter between the two. Then a husky-voiced announcer intones: "Paco Rabanne. A cologne for men. What is remembered is up to you."

For the past month or so, this 30-second commercial has been beamed into America's living rooms courtesy of fragrance maker Puig of Barcelona. Fernando Aleu, a New York neurologist and co-partner in a Puig unit, readily concedes: "We wouldn't have done this even five years ago."

But as the Paco Rabanne commercial suggests, this has become the Year of the Leer on Madison Avenue. Though sex has always moved merchandise, it has never before been so explicit. Advertisers were once content merely to whisper, hint or suggest. Now the veil on the innuendo is being lifted, and sales pitches are downright steamy. Jeans designers, by turning prime time into a sea of undulating posteriors, led the way. But other advertisers quickly fell in step, using sex to push everything from traveler's checks to tea.

"The Last Taboo"

The aim, of course, is to jolt benumbed viewers out of their Barcaloungers. "People are looking for a new stimulant on the subconscious level, and sex is the last taboo," says Arthur R. Ross, creative director of the advertising agency Weiss & Geller Inc. He and other marketers say the newly explicit ads are targeted to reach what they perceive as a jaded, turned-off populace. "Society feels very dead and very pessimistic about the future," Mr. Ross says. Shock value, marketers say, is also useful in pene-

trating the current "clutter" of competing messages bombarding TV screens. (By one estimate, each one of us is exposed to 500 radio and TV commercials a week.)

Suggestive advertising creates headaches for TV networks, whose censors decide whether a commercial oversteps the boundaries of good taste. Often, getting even mildly provocative material by the censors involves considerable ingenuity—or, at the very least, delicate negotiations.

So far, however, there appears to be little backlash against the new ads. "Our commercial isn't horrendously sensual, just keeping up with the times," says Dr. Aleu, who introduced Paco Rabanne in 1975 with what he terms "very plain" print ads. Now, he says, "our TV and print ads have created a lot of noise in a month's time. But it's only the people in Oregon who write that our ads are too sexy."

More Explicit in Print

The Paco Rabanne print campaign is more explicit than its TV commercials. In such publications as New York magazine, Vogue and Esquire, the woman tells her artist-lover: "I'm going to take some (Paco Rabanne cologne) and rub it on my body when I go to bed tonight. And then I'm going to remember every little thing about you . . . and last night." Another magazine ad for the cologne has a woman calling up a handsome young photographer to invite him over to her place. She introduces herself: "We met last week. At the Wexlers'. You were looking down my dress." (The New York Times Sunday Magazine rejected the artist ad but ran the photographer one.)

While soft-focus sensuality has always been a big factor in cosmetics marketing, today it is even creeping into food advertising. The California Avocado Commission supplements its "Love Food From California" recipe ads with a new campaign featuring Angie Dickinson. The leggy actress will sprawl across two pages of some 18 national magazines next month to promote the avocado's nutritional value. The copy line reads: "Would this body lie to you?"

Dannon Yogurt, in an ad featuring a bikini-clad lovely, touts a new yogurt diet under this headline: "More nonsense is written on dieting than any other subject—except possibly sex." And in Lipton Tea commercials, alluring women urge viewers to spice up their lives with the company's line of flavored brews.

Though Dannon Co. and Thomas J. Lipton Inc. stoutly deny any attempt to titillate, Jacob Jacoby, a Purdue University psychologist and marketing consultant, believes otherwise. "Tea is boring as hell," he says, "and the yogurt maker merely chose a provocative value to grab attention."

Symbolism in Action

In any case, he contends, marketers—like everyone else—carry around sexual

symbols in their subconscious that, intentionally or not, they use in ads. He cites the Newport cigaret "Alive With Pleasure" campaign. One such ad features a woman riding the handlebars of a bicycle driven by a man. The main strut of the bike wheel stands up vertically beneath her body, symbolism that Mr. Jacoby says needs no interpretation.

Mr. Jacoby notwithstanding, advertisers suggest that TV-network censors win the prize for turning up sexual connotation where none exists. And, they contend, such primness smacks of a double standard.

"Incest, rape and homosexuality go into programming because the networks realize the pulling power of sex," Weiss & Geller's Mr. Ross says. Jay Jasper, who handles the Paco Rabanne account at the ad agency Ogilvy & Mather Inc., agrees. "By network soap-opera and hit-show standards," he says, "we're pretty tame."

But Mary Lou Jennerjahn, a CBS censor and attorney, argues that while a TV program appears once or twice, often with an advance warning about racy content, "a commercial comes into the home unannounced, over and over again." She neglects to mention, however, the many hit sit-coms that have leaped to the top of the ratings mainly on the strength of their salacious content.

Nonetheless, the censors have the last word, and advertising executives must live with their subjective judgments. To minimize risk, most will show censors an illustrated "story board" of a commercial before it is filmed. "It's the unwise ones who don't," says Julie Hoover, an ABC censor.

Noxell Corp. recently ran afoul of the censors with commercials for Noxzema shave cream. One that showed a man resting his head on a well-endowed showgirl's bosom was turned down. "It was too much for us," says the rejecting censor, who prefers to go unidentified. Another Noxzema commercial that wasn't aired on networks featured Farrah Fawcett helping a lonely woodsman shave. After she murmurs things like "So manly . . ." he remarks: "I haven't seen a woman in nine years." Then, with a nod to Freud, the shave-cream can bursts through the earth's crust, rising like a skyscraper into the forest. (Noxell Corp. officials declined to be interviewed for this article.)

Sometimes, network objections are negotiable. When Ogilvy's Mr. Jasper showed censors the story board for the Paco Rabanne commercial, they insisted that the artists be filmed wearing a wedding ring. Mr. Jasper agreed, but balked at another suggestion. "They wanted to show him wearing pajama bottoms, but we said it wasn't germane," Mr. Jasper says, explaining that the model is shown only from the waist up.

Subjective Decisions

A Citicorp subsidiary squeaked by with a humorous commercial for its traveler's checks that shows a vacationing couple using the public baths in Japan. (The wife cringes in embarrassment as a Japanese man edges closer to strike up a polite conversation with them.) Before approving it, one network censor needed reassurance from the ad agency that in Japan it's customary for men and women to bathe together *au naturel,* as shown on the air. "Still," says the censor, "it was a close call." The Citicorp unit, which previously featured bank tellers in its commercials, has seen its market share "grow substantially" since the campaign began, officials say.

What passes without so much as a blink at one network may be rejected at another. CBS's Miss Jennerjahn concedes that censor decisions are subjective. "I go with my gut," she says. She turned down the Paco Rabanne commercial for network airing because "people beyond the Hudson River might feel it shows promiscuity." Local CBS and ABC stations in New York and other selected markets accepted it for late-night viewing.

In creating the first TV commercial for shoe designer Charles Jourdan Boutique Inc., the ad agency Case & McGrath Inc. "made an end-run around the censors," according to Eugene Case, one of the partners. In the commercial, a female shopper cavorts in a lush country garden with a nearly nude Greek statue, who scoops her up and swings her about.

"It's an elegant and sensual way to promote our image," says Terry Pandel, Charles Jourdan's advertising director. "When the statue moves, he's so strong and overwhelming." (The unspoken assumption is that a statue can take liberties that a male model wouldn't be permitted.)

The new sexy ads reflect another change: Women, as often as not, are shown taking the lead in encounters with men. Heublein Inc.'s Harveys Bristol Cream sherry commercials have young, alluringly clad women confiding to friends on the phone: "A few years ago, it wasn't considered respectable for a woman to ask a man over for a drink. But I figure when I'm serving Harveys Bristol Cream, it's more than just respectable, it's downright upright." A parting line, as a man enters the room: "Nancy, I have to go." Previous commercials for the sherry featured stuffed shirts chatting about yachts in paneled studies.

(Interestingly enough, the two-year-old sex-oriented ad campaign hasn't increased Harveys' sales. But the company blames the advent of imitator sherries that cost about $3 a bottle, competing with the $8 Harveys, and it says it is "very committed" to continuing the commercial campaign.)

Women's Reaction

"Women like it when they're portrayed as taking charge of a situation," says Rena Bartos, a vice president of JWT Group Inc., formerly J. Walter Thompson Co. "It implies power." Mrs. Bartos compares two fragrance ads (neither created by Thompson) that her agency tested last year. One that drew lukewarm—and even negative—response from women was for Aviance. It shows a homemaker stripping off apron and rubber gloves suggestively, as she sings: "I've been sweet and I've been good . . . I've had a whole full day of motherhood, but I'm gonna have an Aviance night." A commercial for Enjoli ("The 8-Hour Perfume for the 24-Hour Woman") drew raves: "I can bring home the bacon, fry it up in a pan," belts the career woman. "I can work till five o'clock . . . and (as she emerges in evening dress) if it's loving you want, I can kiss you and give ya the shiverin' fits!"

The gains women have made in the workplace have actually made them more receptive to overtly suggestive advertising, marketers say. Brenda Harburger, vice president of Charles of the Ritz Group Ltd.'s fragrance division, says the company's Enjoli ad would have been rejected by women 10 years ago "because they were still battling to feel equal to men at work." With one out of two women now working, "people are comfortably recognizing that sex exists, and that it's healthy to desire it," says Sanford D. Buchsbaum, executive vice president for Revlon Inc.'s U.S. cosmetics.

Though barriers are tumbling fast, advertisers still complain they toil under unreasonable restrictions. In TV commercials, for example, live models can be shown in underwear only if it's worn over other clothing.

Pantyhose Ploy

Hanes Corp. circumvented this rule with what one censor calls a "very tongue-in-cheek commercial" for Underalls pantyhose. In 1976, Underalls made its television debut, with cameras focused on the models' fully — if tightly — clothed backsides. One model exclaims: "I feel like I'm not wearing nothin'!" In recently updated commercials, the announcer commands models to "Show us your Underalls." Viewers again see their backsides, and are invited to search out tell-tale panty-lines.

Formfit Rogers Inc. must rely on magazine support for its television advertising in order to "tell our whole story," says Dorothy Tivi Pollack, the lingerie maker's advertising director. In March, Formfit will begin a $4.6 million TV campaign to introduce a panty fashioned from a new polypropylene fabric. The fabric has absorbency and stain-resistant properties that censors generally won't allow to be mentioned on TV, she says.

And if nudity is common in European commercials, it is still anathema in the U.S. market. "We've okayed party scenes where cleavage was visible," ABC's Miss Hoover says. "But we don't want to titillate the audience, and have them oohing over seeing a nipple."

Some advertisers see a pragmatic reason for such reserve. "When the sexual content of a message is very potent, it can overpower the brand name and be very counterproductive," observes Joan S. Holbrook, a creative vice president at the McCann-Erickson ad agency. McCann, which has the Coca-Cola and Tab accounts, uses wholesomely attractive—but never sexy—models. In Mrs. Holbrook's words: "We don't invite America to have a Coke and a smirk."

Working Women: Unmaking the 19th Century

By Peter F. Drucker

We are busily unmaking one of the proudest social achievements of 19th Century reformers, which was to take married women out of the work force so they could devote themselves to family and children.

Historically, women always participated in the labor force at the same rate as men: Women and men alike worked from the time they were able until they dropped. Neither farm nor craftsman's shop can be run alone by either man or woman; both require a couple. And, until recently, all but a tiny fraction of the human race made its living on the farm or in the craftsman's shop. As late as the mid-19th Century, when Dickens wrote his harrowing novel of industrial England, "Hard Times," it was still only a utopian hope that some day in the remote future married women would not have to leave their children to go out to work.

By 1914, however, it had become the mark of the "self-respecting working man" that "his woman" need not work for wages. And by 1950, it was commonly assumed that most women would stop working with marriage and surely when the first child was about to arrive. Until perhaps as late as 20 years ago, "female emancipation" largely meant freeing women from the necessity of taking a paying job. Liberals, progressives, socialists and reformers of all stripes agreed wholeheartedly on the need for laws to protect women by keeping them out of hazardous and "demeaning" occupations. This was, for instance, one of Eleanor Roosevelt's great causes.

Equal to That of Men

Now, all this is considered reactionary and discrimination. And for women under 50, regardless of their marital status and almost regardless of whether they have children, the labor force participation rate is again equal to that of men.

A similar transformation has befallen the other great progressive cause of the late 19th Century: mandatory retirement for older people. Mandatory retirement was an integral part of the Social Security system and was considered a great achievement by social reformers in the early 20th Century. But now mandatory retirement is outlawed altogether in California and for federal employes, and nationwide for almost everyone else until age 70. And the laws limp well behind reality: A large number of those officially "retired" do work, only they know better than to tell Uncle Sam about it, lest they lose many of their Social Security benefits.

But while we are unmaking the great social achievements of the last century, we are not returning to the conditions of pre-industrial times. Historically women, while always sharing fully in work, have never done the same tasks as men. On the farm and in the craftsman's shop the sexes were always equal, but they did different tasks and rarely worked together.

Spinning has everywhere been woman's work; a "spinster" is never male. But weaving and dying were always, and exclusively, tasks for men. In Polynesia men built and manned the ships, and did the fishing; women tilled the fields and grew the yams. Throughout the Old World only women milk cows; in the New World only men do so—why this difference, no one knows. And except for the mythical Amazons, women never took part in organized warfare. Even the female nurse entered the military only in the late 19th Century. But can there be much doubt that women will take part in the next war—perhaps even in combat and next to men?

We are reversing the historic pattern where men worked together and women worked together, but the sexes stayed apart. This is an unprecedented social experiment, surely one of the most interesting ones in history. We are committed to

it, but we won't know for some time, perhaps generations, how it will work out.

Similarly, people used to work full-time as long as they possibly could, and often well beyond. Now the old line between working and idleness is becoming fuzzy. A good many women work part-time. A large number even work full-time for a period and then "take time out" for a baby, only to come back to the labor force, part-time or full-time.

There is as little precedent in social history for the working patterns of older people as there is for men and women sharing the same tasks. It's now possible to retire early and then return to part-time or full-time work. Second careers are both possi-

stance, that the progressive causes of yesterday are today's "hangups of reactionary pigs" and "discrimination"? Will the sacred causes of today's progressives and reformers meet the same fate as demography changes? It is quite conceivable that we are in for a period of rapid change where yesterday's liberal heroes become the rear guard of reaction overnight, just as yesterday's progressive unionist is rapidly becoming Mr. Reagan's supporter.

What will be the impact on the family and on the role and place of the child in the home and in the school? The bourgeois family where Mom stays home with the kids has been one of the favorite topics of sociologists, philosophers, politicians and

---

Drucker on Management

It was once a utopian hope that some day in the remote future married women would not have to leave their children to go away from home to work.

---

ble and necessary now that working-life spans have been lengthened to 50 years from only 25 less than a century ago. Pensions enable older people to take on volunteer work.

For both women and older people, in short, there is increasingly a choice of patterns combining work and non-work, permanent and casual jobs, paid and volunteer work. And these two groups together constitute more than half of all the people in the U.S. labor force, even though many of us still think of "workers" as males under 65 working full-time.

Not all women and older people want to work even when they do, and not all of them want not to work even when they don't. But a large proportion, probably a majority, want *some* work, and they want to be able to make the decision for themselves.

Employers, union leaders, politicians, even those slow-learners the economists are beginning to wake up to the impacts of these changes. One no longer shocks executives by telling them that they need to structure full-time jobs to be permanently staffed by part-time people. Ten, even five, years ago "benefit options" were unheard of; instead uniform benefit plans were imposed on all employes regardless of age, sex, marital status or family situation. Today benefit options are becoming commonplace, though organized labor still frowns on them. Marketers are beginning to realize that the changes in work mean shifts in market segmentation and buying patterns.

But what are the social and political implications? What does it mean, for in-

preachers since before the turn of the century. Depending on one's politics, it was either the bastion of civilization or "total alienation which divorces women from reality." Only 10 years ago Herbert Marcuse still trumpeted the latter theme, which was first played by Flaubert, Marx and Ibsen.

Mothers Now Know as Much

The alienation theme still holds some truth for the young, who are kept out of the world of adult work as they were in the bourgeois family. But mothers and even grandmothers now know as much about the world of work as fathers do. How much longer will TV comedies feature the little woman who cannot balance her checkbook when more than half of all students in accounting courses are female?

What will the family of tomorrow look like, when there are not only two incomes but two parallel and separate careers, a kind of competitive coexistence? I don't know whether it will be better or worse than the bourgeois family but it will surely be different.

Finally, what of all that talk about the disappearance of the work ethic? During the very years that every attitude survey showed a decline in the work ethic, both total labor force and the proportion of the population actively at work have risen spectacularly. Meanwhile, the obstacles to labor force participation for both women and older people have been steadily dynamited.

There's an old lesson to be remembered here: In a good many social matters, attitudes are secondary and attitude surveys are a snare and delusion. What matters is what people do, not what they say they will do.

Another lesson is that the real undermining of the work ethic took place during the latter half of the 19th Century and the first half of the 20th, the years in which non-working for married women and older people were progressive causes. In the last 20 years, the work ethic has returned with a vengeance.

Mr. Drucker is Clarke Professor of Social Science at the Claremont Graduate School. His latest book is "Toward the Next Economics, and Other Essays" (Harper & Row).

Race and Ethnic Relations

7

Minority Report

Integration Is Elusive Despite Recent Gains; Social Barriers Remain

Progress Is More Statistical Than Real as Blacks Seek Housing, Education, Jobs

New Goal: 'Here-Now' Issues

By CHARLES W. STEVENS
Staff Reporter of THE WALL STREET JOURNAL

When court-ordered desegregation came to Atlanta's public schools two decades ago, it was heralded as a great stride forward for integration: The system was 55% white and 45% black, and a thorough racial mix seemed possible. The years since have shown the folly of this hope. Atlanta's whites moved to the suburbs or sent their children to private schools. Now the public-school system is 90% black.

Such has been the dominant course of racial integration in the U.S. Since the civil-rights movement began in earnest 25 years ago, the legal framework that supported segregation has been removed, and blacks have made notable statistical advances in important fields. But progress toward the free and equal association of blacks and whites envisioned by idealists of the 1950s and '60s has been fitful, and much of what mixing has occurred has involved a fairly thin layer of well-educated, well-off members of both races.

Moreover, prospects are dim that this situation will change substantially any time soon. Social barriers to integration are proving far harder to crack than the formal legal obstacles. Also, integration itself has faded as a primary goal of many blacks.

"The issue isn't integration versus non-integration anymore—it's here-now things like jobs," says Selwyn R. Cudjoe, professor of Afro-American studies at Harvard University. "There's a growing realization that integration won't put bacon on the table."

"For blacks, integration has been delayed too long, and it's coming too little, too late," says Ali A. Mazrui, professor of political science and director of the Center for Afro-American and African Studies at the University of Michigan. "It was resisted (by whites) for so long that when whites began saying, 'Let's have it,' some blacks replied, 'Who says we want it anymore?'"

In no area of American life have segregated patterns hung on so tenaciously as in housing. Here and there one can find neighborhoods or suburbs that have achieved some measure of stable racial balance, but they are exceptional.

This is true not only in the aging central sections of the major cities of the East and the Midwest, where black populations have become predominant, but elsewhere as well. Indeed, the maintenance of segregation despite the considerable population movement of the last 20 years has served to underscore its resilience.

Moving to Black Suburbs

The U.S. Census Bureau reports that from 1960 to 1979 the number of blacks living in big-city suburbs grew by 72% to about five million, compared with a 38% growth in the white suburban population in that period. But much of that movement was between mostly black city neighborhoods and suburbs that were already mostly black or were rapidly becoming so.

For instance, the Cleveland suburb of East Cleveland had nearly no black residents in 1960. By 1970 it was 60% black, and by 1980 the figure had climbed to 82%. A study by Pierre de Vise, professor of political science at the University of Illinois at Chicago, showed that all but a handful of the blacks living in the 200 or so suburbs that ringed Chicago were clustered in just 15 of those communities.

Racial discrimination in the sale or rental of housing is banned by law in most of the U.S., but those laws are apparently widely circumvented by both real-estate agents and mortgage lenders. A study of mortgage-lending practices in New York and California, released in June by Harvard and Massachusetts Institute of Technology, found that black applicants were far more likely to be denied a mortgage than whites of similar income and had to pay higher interest rates for the mortgages they did get.

Bank Policy?

"We don't know whether the discrimination is overall bank policy from the top or just done lower down," says Helen F. Ladd, a co-author of the study. "My own sense is that there is a lot of prejudice at the level of loan officer."

In sum, "What we've seen is resegregation, or the extension of previous segregation," says Edward L. Holmgren, executive director of the National Committee Against Discrimination in Housing, based in Washington. "Any progress that has occurred has been halting and slow."

Because public-school enrollments are closely tied to housing, it isn't surprising that integration hasn't proceeded quickly there either. This is true despite the striking down of separate-school laws in the South and the imposition of busing to achieve greater racial balance in some Northern cities.

The extent of integration in the public

schools is a matter of debate, much of which centers on the definition of what constitutes an "integrated" school unit. The U.S. Civil Rights Commission developed a formula based on school enrollments as a percentage of a district's racial population. It concluded that in 1977 46% of the nation's black school-children still attended schools that were "at least moderately segregated," even though the number was down sharply from 76% in 1968.

By another measure, the U.S Department of Education similarly reported that 60% of black children attended schools that were at least half black in 1978, although that was down from 70% of black children 10 years earlier. The department reported that the greatest progress toward integrated schools in that period came in the South, where the proportion of black children attending mostly black schools dropped to 59% from 79%.

In the Northeast, the figure rose to 71% from 68% during these years, reflecting "while flight" to the suburbs and the rigidity of segregated urban housing patterns.

In other areas, progress toward integration has been far more promising. These include higher education and numerous occupations and professions.

Today about one million blacks are enrolled as college undergraduates, a fourfold jump from 1960. Blacks account for about 11% of undergraduates at American colleges, up from 7% in 1970 and 6% in 1960; their college-enrollment proportion almost equals their 12% share of the total U.S. population. Furthermore, only about one-third of black undergraduates attend predominantly black colleges, against about half in 1960.

At the graduate and professional-school level, blacks constitute about 6% of enrollments, up from 4% in 1970.

As more blacks gain access to higher education, their representation in the professions and better-paying jobs generally has risen, although their proportional representation still lags behind that of whites. In the last two decades, nonwhite participation in professional and technical jobs has nearly doubled, to about 9%, and nonwhite representation in the Labor Department's "managers and administrators" category also has doubled, to around 5%. Blacks make up 11% of plumbers and pipefitters, almost twice the proportion of the 1960s, and 8% of machinists and job fitters, four times as many as two decades past.

Currently, there are 9,300 black physicians and surgeons in the U.S., double the number of 1960. The population of black lawyers stands at nearly 12,000, almost six times the number of 20 years ago.

De Facto Segregation Remains

But the reality behind these impressive figures is less heartening to those who desire a colorblind society; where statistical integration exists, it is often accompanied by de facto segregation.

On the nation's college campuses, for instance, some fraternities and sororities remain as vestiges of the formal segregation of past days. More common is an edgy sort of voluntary racial separation that discourages contact between black and white students who would like to make friends.

"Black students eat at the same tables in the cafeteria" and keep to themselves in other ways, says Lee Hockstader, a senior at Brown University in Providence, R.I., who is white and would like easier association with blacks. Race relations at Brown are "a little bit tense," he says, adding, "There's never much interaction outside the classroom."

Sometimes the separation is a reaction to racism. Scott Barnett, a black 1980 graduate of Northwestern University in Evanston, Ill., says he sought black roommates after a white he roomed with "thought that because I was black, I would clean up the room all the time." A less subtle dormitory incident was a sign reading "death to niggers" that someone hung on a dorm room door, he says.

If anything, racial separation is even more prevalent in the professions. In law, medicine and other fields, parallel black and mostly white professional organizations still exist, and partnerships of whites and blacks are rare.

John L. Crump, executive director of the National Bar Association, an 8,000-member black lawyers' group whose activities parallel those of the American Bar Association (which also has black members), says private practice holds so little promise for black lawyers that nearly 75% of them work for government agencies. A recent National Law Journal survey showed that just 12 of the 3,700 partners of the 50 biggest U.S. law firms were black.

Frank S. Royal of Richmond, Va., president-elect of the National Medical Association, a 4,000-member black physicians' group, says he knows of only two private medical practices in which blacks and whites are partners. And he says that in some cities, access to hospitals and other medical facilities remains a problem for the black practitioner. "The American medical profession is just as segregated as American churches," he notes.

(According to the National Council of Churches in New York, some 90% of American blacks belong to black churches. An official of the group says that this isn't surprising "when you consider that churches reflect the residential, social and cultural patterns of the society as a whole.")

Change in Attitude

Probably the main change of the integration front in recent years has come in the way whites regard blacks; if racial integration has lagged in reality, at least the idea of it seems to be taking hold.

Louis Harris & Associates, the polltaking company, has surveyed American attitudes toward race relations since 1963 and has found a steady increase in the acceptance of integration and black-white contact.

In 1978, for instance, a Harris poll showed that 54% of whites wouldn't be upset if blacks moved into their neighborhoods, up from 32% in 1963. Nearly half of the whites polled two years ago said they had regular contact with a black co-worker, up from 32% in 1963, and the proportion of whites who said they had a black friend rose to 40% from 20%.

Sizable majorities of both blacks and whites told the Harris pollsters that their relationships with members of the other race were pleasant and easy, leading the National Conference of Christians and Jews, which commissioned the polls, to conclude that "familiarity has not bred contempt."

And while integration has at least temporarily taken a back seat to other issues among the nation's black groups, there exists no desire to turn back the clock. Says Benjamin Hooks, executive director of the National Association for the Advancement of Colored People, the nation's largest civil-rights organization: "I'm from the South, so there's no point of asking me if *I* want to go back to riding at the back of the bus."

8

Ethnic Groups, Prejudice and Economic Progress

By Thomas Sowell

Many discussions of group differences in income or occupation freely invoke such terms as "discrimination," or the even more emotionally charged (and empirically elusive) term "exploitation." While clear instances of discrimination have been encountered by many ethnic groups at various periods in their history, determining how much of the group differences in income, occupations or housing represent discrimination is complex and uncertain.

The historic prejudice and legal discriminations encountered by the Japanese were at least as severe as those encountered by Puerto Ricans, and yet Japanese incomes are more than double the incomes of Puerto Ricans, and significantly above those of Anglo-Saxons. Not only history but also economics argues against the widespread assumption that group income differences are largely a function of discrimination, rather than human capital differences or differences in age, geographic distribution and other factors.

Translating subjective prejudice into overt economic discrimination is costly for profit-seeking, competitive firms, though less so for government, public utilities, regulated industries like banking, or nonprofit organizations such as universities or hospitals. Just how costly was shown by the repeated failures of white employer cartels to control the wages of newly freed blacks after the Civil War—despite having almost every imaginable economic, legal, political and social advantage.

Statistics which today compare the incomes of ethnic individuals with the "same" education, for example, as members of the general population usually ignore large *qualitative* differences in educational substance and performance. Where these qualitative differences are even approximately taken into account, intergroup differences among comparable individuals shrink dramatically or even disappear.

"The Poor Pay More"

Assertions of consumer discrimination—claims that "the poor pay more"—likewise turn on group differences that are often ignored. Differences in crime rates, for example, affect the cost of running a store in many ways, leading to different prices for the same item in different ethnic neighborhoods. The honest consumer pays costs created by vandals, hoodlums and criminals in his neighborhood, but that is differ-

ent from saying that his neighborhood as a whole is being "exploited" by the store located there or by other ethnic groups. The steady exit of stores from high-crime neighborhoods suggests that there is no great profit being made there.

Ethnic groups also differ in credit repayment, and not always solely by income. Even low-income Italian Americans, for example, are considered good credit risks. The revolving credit devices used by the Chinese, Japanese and West Indians to finance their businesses work only where prompt and full repayment can be relied upon. Groups without the level of dependability that would enable them to use this device to raise capital among themselves are usually unable to raise capital from commercial sources for the same reason. Their failure to develop businesses cannot be arbitrarily attributed to lack of access to banks, for most small businesses (including those of Chinese, Japanese and West Indians) are not launched with bank loans anyway.

In housing markets as well, the high cost of slum dwellings has been denounced for years, going back to the 19th Century immigrant ghettos on the Lower East Side of New York. But despite bitter denunciations of slum landlords there, the actual records show no particularly large profits being made on slums in general. High rents were indeed *charged* for a given amount of space, but profits are made only on the rents actually *paid*—and thousands of evictions per year on the Lower East Side indicate that the two are not only conceptually but empirically very different. Again, the honest renter paid for the others and the average profit rates indicate that the Lower East Side tenants *as a whole* were not "exploited."

Individuals may be devastated by discrimination, even if it does not explain the economic conditions of a group as a whole.

Not only history but also economics argues against the widespread assumption that group income differences are largely a function of discrimination.

W.E.B. DuBois pointed out, at the turn of the century, that "the individual black workman is rated not by his own efficiency, but by the efficiency of a whole group of black fellow workmen which may often be low." Race is one of many sorting devices used because of the costliness of individual knowledge. The question of group discrimination is a question whether the group as a whole is misjudged or underpaid—a question about average performance, not individual variation.

The "representative Negroes" were, according to DuBois, "probably best fitted for the work they are doing," and if the racial prejudices of whites were to disappear overnight it "would not make very much difference in the positions occupied by Negroes" as a whole, though "some few would be promoted, some few would get new places" but "the mass would remain as they are . . ." What DuBois expected the lowering of racial barriers to accomplish was to provide incentives for successive generations of blacks to improve their skills and efforts. Whatever the empirical validity of DuBois's assessment, the important point here is that he distinguished discrimination against the individual from discrimination against the group.

Even where the current capability of the group is accurately assessed in the market, particular individuals in the group may still be grossly undervalued. DuBois himself was perhaps the classic example. But no recitation of such examples provides evidence that discrimination against the group as a whole explains the group's poverty. The galling tragedy of a DuBois or a Paul Robeson—men with superb educations and individual brilliance—was that they were held back solely by racial prejudice, and eventually ended up embittered Communists.

In other groups as well, it has been precisely some of the most acculturated and talented members who have been the most bitter, militant or extreme. The inference made by them and by others was that no amount of *group* acculturation, skills, or efforts would be any more successful than their individual development had been.

Some of the Japanese interned during World War II reached the same despairing conclusion. But however understandable their anger and despair, later events showed that the inference was neither logically conclusive nor historically correct. Within a generation after the internment,

Japanese Americans were among the most affluent, socially accepted and generally respected groups in the United States. This took about half a century from the beginning of Japanese immigration, and many of the virulent racists they encountered along the way could not have been changed by any conceivable thing the Japanese could have done. But the mortality of human beings, and therefore the turnover of individuals in the population, enabled the quiet persistence of the Japanese ultimately to win out on every economic, social and political front.

Nevertheless, this approach which proved successful with the Japanese (and Chinese and Jews) is often dismissed out of hand as naive, while progress is thought to require more confrontationist methods—which failed repeatedly for Irish Americans in the 19th Century, in areas ranging from public school controversies to the military draft during the Civil War to attempts to win economic advancement by terrorism or to procure the independence of Ireland with a military expedition against Canada.

Among blacks in the 20th Century, the initial successes of the non-violent civil rights movement slowed perceptibly as more militant, direct-action tactics stiffened the resistance of the larger society and provoked backlashes extending from simple resentments to the resurgence of such organizations as the Ku Klux Klan (even in Northern communities) and the Nazi fringe.

The point here is not to solve definitively the question of how much of intergroup differences in income, social acceptance and so forth has been due to the behavior and attitudes of particular ethnic groups and how much to the behavior and attitudes of the larger society. The point is that this is a complex question.

The importance of ethnic identity has varied enormously within each group. For some individuals, it has been a badge to be worn proudly. For others, it has been a way of life to be personally treasured, though not made a public issue. And for still others ethnic identity has been incidental, or a curiosity—or a stigma to be forgotten, evaded, or escaped as much as possible. This whole spectrum of individual attitudes has existed historically in all ethnic groups. In short, ethnic identity has been a complex and elusive phenomenon.

Varied With Groups

Its specific content has historically varied enormously, even within given groups. For example, the identity of 19th Century Jewish immigrants centered on their religious observances and their ethnic and national cultural traditions, including the Yiddish language. From their perspective, it would seem incomprehensible how some-

one could be considered a Jew who—like many 20th Century American Jews—pays little or no attention to religious observances, and lives, dresses, and talks like a gentile, and among gentiles. Yet no one would say that post-holocaust, post-Israel Jews have lost their identity. Their voting records alone distinguish them sharply from other Americans of the same economic level. They do not live in the past, but the past is in them.

Ethnic identity has sometimes been thought to be a potent—if not paramount—factor in group progress. But groups with much group identity, in such things as bloc voting or favoritism for political candidates or employes of one's own ethnicity, have not generally done better than groups with less concern over such things.

No one exceeded the favoritism of the Irish for other Irishmen, whether in politics or the church, but in general they advanced no faster than the Italians who showed little of the same spirit in politics or elsewhere. Some groups (such as the Jews and the Japanese) have enjoyed and maintained their own special culture, but without making a public issue of it (as many blacks or Hispanics). It is by no means clear that either cultural persistence or group advancement has been promoted by making cultural distinctiveness a controversial issue. The 19th Century Irish made more fuss about the Gaelic language than the 19th Century Jews did about Yiddish, but Yiddish was far more widely spoken among Jews than Gaelic among the Irish.

With many American ethnic groups, the accumulation of evolutionary changes has made the 20th Century groups very different from their 19th Century ancestors. Many of these profound changes are seldom

---

Both the testimony of contemporaries and the record of epidemics convey the historical fact that 19th Century Irish immigrants lived in filthy conditions. . .

---

discussed, because of current ethnic etiquette and sensitivities. Both the testimony of contemporaries and the record of epidemics convey the historical fact that 19th Century Irish immigrants lived in filthy conditions, both in their homes and in their persons. But modern discussions of ethnicity usually omit any references to either cleanliness or its absence, except for using any mention or complaints along these

lines as proof of the bias or hatred of the person quoted.

Epidemics of filth-related diseases still move very selectively through ethnic neighborhoods, but ethnic differences in life expectancy are axiomatically attributed to the racism of the larger society. Even extremely high automobile accident fatality rates among young men in a group that stresses machismo are automatically attributed to the group's poverty and the older automobiles they drive as a result.

Whatever justification these apologetics might have within a purely moralistic framework, within a cause-and-effect framework they simply blot out major factors at work. Historically, they prevent our knowing or understanding how progress was achieved—or is being achieved—in dealing with internal group problems whose very existence is ignored or denied. A group cannot be getting cleaner over time, if any suggestion that it was ever dirty was only a figment of bigots' imaginations. Their children could not have overcome their educational deficiencies in the schools if their only problems were racist teachers and biased tests. No other internal problems—from alcoholism to violence—could be overcome by any group, if such things were only biased propaganda or the inevitable results of the failures of "society." As a corollary, some of the longest and hardest struggles for self-improvement must be denied—which is to say history itself is denied.

Within the confines of the moralistic approach, progress (like poverty) can only be presented as a product of "society"—now grudgingly granting new "rights" or partial "acceptance." If the Irish were pariahs in the 19th Century and fully accepted in the 20th Century, the moralistic approach sees only society's belated changes to doing the right thing. It ignores the very possibility that the Irish who are accepted today may be very different from the 19th Century immigrants from Ireland whose personal behavior would still be wholly unacceptable to others today, including today's Irish Americans.

The history of American groups—which is to say, ultimately, the history of the American people—is the history of a complex aggregate of complex groups and individuals. It cannot be a simple morality play. It is a story of similar patterns and profound differences, of pain and pride and achievement. It is, in one sense, the story of many very different heritages. In another sense, it is the story of the human spirit in its many guises.

Mr. Sowell is a senior fellow of the Hoover Institution at Stanford University. This piece is from his book "Ethnic America," to be published next June by Basic Books.

9

Simmering Streets

Miami's Liberty City, Site of Riot in 1980, Is Tense, Troubled

Devastated Ghetto Is Bracing For Cuts in Federal Aid, Seeking Private Funding

Drug Deals & Hungry Dogs

By ANTHONY RAMIREZ

Staff Reporter of THE WALL STREET JOURNAL

MIAMI, Fla.—In the tough black ghetto known as Liberty City, things rarely change —but when they do, they get worse.

A riot in 1968, overshadowed by the Republican presidential convention in nearby Miami Beach, was followed 12 years later by last May's devastating riot, which claimed 18 lives and destroyed $100 million in property. Although the latest riot's rubble and ashes have been cleared away now, crime and unemployment remain high and are getting higher. Blacks still view the police as an occupying army whose unchecked brutality ultimately led to the riot. The police, meanwhile, see each summons to this ghetto in the northwestern part of the city as a potential ambush.

"The riot is still going on," says Archie Hardwick, a black community organizer, "except in slow motion."

Now, both black and white community leaders fear that smoldering Liberty City will soon receive more tinder in the form of President Reagan's proposed cutbacks in social services, especially programs designed to spur black businesses. "The President talks about cutting down to the bone," says Annie Love, the head of the tenant council at James E. Scott Homes, a large and troubled Liberty City housing project. "Hell, there ain't no bone for us to cut!"

Troubled Leaders

The President's budget cuts also trouble many white business leaders. "Although I support the overall direction of the President's program, these cutbacks won't particularly help our situation," says Alvah Chapman Jr., president of the Miami Herald and its parent, Knight-Ridder Newspapers Inc.

White business leaders here are looking for private money to help solve Liberty City's problems. One proposal involves City Venture Corp., a Minneapolis-based group of firms whose principal stockholder is Control Data Corp. Although two-year-old City Venture hasn't created any jobs yet, it has gotten commitments for jobs at a Toledo, Ohio, neighborhood revitalization program from such firms as Owens-Illinois Inc. and Libbey-Owens-Ford Co.

The City Venture proposal for Liberty City would cost several million dollars and is aimed at creating 4,000 jobs over the next five years. Using computer educational systems, City Venture trains participants in basic skills such as reading, writing, and arithmetic, as well as how to interview for and keep a job. It also helps minority entrepreneurs obtain loans and run businesses.

Victims' Vows

However, the white businessmen who were located in Liberty City before the riot and who were the riot's principal targets aren't sanguine about the ghetto's future and vow that they themselves will never return. One such businessman is Richard Britt, whose Liberty City plant for overhauling jet-engine parts was looted and partially burned during the riot; Mr. Britt then moved his plant to the suburbs. "Am I supposed to look at those burned-out buildings and those empty lots for the next 10 years?" he asks.

He goes on: "Who's going to build in that area? Nobody. They can talk all the reconstruction they want to. There isn't anybody with any money and any brains that's going to build anything."

By day, there is the look of peace along the shadeless streets of Liberty City (which was named by a white real-estate developer in the 1920s). The riot-razed, bottle-strewn vacant lots are indistinguishable now from similar lots that were vacant before the riot. Street vendors sell fish, turnips and oranges from card tables and from the backs of vans. Women hang laundry from the scratched black railings of ramshackle two-story apartment buildings.

Teen-Agers' Taunts

Late at night, however, viewed from the patrol car of Bill Wolff and Diana Danehart, Liberty City is a tense, angry corner of the world. The two white rookie police officers are with the Public Safety Department of Dade County, and their job on this night is to patrol among Liberty City's estimated 150,000 to 160,000 residents, almost all of whom are black.

As the police car rounds a corner near a crowded saloon, a pregnant prostitute ducks into a house. T-shirted teen-agers glare at the officers as the car cruises past a grocery store. "Are you going to McDuffie me?" street toughs demand, referring to Arthur McDuffie, the black insurance salesman who was bludgeoned to death by white officers in December 1979; the acquittal of four policemen accused of the crime triggered the riot of May 1980.

"Some people step out of their houses and shoot their guns into the air just to scare us—just to watch us react," says Officer Wolff, who is 24 years old. "They think it's a big joke to see the cops run around like crazy."

Although Officers Wolff and Danehart are unfailingly polite to blacks in all the situations they confront this night (mainly screaming "domestic disturbances" and minor traffic offenses), they pass the time privately in bitter remarks about Liberty City and its residents. Watching a stray dog pass by, Officer Danehart, who is 28 years old, says, "It hurts to see the dogs with their ribs sticking out because they can't help themselves—not like the people. They can bring themselves up if they want to."

When told of Officer Danehart's views, a resident of James E. Scott homes is incensed. The resident, a 54-year-old black woman who requested anonymity, blames racism for the ghetto's troubles. She says she works as a maid for two days a week, earning $50 that she doesn't dare report to the welfare authorities lest they cut her $506 in monthly food stamps and other benefits. The woman is raising four young grandchildren by herself, she says, adding: "I need that money to survive."

The Scott Homes are a tough place to live. The concrete complex, sprawling and unlovely, houses some 3,000 people, more than half of whom are under the age of 17. Two-thirds of the families are on welfare, and most of the mothers lack husbands. There is an active drug ring; another operation centers on stolen goods. Residents routinely ascribe shooting deaths to arguments over drug deals or "hot stuff."

Jobs would ease problems here and throughout the ghetto. But black businesses are unable to create the jobs; and white businessmen are reluctant to hire this city's unskilled black teen-agers, perhaps half of whom are unemployed.

Mr. Britt, the owner of the looted jet-engine-parts plant, says he attempted to hire blacks four times before his Liberty City operation was destroyed. Each time, he says, the applicants or their friends tried to burglarize the plant. "Those people aren't unemployed," he says. "They're unemployable." The foreman of his current crew of 26, he adds, is the group's only black.

The few black businesses in Liberty City are unable to provide much help for the ghetto's residents. About the only black business of any size to start up since the May riot is a combination restaurant, lounge and liquor store called the Golden Tornado. And its owner, Ronald Young, voices a familiar complaint of black businessmen: He spent three frustrating years trying to get a bank loan. Finally, last year, he got a $90,-000 SBA loan that was secured by some $200,000 worth of collateral, including the complex's land and building that he already owned.

"I am not a young man—I am 61 years old," says Mr. Young, a college administrator. He adds: "Blacks who want to get into business not only get the runaround, they don't even get to run." (Blacks, who make up some 15% of Dade County's 1.6 million residents, don't control a single bank in the county.)

Relations between the black and white business communities are often icy. Whites "want to deal with tribal chiefs and not with poor folks," says Archie Hardwick, the black director of James E. Scott Community Association Inc., in a reference to an often-stated complaint by whites that there are few black "leaders."

Otis Pitts, the black director of the Advisory Committee on Liberty City Youth, notes that several prominent blacks are members of many committees. Whites, he says, are "looking for super-niggers who can play musical chairs."

Mr. Chapman, the Miami Herald president, is surprised to hear such views and especially to hear attacks on the plan to bring in City Venture Corp. "It's easy for us to become the whipping boy," he says. "Actually, we don't have to do anything. But we are doing something, and it's out of a spirit of public service."

But whatever is done will take time—an increasingly scarce commodity here. Already frustration is mounting that only $62.6 million has been delivered from some $112 million in riot aid promised by the Carter administration. Says Eileen Maloney, a county official coordinating federal aid: "Everybody in the community thought the cavalry, the Army and the Marine Corps were coming to the aid of Liberty City. They weren't."

If President Reagan's proposals for budget cuts are put into effect by Congress, they could mean 1,000 or more CETA workers here out of jobs and back on welfare as early as this October. Among other ramifications, a $6.9 million project designed to encourage commercial development in Overtown, another of Miami's black ghettos, is in jeopardy; and public housing and rent subsidies are likely to be slowed in an area where 20,000 people already are on waiting lists, some for as long as eight years.

"Reagan has fired the shot, but we have yet to feel the wound," says the youth committee's Mr. Pitts. He notes that after the 1968 riot, little was done to change basic conditions in the ghetto. But after last year's devastation, he says, "We won't have 12 years to appease black folks."

An Alienated Generation of Black Students?

By Michael L. King

TUSKEGEE, Ala.—If the students here at Tuskegee Institute are typical, young blacks preparing for professional careers are astonishingly alienated.

This alienation stems partly from the disparity between black America and white America. Black youths resent hearing whites talk about how much progress blacks have made, because they don't think racism has lessened. They fear—no, they are almost convinced—that racism will prevent them from finding a meaningful job in American business.

Despite what the students think, there has of course been progress, and one of its more obvious signs is the emergence in recent years of a black professional class. Trouble is, that class seems as inaccessible to the students as the master's mansion on a Mississippi plantation once did to the field hands.

I discovered this recently when I spent three days talking to students here at predominantly black Tuskegee Institute. I was here as part of a youth motivation task force organized by the National Alliance of Business. The program matches black, Chicano and American Indian professionals with college students who are members of those same minority groups. NAB is financed cooperatively by the federal government and industry. Expenses of task-force participants are paid by their employers.

The Same Questions

I talked to more than 200 students here, individually, in large classes and in small groups. Many asked the same questions: Why would Dow Jones let you come here to talk to us? How did you get your job? Are the people you work with racists? What kinds of questions will a job interviewer ask me? Last summer I couldn't find any other job, so I took a job sweeping floors; did I make a mistake? Should I have gone to summer school instead?

My answers were honest, if predictable: Take advantage of every opportunity to get work experience. An employer will want to know how well you will handle responsibility, and college grades and previous work experience are good indicators. Don't wear a party dress or disco shoes to a job interview. Yes, there are some racists in business and you will run into racism in your careers. Life isn't easy or fair but with hard work others have managed to succeed and you can, too.

Most of these students seemed bright and ambitious, but lacking in the social skills they need to get and keep a profes-sional-class job in white America. To attain any measure of success, blacks typically must learn two distinct cultures—their own, and that of the white majority. Most blacks who now hold professional positions got them because they learned how to live, and gain acceptance, in the majority culture.

But the young blacks I met think learning the majority culture is a waste of time. They are convinced that America has hardened its heart towards them. They dream, but don't make much effort toward realizing their dreams because they fear it is futile. They feel despised by whites and spurned by black professionals.

On a plane back to Atlanta I sat next to Patricia Blackmon, a district staff manager with American Telephone & Telegraph Co.'s Southern Bell unit. She was on the Tuskegee task force, too, and she came away with similar feelings. "I am really afraid when I think what's going to happen when they graduate," she said sadly. "When they apply for jobs and don't get them they'll think it's racism. But I wouldn't hire most of them either."

Most of these students seemed bright and ambitious, but lacking in the social skills they need to get and keep a professional-class job in white America.

Ms. Blackmon and I puzzled about how and why these students—only 10 to 15 years younger—are so different from those of us who came of age in the 1960s. We ruminated about our own experiences growing up black and poor — she in Newnan, Ga., and I in Greenville, Miss.

Our generation, we agreed, had grown up with little television and much responsibility. From our earliest years we'd been actively involved in everything around us. We had chores to do after school, but there was never a hint of getting paid for them. Ms. Blackmon's father was a storekeeper, and after school she was required to work in the store.

I recalled to her that on Sunday nights my sister Esther would play the organ, while my father, my sister Helen, my two brothers and I served as the church choir. "That was us," she said excitedly, also remembering. "That was me playing the organ."

But the students' memories are sparser and paler. For some reason—too much television, I suspect—they are passive in many ways. Without that bent toward active participation, they have little sense of origination, conclusion or accomplishment.

My generation always seemed to have a sense of purpose, even when—as frequently occurred—we charged off in the wrong direction. We spent our days demonstrating against racial injustice, and our nights boning up on revolutionary rhetoric by studying the writings of Jomo Kenyatta and Frantz Fanon. Reading was a joy, because to wrestle successfully with such concepts as colonialism and nationalism gave us a sense of accomplishment and precluded feelings of isolation.

We even managed to pass our college courses. We were too ornery to flunk. Administrators told us that failure was certain for students who committed such vile acts as imprisoning the chancellor's family in their own residence at the University of Mississippi, or taking school trustees hostage at Tuskegee. We were determined to prove them wrong, and we did.

By contrast, the students I met seemed to have no clear sense of purpose and no unswerving determination to accomplish anything.

Most important, we who grew up in the Sixties felt a sacred indebtedness to those who had gone before us. Our successes, we believed, occurred in large part because we'd been hoisted high atop the shoulders of the generations past. When my mother was a small girl, my grandparents lived and worked on a plantation in the Mississippi delta. They ran afoul of the plantation boss when my grandmother decided my mother should attend school. The plantation boss felt that children of the field hands also owed him a day's work. My grandparents disagreed. So they crammed their meager possessions in a broken-down wagon and moved on. If my grandparents had done otherwise, I thought years later, my own career goals and life accomplishments would have been far lower.

That today's black college students seem to feel cut off from their predecessors, rather than linked to them, says much about the shortcomings of my generation. We haven't done very well by younger blacks. To many of us, social responsibility has come to mean a yearly contribution to the United Fund, an every-other-year contribution to the United Negro College Fund, and an occasional trek into the inner city for ribs. Evidence of our aloofness is that the eight persons who traveled here for the youth motivation task force were less than half of those the NAB asked to participate.

Both Ms. Blackmon and I were adults before we met blacks who hold the kind of jobs we now hold. In those days there weren't many black professionals and most of them were physicians.

More Interaction Needed

Now, there are many. But we haven't interacted with black youth as we should have. In the white culture there is much interaction between youth and professionals. Often this interaction—around the neighborhood, in churches, family get-togethers—is unintentional and simply is part of the milieu in which white youths grow up. In much of the black community, such coincidental interaction isn't possible. It must be planned. And thus far, we've failed to do that.

I don't worry about the Tuskegee students I met. Most of them will make it. But I am deeply worried about the students who have no encouragement and no one with whom to share their plans.

Once, at Tulane University, I spent the better part of a Saturday in the library sweating over chemistry books. By evening, I had resigned myself to failing the exam the following Monday. I walked downstairs in the University Center to get a glass of beer. Before I entered the Rathskeller I was approached by a janitor whom I knew only as Joe. "How's it going?" Joe asked.

"Bad," I groaned. "This chemistry course is getting the best of me."

Joe wrapped his arm around my shoulder. "It ain't bad as you think," he said. "You know, when I was a boy they wouldn't let me near this place. If I crossed Jefferson Street they'd put me in jail. It ain't that hard. You'll make it. You gotta."

I was too choked up to drink beer. I went back to my room and studied for the remainder of the weekend. I made an A on that exam—partly, I think, because someone was there to encourage me and to keep me from quitting.

I'm glad I participated in NAB's program at Tuskegee. I believe such programs change lives, and I wish that other black professionals would recognize this and find a way to get involved.

Mr. King is a reporter in the Journal's Cleveland bureau.

The Situation for Blacks in the Reagan Years

This week's issue of the Economist of London summarizes the situation nicely: "A counter-revolution in civil rights is under way in America. During the Reagan years federal government support for efforts to end racial segregation and to promote opportunities for disadvantaged minorities cannot be taken for granted. The new, harsher climate represents a victory for some of the nastier forces on the American right which have always balked at civil rights laws. But it has been given an intellectual underpinning by those free market economists with good White House connections who argue that government

---

Viewpoint

by Morton M. Kondracke

---

aid to minorities has been useless, perhaps even harmful. The Reagan administration's enthusiasm for this logic heralds an end to the bipartisan consensus on civil rights that has prevailed for the past 20 years."

What should blacks and black leaders do about this counter-revolution? Recent polls suggest that one reaction is a growing sense of pessimism in the black community.

There are two other major strains of black leadership reaction to the Reagan counter-revolution. Traditional organizational and political leaders seem intent on railing at Mr. Reagan, taking him to court and trying to get Congress to salvage government's 20-year social and civil rights agenda. This group is sticking by standard liberal doctrine that black poverty fundamentally is the result of white racism and should be remedied by government programs which both end discrimination and attempt to improve the economic circumstances of black people.

This view is now under challenge from a small group of black conservatives led by Thomas Sowell of Stanford University's Hoover Institution, author of two recent books, "Markets and Minorities" and "Ethnic America: A History." Mr. Sowell acknowledges that blacks have suffered discrimination, but denies that it is the basic cause of black poverty. More important, he says, are cultural patterns of illegitimacy, illiteracy and dependency, the unfamiliarity of recent Southern migrants with urban living and the facts that the average age for blacks is lower than for the population as a whole (hence their average income is lower) and that half of all blacks live in the South (where the average wage for all groups is lower than for the nation).

Most of all, Mr. Sowell condemns the notion that blacks should look to government for their salvation. "At particular junctures," he writes, "government policy may be beneficial to particular ethnic groups. It is the long run reliance on political action that is questionable in view of the unpredictability of political trends in general." He cites as examples the shift from Reconstruction to the era of Jim Crow, from desegregation of the federal civil service to re-segregation under Woodrow Wilson and back again.

Traditional civil rights leaders and the black conservatives are battling back and forth. The former accuse Mr. Sowell of blaming the victims of their poverty and of providing Mr. Reagan with a rationale for racial retrenchment. Meanwhile the conservatives charge that the traditional leadership is an elite which maintains its status by promoting government programs which actually prolong black dependency.

Is it necessary to side with one group or the other—or to give in to despair? I think it's not. A sound middle road is available for black leadership, which is spelled out by black Harvard Professor Martin Kilson in the summer 1981 issue of the quarterly The Public Interest.

Mr. Kilson contends along with the traditional leadership that "racism, though diminished, remains a problem and complicates the task of ending intergenerational poverty among Afro-Americans. A new conservatism aids a persistent racist response toward black poverty by too many whites. Its spokesmen often suggest, implicitly or explicitly, that the claims of lower-class Afro-Americans on public resources are less worthy than the claims of white lower strata at earlier periods."

Mr. Kilson also agrees that political and government action has been vital to blacks in the past—protecting them against racial violence, securing their political rights and making possible many of the educational and economic gains that blacks (and particularly middle class blacks) — have achieved during the past two decades. Mr. Kilson says that black leaders have a right and responsibility to rail at Ronald Reagan and to protect the most important gains of the past against erosion.

But he also says that black leaders should diversify their activities by paying more attention to the black underclass and its cultural infirmities, including delinquency, crime, unwed motherhood, drugs, lack of educational motivation and unemployment. According to Mr. Kilson, the most important factor in the persistence of black poverty is the "seemingly endemic incapacity" of female-headed families "to foster social mobility comparable to husband-wife and male-headed families." And in the black community there has been "an enormous expansion of female-headed households during the past two decades"—from 23% of the total in the early 1960s to 41% today. According to Mr. Kilson, "it must be a part of any serious strategy" for black leaders "to devise ways . . . for reducing certain cultural or societal pathologies widely prevalent among lower-class blacks. . . . above all, becoming mothers and fathers while still in one's teens."

Mr. Kilson suggests that black leaders ought to fight racism and Reaganism, yes, but also get busy in their own communities combating drugs, crime, promiscuity and illiteracy.

Mr. Kondracke is executive editor of the New Republic magazine.

The Ideas Around Us

Learning Wisdom From The Federalist

By WILLIAM KRISTOL

One reason we read old books like The Federalist—the series of 85 papers written in defense of the new Constitution in 1787-1788 by Alexander Hamilton, James Madison and John Jay—is to find quotations with which to adorn our discussions of contemporary issues.

Friends of supply-side economics, for example, can gain points for elegance by quoting Hamilton (from Federalist No. 21): Many taxes "prescribe their own limit, which cannot be exceeded without defeating the end proposed—that is, an extension of the revenue. When applied to this object, the saying is as just as it is witty that, in political arithmetic, two and

The Bookshelf

"Explaining America: The Federalist"
By Garry Wills

two do not always make four. If duties are too high, they lessen the consumption; the collection is eluded; and the product to the treasury is not so great as when they are confined within proper and moderate bounds." There is much in The Federalist that is similarly notable and quotable.

Another reason to read The Federalist is patriotism. Madison argues in No. 49 that even the "wisest and freest governments" require the veneration of their citizenry if they are to have "the requisite stability." How better inculcate that veneration than to consider this impressive product of our Founding Fathers, embodying their deep and coherent reflection on the principles and problems of free government? Our admiration for this work of the Founders invites pride in the fact that they are *our* Founders, and instills a determination to live up to their high standards of thought and deed.

But the real reason to read The Federalist is, of course, to learn from it. The decline in the quality of American political thought has been so marked that even a cursory reading of The Federalist cannot help but be of benefit, and a careful study can be a liberating experience. It is virtually a necessary experience for one seeking to think seriously about fundamental questions of American politics; for to try to learn about the broad issues of politics by reading only 20th Century political science is like trying to learn to appreciate music by listening only to 20th Century music.

How helpful is Garry Wills's new book, "Explaining America: The Federalist" (Doubleday, 286 pages, $14.95), to the task of learning from The Federalist? The answer is mixed. Mr. Wills, a political journalist and author of a recent book on Jefferson's Declaration of Independence, is more successful in showing that "much that has been written about The Federalist

must be discarded" than in providing his own coherent and convincing analysis.

The thrust of Mr. Wills's interpretation of The Federalist is to find in the work far more concern for the character of the citizenry and the virtue and wisdom of the rulers than is usually acknowledged. It is mistaken, Mr. Wills argues forcefully, to see the authors of The Federalist as bowing before the power of self-interest, and as relying almost exclusively on quasi-mechanical contrivances such as the size of the nation and checks and balances to preserve liberty. Mr. Wills asserts that The Federalist expects a virtuous people to "choose wise and virtuous rulers who would exercise power benignly"; and that rather than setting "interest against interest in a constructive process of self-correction," The Federalist expects "that interest is to be eliminated from the political arena, distilled out of the process."

Mr. Wills's challenging argument may serve as a useful corrective to other interpretations. But it is not entirely satisfactory. Perhaps because of his training as a classical philologist, Mr. Wills is most interested to discover the sources for various passages in The Federalist (usually in the essays of the Scottish philosopher David Hume). His concern for sources and his method of interpreting statements of Madi-

son and Hamilton through the prism of Hume produce occasional insights, but they divert Mr. Wills from the task of trying to understand how the various parts and various aspects of The Federalist fit together as a complex but unified whole.

A coherent understanding of The Federalist would show in particular how its hard-headed and its elevated aspects are knit together. It would show how The Federalist's appreciation of the harsh necessities of politics is consistent with its high expectation that Americans would vindicate "that honorable determination which animates every votary of freedom to rest all our political experiments on the capacity of mankind for self-government." And it would suggest how The Federalist's emphasis on the fact that we Americans are not exempt from "the natural and necessary progress of human affairs" does not preclude our following "a new and more noble course."

Mr. Wills's book does not provide such a coherent understanding, but at least it invites us to reconsider The Federalist and achieve such an understanding ourselves.

Mr. Kristol is assistant professor of political science at the University of Pennsylvania.

Thinking Things Over

———— By Vermont Royster ————

Equality—and Difference

Of all the enduring controversies of my time (evolution, for example) none is more puzzling than that over the roles of heredity and environment. And none more emotion-laden.

The emotion arises because it has spilled over into current arguments about race and, more recently, the relation between men and women. It thus intrudes into debates about child-rearing, education, the role of women in society in everything from jobs to military service. So heated is

the emotion that anyone who dares a comment is sure to be assailed from all sides.

What makes it puzzling is that people have really known for centuries that among living things both genetics and environment play their parts in the development of species and of individuals within the species. Each contributes to making living things what they are.

Primitive farmers knew that grain grown under some conditions of rain and sun thrived better than that with a different environment. They also knew, long before they knew why, that some strains of grain survived better in an adverse environment.

They knew, too, that a well-trained horse runs faster than one that isn't. This leads no one to suppose, even today, that a Kentucky Derby winner can be made by training alone. Its speed is a function of both its heredity and its training.

The situation is no different in a schoolroom, where good teaching in a good environment benefits every child. Or in the rearing of boys and girls and where the

manner makes a difference in the adults they will become. But no amount of teaching will make an Einstein out of everyone, nor any rearing make a female out of a male.

All this, I'm sure, we all know without modern genetics to tell us so. Yet it's a little startling to see Newsweek, in a recent issue, announce the discovery that there are genetic differences between men and women. And then see it twist and turn to minimize those differences, knowing the topic to be so emotion-laden.

* * *

The emotional weight begins when we begin to attach to differences, racial or sexual, such words as "superiority" or "inferiority." Which is "superior," a Pygmy or an Eskimo? Each would answer differently, but the question is meaningless. Superior in what and for what?

The natural superiority of women in many particulars is shown by experience. Physically, they live longer than men; they survive better than men certain hardships, such as near starvation and have greater endurance under strain. Mentally, girls learn to talk earlier than boys. The experiments cited by Newsweek show what folklore long understood, that girls have a better developed tactile sense and manual dexterity.

In other areas the situation is different. Boys are taller, develop stronger upper-torso muscles. By the time they reach puberty they can run faster, lift heavier weights, throw objects farther than girls given the same exercise training. Little boys, as every mother knows, are more apt to take things apart (tear them up), which suggests a greater curiosity about what makes things work, such as bows and arrows and rock-throwing catapults, and may account for success in science and technology.

On the average, that is. I'm male, five-feet-six, 140 pounds. So there are many women stronger than I, who can beat me at tennis, hit a golf ball farther, run faster. On the other hand, so I'm told, I talked earlier than neighboring girls, suggesting a verbal aptitude commonly thought of as "female."

* * *

Folk wisdom also understood that such inborn traits could be modified by environment. Our ancestors may have erred in rearing boys one way, girls another, although that's a modern judgment. Certainly in earlier times there were good reasons for reinforcing the maleness of boys, the femaleness of girls. But in so doing those ancestors recognized the innate traits of sex could be tempered. It was just they thought it wiser, given their conditions, to reinforce rather than to alter.

All science has added to folk wisdom is to explain the differences. We understand better today the working of genes, or the role of hormones, in making each of us different.

Unfortunately the new knowledge hasn't added to our wisdom. We, or at least a great many of us, think that in order to proclaim our equality as human beings, regardless of pigmentation or gender, we must deny the differences. To admit genetic differences which limit what can be changed by environment strikes some people as an outrage. To admit unalterable differences, so they fear, is to brand some as "inferior."

In education this has led to the idea of the monolithic classroom. All children, regardless of natural aptitudes, must be taught the same things in the same way. To teach differently is elitism, a pejorative term with its implication that education in some things is "better" than others. Try to shape the individual to the education rather than the other way around.

The same idea has taken hold of child rearing. Boys and girls should be raised as if they were the same. And note that the standard chosen is subtly insulting to the female. Raise the girls in pants, not the boys in pinafores. There are even those who say women won't be "equal" until they play football for the Chicago Bears or lug 50-pound packs through the mud as combat infantrymen.

It's gotten pretty ridiculous. We're all born white, black or yellow, destined to be six feet tall or five-feet-six, male or female. Instead of bemoaning such destiny, we should make the most of it and revel in our differences. But given the modern mood, I doubt we will.

The Conservative Ideas in Reagan's Victory

By Leopold Tyrmand

As the Reagan presidency sails into actuality, it may be proper to consider whether this circumstance is the victory of a man or of an idea. Ever since November 4, plenty has been said about the man and very little about the idea.

Somehow obscured by the media's portraiture of Mr. Reagan's triumph is the question of how much of it can be attributed to his skills, his charms and the timeliness of his message—and how much should be ascribed to the ideas he has invoked for the last two decades. Yet Mr. Reagan's achievement cannot be divorced from the political pogroms in South Dakota, Idaho and elsewhere in which the important thing was not who won but what won.

Reagan's Opinions

Much reporting told the country everything about Mr. Reagan's chemistry and magic, but practically nothing about the ideas he proclaimed. Instead, the media repeated his stands on regulations, foreign policy, inflation, spending, bureaucracy and unemployment. These are his opinions on issues; they are not ideas. Ideas are often concepts for how to perceive, feel about and deal with issues. Accordingly, except

for the economic idea of a radical tax cut and the suggestion of getting tough with the Soviets (a sort of geopolitical idea), Mr. Reagan just affirms that his ideas are conservative. His stance somehow feeds the conviction of columnists who believe that one is a conservative if he is against big government and for free enterprise and a strong defense. Yet a sympathy for business, or for a well-armed America, are sociopolitical preferences, not ideas — the theory of the free market or of America's global responsibility are ideas.

Some voices in the press have already tried to present the anticipated splendor and the Adolfo dresses of the Reagan White House as a conservative idea. The New York Times Magazine ran a piece titled "Living Well Is Still the Best Revenge," as if the Times were attempting to

set the tone for an era of conservative ethos in which wealth is a moral and existential measure. This is a doleful misunderstanding, especially in view of the fact that the polyester-clad Moral Majority provided perhaps the most powerful infusion of ideology into the 1980 political season.

Therefore, what are those ideas which, translated into a political landslide, have made Mr. Reagan who he is?

It's uncertain whether Mr. Reagan ever read Von Mises, Weaver or Strauss. Their ideas came to him via cultural osmosis, from conservative publicists and pamphleteering over the last 40 years.

Modern American conservatism is an elastic notion: Anyone who liked Hamilton and John Adams during his college years can claim a conservative bent; but actually an admirer of Jefferson may claim the same label today. Scholars generally see two brands of contemporary conservatism: libertarian, whose priority is freedom and its application to our social existence; and social-ethical, which, next to liberty, is equally concerned with other components of our common destiny—like an individual's rights and duties, Western civilization, societal bonds. The social-ethical variety of conservatism owns a larger portfolio of mankind's thinking and looks for help from sources that include religion, reason, tradition, historical experience and the continuity of values. Conservative ideas are scarcely new; in the language of philosophers, they are the ideas of social contract, natural law and equality of rights.

The Judeo-Christian mind has long been involved with these themes. If the libertarian, or secular, conservatism traces its immediate heritage to John Locke and Montesquieu, the favorite reference of social ethical conservatives is Edmund Burke, a thinker less honored by historians. Dr. Johnson called Burke a Whig, which then meant one of liberal persuasion. However, one who considered himself a liberal in 18th- or 19th-Century England and France would have a hard time reading The New York Times or listening to Senator Kennedy's speeches.

Classical liberals firmly believed that man's social happiness lay in curtailing the arbitrary powers of politics and culture, in the decentralization of the state's functions, in economic freedom, in voluntary associations, in "family, neighborhood, guild, church." In our time, "liberal" has come to mean the collectivization of social objectives and a manipulative government whose benevolent omnipotence is assumed to be for the societal good. Jefferson, de Tocqueville and Lincoln would wince if faced with such an assumption.

At this century's outset a dynamic brand of prescriptive liberalism gained vast influence in America's politics, economy and culture, and was declared to be a social panacea. Culminating in FDR's victory, it turned into an intellectual faith, ritual and superstition, and determined public affairs for decades. To this kind of liberalism, "social contract" meant a prescription for how to distribute wealth in keeping with the rules of compassion devised by a federal bureaucracy; liberty was isolated from moral principle or civic assent and turned into behavioral laissez-faire-ism presented as human rights. On the philosophical plateau, American liberalism dismissed reason—the tool of Locke, Jefferson, Franklin and Burke—and installed conscience alone as the informing agent for how to live, prosper and progress.

The reaction to this set of beliefs began before World War II, but only later did it coalesce into what became known as the conservative intellectual movement. The conservative response to the prescriptive dogmas of enforced egalitarianism and social justice was strictly antitotalitarian; conservatives challenged the tyranny of recipes for how to love, what to believe in and how economy and culture should perform. However, the conservative fight for the meaning of democracy and civilization was doomed to obscurity; the academy, the media, the literary salons were firmly in the hands of the liberal true believers. Thus, the conservatives became an inbred group, ostracized by their liberal colleagues and by enlightened opinion at large. They attracted some support from a few businessmen who were interested in their defense of capitalism, and from segments of young academic intelligentsia in search of intellectual nonconformism and a rational critique of the liberal orthodoxy. The giant middle class, whose sense of the permanence of values they championed, was ignorant of their existence—and it still is, thanks to the silence of the media. Still, despite all odds, those social-ethical conservatives developed a sort of adversary underground culture. They took to the pamphlet, that old vehicle for independence of mind and free inquiry, they had lecture circuits, symposia, seminars and newsletters. A network of small, unprofitable scientific and literary reviews eventually became their wonder weapon. It can safely be asserted that the seeds of the 1980 election were planted in the tiny scholarly journals of the 1940s and watered by abstruse philosophical ruminations.

Many names could be cited, but five should be mentioned as perhaps having a pervasive influence in the formation of future answers to the complexity of social and moral concerns. Those are Ludwig von Mises, Richard Weaver, Leo Strauss, Gordon Keith Chalmers and John Hallowell.

All were university professors—political philosophers, economists, moralists. Von Mises and Strauss were Europeans, escapees from Hitler. Weaver was the father of the conservative philosophy of culture (few today who repeat the phrase "ideas have consequences" know that it's the title of his book, still in print). With books such as "Human Action," Von Mises devoted his life to proving that capitalism and free enterprise are sources of humanity and virtue (which makes him an ancestor of supply-side microeconomics), and that any form of collectivism and statism must end in totalitarian oppression.

Strauss taught, at the University of Chicago and in his "Natural Right and History," that freedom, pluralism and democracy can survive only if words like authority, duty, responsibility and common sense "are deeply ingrained in individual and social consciousness."

Chalmers and Hallowell maintained that the conservative impulse is man's only defense against dehumanization in a culture erected on moral relativism and the eradication of both natural and revealed law. They argued against value-free education, against the "liberation of instincts" and for normative standards of social and personal conduct, for a sensible balance between civic rights and civic obligations, for America's spiritual and social institutions as bulwarks against despotism. Hallowell's best-known work is "The Decline of Liberalism as an Ideology"; Chalmers's "The Public and the Person" is no longer in print.

To many it's evident that 1980 brought about the victory of those ideas. American institutionalism was pitted against the idea of social engineering, and it won hands down. The modern conservative message that freedom is a condition under which life can best improve ran against the concept of unbounded permissiveness as a prescription for a better society, and the voters made the obvious choice. Finally the need for common sense and normalcy of mores (the ethics of natural law) as the prime conditioners of our everydayness has emerged as a powerful factor of the voters' response: The desire for the restoration of standards established by six millennia of civilization sealed Mr. Reagan's triumph.

Ideology Won't Go Away

It's uncertain whether Mr. Reagan ever read Von Mises, Weaver or Strauss. Rather, their ideas came to him via cultural osmosis, from conservative publicists and pamphleteering over the last 40 years. This guarantees that if Mr. Reagan's tenure results in ideological cosmetics in lieu of a more profound reform of public affairs, the ideology he espouses won't go away. Ideas can only be defeated by antithetical ideas; this is the gist of what happened in 1932 and in 1980—the rest is politics as usual.

None of those philosophers of economics and culture is mentioned in the Columbia Encyclopedia or the Random House Dictionary; only one has a few lines in the Encyclopedia Britannica. Their names pop up in neither Time nor the New York Review of Books. However, anyone who doubts that they engendered a political upheaval has an obsolete understanding of history.

Mr. Tyrmand is editor of Chronicles of Culture, published by the Rockford Institute.

Neo-Conservatism and the Class Struggle

By Arthur Schlesinger Jr.

Is class warfare what we really want in America? One would have supposed that this is the last thing our already tense society, streaked as it is with anger and violence, needs. Yet this is the direction in which the "neo-conservatism" of the Reagan administration is taking us.

Conservatism, like liberalism, is a house with many mansions. The older tradition of Anglo-American conservatism goes back to Edmund Burke. This tradition, the ethical afterglow of feudalism, was inspired by a belief in the organic character of society. Power was held to imply responsibility, and all classes were to be brought together in harmonious union by a sense of reciprocal obligation. Political leaders in this tradition saw society, not as a bundle of cold and commercial relationships, but as a living moral unity. 19th Century Tories, like Shaftesbury and Disraeli, had no hesitation about calling in the state to redress the social balance on behalf of the poor and thereby to strengthen the ties of community.

In essence, this was the ethos of the landed aristocracy. The rising business classes in the 19th Century had a different view. They sought to strike off the old bonds of prescription and hierarchy and to set the individual free. Their creed was laissez-faire—every one for himself and the devil take the hindmost—and they fiercely opposed intervention by the state to protect those who fell behind. Their goal was to replace the old society of status with the new society of contract. Their interest was not in social cohesion but in pecuniary opportunity, though they appended the self-serving argument that the pursuit of private interest was the best way to promote the general welfare.

The Root of All Evil

The United States never had a feudal system and thus does not have feudal sentiments. Some contemporary American conservatives—Russell Kirk and George Will, for example—are of the Burkean school. Mr. Will admonished his fellow conservatives the other day that they can carry their vendetta against government too far. But our contemporary neo-conservatives are mostly not conservatives in the older sense. Rather they are 19th Century Manchester liberals sworn to two basic propositions: that government is the root of all evil; and that, once we get government off our backs, our problems will solve themselves.

They add to these general thoughts a specific economic strategy—the old trickle-down theory, or, as it has been rebaptized

recently, supply-side economics. According to this creed, the business of tax policy is to allocate more money to the rich in the expectation that they will use it to produce jobs and income for the rest of us. The consistent supply-sider opposes across-the-board tax reduction. The whole point is to redistribute income to the rich on the theory that only the rich can do the saving and investing essential for economic growth. At the same time, the role of government must be systematically diminished. The result is the Reagan policy of cutting taxes for the rich and social programs for the poor.

So the administration proposes to take from our cities a quarter of their federal

the poor, not to the rich. The rich send their children to private schools; the poor have no alternative but public education. Occupational safety and health regulations protect the poor, not the rich. The rich buy books and pictures; the poor need public libraries and museums. The rich have estates; the poor go to public playgrounds, swimming pools and parks. The rich have doctors on Park Avenue; the rest of us look at mounting medical bills and yearn for national health insurance.

The neo-conservatism of laissez-faire invites political and social risks that the older Burkean conservatism avoided. By placing pecuniary opportunity above social cohesion, it invites the risk of intensifying

---

Board of Contributors

Capitalism has survived because of a campaign, mounted by liberals, to reduce the suffering…of those to whom the accidents of birth deny an equal chance.

---

aid, to take a million or more persons off food stamps, to reduce federal support for education, for dependent children, for mass transit, for subsidized housing, for Medicaid, for nutrition, for the arts, to slash federal programs for jobs, job training and welfare, to retreat from civil rights enforcement, to end legal services for the poor and black lung benefits for coal miners.

Such policies may have some higher justification. But it is idle to suppose that they will not bring suffering to those living on the margin of subsistence in our land. There may be an argument for purification through suffering. There is something distasteful, however, when rich people call for purification through poor people's suffering.

Of course, the rich assure the poor that economic insecurity is the great stimulus to accomplishment. Yet the proposition that economic security saps initiative and self-reliance is one the rich apply freely to others, rarely to themselves. If they really believed their guff about the bracing effect of economic insecurity, they would favor a 100% inheritance tax so that their own children would not be denied this great moral benefit.

The massacre of public programs is of course a socially discriminatory policy. For, as J.K. Galbraith has so eloquently pointed out, public services are essential to

the divisions within our society. Neo-conservatism is based on a long-odds gamble—that the release of productive energy allegedly to be wrought by tax reduction will increase benefits for all, and do so before the withdrawal of public concern causes the poor and powerless to lose faith in the justice of the social order.

I do not make this elementary point out of sentimental concern for the less fortunate; nor out of the theory that moves David Stockman to such excited indignation that (in his words) "almost every service that someone might need in life ought to be provided, financed by the government as a matter of basic rights." I would suggest rather the explosive possibilities when an economic establishment pursues a class war against the poor.

For, as Mr. Galbraith and others have pointed out, capitalism has not triumphed over the prophecies of Karl Marx by loyalty to the gospel of devil-take-the-hindmost. Capitalism has survived because of a continuing and remarkably successful effort to humanize the industrial order, to cushion the operations of the economic system, to combine pecuniary opportunity with social cohesion. It has survived because of a long campaign, mounted by liberals, to reduce the suffering—and thereby the resentment and the rebelliousness—of those to whom the accidents of birth deny an equal chance.

What Marx failed to foresee was precisely the ability of modern democratic society to develop a sense of social responsibility, a working sense of community. Those who would now have us abandon social responsibility in the name of unbridled individualism are doing Marx's work for him—and, it may well be, more effectively than a squalid generation of Communist parties has been able to do. Social responsibility is indispensable to the preservation of a free political order. This is not, I repeat, the talk of a sentimental liberalism. It is the injunction of a wise conservatism —as I imagine Edmund Burke would agree.

The Day of Reckoning

President Reagan is following a dangerous course. To some degree, ironically, the liberal reforms of the welfare state he so volubly deplores will postpone the day of reckoning. But, despite Social Security and unemployment compensation, ordinary Americans will begin to wonder about a society in which (according to the economic unit of U.S. News & World Report) executive salaries in 350 of the nation's largest corporations rose nearly 10% in 1980, in which 15 corporate leaders award themselves more than a million dollars a year (and often double or triple that through stock options or stock appreciation rights) and in which the median compensation for board chairmen—$445,158—is 30 times that of the average factory worker—all this in a day when the deliberate policy of government is to enrich the already rich and to deprive the poor of essential services.

American conservatives in their desire to establish a native tradition often invoke the name of the 19th Century writer and philosopher Orestes A. Brownson. They might well recall Brownson's own words a century ago in that robustly conservative work "The American Republic": "The men of wealth, the business men, manufacturers and merchants, bankers and brokers, are the men who exert the worst influence on government in every country.... They act on the beautiful maxim, 'Let the government take care of the rich, and the rich will take care of the poor,' instead of the far safer maxim, 'Let government take care of the weak, the strong can take care of themselves.' "

Mr. Schlesinger is Albert Schweitzer Professor of the Humanities at the City University of New York, winner of Pulitzer Prizes in history and biography and a member of the Journal's Board of Contributors.

Suffrage and Voter Turnout

Who Cares?

Small Vote Expected; Could Help GOP Win But Hinder Governing

Slip From '76 Would Bolster Special Groups' Influence, Add to Voters' Cynicism

Hostage News Fogs Outlook

By Dennis Farney
Staff Reporter of The Wall Street Journal

WASHINGTON—Americans are expected to vote with their feet today, walking away from the Carter-Reagan-Anderson choice in droves.

After one of the most lackluster campaigns in recent political history, pollsters and party professionals think there is an outside chance that voter turnout today could drop below 50% for the first time since 1924. That's still considered unlikely. But it appears almost certain that turnout—the percentage of eligible voters who actually vote—will fall below the 54.4% of 1976. And it's possible that it could be the lowest since the 51.1% of 1948.

"There'll be more blank presidential ballots this year than at any time in modern history," predicts Peter Hart, a pollster.

In the short-run, tactical sense, all this is encouraging news for Ronald Reagan and Republican candidates generally. That's because the nonvoters tend to lean Democratic: They are the young, the minorities, the less-well-educated, the blue-collar workers.

Turnout "Crucial" for Democrats

"If national turnout drops below 50% we're absolutely in trouble," says Tracy Gallagher, director of voter registration for the Democratic National Committee. "Turnout is crucial this year." The Democrats are pinning their hopes on get-out-the-vote drives by organized labor and a voter-registration project that has signed up more than one million new voters in 13 key states.

But the longer-term implications of lagging turnout are troubling, for Republicans as well as Democrats: The nation becomes harder and harder to govern.

"When voter participation declines, two things happen—both bad," says Curtis Gans, director of the Committee for the Study of the American Electorate.

"Special-interest groups then have a disproportionate influence on policy. Take public employes, for example. Public employes make up about one-sixth of the electorate. But public employes vote pretty heavily. So if national turnout drops to 50%, their vote amounts to almost one-third of the total. And in a congressional election, where turnout can be as low as 33%, they're one-half."

Cynicism Breeding Cynicism

At the same time, Mr. Gans continues, low turnout not only reflects public cynicism, it also sets the stage for more cynicism. Nonvoters have no stake in the elected President, so they are quicker to criticize whatever he does. Their cynicism makes it harder to mobilize the country behind specific policies, creating a semi-paralysis that leads to more cynicism.

Of course, it's possible that today's turnout could surprise the experts and reverse the decline that began in 1964. The news from Iran, indicating progress toward resolving the year-old hostage crisis, may bring more voters to the polls. Moreover, says pollster Robert Teeter, voters are in an odd mood this year.

"They're apathetic about the choice they have between Carter, Reagan and Anderson," he says. "But they aren't apathetic about the problems they see facing the country. They're frustrated, upset, anxious, worried. All the data we see suggest a low turnout, but I'm not certain it'll work out that way. Voters may just decide that they've got to vote, just to do what they can."

The Census Bureau estimates the voting-age population at 160.5 million: about 140.6 million whites and just short of 20 million nonwhites. But these bland figures disguise a mosaic of differing groups and subgroups, a mosaic that slowly changes shape from election to election as groups continue drifting toward or away from the two major parties. It isn't an exaggeration to say that the next President will be determined by what several of these groups do today.

The "Sleeping Giant"

The most fascinating are the children of the post-World War II baby boom, the electorate's "sleeping giant."

They have enormous potential power: More than 40% of the total voting-age population is in the under-35 group. But they aren't exercising that power. In 1976 only 42% of those 18 to 24 bothered to vote; the 25-to-34 category did better, at 55.4%. In the 1978 congressional elections, voters over 65 were nearly three times as likely to vote as 18-to-20-year olds.

Some political professionals — pollster Robert Teeter for one—visualize the under-35 group as a kind of avalanche waiting to happen. Should some cause or some politician galvanize this inert mass into concerted action, Mr. Teeter thinks, it could reshape politics for a generation or more. But nobody expects that to happen this time around.

"The under-35 group is a sleeping giant, in terms of its potential to transform politics," says Richard Wirthlin, Ronald Reagan's pollster. "But there's every indication that it will keep on sleeping this year."

So, in this election as in every other, older voters will wield influence all out of proportion to their numbers. This fact isn't lost on politicians when they set policy—for example, in deciding how much to tax younger workers to support the Social Security system. And in coming decades, as the children of the 1945-to-1964 baby boom grow older themselves, the young will have less and less power.

"It seems clear that the country is capable of growing more conservative for demographic reasons alone," says Bryant Robey, editor of American Demographics magazine. "The youth culture is ending and the middle-age culture is beginning."

Women are another group with growing power, and this year they are a trouble spot for Mr. Reagan.

Potential female voters currently outnumber men by seven million, a margin that is expected to widen in the years ahead. And polls indicate that women lean toward President Carter while men prefer Mr. Reagan. A recent poll for Time magazine by the firm of Yankelovich, Skelly & White Inc., for example, found the preferences almost exactly reversed: Men preferred Mr. Reagan 49% to 36%, women Mr. Carter, 49% to 33%.

Pollsters generally think such results indicate that the President has succeeded among women by portraying Mr. Reagan as a trigger-happy man who might get the U.S. into a war; women traditionally have leaned toward the "safer" candidate. But Ruth Clark, a Yankelovich analyst, questions this conventional wisdom. "The key issue is the Equal Rights Amendment," she says. Mr. Reagan opposes the ERA, as does the GOP platform.

Two Groups to Watch

Keep your eye on two additional groups as the vote comes in tonight.

The first is white Southerners. This group has been drifting away from the Democratic Party for decades, a trend arrested by friend-and-neighbor Jimmy Carter in 1976. Mr. Carter came close to winning half the white Southern vote; overwhelming support among black voters then put him over the top. But this year, many analysts think white Southerners will resume their drift toward the GOP.

"Regional pride is a one-shot thing," reasons Ben Wattenberg, a political analyst. "Southerners have already proved a Southerner can be elected President. There's bound to be attrition this time, and it wouldn't take much to make a big difference. Shift 3% of the white Southerners and you could cost Carter 100 electoral votes."

The other key group is Hispanic-Americans. Hispanics are overwhelmingly Democratic—a Robert Teeter poll for the Republican National Committee found they prefer the Democratic Party over the GOP by a 65% to 6% margin. But they haven't voted heavily in the past. Democrats are making a strenuous effort to change that pattern this year.

In the battleground state of Texas, the number of registered Hispanic voters has jumped to an estimated 800,000, roughly 12% of the state's voting population, from 488,000 in 1976. That year, Jimmy Carter carried 87% of Texas' Hispanic vote; he isn't expected to do that well this time. Still, maintains the Democratic National Committee's Mr. Gallagher, "if we can take 75% of the Chicano vote, we can win Texas."

"An Inside-Out Election"

Analysts do expect some longtime voting patterns to change this year. "This will be an inside-out election," predicts Mr. Hart, the pollster. "Reagan will do better among blue-collar voters than Republicans usually do, and Carter will do better among white-collar voters than Democrats usually do."

But the overriding questions concern turnout. What percentage of the electorate will bother to vote? Which groups will be highly motivated this time, which apathetic? The answers will do more than determine who the next President will be; they will also help define the difficulty of the task of governing that faces him.

"In 1976, Jimmy Carter was elected by 27.2% of the voting-age population," says Mr. Robey of American Demographics. "That was better, I guess, than Martin Van Buren, who was elected in 1836 by only 11.4%." (The Van Buren percentage suffers because women didn't have the vote in his day.) "But when nonvoters outnumber the voters who put you in office by almost two to one, it's awfully hard to claim a mandate."

Turnout Falls to 52.3%, Lowest Since '48 Election

By a WALL STREET JOURNAL Staff Reporter

WASHINGTON—The voter turnout in Tuesday's presidential election was the lowest since 1948.

The percentage of eligible voters who actually voted fell to 52.3% from 54.4% in 1976. Of the 160.5 million potential voters, about 84 million went to the polls. The turnout percentage now has declined in every presidential election since 1960, when 64% voted in the close Kennedy-Nixon race. The 1948 turnout—the Truman-Dewey race—was 51.1%.

Turnout Tuesday apparently rose slightly in the South while declining in every other region, says Curtis Gans, director of the Washington-based Committee for the Study of the American Electorate. And although Ronald Reagan will undoubtedly claim a mandate in his landslide victory, only a little more than one-fourth of the eligible voters cast ballots for him. The rest voted for someone else or stayed home.

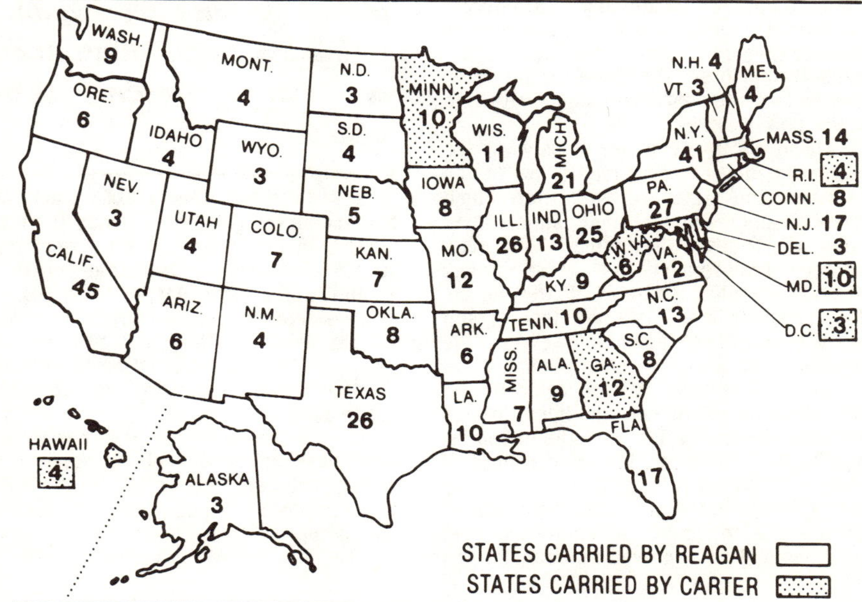

The Voting Rights Act Is Still Needed

The stench of hypocrisy hangs over the gathering battle to renew the Voting Rights Act when it expires next year.

Most of the politicians and pundits who vigorously oppose renewal of the act in its present form are those who have never supported civil rights legislation of any kind.

Now they furrow their brows, intone sonorously about fairness and attempt to

Viewpoint

by Hodding Carter III

blot out history—their own as well as the South's and the nation's. They wish to kill in early maturity that which they tried desperately to strangle at birth.

To hear Sen. Strom Thurmond, Ole Dr. Dixiecrat himself, or James J. Kilpatrick, the columnist who played Dr. Frankenstein to massive resistance, now piously make the case against the strict requirements of the voting law is to understand that the mind-set which made the measure imperative in 1965 is a long way from dead in 1981.

Such advocates do not come into court with clean hands. They accepted only grudgingly the notion that equality of all citizens is a matter of legitimate legislative and judicial concern. They fought a long, rear guard action against the nation's growing commitment to racial justice. They gave aid, comfort and leadership to the South's most virulent racists at a time when moderate leadership was sorely needed. And now, sensing a moment of conservative renaissance, they are apparently trying to set the stage for the reassertion of white supremacy and a return to black powerlessness.

All so carefully, so unctuously, in the name of "equity," of course. It "isn't fair" to make some states live with a law which doesn't apply equally to all states, they complain. Remove the Voting Rights Act's onerous requirement that those states' election law changes be precleared by the federal courts or the Attorney General, and nothing would change, they claim. We don't long for a second redemption.

As a white Southerner, I would like to be able to agree. As one who lived through the vast changes which were the forced result of the civil rights laws and rulings of the past 27 years, I know that many of my fellow Southerners have gladly thrown off the oppressive mantle of legally enforced injustice and have proved that racism and the white South are not and need not be synonymous.

But theirs are not the clamorous voices insisting that it is past time to stop penalizing the South. Certainly there are few, if any, black Southerners who come forward to plead that the Voting Rights Act cup be taken from their lips and lives. They know how long and how brutally they were deprived of basic political rights, they know the faces of their still-living oppressors and they are not about to invite a return to the desert quite yet.

Just how parched a land it was—just how incredibly successful the segregationist white South was in denying the vote to black Southerners—is best illustrated by the following figures:

In 1964, there were 29,000 black adults allegedly registered to vote in Mississippi, a state of almost one million blacks of all ages. Roughly 10,000 of these mustered enough courage to risk death by actually voting in state elections that offered them no real choices. The Voting Rights Act was passed a year later. Fifteen years after that, there are about 330,000 registered black voters in Mississippi, with no significant change in the black adult population. There are also some 400 black elected officials in the state, compared to the 10 or less in 1964.

While there is at least one full generation of white Southerners who know nothing of de jure segregation's forbidden perversions, there are many preceding them who do.

In 1964, there were 110,000 black Alabamans on the poll books; today there are 350,000. In Louisiana, the total went from 165,000 to 465,000 in the same period; in South Carolina, from 144,000 to 320,000.

President Reagan, not precisely a roaring enthusiast for the act in 1965, recently released the text of a letter to Attorney General Smith, asking for his assessment of the matter.

"I am sensitive to the controversy which has attached itself to some of the act's provisions," he wrote, "in particular those provisions which impose burdens unequally upon different parts of the nation."

"But," he added, "I am also sensitive to the fact that the spirit of the act marks this nation's commitment to full equality for all Americans. . . ."

The latter is gross understatement. The act doesn't "mark this nation's commitment to full equality." It is absolutely basic to that commitment, and for one clear reason which any conservative should recognize. It's called human nature.

While there is at least one full generation of white Southerners who know nothing of de jure segregation's forbidden perversions, there are many preceding them who do. From those generations come politicians and nonpoliticians who like the old ways very well, thank you, and would quickly revert to them if circumstances permitted. Not enough people have died to guarantee otherwise—not when one of the most powerful politicians in Mississippi today manned Gov. Ross Barnett's command post at the University of Mississippi when the governor sparked an insurrection against the university's court-ordered integration in 1962. Not enough, either, when another high-ranking white politician there is best remembered as the college snitch of the late 1950s who turned over the names of "integrationist" professors to the rabidly racist (and politically powerful) White Citizens Council, the better to hound them from the state.

Even if men such as these were willing to sign a blood oath that they would resist any effort to recreate the "way of life" they once swore mightily they would die to preserve, Congress could not weaken the Voting Rights Act in good conscience.

But they will sign no such oath, and some of them could not be believed if they did. The reason for disbelief would once again be human nature, as best explained in an old conservative saw of the early civil rights days. As the segs repeated ad nauseam, you "can't legislate morality;" you can't change people's hearts and minds by passing a law.

Given the way some of them still talk and feel, they may have been right—and that is the compelling justification for keeping the Voting Rights Act on the book. Whatever its effect on hearts and minds, it had and has a massive effect on behavior. That, after all, is precisely what was needed in 1965 and is still needed today.

Mr. Carter, formerly assistant secretary of state for public affairs in the Carter administration, is a regular contributor to "Viewpoint."

Congressman Offer Access To Raise Cash

By Jerry Landauer

WASHINGTON—It says in the newspapers that the Libyans gave or lent money to Billy Carter in the expectation that they might thereby obtain influence in the U.S. government.

The case of the President's brother has become a cause celebre, with major political and legal complications. But one aspect of it—the notion of purchasing access—or the illusion of access—to power isn't new to Washington.

The current crop of fund-raising endeavors is illustrative. Consider the efforts of Sen. John Heinz, chairman of the Republican Senatorial Committee and the man in charge of raising millions of dollars for GOP senatorial candidates to spend in the fall campaign.

Sen. Heinz is offering "personal relationships" with Republican Senators to donors of at least $1,000. These contributors are promised "give and take" meetings at private buffets; dinners and cocktail parties; a "confidential" telephone number providing a "clear channel" of communication to every GOP Senator, and "substantive information" about what is going on in Congress.

Record of Compliance

Sen. Heinz says his fund-raising is entirely proper. People donate not in quest of political favors, he says, but because they want to elect Republicans. "I'm happy to say that our committee has an exemplary record of compliance with the federal election laws," he says, "and since our contributions are pooled, no candidate or senator is beholden" to any donor.

Mr. Heinz might be right. The language of political solicitation is alive with hints of influential access—but lacking in promises of tangible results. For instance, $1,000 contributors to the GOP senatorial campaign become members of the Inner Circle, a new organization designed—rather vaguely "to give members access on a face-to-face basis with every Republican in the U.S. Senate."

Inner Circle membership includes the right to "advise us about important issues," promises Mr. Heinz. Bigger donors get bigger access. Donors pledging $5,000 a year already have dined at the homes of five GOP Senators. The lesser contributors, down to $10 or $100, may have to content themselves with periodic newsletters from the senatorial committee.

Alluring Invitations

If the prospective donor wants to conclude that he is purchasing legislative favors, that obviously is his own doing. What politicians mostly hold up for sale is the alluring possibility of influence, rather than the real thing.

Thus the cozy tone of Sen. Russell Long of Louisiana, seeking donations for another Democratic heavyweight, Chairman Warren Magnuson of the Senate Appropriations Committee. "I am inviting you and a limited number of others to join me," writes Mr. Long, reminding that the honored guests should bring $500 for a continental breakfast with the Senator from Washington State. "We intend this to be a small and informal gathering so that we will be able to meet and talk personally with everyone who attends."

Campaign collectors for Sen. Bob Dole (R., Kans.) get more specific, reminding donors of Mr. Dole's labors for the insurance, real estate and other industries. "Of course," they write, "Bob Dole's views on key economic and tax issues carry great weight in the Senate since he sits as the ranking Republican member of the Senate Finance Committee."

Pitch to PACs

Sen. Thomas Eagleton (D., Mo.) gears his pitch to corporate Political Action Committees. "As you may already know," he tells them, "I am a senior member of the Senate Appropriations Committee and I am in line to become chairman of the Governmental Affairs Committee at the beginning of the next Congress."

On the House side, Republican leader John Rhodes of Arizona spares potential contributors the elbow-jostling of "crowded" fund-raising affairs. Acting as a host for a dinner to benefit Rep. Matthew Rinaldo (R., N.J.), he promised donors that attendance would be "strictly limited" so that "we can have a frank, rewarding exchange of views" in which "no topic will be excluded nor will discussion be limited."

A Small Party

More recently, Mr. Rhodes invited donors to spend a $500 evening with the GOP congressional leadership. "I've asked that attendance be limited to 125 persons," he wrote. "I know you will especially appreciate the nature of this small influential group."

For junior members of Congress, a favored tactic is the sale of access to influential seniors. Thus for just $125 a lobbyist representing defense contractors, for instance, could obtain a word with Chairman Melvin Price of the House Armed Services Committee. Mr. Price (D., Ill.) recently acted as chief host for an affair benefiting Rep. Bob Stump (D., Ariz).

House Speaker Thomas O'Neill allows the use of his name on scores of fund-raising invitations. But the Massachusetts congressman has time to drop in on only a few, so Democratic candidates must scrounge to deliver other big names for donors. On a given day as many as a dozen congressmen or candidates may vie for fund-raising attention at receptions, dinners, buffets, breakfasts or lunches.

Bid for Access

Hedging Political Bets, Firms Give to Liberals In Positions of Power

Campaign Units Back Bayh, Magnuson and Cranston, Slight Some Republicans

Aid the Healthy, Kill the Sick

By JERRY LANDAUER

Staff Reporter of THE WALL STREET JOURNAL

WASHINGTON—Rep. Dan Rostenkowski, a veteran Democrat from Chicago, rarely needs campaign contributions. In 1976 and 1978 he flattened Republican opponents with better than 80% of the vote. In this year's Democratic primary, he got 45,079 votes to his opponent's 5,286. And even his current GOP rival all but concedes the Congressman will roll up another big victory in November.

But though he doesn't need the money, Rep. Rostenkowski's campaign treasury is flush, and much of the cash is coming from what seems to be an unlikely source: political-action committees, knows as PACs, organized by corporations or sponsored by business-related trade associations. These committees are willing to overlook Mr. Rostenkowski's 89% pro-labor voting record since he came to Congress in 1959.

The reason: Rep. Rostenkowski is the second-ranking Democrat on the tax-writing House Ways and Means Committee. From that powerful post, he occasionally throws a bone to business. And in turn, business people seem eager to befriend him.

This pattern—substantial business support for entrenched Demcrats who vote with labor on most issues—appears prevalent throughout the country. It suggests that corporate strategists don't expect the Republicans to win a congressional majority. So instead of trying to beat pro-labor Democrats, numerous business PACs are scurrying to curry favor with them.

Buying Access

The campaign-giving runs counter to urgings by some business leaders and PAC officials that increased emphasis should be put on electing a more pro-business Congress.

"Business should quit trying to buy access and start buying a new forum for private enterprise," says Richard Lesher, president of the U.S. Chamber of Commerce. "A lot of companies are putting their narrow, selfish interest ahead of the broader interests of the business community," he asserts.

Whatever their reasons, hundreds of corporate PACs are giving most of their donations to Demcratic candidates for the Senate and House. In fact, a recent tabulation by the Federal Election Commission shows that 867 registered corporate PACs actually gave more money to Democrats, $3.8 million, than to Republicans, $3.6 million through June 30. (Labor PACs gave Democrats $4.9 million while spreading only $400,-000 among Republicans.)

But as the campaign progresses, business giving is likely to tilt toward the GOP. The Democratic Study Group, an organization of House liberals, expects the corporate PACs to pounce on vulnerable Democrats "while continuing to buy access to those Democrats who have safe seats and who are generally responsive to business concerns." In other words, predicts Richard Conlon, the study group's staff director, corporate PAC "will help the healthy and shoot the sick."

Going With a Winner

Much of the early business money is going to the campaigns of secure, pro-labor Democrats who also hold leadership posts in Congress. In Illinois, for example, 84 corporate political-action committees already have donated $53,900 to Rep. Rostenkowski's campaign. Trade-association PAC's sent $33,500, and five committees representing doctors, dentists, oral surgeons, podiatrists and chiropractors contributed $11,800; these interests want to be remembered when Rep. Rostenkowski's Ways and Means Committee writes federal health legislation.

Back in February, Mr. Rostenkowski's 75-year-old Republican opponent, Walter Zilke, filed a statement with the Federal Election Commission indicating that he can't expect to win: "I do not expect any contributions," Mr. Zilke stated. But even that concession didn't stanch the flow of business dollars to Democrat Rostenkowski.

The National Automobile Dealers Association gave $5,000 (the maximum) for Rep. Rostenkowski's runaway primary victory. American Family Corp. donated $5,000 for the Congressman's general-election noncampaign against Mr. Zilke. And gifts of $1,-000 or more arrived from PAC's sponsored by such major companies as Bethlehem Steel, American Telephone & Telegraph, International Harvester and United Airlines.

Drinks on Me

Mr. Rostenkowski uses the unneeded business dollars to strengthen the Chicago Democratic machine, to make donations to charity, to aid hard-pressed House colleagues such as liberal Democratic Rep. James Corman in California and to buy food and drink for political pals. Since March the Rostenkowski campaign has paid 14 entertainment tabs for "advisers" or "campaign workers," including one bash at the Como Inn in Chicago that cost $2,197.85.

A similar case is that of Sen. Warren Magnuson of Washington, a pro-union, free-spending liberal. According to the AFL-CIO's Committee on Political Education, Mr. Magnuson has sided with labor on 230 of 249 important votes since he was elected to the Senate in 1944. Yet his donor list of over 100 business PACs reads like a "Who's Who" of industry: Alcoa, Braniff, Coca-Cola, Lockheed, Rockwell International, Standard Oil (Ohio), Westinghouse, U.S. Steel.

In all, corporate political-action committees have given $200,000 to Sen. Magnuson—the chairman of the Senate Appropriations Committee.

In California, Senate Democratic whip Alan Cranston rates 91% approval on the AFL-CIO scorecard. Mr. Cranston opened his reelection drive with a $1 million war chest, "much of it from business," the U.S. Chamber of Commerce says. He got donations from many of the business PACs that appear on Sen. Magnuson's list, plus such others as Anheuser-Busch, Atlantic Richfield, Hughes Aircraft and Occidental Petroleum.

In general, big business appears to feel relatively comfortable with a Democratic Congress. "The PACs run by corporations have absolutely no principles," one business leader contends. Often big business gives to both sides in a congressional race, and a liberal-leaning Democrat who occasionally aids business can be well rewarded.

"If a Democrat looks like he's going to win and he's done us a couple of favors we'll throw him some dough, especially if he's in a position to screw us if we don't," says one PAC insider who doesn't want to be identified. "I know this doesn't sound very principled, but that's the way it is."

The business PACs also appear reluctant to finance Republican challengers to Democratic hierarchs who are considered vulnerable at the polls. In Oregon, Republican Dennis Smith is getting only scattered business support in his drive to unseat Ways and Means Chairman Al Ullman; some 120 business PACs have rallied to Mr. Ullman's standard.

Support for Jim Wright

In Texas, most business groups are stiff-arming Republican James Bradshaw, who is thought to have a chance to unseat House Democratic Leader Jim Wright. The PACs fear that Rep. Wright's successor as Democratic floor leader would be Rep. Phillip Burton of California. Mr. Wright's AFL-CIO approval rating is 74%; Mr. Burton's is 94%.

In Indiana, Republican John Patrick Hyler is challenging House Democratic whip John Brademas. Mr. Hyler, a businessman, won the GOP primary on May 6. In the next three months he got just one business PAC donation, $400 from Whirlpool Corp. "Brademas had more money in the war chest at the beginning of the campaign than we expect to raise" during the whole race, says Richard Schmitt, Mr. Hyler's treasurer.

In the Indiana Senate race, Democrat Birch Bayh is running scared for a fourth term. He ranks high on conservative "hit lists." On important Senate votes Sen. Bayh nearly always sides with labor; the AFL-CIO gives him a 94% approval rating. But on other issues he sometimes helps business.

This year, for example, Sen. Bayh rammed a bill through the Senate that protects the territorial franchises of soft-drink bottlers against antitrust challenge. Contributions to his campaign rolled in from bottlers as far away as California, and Pepsi-Co's Concerned Citizens Fund added $500 to an earlier $1,000 gift.

"Bifocal" Beneficence

According to a candid 1978 memorandum from PepsiCo's chairman, Donald Kendall, the company PACs "primary criterion" in picking recipients is whether the candidate might help on issues "of paramount importance to our company." At the same time, though, Mr. Kendall urged corporate PACs to adopt a "bifocal approach," one that avoids excessive business giving to pro-labor "hard-liners."

In Mr. Kendall's view, too many corporate strategists view campaign donations as a way of "keeping congressional doors open"—to officeholders who often oppose the business community on "broader, free-enterprise issues."

John Dolan, chairman of the National Conservative Political Action Committee, which is spending several million dollars to defeat congressional liberals, couldn't agree more. "Business people who contribute to Warren Magnuson or Alan Cranston or Birch Bayh should be ashamed of themselves," Mr. Dolan asserts. "To give Alan Cranston a thousand bucks in the hope that he'll open his door is an insult not only to the Senator but to the people who contribute to the PAC."

Some large business PACs are responding to such criticisms by channeling more contributions into the campaigns of conservative challengers to pro-labor Democrats. But this is happening chiefly in rural states where there is little big-business presence and where the incumbent has few chances either to assist or to punish the business community.

It's no coincidence that two of the biggest Republican recipients of corporate PAC dollars are Rep. James Abdnor in South Dakota and Rep. Steve Symms in Idaho. Neither of the Democratic office-holders they are challenging, Sen. George McGovern and Sen. Frank Church, holds a Senate committee assignment deemed vital to business interests.

But in the more industrialized states, liberal Democrats often seem to share a community of interests with business. This is especially true in industries dependent on government spending, reliant on federal favors or protected by bureaucratic regulation.

One illustration is the Good Government Fund sponsored by McDonnell Douglas Corp., a major aircraft maker and U.S. defense supplier. James S. McDonnell III, the company's vice president for marketing, is one of the few big-business donors to Mr. Dolan's grass-roots conservative movement. But the three largest donations from the company's political-action committee have gone to Democrats Bill Burlison of Missouri, a member of the house defense appropriations subcommittee; Melvin Price of Illinois, chairman of the House Armed Services Committee; and Charles Wilson of California, who ranks right behind Mr. Price on the panel's procurement subcommittee. The three Democrats vote with labor on four of every five important issues, the AFL-CIO scorecard shows.

Besides making hefty donations to liberals, the business PACs are showering huge sums on more-conservative Democrats high in the congressional hierarchy. Ernest Hollings, chairman of the Senate Budget Committee, is running easily for reelection in South Carolina; business committees nevertheless sent him $200,000.

The single biggest recipient of business political-action-committee dollars is Louisiana Sen. Russell Long, chairman of the Senate Finance Committee; such contributions to his campaign exceed $400,000.

Teachers Tie Election Cash To Single Issue

By Albert R. Hunt

Staff Reporter of The Wall Street Journal

The National Education Association, an organization of 1.8 million teachers that takes its liberal politics seriously, has adopted a curious approach to campaign financing.

The group is contributing funds this election season to a number of conservative Republican congressmen who vigorously oppose most of the principles the NEA favors —such as fair housing, the Equal Rights Amendment and labor law reform. At the same time, the teachers' organization has withheld campaign contributions from several liberal Democrats who for years have stayed loyally in the NEA's corner.

The reason: NEA financial support in 1980 is being pegged almost exclusively to how lawmakers voted last year on the teachers' No. 1 legislative priority—a bill creating the Department of Education. Most congressmen who voted for the department are getting help from the NEA's political war chest, no matter how they stand on other issues. Almost all who voted "no" have been cut off from NEA funds.

Election-Year Pressures

The NEA's criterion for campaign aid is noteworthy in an election year when many politicians, especially Democrats, have been hounded by special-interest groups that support or oppose candidates solely on the basis of one issue: abortion or women's rights or gun control, among others. An NEA official says campaign contributions from the teachers' organization are tiny compared to the funds flowing from the "right-wing, single-issue groups we're fighting."

But the NEA's complaints about "single-issue" politics haven't prevented it from adopting its own "single-vote" standard. House and Senate candidates who qualify are sharing a campaign treasury raised by teachers that already totals about $250,000.

Recipients include such conservative Republican congressmen as James Quillen of Tennessee, Tom Corcoran of Illinois, and Floyd Spence of South Carolina. Each has opposed most liberal-sponsored education measures embraced by the NEA, as well as such teacher-favored bills as the Equal Rights Amendment and a revision in the labor laws that would have made it easier for employes to join a union.

A Small Donation

Each, however, supported creation of the Education Department. Mr. Spence cast several votes against the department but voted for it on the final roll call that cleared the House, 210 to 206. He has received a small NEA contribution, but he hasn't been endorsed for reelection by the group.

But missing from the NEA contribution list—as of its last report Sept. 20—are such liberal House Democrats as Patricia Schroeder of Colorado and Benjamin Rosenthal of New York. Both supported the labor-law bill and the ERA, as well as most liberal education measures. But they voted against the Education Department.

In all, the teachers have contributed to 20

incumbents in Senate contests; all 20 voted for the Education Department. In races for the House, where the real fight over the department was waged, the pattern is almost as striking. Contributions have gone to 96 in-cumbents and 94 of them voted for the department. These range from liberal Democrats to die-hard Republican conservatives.

Schroeder Is Irked

This isn't coincidence, says Rep. Schroeder, who received $2,700 from the NEA in 1976 and $1,500 two years ago. "They told me they're single-shooting this campaign," she says. "It all depends on how you voted on the Education Department."

That annoys the Colorado Democrat: "On every other issue, I've been on NEA's side, but they went nuts on this one." Before the crucial vote last year, she says the teachers association "strongly intimated they wouldn't support me if I voted the wrong way."

The NEA insists it looks at a series of votes before contributing to a candidate, but it acknowledges the Education Department vote is a critical factor. "This was our major issue," says Kenneth Melley, the NEA's director of political affairs. "We want to show appreciation either by endorsement or a contribution."

A liberal congresswoman who voted against the Education Department complains that the NEA "went nuts on this one."

The two House members who opposed the Education Department and still received NEA contributions are David Obey, a Wisconsin Democrat, and William Clinger, a Pennsylvania Republican.

NEA officials say support from local teachers' associations helped persuade the parent group to support such conservatives as Reps. Quillen and Corcoran. But the NEA doesn't always heed the advice of its grass-roots affiliates.

In Youngstown, Ohio, the local teacher's group wanted NEA support for Harry Meshel, a Democratic state senator who led legislative efforts for public employes and is running for Congress. His opponent is Rep. Lyle Williams, a first-term, moderately conservative Republican.

But the NEA balked. While it hasn't endorsed a candidate, the NEA did contribute $2,000 to Republican Williams' campaign. In May 1979, the Education Department measure cleared the House Government Operations Committee by one vote with Rep. Williams, at the last minute, casting the decisive vote. "Lyle Williams' vote was the difference and with that historical perspective we rejected the recommendation of our state affiliate," says Mr. Melley.

Presidential Nominations

New Hampshire Vote

Carter Beats Kennedy Impressively And Reagan Has Stunning Victory

By Albert R. Hunt
Staff Reporter of The Wall Street Journal

BEDFORD, N.H.—Jimmy Carter scored an impressive victory in his chief rival Ted Kenndy's backyard here, but that was overshadowed by the stunning win of Republican Ronald Reagan only hours after he fired his top campaign command.

President Carter's victory in the New Hampshire Democratic primary was widely expected, with pre-election polls showing him running almost two-to-one ahead of Sen. Kennedy (D., Mass.). The actual margin was smaller, with the television networks last night projecting Mr. Carter would garner close to 50% of the vote, and Mr. Kennedy a little less than 40%. Nevertheless, the loss jeopardizes Sen. Kennedy's ability to muster sufficient financial and political support to wage any serious campaign over the next month against the incumbent President.

Also last night, President Carter apparently won a decisive victory over Sen. Kennedy in the Minnesota caucuses, although the actual size of the win and the delegate breakdown couldn't be determined yet.

But the big surprise was Mr. Reagan, who was thought to be in a neck-and-neck race with former Central Intelligence Agency chief George Bush. Instead, the former California governor, according to TV network estimates, captured about 50% of the vote and trounced Mr. Bush by better than a two-to-one margin.

Frontrunner Again

This victory refurbished Mr. Reagan's image as a popular Republican vote getter, which had been tarnished by his unexpected loss to Mr. Bush in last month's Iowa presidential caucuses. In the process, the 69-year-old Mr. Reagan re-emerges as the GOP front-runner in this topsy-turvy political year.

Mr. Reagan's remarkable showing here was rivaled by yesterday's decision to overhaul his top campaign staff. Most significant was his decision to fire campaign manager John Sears, widely considered one of the ablest political practitioners in the country.

Mr. Sears drew fire ever since the Iowa loss from many other Reagan supporters who charged that his "pragmatism" was stifling the old Reagan zest and verve. Mr. Sears will be replaced as campaign chief by William Casey, a New York attorney and former chairman of the Securities and Exchange Commission. But the Reagan campaign is likely to be dominated by many of the candidate's old California confidants.

The result, some campaign insiders say, is that the Reagan campaign may take on a more conservative ideological tone.

Differences With Bush

Some long-time Reagan advisers have been urging him to delineate more sharply his differences with Mr. Bush, both on economic issues, particularly his proposals for massive federal tax cuts and spending reductions, and on such social issues as abortion and gun control.

But there are risks in yesterday's move too. Several other top campaign aides will leave with Mr. Sears and this could disrupt the carefully crafted political apparatus that the Reagan forces built over the past year.

For now, however, Mr. Reagan's spectacular New Hampshire victory provides his campaign with a timely shot in the arm. And even before last night, the Reaganites expected to dominate the four southern primaries held early next month. "We're back in charge now," exclaimed one Reagan aide.

Conversely, the size of his defeat was a serious blow to Mr. Bush and is sure to slow the impressive political momentum he was building following victories in Iowa and Puerto Rico. Bush strategists were counting on at least a strong second place showing in New Hampshire, and none anticipated a massive defeat.

Although the crazy-quilt patterns of this particular presidential year make any historical analogies risky, nobody has ever been elected President without winning the New Hampshire primary since the Granite State initiated a presidential preference contest in 1952.

Damage for Bush

Moreover, Mr. Bush is likely to be damaged further by the impression he hurt his prospects with some unimpressive late campaigning here. Last Saturday night, he faltered in a debate with Mr. Reagan when it appeared that he had participated in excluding four other candidates from that session.

The 55-year-old former CIA chief hopes to rebound quickly with a victory in the friendlier environs of the Massachusetts primary next Tuesday; before last night's win, Mr. Reagan wasn't planning any effort in Massachusetts, although that may be altered now. Further, Bush strategists argue they will fare better if the Republican race narrows to a two-man contest with Mr. Reagan. "We just can't pick off any of Reagan's hard-core vote, but I think we can win most of the votes going to the others," Bush pollster Robert Teeter said after yesterday's results.

But that two-man race possibly won't occur as soon as the Bush forces would like. Sen. Howard Baker (R., Tenn.) finished third in New Hampshire, and although his showing wasn't impressive, Baker strategists say the decline of Mr. Bush will encourage their candidate to stay in the race. Also, Rep. John Anderson (R., Ill.), who finished fourth yesterday with about 10%, hopes to make a big effort next week in Massachusetts where his more liberal views could receive a warmer reception.

Two other Republican hopefuls, Rep. Philip Crane (R., Ill.) and Sen. Robert Dole (R., Kans.), both received only a miniscule vote yesterday and are likely early casualties in the presidential contest. Similarly, former Texas Gov. John Connally suffered a dismal showing in New Hampshire and faces an uphill fight to stay politically alive in the South Carolina primary next month.

On the Democratic side, President Carter continued his dominance of the contest that started with a huge victory in Iowa last month. The Carter forces are confident that, except for the primary in Sen. Kennedy's home state next week, they are running away from the Massachusetts Democrat in every other contest in sight.

Although the Kennedy forces maintain that the race was closer than expected, the challenger's inability to win in his neighboring state is ominous for his candidacy. The Kennedy campaign already is experiencing money problems—it is raising about $200,000 to $250,000 a week, or only about half what is needed to wage a full-scale campaign, and those woes are likely to grow with the New Hampshire loss. "We have enough money to make it through Massachusetts but after that it's tough," says a top Kennedy campaign aide.

One possibility under serious consideration is to have Sen. Kennedy scale back his effort and select only a few spots, and to replace his constant campaigning with more carefully prepared criticisms of Carter policy. But Kennedy operatives concede that there isn't any strategy that's likely to succeed until public passions over the Iranian hostages and the Soviet invasion of Afghanistan subside and public attention returns to domestic economic problems. But, privately, most of these Kennedy aides doubt this will occur soon enough to revive their candidate.

The other major Democratic candidate, California Gov. Jerry Brown, finished a distant third yesterday, with about 10% of the vote. Mr. Brown has announced that he'll skip all the primaries and caucuses over the next month and won't resume his long-shot quest for the nomination until the April 1 Wisconsin primary.

New Hampshire elects less than 1% of the delegates to the Democratic convention and a little more than 1% of the delegates to the Republican convention. As of late last night, the indications were that President Carter would win 10 or 11 delegates and Sen. Kennedy would capture eight or nine delegates in New Hampshire. On the Republican side, it looked like Mr. Reagan would win 13 or 14 delegates, Mr. Bush would win four or five, and four more would go to other candidates.

There was a big turnout in both party primaries yesterday. It was estimated that more than 100,000 Democrats voted, up about 10% from four years ago, while the Republican turnout was an estimated 145,000, up more than 20% from 1976.

The GOP Ticket

Reagan Picks Bush To Be Running Mate As Ford Deal Fizzles

Former CIA Chief Emerges After Evening of Rumors That Ford Would Accept

Drama at the Convention

By ALBERT R. HUNT and JAMES M. PERRY
Staff Reporters of THE WALL STREET JOURNAL

DETROIT — Ronald Reagan negotiated all day and all evening to put Gerald Ford on the ticket as his running mate, and then, to the astonishment of this convention, came to the floor and said his choice was George Bush.

The negotiations with Mr. Ford broke down over the former President's insistence that he be given almost coequal status in a Reagan administration.

Mr. Bush, all along, had been the fall-back candidate should Mr. Reagan be unable to strike a deal with Mr. Ford.

Political veterans couldn't remember such an astonishing turnaround. As the news spread through the convention hall that Mr. Ford was the likely choice, the delegates reacted with euphoria. The Reagan-Ford ticket was the "dream ticket" that Mr. Reagan's advisers had been planning for weeks.

Late last evening, rumors swept the hall that Mr. Reagan and Mr. Ford would appear together in one of the most unlikely developments in history, a script no Hollywood studio would ever have bought.

Somehow, though, Mr. Reagan's managers turned the jubilant script into what was almost a political tragedy.

"It's in the nature of political campaigns to have topsy-turvy days," said Sen. Paul Laxalt of Nevada, the Reagan adviser. No one, though, could remember anything quite so topsy-turvy as this one.

Mr. Ford had won grudging support from conservatives at the convention. Sen Jesse Helms of North Carolina said he could live with a Reagan-Ford ticket. But he had said earlier he would challenge Mr. Bush and seek the vice presidential nomination himself. It is likely he'll take that step now.

Mr. Ford began the speculation himself when he appeared on CBS News and said he was willing to return to Washington if he could be convinced he would "play a meaningful role across the board in the basic and the crucial and the important decisions that have to be made in a four-year period."

Even his wife, Betty, always thought to be the stumbling block to his return to public life, said she supported Mr. Ford's apparent decision to run for Vice President. "OK with you?" asked Barbara Walters. "You know that," Mrs. Ford replied.

Frantic negotiations had gone on all afternoon yesterday and into the night at the campaign suites and campaign headquarters on the 68th and 70th floors of the Detroit Plaza Hotel.

The pressure exerted on Mr. Ford was overwhelming. The entire leadership of the party, it seemed, was asking him to run to elect the top of the ticket and turn 1980 into one of the great GOP victory years.

Most Republicans thought they could win with Mr. Bush, but there had been some lingering doubts. The choice of Mr. Ford was supposed to change all that, for he is a moderate, a man with Washington experience, and an expert in foreign policy.

Sen. Charles Percy of Illinois summed up the feelings of almost everyone when he said: "It would be a magnificent ticket. It would wrap up the election."

But the dream of Mr. Reagan's advisers somehow faded away as midnight approached and the convention waited to hear the stunning, marvelous news that they had a ticket with a former President on it running for Vice President, something the country had never seen before.

One top Reaganite explained early this morning that the Ford deal was "90% done" and then it "fell through" on the important detail of sharing power. Then, according to this informed source, top Reagan aides felt they had to go quickly to their main fallback candidate, Mr. Bush, to avoid the appearance of a clumsy and counterproductive early-morning decision.

In a post-midnight appearance before the convention, Mr. Reagan said Mr. Ford had finally decided "he can be of more value to the ticket . . . campaigning his heart out, which he has pledged to do, and not as a member of the ticket."

Then Mr. Reagan announced that his choice was former United Nations Ambassador Bush. The delegates interrupted him with cheers.

He noted before he got to the heart of his message that he was breaking with precedent coming before the convention. But he said it was necessary, "seeing the rumors that were going around and the gossip that was going on here."

Mr. Reagan admitted a "number of Republican leaders" had believed "a proper ticket would include Gerald Ford." He said: "We have gone over this and over this and over this." It wasn't enough. The great "dream ticket" collapsed somewhere on the top floors of the Detroit Plaza Hotel late in an evening that once had looked so promising.

What the political fallout would be from the march up the hill with Mr. Ford and then the sudden march down it with Mr. Bush was anyone's guess. It was hardly calculated to enhance the reputation of Mr. Reagan's campaign team. Nothing in politics is much worse than raising hopes of a great victory and then putting them in sudden jeopardy.

Democrats, braced for the strongest Republican ticket in recent history, probably can take a deep breath of relief. Mr. Carter's strategists had said they would have trouble enough with a ticket including Mr. Bush, much less one headed by a popular former President.

---

24   *August 1, 1980*

Panicky Pols

More Democrats Fear An Anti-Carter Sweep, But Who Else Is There?

President Slips, Yet Kennedy And Jackson Have Flaws; Muskie, Mondale Demur

---

Convention Could Be Bloody

By ALBERT R. HUNT AND JAMES M. PERRY
Staff Reporters of THE WALL STREET JOURNAL

WASHINGTON—"Free the delegates!" stormed Edward Bennett Williams, the well-known lawyer, at a press conference yesterday in a House office building. He called for an "open" Democratic convention.

Over on the Senate side of Capitol Hill, Democratic Sen. Edward Kennedy and independent presidential candidate John Anderson suddenly called a joint press conference to hint that Rep. Anderson might drop out of the race if the Democratic convention nominates someone other than President Carter. Meanwhile, Democratic Senators rushed from one meeting to another, wringing their hands over what might happen to them in the election this fall.

And hovering over all of them is the rollicking figure of Billy Carter, the President's bad-boy brother, who yesterday said a top Justice Department official—who had accused him of lying—is "full of s—."

Thus the Democrats' political panic spreads, just 10 days from the opening of their national convention in New York City. Hour by hour, fed by fire-breathing rhetoric on all sides, the hullabaloo is growing. It promises to make the convention stormier than most, maybe even rivaling the 1968 firestorm in Chicago.

The Real Issue: Jimmy Carter

Behind the rhetoric, the real issue is President Carter himself. His ratings are the lowest the polltakers can remember, plunging to the bottom of their charts over his brother Billy's Libya connections. (For a story about intelligence reports that Libya engaged in a broad effort to influence U.S. policy through Billy Carter and others, see story on page 14.) Some Democrats fear that the President could be on his way to a crushing defeat in November. Maybe more important is the growing realization among many congressional Democrats that they could be swept out of office along with Mr. Carter.

So the remedy, in the view of these Democrats, is to open the convention and allow the delegates to make another choice. Sen. Kennedy thinks the convention, free to vote its conscience, might turn to him, wishful as that thinking may be. Mr. Williams seems to be thinking of still another possibility, perhaps Secretary of State Edmund Muskie, one of his oldest friends.

It still isn't likely that Mr. Carter can be denied the nomination he thought he had locked up in the caucuses and the primaries. The problem for the Democrats who are terrified over the prospects of the Carter ticket is finding someone else.

Many congressional members think Sen. Kennedy, who will take about 1,250 delegates to the convention, could be as bad for them as Mr. Carter.

What About Jackson?

Mr. Kennedy is said to have told Sen. Henry Jackson of Washington that if he fails, the next choice should be Mr. Jackson. But many of Mr. Kennedy's supporters are old-line liberal Democrats, and most of them would have trouble swallowing Mr. Jackson's hard-line defense and foreign-policy positions.

That seems to leave Secretary of State Muskie. Mr. Muskie says he supports Mr. Carter "all the way." But he doesn't quite say he wouldn't accept the nomination that he sought so hard in 1972. It would be difficult for Mr. Carter's own Cabinet official to be part of such a disloyal proceeding. It would be even more difficult, of course, for Vice President Walter Mondale, another possibility. Rep. Morris Udall of Arizona, still another, says he would head for the Mexican border if he was nominated.

So the odds remain with Mr. Carter, who will take almost 2,000 delegates to the convention, over 300 more than he needs to win the nomination. "He's been hurt badly," says one party professional, "but he's still the heavy favorite."

Desperate to Dump Carter

Many of the people who are talking most loudly about denying President Carter the nomination — mostly junior Democratic House members—aren't even delegates to the convention. But they are keenly interested in keeping their jobs, and they desperately believe that the only way for them to stay in office this fall is for the delegates to dump Jimmy Carter.

Here is why, according to Joe Rothstein, a Washington-based political consultant who is managing the campaigns of 11 House Democrats and three Senate Democrats.

"Carter at the top of the ticket costs all my people five to 10 points," he says. "I think it's going to be 1932 in reverse" (when the Republicans, led by Herbert Hoover, were routed).

But is it practical to "dump" the President of the United States?

"Is it practical," Mr. Rothstein replies, "to nominate a President with a 77% negative rating, a President who's two to one behind his Republican opponent, a President who has a growing scandal involving his brother? Is it practical not to dump him?"

That's the sort of talk that is spreading across Washington. Polls are coming in from around the country, and some of them show Mr. Carter running third, behind both Ronald Reagan and Mr. Anderson. In one rural House district, Mr. Rothstein says, a poll shows Mr. Carter collecting less than 15% of the vote. "Carter isn't coming back," he says. "I can't think of anything I could do for my people that would be more important than getting Carter off the ticket.''

If Mr. Carter really is going to be dumped, the test will come early in the convention when delegates vote on a proposed rule called F3c. It would require delegates to vote on the first ballot for the candidate they were elected to support. A Carter victory on that test almost surely would lock up his nomination. But losing the test vote would create the possibility that Sen. Kennedy or another candidate could stampede wavering Carter delegates and snatch the nomination from the President.

The forces calling for an ''open'' convention have won big points by seeming to make the rules fight a moral issue—the right of delegates to exercise a free choice—rather than the political one it really is. Mr. Williams, the chairman of the Open-Convention Committee, in denouncing the rule yesterday talked about the Constitution, the Bill of Rights and the traditions of the party.

The pressure on Mr. Carter and his managers to back down on their support of the rule was growing by the hour. It began with Mr. Williams' red-faced demand. It picked up steam later in the day when it was reported that Sen. Warren Magnuson, one of the powerful old Democrats in the Senate, was urging Mr. Carter to back off.

The Carter people were resisting because they have spent so much time and effort telling their delegates not to give an inch on the rule. They fear that if they back away now, it would be seen as a sign of weakness. Kennedy strategists think if the Carter people do back away, they will do it at the last moment.

Carter's Support on Rules Slips

Despite denials by top Carter campaign officials, support for the President's position on the rules fight clearly is slipping. One well-placed New York Democrat currently estimates that 40 of the 118 pro-Carter delegates from that state would support the ''open-convention'' move, and other prominent Illinois Democrats may join them. Similar defections are taking place in such major states as Ohio and Pennsylvania. Yesterday pro-Carter Kansas Gov. John Carlin endorsed the open convention; he can probably deliver more than a dozen Carter Kansas delegates on that issue.

Last night the presidents of 35 unions announced jointly that they support an open convention. The union chiefs said they don't want Mr. Reagan to be President and they don't believe President Carter can defeat him, according to Edward Carlough, president of the Sheet Metal Workers' Union.

Kennedy strategists figure they are about 100 votes short of winning this battle. But they believe they are picking up support daily.

Even if this rules fight is somehow avoided, there will be other bitter battles in New York. The Kennedy forces are planning three or four major platform fights. They support planks for an economic-stimulus package, a promise not to fight inflation with unemployment and opposition to the MX missile system.

All of these would be politically embarrassing to President Carter, but it's far from certain he can control all his delegates. ''On the economic issues particularly, a lot of the Carter delegates are more liberal than Carter,'' contends one Washington Democrat.

The hope of the anti-Carterites is that these platform battles will create a political chemistry in New York that would cause enough defections among the Carter delegates that the President would lose when the convention finally gets around to nominating a candidate.

''You're going to have a mix of alcohol, TV cameras and bad polls,'' says pro-Kennedy Massachusetts Rep. Edward Markey. ''Anything can happen.''

Sen. Kennedy's surprise, 45-minute meeting yesterday with Rep. Anderson, who is expected to siphon presidential votes from both the Democrats and the Republicans, seemed calculated to stir further the dump-Carter debate. After the meeting Mr. Anderson told reporters, ''It would only be prudent to reconsider what my position then would be (if Mr. Kennedy or anyone else defeated Mr. Carter at the convention).''

Mr. Anderson's strategists don't expect Mr. Kennedy to win the nomination. If he loses, they hope to pick up some of his supporters.

White House is Confident

The White House dismisses all the dump-Carter talk as wild speculation, contending there is no way the President can lose 300 delegates. Moreover, they note that the President won 24 to 34 primaries this year and has rebounded from the political doldrums before.

Yesterday, two pro-Carter Democratic Senators, Joseph Biden of Delaware and Walter Huddleston of Kentucky, were trotted out to say there isn't any loss of support for the President. They said they had talked to 15 to 20 Democratic Senators who they said are sticking with Jimmy Carter. And they warned the ''open-convention'' move is ''hurting the party'' and ''delaying the time we can focus on defeating Ronald Reagan.''

A big problem still gnawing at Mr. Carter's supporters is what may be revealed next about Billy Carter's antics.

The controversy began on July 14 when the President's brother settled a Justice Department lawsuit by registering as a foreign agent of Libya—and disclosing his advocacy role for that pro-terrorist nation and what he got for doing it. Payments came to $220,000. which Billy Carter says is a loan.

Then it was revealed that Billy Carter was used to set up a meeting between Mr. Carter's national security adviser, Zbigniew Brzezinski, and a Libyan diplomat.

Questions were raised about whether White House officials warned Billy Carter of a Justice Department investigation. Then Attorney General Benjamin Civiletti admitted he told President Carter in a private conversation that Billy was ''foolish'' not to register as a foreign agent and that he probably wouldn't be prosecuted if he did. The most recent flap was the Justice Department's statement that Billy Carter told its investigator he had possession of government cables about his first trip to Libya in 1978. A Senate committee is looking into the matter, and President Carter says he is ''eager'' to tell the committee his side of the story.

The Process Is Out of Kilter

By Albert R. Hunt

WASHINGTON—James Brady, the resourceful public-relations adviser to Ronald Reagan, felt the presidential election was sewed up the day after the Reagan-Carter debate.

''When I saw headlines 'Reagan Wins 2-to-1' that was it,'' he recalls. Those headlines were based on an ABC-TV national phone-in setup to get public reaction to the debate. The device was unscientific and highly irresponsible, yet it exemplifies the superficiality of our presidential elections.

One of the few benefits this time is that the voters did produce a clear-cut winner. But whether pleased or displeased with that outcome, political analysts in both parties agree that the process is out of kilter. It's too long, it's too shallow and it inadequately tests the ability of a future President to govern.

That's a consensus embraced both by many conservative supporters of Ronald Reagan and by many shell-shocked liberals. Of course, it's not unusual for politicians to wring their hands about "the process" and then do nothing about it. But with one election just completed and the next one almost too far away to consider, the time is ripe to think about ways to make the presidential election system more sensible.

Both party chairmen have privately endorsed the need for such an examination; if it isn't started soon, though, it will get caught up in the exigencies of the next election. Here are some of the more serious possibilities that thoughtful political participants are discussing:

The Nominating Process

A non-incumbent running for President must start two years ahead of Election Day. Thus, like Jimmy Carter four years ago and Ronald Reagan and George Bush this year, it helps if you're unemployed; job-holders suffer a disadvantage. Once the race begins, candidates face three dozen primaries; they often wake up wondering what state they're in, as well as what they want to say or think.

The solution of one national primary is rejected by most experts, who worry it would destroy whatever minor importance political parties still enjoy. Further, while the current election marathon lasts too long, a series of tests is healthy for both the voters and the candidates; the better a candidate does, the more scrutiny he or she faces.

But a balance is possible. There could be four regional primaries, held every three weeks from mid-April through mid-June. As Sen. Howard Baker (R., Tenn.) has suggested, each could be held in a separate time zone—Eastern, Central, Mountain and Pacific; by including Northern and Southern states in one primary, this arrangement would help avoid worsening regional tensions. And as Rep. Morris Udall (D., Ariz.) proposes, every state should have the option of devising its own separate caucus system in that period. But if a state wanted to hold a primary, it would have to be held on that day.

A regional-primary system wouldn't prevent some states from holding meaningless straw ballots months earlier; Florida and Maine did that in late 1979 for the benefit of news-hungry political reporters. However, this change would compress the formal primary season by several months and result in a more orderly process.

Peer Review

Simultaneously, political leaders should be given an enhanced role in picking presidential nominees. Says veteran Republican political strategist John Sears, "Under the current system, only the press analyzes whether anyone is up to being President."

This absence of peer review, as the case of Jimmy Carter so sadly showed, takes its toll later. "The skills and coalition required to get the presidential nomination," notes political scientist Austin Ranney, a Democrat, "are separate and different from the skills and coalitions required to govern."

A return to the smoke-filled room would be greeted with much cynicism by an already-suspicious public. Again, a middle ground looks attractive. A certain automatic percentage—probably around 25%—of delegates to the nominating conventions

---

With one election just completed and the next one almost too far away to consider, the time is ripe to think about ways to make the presidential election system more sensible.

---

should consist of all that party's members of Congress and top state and local officeholders and party officials; the rest of the delegates would be elected in the primaries or caucuses. This way a presidential candidate could ill afford to ignore the politicians he or she would encounter if elected. And the elected officials could ill afford to ignore any clear-cut expression of voter opinion in the primaries.

Efforts ought to be made to institutionalize a series of debates in every general election. The value of such encounters is exaggerated, but they provide some additional knowledge to voters. And there should be more than one such face-off in each campaign.

Debates should be run by professional news organizations, however. This year the League of Women Voters, with its on-again, off-again declarations on including an independent candidate and its penchant for devising the least informative formats, demonstrated that it isn't up to the task. Since presidential debates are television extravaganzas, it seems the best option is to have the TV networks run them.

But if the networks are to get this bonus, a good trade would be to force them to give the candidates—or even better, the political parties—a free half-hour of prime TV time every week during the fall campaign. The candidates or parties could use this 30 minutes in any way they wanted. Some sort of arrangement could be devised to accommodate third-party or independent candidates.

"This would force the candidates to be more substantive and at the same time force the networks to give more substantive treatment to the candidates," suggests Greg Schneiders, media consultant to Jimmy Carter. In return, says Mr. Schneiders, it might be a good idea then to outlaw most of the 30- and 60-second TV spots used in presidential races.

Money

If the networks were forced to give free time, money wouldn't be a problem for presidential candidates in the general election. But, under the current system, the financial rules affecting the primaries ought to be overhauled.

First, the $1,000 limit on individual contributions ought to be raised at least to $5,000; with inflation, it's pretty hard to "buy" a presidential candidate for $5,000. Spending limits, which forced candidates like Mr. Reagan to run a bare-bones operation the last three months of the primary season, ought to be eliminated. And the hundreds of petty regulations imposed on presidential campaigns ought to be significantly simplified; politics is too important to be left to the accountants.

Such proposals, if adopted, wouldn't amount to a panacea. The election process still would be too long and many candidates still would stress style over substance. But at least these changes might give the public more opportunities to assess the candidates, and they might prepare the candidates better to serve as President.

Mr. Hunt, a member of the Journal's Washington bureau, covers politics.

Crisis of the Party System: I

By Arthur Schlesinger Jr.

Something has gone badly wrong with the American party system. All gauges register trouble. The steady decline in voter turnout, the steady increase in ticket-splitting, the multiplication of voters styling themselves independents, the growing tendency of candidates to conceal rather than emphasize party affiliation, the substitution of television for party organization, the rise of personalist political movements—these are surely characteristics of a party system in an advanced state of decay.

Many observers, moreover, see the decay of the parties as a basic cause of the larger crisis of ungovernability. Historically, it is said, the party has brought disparate voters together into coherent combinations, contained explosive issues through brokerage and compromise and provided the means of concerted action in a government based on the separation of powers. With the party system no longer channeling the energies of our politics, these energies shoot off in all directions, and nothing gets done at the center.

Many factors are adduced to explain this crisis. I would like to offer an historian's thoughts as to what the crisis is *not* about and then as to what, in my judgment, it *is* about.

We hear, for example, that supposedly novel and untoward developments — the fragmentation of Congress, the power of lobbies, the spread of single-issue movements—help account for the decline of the parties. One wonders whether these phenomena are really all that novel, and whether their existence explains very much.

Lapse From a Golden Age?

Take Congress. Columnists write weighty pieces implying that the current incorrigibility on Capitol Hill represents a terrible lapse from some golden age when legislators unquestioningly obeyed party whips. But there never was such a golden age. Even Franklin Roosevelt, in the era of the so-called rubberstamp Congresses, had to fight for every New Deal measure after the Hundred Days and, with all his craft and popularity, was not uncommonly defeated on cherished initiatives, such as

discretionary neutrality and the Supreme Court.

Nor was party indiscipline new in the days of FDR. It is inherent in the American political order. Partly because of the constitutional separation of powers, partly because of the size and diversity of the country, American political parties, as Tocqueville observed 140 years ago, "are impatient of control and are never manageable except in moments of great public danger."

This innate unmanageability, Tocqueville pointed out, resulted from the dependence of the legislator on his constituents. "A representative," he wrote, "is never sure of his supporters, and, if they forsake him, he is left without a resource. . . . Thus it is natural that in democratic countries the members of political assemblies should think more of their constituents than of their party. . . . But what ought to be said to gratify constituents is not always what ought to be said in order to serve the party to which representatives profess to belong." Party indiscipline, far from being a novelty of our own fallen times, is one of the conditions that American democracy has endured from the start.

The same reflection applies to the theory of lobbies as some new and ghastly menace to the republic. We have had lobbies ever since we have had Congress. And lobbies were never more powerful than in those years after the Civil War when we came as near as we ever have to the beatitude of party discipline. Those who think that private-interest lobbies are a horrid invention of the late 20th Century ought to read "The Gilded Age" by Mark Twain and Charles Dudley Warner (1873) or meditate the gaudy career of Sam Ward (1814-1884), the King of the Lobby. On the other hand, the public-interest lobby has never been more effective than it is today; and to some degree this development offsets the private-interest groups. Ralph Nader is the modern response to Colonel Sellers and Sam Ward.

Nor are single-issue movements the appalling innovation that columnists, contemplating the anti-abortionists, the anti-gun-controllers, the ecologists, the homosexuals, and so on, evidently suppose

them to be. What Madison called the "mischiefs of faction" has been an abiding concern in American history. Single-issue movements have flickered across the political landscape from 1787 to 1979, whether devoted to the extirpation of Freemasonry, the abolition of slavery, the restriction of immigration, the issuance of greenbacks or the enactment of prohibition. American democracy has survived these movements too.

When the Know Nothing party was at its height, Horace Greeley predicted accurately that it would "run its career rapidly, and vanish as suddenly as it appeared. It *may* last through the next presidential canvass; but hardly longer than that. . . . It would seem as devoid of the elements of persistence as an anti-cholera or an anti-potato-rot party would be." The Know-Nothings, it should be noted, had a far greater success in elections than any of the one-eyed movements of our own day have had.

It would appear that commentators are getting inordinately excited about what are in fact the routine conditions of American politics. Yet there must be some reason for this excitement. The reason obviously is the greater salience these conditions appear to have today. And here is where the diagnosticians get the order quite wrong. They argue, for example, that these conditions account for the feebleness of the presidency. On closer examination, I think it will appear that the feebleness of the presidency accounts for the salience of these conditions. Or at least in good part. There is a more organic problem, which I will get to in a second article.

The absence of presidential leadership creates a vacuum in the center of our politics. It is this vacuum that disorganizes Congress and that the single-issue movements and lobbies rush to fill. The vacuum exists today not for structural reasons but for personal reasons—the limitations of the man in the presidency—and for historical reasons—the limitations of the epoch.

Mr. Carter is a highly intelligent man, but his is the intelligence of an engineer, not of a political leader. Our effective Presidents have understood that politics is ultimately an educational process. They have had a conviction about the direction in which they want to take the nation and a capacity to persuade their countrymen that this is the best direction for the nation to go. They have possessed, and had the power to convey, a vision of the future.

Mr. Carter sees himself as general manager of a government, not as President of a Republic. After two years of the Carter presidency, no one can tell the direction in which he wants to lead the country. He shows no discernible interest in the tasks of public education. Or perhaps he simply has little to say. Who can tell? In any event, his non-leadership leaves the special interests and the single-issue zealots a fairly clear field.

The Depressive Phase

In fairness, one must add that, even if he understood what the Presidency is all about, he is in office at an unpropitious time for an exercise of leadership. For, in the inherent cyclical rhythm of American politics, we are today in the depressive phase. We habitually go through seasons of action, passion, reform and affirmative government, until the country is worn out; whereupon we long for respite and enter

into seasons of lull, apathy, cynicism and negative government. Our contemporary passivity after the turbulent sixties and early seventies recalls the passive fifties after the demanding thirties and forties,

---

Board of Contributors

Party indiscipline, far from being a novelty of our own fallen times is one of the conditions American democracy has endured from the start.

---

and the passive twenties after the active first two decades of the century.

Two things, however, happen during these periods of rest and recuperation. The national batteries recharge themselves, and the problems we neglect threaten to become unmanageable. Sometime in the

eighties the dam will break, as it broke in the sixties, the thirties and at the turn of the century. There will arise a new passion for reform, innovation, experiment and a new opportunity for strong national direction. Competent presidential leadership will begin to fill the vacuum, and such chronic ailments of our history as fractious Congresses, greedy lobbies and single-issue pests will dwindle once again to their proper proportions.

If these historic afflictions were our only worry, we could be reasonably optimistic about the party system. But there is the organic problem mentioned a moment ago. And the organic problem is what I think the crisis of the party system is really about.

Mr. Schlesinger is Albert Scweitzer Professor of Humanities at the City University of New York, winner of Pulitzer Prizes in history and biography and a member of the Journal's Board of Contributors. This is the second of two related articles.

  May 14, 1979

Crisis of the Party System: II

By Arthur Schlesinger Jr.

In an earlier piece I suggested that the chronic afflictions of the party system — congressional fragmentation, lobbies, single-issue movements—can be overcome, as they have been in the past, by competent presidential leadership. The reason for the deep and perhaps incurable crisis of the system lies elsewhere. It lies above all in the organic changes wrought in the political environment by the electronic revolution.

The party system had already begun to lose historic functions well before the advent of electronic technology. The decline of immigration deprived the political organization of its classic clientele. The rise of civil service limited its patronage. The New Deal took over its welfare role. But today two modern electronic devices—television and the computer—are having a devastating and possibly fatal impact on the traditional structure of American politics.

The traditional structure had three tiers: the politician, the voter and, in between, a cluster of intermediate agencies—most significantly the party organization; but also the trade association, the labor union, the farm organization, the ethnic brotherhood—negotiating between the politician and the voter, interceding for each on behalf of the other and providing the links that held the party system together.

The electronic revolution has abolished the mediatorial function. Television presents the politician directly to the voter, who makes his judgment more on what Walter Cronkite and John Chancellor show him than on what the party leaders tell him. Moreover, television, as Austin Ranney suggests, has become the main source not just of information but of ''reality'' for the voter.

At the same time, computerized public opinion polling presents the voter directly to the politician, who judges opinion more by what the polls show him than by what the party leaders tell him. The political organization is left to wither on the vine.

The organization has thus lost its domination of the lines of information and communication between government and public opinion. It has lost most of its power to

select top candidates too. This loss is often blamed on the spread of presidential primaries. But presidential primaries have been around for a long time. It took television to transform them into the controlling force they are today. Television has given the ordinary citizen a new sense of entitlement in the political process. Presidential nominations are no longer settled by party leaders in smoke-filled rooms but by primaries and caucuses at the grassroots. Political conventions have become ceremonies of ratification. A person born the last year that a convention required more than one ballot to nominate a presidential candidate would be 27 years old today.

'Photo Opportunities'

Television stimulates political activism. Every rebel group knows about ''photo opportunities'' and schemes to get itself on camera. What Sam Lubell has called the ''struggle for political visibility'' is the means by which a newly demanding electorate presses its claims. All this has further weakened party identification and intensified the distrust of politicians and organizations—a distrust that, substantiated by spectacular policy disgraces at home and abroad, has turned into rabid hostility.

Political loyalties, once as sacred as religious affiliations, are steadily fading away. Campaign billboards in our heterodox age play down the party of the candidate—a profound change from the time when Thomas B. Reed could say, "A good party is better than the best man that ever lived."

The party organization is in addition losing its control over campaigns. Television and polling have bred a new profession of electronic manipulators. Assembled in election-management firms, the media specialists, working indifferently for one party or the other, reduce campaigns to displays not of content but of technique.

Can the traditional party system be saved? I must confess skepticism about many of the proposed remedies. The suggestion is made, for example, that party professionals be allocated a fixed proportion of seats in nominating conventions, that campaign funds should go to party organizations rather than to individual candidates and that other guarantees should be sought for party organizations against the depredations of electronic mercenaries, on the one hand, and citizen activists on the other.

Some of these proposals seem to me doubtful on the merits. It is hard to justify the proposition that the interests of American democracy would have been better served through history had political funds been entrusted to party bosses rather than to issue-oriented candidates. Let us not in our adversity succumb to a romantic myth of party organization. New ideas have won access to politics precisely through crusaders like T.R., Wilson, F.D.R., who had to take the party away from the organization in order to move the nation ahead. The crusaders were responsive to needs and issues; the bosses to boodle and survival.

Nor are larger proposals to centralize and discipline the parties more persuasive. This effort is against the grain of American parties, for reasons observed long since by Tocqueville, as well as against the spirit of the electronic age.

Nor is discipline necessarily all that transcendent a virtue. The reputation of Congress was never lower than in the second half of the 19th Century when parties were most disciplined. Those were the times that led Mark Twain to write "Reader, suppose you were an idiot. And suppose you were a member of Congress. But I repeat myself."

Strict party discipline is likely to mean a preponderance of idiots following the leadership like sheep. My guess is that we have had in recent Congresses fewer idiots and more informed, educated and independent-minded legislators than we have had

since the early Republic. But the price we pay for independent-minded legislators is their determination to make up their own minds. We can't have it both ways—a high quality Congress and sheeplike discipline. The improvement in quality also explains, I would think, the increased defection rate, for there are fewer time-servers today and more people who, coming to Congress to accomplish things, then retire in frustration when they discover that they are not getting very far.

Some political scientists blame the decline of the parties on the reform movements of the last decade. But party reform was a response, not a cause. Many of the "reforms"—the modernization of proce-

---

Board of Contributors

Today two modern electronic devices — television and the computer—are having a devastating and possibly fatal impact on the traditional structure of American politics.

---

dures, for example, and the larger representation of women and blacks—strengthened the parties. Other "reforms" carelessly or deliberately ignored the interests of parties as institutions. But the idea that procedural reforms caused the crisis, or that repealing these reforms will cure it, is akin to the delusion of Rostand's Chanticleer that his cock-a-doodle made the sun rise.

Obviously we should do what we can to avoid weakening the party system further. Such proposals as the direct election of Presidents, a national primary, a national initiative and referendum, might well administer the *coup de grace* and must be resisted. The provision of free television time to the national party committees would be modestly useful in propping the parties up. But most structural remedies are beside the point. The attempt to shore up structure against loss of function is artificial and futile.

Restoration of Serious Function

The party system is simply no longer effective as an agency of mass mobilization, or as an agency of candidate selection, or as an agency of information and communication, or as an agency of brokerage, or as an agency of welfare and acculturation, or as an expression of the politi-

cal culture. It can be saved only by the restoration of serious function. At present, the party organization does little more than certify platforms and provide labels for the organization of elections and legislature.

Two things alone can give these decrepit parties a lease on life: the incubation of ideas that give promise of meeting the hard questions of our age, especially inflation and energy; and the election of competent Presidents who will thereafter act to revitalize their parties in the presidential interest. The best hope for the party is as an instrument of Presidents who need to overcome the separation of powers and to mobilize mass support in order to put new programs into effect.

Otherwise we may be beginning a slow, confused descent into an era of what Walter Dean Burnham has called "politics without parties." Political adventurers will roam the countryside like Chinese war lords or Iranian ayatollahs, recruiting personal armies, conducting hostilities against some rival warlords and forming alliances with others, and, as they win elections, striving to govern through ad hoc coalitions in legislatures.

The prospect is not inviting. The crumbling away of the historic parties would leave political power in America concentrated in the adventurers, in the interest groups that finance them and in the executive bureaucracy. The rest of us might not have even the limited entry into and leverage on the process that the party system, for all its defects, has made possible. Without parties, our politics would grow angrier, wilder and more irresponsible.

Still we cannot restore the past by act of will. "The sum of political life," wrote Henry Adams, "was or should have been the attainment of a working political system. Society needed to reach it. If moral standards broke down, and machinery stopped working, new morals and machinery of some sort had to be invented." This seems to be our problem—not to engage in artificial resuscitation of a system that has served its time but to invent the morals, machinery and ideas required by the last quarter of the 20th Century.

Mr. Schlesinger is Albert Schweitzer Professor of the Humanities at the City University of New York, winner of Pulitzer Prizes in history and biography and a member of the Journal's Board of Contributors. This is the second of two related articles; the first appeared last Thursday.

The Republican Revival

By Norman C. Miller

DETROIT — It's hard to remember, amid the cheerful and confident Republicans assembled here, that just a few years ago there was a serious question, raised by some Republicans themselves, whether the Grand Old Party could survive.

Well, the often beleaguered Republicans have more than survived. They will close their convention tomorrow, after crowning Ronald Reagan as their presidential nominee, in better shape than anyone could have dreamed as recently as 1974. Then, the Watergate scandal not only drove a Republican President out of the White House but plummeted the party of Richard Nixon to devastating depths. After suffering huge losses in the 1974 congressional elections and losing the White House in 1976, some wondered whether the Republicans might go the way of the Whigs.

Now, wonder of wonders, the Republicans find themselves with an excellent chance of electing Ronald Reagan to the White House and also scoring big gains in Senate, House and state elections. The prospect of an across-the-board GOP comeback is all the more remarkable when you consider that Mr. Reagan and most other GOP candidates are espousing conservative positions that Barry Goldwater could have embraced happily in 1964, when the Republicans suffered their greatest defeat since the Democrats established their political dominance in the 1930s.

What was extreme conservatism 16 years ago, now is politics with mainstream appeal—not only for Republicans but for large numbers of independents and nominally Democratic voters.

This by no means guarantees that Republicans are sure-fire winners. As they have demonstrated over and over, they are experts at finding ways to lose. Here in Detroit, they doubtless lost votes among the white-wine-and-brie set by refusing to endorse the Equal Rights Amendment; more important, the needless ERA flap deflected attention from potentially popular Republican positions on the major pocketbook and foreign-policy issues.

Still, the conditions exist for a big GOP win, if Mr. Reagan and other Republicans have the savvy to exploit their opportunity. The critical issues all break in favor of the Republicans.

Heirs of Herbert Hoover

To their own amazement, they now are in striking distance of persuading voters that the heirs of Herbert Hoover would do a better job of reducing unemployment than the Democrats. A recent survey by Robert Teeter, a respected GOP pollster, shows the Republicans closing within three percentage points—38% to 41%—on the question of which party would do better in handling unemployment.

The Teeter poll, which is generally confirmed by other surveys, has a lot of good news for Republicans. By a huge 58%-25% margin, people say Republicans would do a better job than Democrats of bringing down double-digit inflation. By similarly big margins, Republicans are favored on the issues of holding down taxes and maintaining military security. They run narrowly ahead on the issues of maintaining the peace and insuring adequate energy supplies.

On major issues, then the Republicans are in strikingly good shape. For this, in large measure, they can thank Jimmy Carter. Elected on promise of restoring competent government, Mr. Carter has presided ineffectually over skyrocketing inflation, rising unemployment and the decline of U.S. prestige and power in the world. The President is widely viewed as a weak and uncertain leader. Thus the Republicans have that elemental and powerful political war cry—it's time for a change—working for them.

There also is some evidence that Republicans may succeed in tying congressional Democrats to the President's inept record. The Teeter poll shows the most positive attitudes toward Republican congressional candidates—and the most negative attitudes toward Democrats—since 1966, the last time the GOP scored major gains (47 seats) in House elections. In Senate races, even some Democrats concede the Republicans may score a net gain of five or six seats; there is a remote chance they may pick up nine seats needed for Senate control.

No one is suggesting there is a mass movement of voters into the Republican Party; it still can claim allegiance of only about one of five voters. Indeed, if anything a worried and distrustful electorate is increasingly in an anti-party mood.

But it seems clear the Democrats have worse problems than the Republicans. The voters no longer are buying the old liberal Democratic prescriptions; witness the rejection in the primaries of Ted Kennedy's candidacy. President Carter has failed to develop credible policies in place of worn-out liberalism. And the Carter-Kennedy battle has left the Democrats badly split, a split that may get worse instead of better during and after the Democratic convention next month.

While disillusioned Democrats and independents aren't signing aboard the GOP, the issue attitudes of many of them converge with Republican views. Big majorities want income taxes cut and government spending and regulations curbed. Big majorities also favor more defense spending and a get-tough policy with the Soviets. Republicans — especially Ronald Reagan—are out in front of the Democrats on these cutting issues.

In Mr. Reagan, the Republicans have a formidable candidate, whom Democrats have tended to underestimate ever since he was elected Governor of California in 1966. Mr. Reagan isn't a rigid right-winger, although ideological conservatives form his core of support. In his California campaigns, and in this year's Illinois and Wisconsin primaries, Mr. Reagan has demonstrated he can win blue-collar votes—and the Democrats are dead if large numbers of working-class voters turn away from Mr. Carter.

Right now, Republican pollsters say Mr. Reagan is leading Mr. Carter and independent John Anderson in some key industrial states—Illinois, Michigan, Ohio and Pennsylvania. With Mr. Reagan's strong base in the West and winning poten-

Perspective on Politics

tial in such Southern states as Texas and Louisiana, he has the makings of an electoral majority if he can hold the lead in those four big Northern states.

That, of course, is a big if. Mr. Reagan probably will have to offer the voters a good deal more than he has so far to win the election.

Simply attacking Mr. Carter isn't likely to work. John Anderson's strong showing in the polls carries a message for Mr. Reagan as well as for the President. Huge numbers of voters—more than one-third of them—are telling pollsters they don't like either of the major-party candidates. Mr. Reagan, as the nonincumbent, has a better chance than Mr. Carter to woo those turned-off or Anderson-inclined voters. But he needs to give them positive reasons to vote for him.

Held in Low Regard

For while Jimmy Carter is held in low regard, many people also doubt Mr. Reagan's abilities. His habit of disposing of complex issues with snappy one-liners, while effective in the GOP primaries, probably won't wash in a general-election campaign. To gain the confidence of doubtful voters, Mr. Reagan needs to deal effectively with the charge that he is simplistic and reckless—a charge the Carter campaign is certain to emphasize.

Mr. Reagan is vulnerable to that charge because so far his rhetoric on key issues *does* seem simplistic and even reckless. Can he really cut taxes sharply and increase military spending massively without making inflation worse? Is a dramatic arms build-up and a hard-line stance against the Soviets the way to make the world safer?

Perhaps Mr. Reagan has convincing answers to these critical questions, going well beyond the superficialities that marked his primary campaign. His staff promises he will spell out reasoned rationales for his positions in a series of speeches. Still, the fact that troubling questions exist about Mr. Reagan's dept after 14 years in public life is a dangerous political problem.

Mr. Reagan's choice of a vice presidential candidate and the themes he sounds in his acceptance speech tomorrow will be vitally important to his effort to broaden his constituency. He needs a moderate running mate with appeal both to Anderson-inclined independents and wary working-class Democrats. And the 69-year-old candidate needs a running mate clearly qualified for the presidency; otherwise, the age issue, which faded in the primaries, might become a serious liability again.

The acceptance speech will give Mr. Reagan a matchless opportunity to impress millions in the TV audience with his leadership abilities on the decisive pocket-book and peace issues. If he yields to the temptation to merely entertain artisans in the convention hall with denunciations of Jimmy Carter, he probably will turn off many voters who want something more from politicians than name-calling.

But however things work out, at this moment Mr. Reagan and the conservative faithful who now dominate the GOP are entitled to savor their triumph here. For Mr. Reagan, whose vigor belies his age, it is a grand accomplishment to win his party's nomination after two unsuccessful bids. Equally remarkable is the revival of a vigorous Republican Party after all its travails. Win or lose in the fall, you have to admire a man and a party that won't quit.

————————

The Collapse of Consensus

By Norman C. Miller

NEW YORK—There's nothing unusual about the brawl the Democrats are having at their convention. Democrats wouldn't be acting like Democrats unless they were brawling.

The party's genius—the reason it has prevailed for nearly five decades as the dominant party—has been the ability of its often-warring factions to submerge their differences, after convention battles, and unite against the Republicans.

But this time it will be very difficult for the Democrats to truly unite after a divisive convention. The reasons run much deeper than the bitter antagonism of some Carter and Kennedy backers, an antagonism that extends to President Carter and Senator Kennedy themselves.

An Eroded Consensus

Bitter feelings are a serious problem for the Democrats. But a more fundamental problem is the collapse—or at least the near-collapse—of the basic consensus the party's factions once shared on the great foreign policy and economic issues at the heart of American politics.

The Vietnam war ruptured the Democrats' consensus on foreign policy and the division has never been repaired. It is a basic reason Hubert Humphrey and George McGovern lost to Richard Nixon in 1968 and 1972. Jimmy Carter, elected mainly because of the Republicans' Watergate hangover, has done nothing to restore the Democrats' lost foreign-policy consensus.

Indeed, in his fumbling fashion, the President has exacerbated their party's split over foreign policy. On assuming office, he clearly sided with what may roughly be termed the party's McGovern wing. That is, he established as an overriding objective a detente policy emphasizing arms control and general accommodations with the Soviets—declaring in his first major foreign-policy speech in 1977 that we must free ourselves of "inordinate fear of Communism."

Thus President Carter and his principal foreign-policy makers insisted that Kremlin objectives were essentially benign even as the Soviets relentlessly built up their military might while the administration cancelled new strategic weapons. And the

————————

Perspective on Politics

————————

Carter administration continually explained away Soviet-backed aggression in Ethiopia, Yemen and Cambodia.

The result was a deepening estrangement of Democrats who fundamentally distrust the Soviets and advocate a U.S. defense buildup — exemplified by party leaders such as Sens. Moynihan, Jackson and Nunn and labor leaders such as Lane Kirkland of the AFL-CIO. But this wing of the party couldn't find a candidate to challenge the President in the primaries. Anyway, Mr. Carter's shocked reaction to the Soviet invasion of Afghanistan—when he seemingly switched to a hard-line policy—encouraged these Democrats to think that their view of foreign policy finally was in the ascendancy.

But the President's wavering course since the Afghanistan invasion last November has left the hard-line Democrats basically dissatisfied. "He speaks as if there has been a change (but) will he act?" complains Sen. Moynihan.

Ironically in foreign-policy terms, the challenge to Mr. Carter's renomination came from the left. Ted Kennedy basically agreed with the original Carter foreign policy and — speaking for the McGovern wing — even criticized the President's pledge to defend the Persian Gulf after the Afghanistan invasion.

But the Kennedy campaign, emphasizing economic issues, has exposed the second great division in the party. Mr. Kennedy bases his candidacy on the old-line liberal economics that have controlled Democratic politics since the New Deal. Mr. Carter, it is clear after four years, doesn't have a coherent economic philosophy. But, in company with many other Democrats, the President apparently believes that double-digit inflation has destroyed liberal economic doctrine as a viable policy.

Mr. Carter's problem, of course, is that his constantly changing economic policies have become a laughingstock. And the results have been awful: horrendous inflation and rising unemployment. All factions of the party are appalled by the prospect of running on the Carter economic record.

Sen. Kennedy, although his liberal policies are shopworn, still offers an alternative economic platform that could enable worried Democrats to distance themselves from the hapless Carter record. So, even though Mr. Kennedy last night withdrew as a presidential candidate, it is possible that the convention tonight may repudiate parts of the Carter economic policy by voting for a Kennedy-sponsored jobs scheme.

The disarray among Democrats over fundamental economic issues is their worst problem in the campaign against the Reagan-led Republicans. Sen. Kennedy and other old-line liberals are quite sincere in their opposition to Carter policies; they will support a renominated Mr. Carter, if they do, without enthusiasm. Other Democrats, who believe the party must develop a new economic philosophy, are hard pressed to argue convincingly that the uncertain Mr. Carter is a leader who will shape viable policies.

Thus, on gut economic issues, the Democrats now are badly split between the Kennedy-led faction that still insists on the old liberal policies and an inchoate faction that is groping for something new. Meanwhile, the Republicans are pretty much united on tax-cut policies with potentially powerful political appeal even if they turn out to be irresponsible economics.

Opportunity for GOP

Indeed, on basic approaches to both economic and foreign-policy issues, Ronald Reagan and other Republicans now are emphasizing policies that strike responsive chords among some traditional Democratic constituencies and independent voters.

The Reagan-led Republicans have a rare opportunity to score sweeping gains based on both a hard-line foreign policy and a new economic policy emphasizing tax-cut incentives.

The Democrats' main hope is that Mr. Reagan will make enough blunders that they can successfully attack him as simplistic and reckless. That could happen. If it does, the Democrats could wind up holding the White House once again despite their basic divisions and Jimmy Carter's inept record.

But the Democrats' split on great issues would remain in any case. Neither this convention nor the campaign is likely to help restore the Democrats' lost consensus. It may take several years—and the loss of elections—before the Democrats can develop new leaders and sort out a new consensus.

30

The Democratic Attack Still Lacks Teeth

Suddenly, the Democratic opposition is as close to being ecstatic as it has been since Nov. 4. The President seems to be retreating and reneging. His televised address a week ago was far more tentative and tenuous, far more indefinite, than his earlier vigorous assertions of purpose and program. There is the smell of political trouble for the Republicans in the air, if not of outright disaster, and long-quiet

---

Viewpoint

by Hodding Carter III

---

voices are being raised against much of what has happened since Jan. 20. Even the press seems to be coming out of its kennel and snarling a bit, here and there.

From the point of view of a healthy functioning democracy, such critical zeal is welcome. But from a slightly longer-term perspective, there is much less in the new assertiveness than meets the eye. The President may have stumbled, but the opposition has yet to regain its feet.

The surface facts seem clear enough. The President over-promised from the start, so that even when he forced the legislative process to produce prodigiously, it could not begin to match the expectations raised by his rhetoric. Thus, while he can complain with some justification that much of his allegedly failed program has not yet been put into effect, his complaint misses the point. If you seem to suggest that the millennium is at hand, you begin to look foolish as the days drag on without the Second Coming.

Beyond that, his public persuasiveness could paper over only temporarily his policy's glaring internal contradictions, most notably the wide disparity in approach of the monetarists and supply-siders who staff the administration's higher economic reaches. That gap, plus the concern that it won't be spanned anytime soon, are the proximate cause of the money markets' near-hysterical disaffection. Stocks and bonds have been on the skids for months, whatever their short-term ups and downs, and will apparently remain depressed until the trumpet sounds a single refrain at the White House.

Finally, people are beginning to notice that what the new administration really offers is a distorted mirror image of the old big government way of doing business. The state isn't really fading away; it's simply redirecting its emphasis from social welfare to defense spending. The budget will continue to grow, if more slowly, because no matter how drastic the domestic cuts, the President is adamantly committed to a record-shattering increase in defense spending. Fond hopes notwithstanding, there isn't going to be a balanced budget in the foreseeable future, and everyone knows and acknowledges it except the administration's spokesmen. Having erected a balanced budget as the totem of fiscal sanity, the President's men are stuck with the psychological downside of their failure to achieve it.

The President is absolutely correct when he says that Main Street isn't half as disturbed about all this as Wall Street. But he must know that when the social service cuts begin to bite after Oct. 1, when middle-class and lower middle-class Americans learn that they aren't exempt from the call to sacrifice (which they presently believe is meant for welfare chiselers alone), they will begin to squeal also. That won't necessarily make Main Street any more right than Wall Street is today; it will simply add another weight to the previously weightless administration balloon. Except in their most hallucinatory projections, the supply-siders do not claim that the tax cuts will have an overnight effect. The budget cuts will.

All of which could be the prescription for Democratic Party rejuvenation if the patient had any notion of what it means to do after leaving the hospital. The party doesn't, however, being still torn by schisms which make the monetarist-supply-side friction seem insignificant. Solidarity Day was a gigantic success, but it held together because the various groups which joined organized labor on the Washington Mall self-consciously papered over their differences. Their theme was attack, attack and attack the President's policies once again, which was useful as far as it went, but will not hold the American electorate's interest or respect if it is not quickly replaced with something more constructive.

But what is the grand old party of innovation offering in the way of new ideas, or even interesting refinements of old ones? The answer can be found in its approach to the Social Security mess. Congressional

Democrats make hay out of President Reagan's waffling on the subject, then try to pretend that the nation's most important economic safety net is not in serious trouble.

And who is their chief spokesman in riposte to the administration's economic program? Why, Wall Street, their old nemesis, now given the responsibility for providing the final word to Reagonomics. That is downright suicidal, the canyons of downtown New York not being traditional Democratic territory. What the market gives in the way of solace today it can and will take away tomorrow. The essential task for Democrats is to offer an alternative to the President's program, not desperately attach themselves to temporary allies who have no lasting interests in common.

It is the tragicomic spectacle of left-liberals approvingly quoting Barry Goldwater on the inequity of right-wing single interest groups, which best illustrates the opposition's bankruptcy. The President need not fear the teeth of such enemies. This administration's most cherished policies may prove wrong, but that is no reason to bet they will be replaced. You can't beat something with nothing.

———

Mr. Carter was assistant secretary of state for public affairs in the Carter administration.

———

Campaigning for Office

Carter and Reagan Each Claim Victory In Debate; Little Convincing Proof Is Seen

By a WALL STREET JOURNAL *Staff Reporter*

WASHINGTON — President Carter and Ronald Reagan breathed sighs of relief that the Great Debate was over, took comfort in what they accomplished during it and then plunged on into the final six days of the presidential campaign.

Both sides insisted they won the debate, but no one was able to produce very convincing evidence.

Richard Wirthlin, Mr. Reagan's chief poll taker and strategist, said the overnight surveys he commissioned showed Mr. Reagan went into the debate with a five-point lead over the President and came out with a 10-point lead. Mr. Wirthlin cautioned, though, that gains and losses registered in these presidential debates usually are only temporary. What it does, he said, is "give us a little more cushion."

Jody Powell, the President's press secretary, told reporters about a complicated procedure in which that campaign's poll taker, Patrick Caddell, arranged for measurements of 50 undecided voters in the state of Washington, half leaning to the President, half leaning to Mr. Reagan. The debate made the Carter leaners lean more heavily to the President and the Reagan leaners lean less heavily to Mr. Reagan.

Nationwide Canvass

Perhaps the most reliable poll was taken by the Associated Press. In a nationwide canvass of 1,062 voters who watched the debate, AP reported that each candidate picked up six points, with Mr. Reagan leading Mr. Carter, 49% to 39%.

The most controversial survey was taken by ABC news. Nearly 700,000 people called special telephone numbers to register their decision on who won the debate. The network conceded there was nothing scientific about it, but reported anyway that Mr. Reagan was the winner, two to one. The Carter people were incensed that some newspapers decided to carry the results as important news.

The Reagan campaign pointed with some pleasure at a technological game played in Seattle, Wash., with 200 households hooked up to a computer. People watching the debate could push any of eight buttons, registering various reactions to what was being said. The operation is run by Roger Percy, Illinois Sen. Charles Percy's son, and both campaigns subscribe to the results. Mr. Wirthlin, Mr. Reagan's man, says Mr. Reagan defeated Mr. Carter on the "vox boxes," four rounds to two, with two even. But Mr. Percy says it really was an even split, with Mr. Carter picking up points at the end.

Independent candidate John Anderson, who was frozen out of the debate, said the performances of both the President and Mr. Reagan were "shallow." He conceded that it currently looks as if this is a two-candidate race. He said he would try the best he could to "remedy" that in these next few days.

Irrespective of what the polls might have indicated, the Carter and Reagan campaigns cleared out of Cleveland in buoyant moods.

Post-Debate Stop

The Carter campaigners said the President raised all the issues he needed to raise to win over traditional Democratic constituents who have been wavering—blue-collar workers, Jews, suburbanites.

In his first post-debate stop, another town meeting, held in an Episcopal cathedral in Pittsburgh, Mr. Carter repeated his charge that Mr. Reagan wasn't concerned about the possibility of terrorist nations developing atomic weapons. He also attacked Mr. Reagan's positions on the minimum wage and Social Security. He continued to plead with Democrats to come home to their own party.

Mr. Reagan flew out of Cleveland to Houston. Texas and Florida are the two big Southern states Mr. Reagan hopes to steal away from Mr. Carter. Wins in those states would give Mr. Reagan breathing room in the North.

In Houston, Mr. Reagan gave his standard speech, adding that Mr. Carter refused to talk about his own record during the debate. "You can see why," Mr. Reagan said.

Mr. Reagan moves on today to Arkansas, Louisiana, New Jersey and Pennsylvania. Later in the week, he'll hit the industrial Midwest. Mr. Carter will be campaigning in the big industrial states too, with side trips to Texas and other states in the South to fend off Mr. Reagan. He'll take a real gamble in the final hours of the campaign by invading Mr. Reagan's home state, California.

———

The Campaign and Presidential Character

Reagan and 'Depth'

By ALBERT R. HUNT

WASHINGTON—Last spring I wrote a front-page profile of Ronald Reagan which if not especially memorable, was balanced. It depicted Mr. Reagan as a decent, reasonably bright and often pragmatic politician who is neither a particularly deep nor innovative thinker and seems firmly rooted in the values and virtues of the past.

Immediately, my liberal friends accused me of "going into the tank" for the Republican leader. How could the term "bright" be applied to such an intellectual lightweight? Or decent and pragmatic to such a reactionary warmonger? And—most painful of all—why was I such a simpering sycophant for the editorial-page policy of this newspaper?

This reaction underscored one of the most important elements in Ronald Reagan's political success: He is very well served by his political enemies.

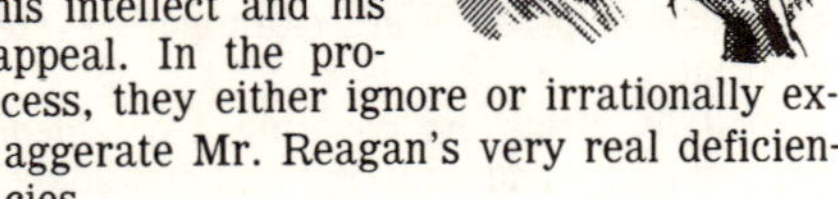

From his first opponent, former Gov. Pat Brown of California, on through Jerry Ford and Jimmy Carter, they have repeatedly misread and underestimated him. They have been contemptuous of both his intellect and his appeal. In the process, they either ignore or irrationally exaggerate Mr. Reagan's very real deficiencies.

The simple truth, whether liberals like it or not, is that "the Gipper"—he once played Notre Dame football great George Gipp in a movie—is a genuinely nice man whose humor and personal generosity charm even many political opponents. "He genuinely believes there's some good in everybody," says his close aide, Michael Deaver. While that sounds like what any close aide would say, anyone who spends any time around Ronald Reagan can see that, unlike that other *bete noire* of liberals, Richard Nixon, the Gipper isn't a hater.

Mr. Reagan also is a secure man. A campaign staff, it is said, is a "mirror reflection of the candidate." And with one or two exceptions, the men (unfortunately, there are few women) around Mr. Reagan display little of the paranoia that was so characteristic of the Nixon entourage.

Nor is Mr. Reagan stupid. No one can survive on the national political scene for 14 years, winning elections and scoring well in debates, with an inferior mind. Opponents can disagree with Ronald Reagan's conclusions, but he does talk with knowledge about a wide array of subjects.

Thus it's nonsense to say, as Time magazine recently did, that the central question about Mr. Reagan remains: "Is he smart enough to be President?" Two of the smartest men, in the I.Q. sense, to occupy the Oval Office in recent times have been Richard Nixon and Jimmy Carter. Conversely, nobody ever called Harry Truman or Jerry Ford intellectual giants. Which pair would you prefer?

The image of Mr. Reagan as a rigid ideologue is equally erroneous. When on the banquet circuit, talking to the philosophical true-believers, he certainly feeds that impression. But a better guide is his eight-year record as governor of California. Even Democratic critics admit he governed far more moderately than his rhetoric—then and now—would have you believe.

And during this campaign he has seemed very comfortable with the much-advertised "moderating" of his views on such issues as federal aid to New York City and to Chrysler Corp. He believes he adheres to his basic conservative principles on the major issues of the government's role in society and the need to counter the Soviet Union around the world. Therefore, aides say, it doesn't bother him to hedge a little on some politically sensitive specific issues. Whether this position is right or wrong, it isn't the mark of a hard-line ideologue.

So, after spending the equivalent of several months watching Ronald Reagan during the last year, I think he is smart enough, decent enough and sufficiently flexible to be President. Still, there are nagging problems about the man.

On one level, it's irritating to see Ronald Reagan pandering to the "Moral Majority'" fundamentalists, for there's a certain hypocrisy involved. In talking about restoring the old values, he presents himself as a positive prude; the best form of birth control, he has said, is to "say no."

This comes from a man who was divorced and, before his second marriage, was one of Hollywood's well-known lady-killers. Moreover, his four children live very modern lifestyles—something which, I think admirably, he has accepted. But it's disingenuous for the Gipper to pretend he's a moral cousin of the Rev. Jerry Falwell. After the last four years, the last thing we need is more moral hypocrisy in the White House.

On a more serious level, there is Mr. Reagan's penchant for seeing things in simple terms. That penchant, often a virtue in a political campaign, becomes worrisome when one imagines him in the Oval Office. If he makes it to the White House, his tendency to ignore complicated relationships will be troubling, especially in foreign policy. As my colleague, Karen Elliott House, wrote five months ago, the worry here about Ronald Reagan isn't that he's reckless; it is that he shows "little grasp of complex international issues and seems unable to relate specific problems to his broad philosophical design."

Mr. Reagan likes to see the world in black-and-white terms. Thus the Iran-Iraq conflict must drive him up the wall. The Israelis, good guys in the Reagan book, and the Libyans, bad guys, are siding with the Iranians; on the other side, the Saudi Arabians and the Soviets are with the Iraqis. How a President Reagan would respond to such an anomaly is a question mark.

Further, for all his personal charm, Ronald Reagan is a creature of California's media politics who isn't comfortable with one-on-one cajoling or negotiating. But the standard campaign speech, replete with the one-liners, won't count for much when he's trying to deal with a congressional power like Chairman Russell Long of the Senate Finance Committee.

Finally, I'd feel better if Ronald Reagan were more versed in history. He doesn't read many books and most of his historical references come from either personal memory or a newspaper or magazine article he has read. (He has an incredibly retentive mind, which sometimes gets him in trouble when he recalls and repeats some of the extreme notions he has read.) The nation's earlier Presidents were well served by an appreciation of historical frameworks, a quality that has been sadly absent from the White House in recent years.

I have watched and thought about Ronald Reagan a lot during the past year. Still, I'm uncertain whether he would be a good or bad President. But I do feel confident that at least two groups would have their expectations dashed by a Reagan presidency. They are his harshest critics and his most zealous supporters.

Mr. Hunt, a member of the Journal's Washington bureau, covers politics.

Carter and 'Meanness'

By Timothy D. Schellhardt

WASHINGTON—In the two years I've watched him closely, Jimmy Carter has emerged as two distinct personalities.

The first Jimmy Carter is the man who perched atop a stool recently at the Lyndhurst, N.J., fire station before a small audience of area residents.

Calmly and with self-confidence, he answered the voiced concerns of the group—their worries about inflation and national security, among other things. He did so with a firm grasp of the issues, with warmth and a touch of humor when appropriate, putting his audience at ease. This Jimmy Carter, you sense, is a good and decent man with a compassionate heart who, despite major failings, desires to do the right thing as President.

The other Jimmy Carter is the one who stood before a raucous crowd recently in Waco, Texas, attacking Republican rival Ronald Reagan with one cheap shot after another. This Jimmy Carter appears mean, vindictive, humorless; he projects a smallness of character that suggests he's a mere opportunist.

Which comes closer to being the "real" Jimmy Carter? It's an important distinction since, in many ways, the presidential election tomorrow may hinge not so much on the issues as on the characters and personalities of the two major contenders. As my first days of observing this President have turned into months and years, I've grown increasingly concerned that the true Jimmy Carter may be more the latter personality than the former.

This is a troubling assessment and one I wouldn't have drawn during my first year of following Mr. Carter, from mid-1978 through mid-1979. I recall vividly some of my early experiences watching this President. One came at the Ebenezer Baptist Church in Atlanta, the home church of Rev. Martin Luther King Sr. Here was a President, a white man from the deep South, accepted as a brother to the black congregation who with their families and ancestors had suffered lifetimes of racial discrimination. When Mr. Carter and the congregation, arm in arm, sang "We Shall Overcome," it was a moving experience. Since then, I've often thought: "I can't imagine a President Reagan doing that."

Another early memory concerns a Carter trip to the West Coast, where he strongly attacked the medical and legal professions for battling social progress. It was a message that then seemed necessary and appropriate for a President seeking overhauls of the health care and legal systems. He delivered the message effectively.

Since then, however, the President's frequent criticisms of special-interest groups or of political opponents often have rung hollow. They have suggested that Mr. Carter seeks only to place the blame for his own failures on someone else's shoulders. In often-strident tones, Mr. Carter blames the persistent high inflation on Mideast oil sheiks rather than on his own shortcomings. High interest rates are due to big banks or to that nasty Federal Reserve Board, he contends. His inability to move pet legislation through Congress, the President growls, reflects only the powerful lobbying of the oil industry or some other influential special interest.

And in the summer of 1979, when he emerged from his puzzling week-long seclusion at Camp David, Md., Mr. Carter went so far as to place most of the blame for his troubled presidency on a national "crisis of confidence"—without acknowledging his own failures to govern effectively.

A lot of my doubts about Mr. Carter have crystallized during this year's campaign. It's difficult to be less than cynical toward the President who refers, as he did recently, to Edward Kennedy as "one of the greatest people ever to live on this earth." This is the same President who, along with his chief aides, vilified Democratic challenger Kennedy last spring as being practically unfit for the presidency.

Mr. Carter's verbal assaults on Mr. Reagan, too, frequently have exceeded acceptable bounds this fall. That impression intensified last month when the President appeared with Mr. Reagan at the annual Alfred E. Smith dinner in New York. As is the custom at this affair, Mr. Reagan made some light self-depreciating jokes and then delivered a warm, serious message about the legacy left by the defeated Democratic presidential candidate of 1928.

President Carter, however, used the occasion to ridicule his opponent with some snide jokes. Then he went on to denounce Mr. Reagan's "ties" to the Moral Majority, that group of fundamentalist preachers who are active politically this year. The President's remarks drew gasps and even boos from the smartly dressed audience, and that response seemed altogether appropriate.

Usually, reporters covering a presidential contender end up liking that candidate, even though they may not vote for him. That was the case among reporters who covered Jimmy Carter and Gerald Ford in 1976 and those who have traveled with Mr. Reagan this year. Not true with the Carter of 1980. His antipathy toward the press is quite apparent and this feeling is reciprocated among White House reporters.

Moreover, his Secret Service detail generally dislikes Mr. Carter; agents feel he seldom appreciates the long hours they put in. You hear occasionally, too, that the domestic staff at the executive mansion yearns for the return of a friendlier first family. Certainly Mr. Carter rarely praises his official aides, and he takes hard work by subordinates for granted, usually neglecting to thank them.

The private Jimmy Carter, I've discovered, is unlike the public perception. He can swear and snarl with the best of them and he can care more about getting even with a critic than winning him over. Aides say, sometimes even publicly, that in a second term Mr. Carter won't forget those who crossed him this year and those who wrote or said critical things about him. I believe them, remembering an off-the-record session with Mr. Carter on the Delta Queen river boat where he lashed out at critics in the press and in politics.

It may well be that a presidential campaign, and particularly this year's struggle for vindication through re-election, tends to bring out the less appealing side of Jimmy Carter. Recently he has seemed more concerned with winning the political battle than with anything else. But if he's re-elected tomorrow, and is freed of the need to run for office again, Mr. Carter's better side just might grow dominant; he might become more the warm, compassionate, good-hearted leader. That, at least, is what Americans can hope.

Mr. Schellhardt, a member of the Journal's Washington bureau, covers the White House.

Casting a Vote for Anderson

By ARTHUR SCHLESINGER JR.

As a lifelong Democrat, I have been watching the Reagan-Carter-Anderson contest with serene detachment. Confronted with a real Republican nominated by the Republicans, a crypto-Republican nominated by the Democrats and an ex-Republican nominated by himself, this Roosevelt-Truman-Kennedy Democrat doesn't see an obvious way out. Any choice is difficult, and political disagreements in 1980 are not worth breaking friendships over.

I do not find it easy to abandon lifetime habits of Democratic regularity. But I cannot see that on his record President Carter has earned 20 more seconds—not to speak of four more years—in the White House. He has shown no steadfast purposes either in domestic or in foreign policy. This is the end of his term, but no one yet knows the direction in which he wants to take the country. He alters course with every prevailing wind. He has had half a dozen anti-inflation policies. His recent economic program is his third in eight months. He has no compunction about basing a policy on premises he had grandly rejected a short time before. Lacking any unifying vision, displaying no interest in the way specific policies relate to each other, he ad hocs it all over the place, while the country sinks ever deeper into the morass.

This waywardness is especially disturbing in foreign affairs. Yesterday's righteous dove has become today's righteous champion of limited nuclear war, the MX and the Rapid Deployment Force. Mr. Carter's rattled overreaction to the Soviet invasion of Afghanistan (the "gravest threat" to world peace since 1945, he solemnly told us) hardly inspires one to wish his finger on the button for another four years. Sen. Jackson has wisely warned us to beware of born-again hawks.

Incoherent and Incompetent

The Carter administration is not only exceptionally incoherent. It is also exceptionally incompetent. ("Although he is a poor hitter, he is also a bad fielder.") Tom Wicker has accurately written that Mr. Carter's record of ineptitude stands unmatched since Warren G. Harding. One of Carter's few accomplishments has been the rehabilitation of Gerald Ford: depicted by night-club comedians four years ago as

---

Board of Contributors

I do not find it easy to abandon lifetime habits of Democratic regularity. But I cannot see that on his record President Carter has earned 20 more seconds in the White House.

---

a stumbling buffoon, now elevated by the really impressive bungling of his successor into beloved elder statesmanship.

Incoherence and incompetence might not be decisive disqualifications if Mr. Carter showed any signs of learning from his blunders. Quite the contrary, he gets worse every year. At this rate one shudders to think what four more years might do to the republic. Experience is a meaningless claim unless it implies a capacity to grow.

Instead of learning from error, Mr. Carter digs in all the deeper, withdraws all the more from face-to-face argument and attacks the motives of his critics. Underneath that brittle mask of control one senses an uptight and agitated psyche, filled with repressed anger and venom. His meanness of spirit and heart has come out in the campaign, especially in the pattern of cowardice displayed in his flight from debate and in his truly Nixonian facility for piously saying nasty things while piously denying that he is saying them.

His abiding theme is self: the justification of self, the celebration of self, the substitution of self (_my_ sincerity, _my_ piety, _my_ never lying to you) for discussions of direction and policy. Re-election would come as the ultimate vindication of self and very likely produce a dangerous euphoria. The most deluded people in this campaign are those liberal Democrats who think that effort on Mr. Carter's behalf would be repaid by presidential attention to their concerns in a second term. As he would attribute defeat to their iniquity, so he would attribute victory to his own virtue, and he would pay them no more heed after the election than he did before the convention.

Mr. Carter's dismal presidency offered the Republicans a splendid opportunity. Typically, they have botched it. With their genius for self-destruction, they have found the one man capable of convincing the electorate that he is even more incoherent and incompetent than Mr. Carter. Before the campaign began, a sort of case could be made for Mr. Reagan. There might be an advantage, it could be argued, in replacing a tense, unstable, unpredictable President by an affable, relaxed, indolent 70-year-old with an accommodating personality who talks wild but doesn't (or at least as governor of California didn't) do much about it. This was the theory of Mr. Reagan as a kind of sub-Eisenhower.

But Eisenhower concealed astuteness and craft under surface imprecision. Mr. Reagan, it is evident, is shallow all the way down. His incurable penchant for gaffes almost ruined him until his staff put him under virtual house arrest and sealed him off from the press. Irresponsible babble might not have mattered in the White House in a time like the 1920s. It will not do in the dangerous 1980s. Even in the 1920s, as Calvin Coolidge used to say, the first lesson a President has to learn is that every word he says weighs a ton.

The single argument seriously advanced for Mr. Carter is that Mr. Reagan would be worse. We must return the President with all his infirmities, we are told, because otherwise America will start sending troops all around the world. The last time we heard that argument was in 1964, when people returned Lyndon Johnson in order to avert the escalation of the war in Vietnam. Or we must rally around Mr. Carter to save the Supreme Court. This is a more substantial argument. Still, the basic issues about the reach of federal power have long since been resolved, and a Senate Judiciary Committee led by Sen. Kennedy and (we trust) Sen. Bayh will be as capable of stopping bad appointments as it was when Mr. Nixon came up with Judges Haynsworth and Carswell. Who can really know what the difference would be between this demonstrably poor President and this speculatively hopeless aspirant? "Sir," said Dr. Johnson, "there is no settling the point of precedency between a louse and a flea."

So we are left with John Anderson. Mr. Anderson is another one of those twice-born fellows. In public discourse he is often preachy. In private he seems a talker rather than a listener. Yet he is not without humor, and he is a man of high intelligence. He rivals Mr. Carter in command of detail and, unlike Mr. Carter, sees particular policies as part of a larger framework. His foreign policy is sober and realistic.

He is, moreover, a man of authentic independence. In a time when the country has moved to the right, he has moved to the left—not very far left, but definitely to the left of Mr. Carter and Mr. Reagan. His platform lacks the boldness of new ideas that has marked some other third party efforts in American history, but it is unfailingly intelligent and thoughtful. Organized labor still affects to see Mr. Anderson as the right-winger he was when he first entered the House. Yet he is the only one of the three candidates with a Rooseveltian belief in affirmative government. Long before 1980 Mr. Anderson said of Mr. Carter's demagogic assault on the Roosevelt tradition, "He campaigned against Big Government and he has planted the seeds of doubt in the minds of the American people on the ability of government to solve problems. It may be almost something that comes back to haunt him." People change and grow. The absurd constitutional amendment Mr. Anderson proposed declaring the U.S. a Christian republic is as relevant to his present views as Hugo Black's membership in the Ku Klux Klan was to his work on the Supreme Court.

Would Mr. Anderson make a good President? One is reminded of the old joke: Two friends meet after many years; one asks the other, "And how is your wife?"; he replies, "Compared to what?" Compared to Mr. Carter, a demonstrated failure, and to Mr. Reagan, a monumental gamble, Mr. Anderson looks pretty good.

Guilty Party

But he has little chance of winning. Can a lifelong Democrat support him at the risk of electing Mr. Reagan? The Carter people are already trying to set up disaffected Democrats as the guilty parties if Mr. Reagan should win. This blackmail can be ignored. If Mr. Carter loses, there is only one man to blame; and that is himself. If after four years in the White House, with all the resources of incumbency, he has miserably failed to win the confidence of the electorate, and even of fellow Democrats, *he* is the guilty party. The invocation of 1968 is irrelevant. Mr. Carter is no Hubert Humphrey, and Mr. Reagan, even if he is no Eisenhower, is presumably not a Nixon either. And the worse Mr. Reagan looks, the more Mr. Anderson will draw disaffected Republicans as well as disaffected Democrats.

Some think that a vote for a man who is not likely to win is by definition a wasted vote. This is surely wrong. A vote for Mr. Anderson is the only way to rebuke the major parties for offering us Mr. Carter and Mr. Reagan. Brooks Hays, for many years a Congressman from Arkansas and the best of political raconteurs, tells of an aged woman he encountered when running for re-election. "I hope you will vote for me," he said. "Nope," she replied. "Why not?" he asked. "I don't vote," she said. "I've never voted in my life." "You mean that you are 86 years old and have never once voted? Why in the world not?" "Because," the old woman replied, "it only encourages 'em."

If most Americans wearily accept the choice between Mr. Carter and Mr. Reagan, it will only encourage the major parties to believe that they can get away with nominating third-raters in the future. Non-voting is no remedy. The best way to discourage the major parties from imposing such ridiculous alternatives on the country is to register a mighty outpouring of popular disgust through the Anderson-Lucey ticket.

Mr. Schlesinger is Albert Schweitzer Professor of the Humanities at the City University of New York, winner of Pulitzer Prizes in history and biography and a member of the Journal's Board of Contributors.

GOP Mandate

Reagan Buries Carter In Roaring Landslide Throughout Country

Republican Cuts Deeply Into Democrats' Traditional Bastions, Including South

Anderson Was Not a Factor

By James M. Perry and Albert R. Hunt
Staff Reporters of The Wall Street Journal

WASHINGTON — Ronald Reagan was elected the 40th President of the United States in a thundering landslide that buried Jimmy Carter in every section of the country.

The 69-year-old Republican won what almost no one expected anyone could win in 1980—a mandate to govern a country that seemed to be asking for stronger, more forceful leadership in the conduct of both domestic and foreign policy.

Early voting analysis indicated that Mr. Reagan wrecked the old Democratic coalition — cutting deeply into the traditionally Democratic blue-collar and union-member vote. He was doing almost as well with Catholics as Mr. Carter and he was running far ahead of even his own people's projections in the South, supposedly Mr. Carter's stronghold.

Democrats feared the Reagan landslide might bite deeply into their numbers in the Senate and the House, and it began to look as though the fears were well-founded. Early casualties were Sens. George McGovern of South Dakota, Frank Church of Idaho, Birch Bayh of Indiana and John Culver of Iowa. Several other liberal Democrats were in trouble, raising Republican hopes they could come at least close to winning control of the Senate.

Results were coming in more slowly in the House, were Republicans had a lot farther to go, but in one early dramatic development House Democratic Whip John Brademas was swept out of office in the Reagan landslide in Indiana.

By a little after 8 p.m. Eastern time, NBC had predicted that the former California governor and former movie actor had won a stunning victory, defying preelection predictions of a close contest.

Shortly before 10 p.m., when the polls were still open on the West Coast, Mr. Carter appeared before his friends and associates at a Washington hotel to concede defeat.

Standing in front of a large American flag, he smiled and waved and reminded his listeners he promised four years ago never to lie to them. "I can't stand here tonight and say it doesn't hurt," he said.

He told the audience he had called Mr. Reagan in California to congratulate him on his "fine victory" and to promise him a "fine transition" in the next few weeks.

Independent candidate John Anderson finished a distant third, but he seemed certain to win more than the 5% of the vote he needed to qualify for federal funds to pay off his campaign debts. Exit polls indicated he hurt Mr. Carter a little more than he hurt Mr. Reagan, but he didn't turn out to be a factor in the outcome at all. Still, in his concession speech, Mr. Anderson hinted he may run for President again in 1984, saying his defeat was "a decision deferred."

Carter strategists say they realized Monday night the President's hopes for second term were doomed when campaign pollster Patrick Caddell reported that public focus on the Iranian hostages was damaging the President. Some Democrats hoped the potential release of the hostages would tilt the election to Mr. Carter, but apparently it worked the other way.

Going into the last two days of the campaign, Mr. Caddell said, the race was about even, but then "it just blew up. . . . It was the hostages. The hostages tended to focus the voters on their enormous frustrations."

The Reagan camp agrees the hostage issue may actually have helped the Republican nominee, but they disagree that it made the difference. "We had it won anyway, and all that (the hostage issue) did was add a little icing to the cake," said one top Reagan aide. (The final Reagan national poll put him ahead by six points.)

And, in the same vein, Reagan polltaker Richard Wirthlin said while the hostage situation "caused us some pause," in the end it didn't affect many voters. Instead, he said, Mr. Reagan won because he was able to "go to the roots" of the Democratic constituency, siphoning off large numbers of blue

collar and Catholic voters. Moreover, he said the GOP nominee improved his standing in the closing days among women voters, who earlier had been more skeptical than men of Ronald Reagan.

Since last week's debate, the Reagan camp's surveys showed voters moving to the GOP candidate; this was confirmed in other surveys, too, such as a final check by the United Auto Workers union in Michigan showing their undecided voters going almost three to one for Ronald Reagan in the closing days.

The Reagan aides believe the economic issue was what really won it for them in every section of the country. Going into yesterday's election, they were convinced they would win a majority of the big industrial states, hold almost their entire base in the West and cut into the President's Southern base to at least some degree.

But it became evident very early last evening that the tide was going to be even stronger than they anticipated. The television networks predicted Mr. Reagan would win Indiana, as expected. But then NBC, shortly after the polls closed in these states, projected Mr. Reagan would win Florida, Alabama and Mississippi—suggesting the President was being routed in his home base. In 1976, for instance, he carried Alabama by a decisive 56% to 43%.

In short order, the big industrial states started rolling in for the GOP nominee. New Jersey, Pennsylvania, Ohio, Michigan and Illinois—with a total of 116 electoral votes—all were declared by NBC for Mr. Reagan by about 8 o'clock. A few minutes later, Texas, with its 26 electoral votes, was put into the Reagan column.

All of the television networks did "exit" polls of voters leaving the voting booths around the country. These confirmed the sweeping Reagan victory was largely due to dissatisfaction with Jimmy Carter, especially over the economy in general and inflation in particular. CBS said the overriding finding in its exit polls was a "loss of faith" among voters in Jimmy Carter. One of every three voters who went with Mr. Carter four years ago rejected him yesterday, CBS said.

The networks also reported that voters disapproved of Mr. Carter's "weak" handling of foreign policy, a feeling that was intensified by the recent surge of news from Iran that the parliament had set terms for the release of the 52 American hostages, who had been held for exactly one year yesterday.

Mr. Reagan cut heavily into traditional Democratic Party constituencies. One ABC survey indicated he won about 40% of the vote of union members in Pennsylvania. Other surveys showed less than half of the Jewish voters was supporting the President and more than one-third of this vote was going for Ronald Reagan; traditionally,

Democratic presidential candidates win about 70% of the Jewish vote, a critical element in such key states as New York, Florida and New Jersey. The black vote apparently was going heavily for the President, but there were indications the turnout wasn't very heavy.

The networks generally indicated the economy was a more important factor than the disagreement between the Reagan and Carter camps over the impact of the hostage issue. But ABC, in its exit poll, reported that about a quarter of the voters said the hostages were the most important factor in their final decision, with it seemingly cutting in Mr. Reagan's favor.

The ABC exit poll indicated Mr. Reagan was picking up about 25% of the Democrats and more than half of the Independents while holding almost 90% of the Republican voters. These interviews also indicated that John Anderson took slightly more votes from the President than from the challenger.

Further, the network said 25% of the voters said they made up their minds in the last week of the campaign. Of these late deciders, 44% went for Mr. Reagan, 38% for Mr. Carter and 13% for Mr. Anderson.

For Ronald Wilson Reagan, it was the culmination of an effort to win the presidency that began 12 years ago and of a political career that began 16 years ago when he gave a stirring speech for losing presidential candidate Barry Goldwater.

Democrats had hoped to paint Mr. Reagan as some kind of progeny of the conservative Mr. Goldwater, but it apparently didn't work. ABC exit polls seemed to indicate that Mr. Carter's tough line hurt him more than it helped. Asked to name which candidate they thought made especially unfair charges during the campaign, 40% named Mr. Carter, 23%, Mr. Reagan.

Mr. Reagan spent most of his time attacking Mr. Carter's handling of the economy, appealing from the start to blue-collar Democrats and union-member Democrats. All that paid off yesterday.

In the final days, Mr. Carter desperately tried to call Democrats home to the party of FDR and John Kennedy. But Edward Kennedy had run against him in the primaries and much of that traditional Democratic support never warmed to Mr. Carter. And in the final hours, he pleaded with supporters of Mr. Anderson to vote for him to prevent a Reagan presidency.

Looking ahead, the Reagan camp indicated it will move quickly on planning its transition into power. Mr. Reagan will lunch with Vice President-elect George Bush today and hold his first post-election news conference tomorrow. Over the weekend, aides say, he'll go to his ranch near Santa Barbara, Calif., to relax and start thinking about plans for his administration.

The initial priority, some aides said, would be the appointment of a Cabinet and top White House aides. Curiously, Reagan adviser Richard Allen resurfaced at the Los Angeles campaign headquarters yesterday wearing a staff pin. Last week Mr. Allen "withdrew" as Mr. Reagan's national security adviser following a Wall Street Journal story that said he had used a White House job in the Nixon administration to further private business interests. Neither he nor the campaign officials would say whether he was back on board.

On another note, Reagan staff chief Edwin Meese said the Reagan administration will attempt "to reach some sort of accommodation" with Federal Reserve Chairman Paul Volcker. He didn't elaborate.

Groups in the Political Process

 January 11, 1980

Two, Four, Six, Eight: Ready, Set, Associate! Welcome to the Club

* * *

More Associations Sprouting As Interests Proliferate; Shoe-Swap for Amputees

By David J. Blum
Staff Reporter of The Wall Street Journal

Glen Plaisted runs a funeral home in Finley, N.D., and he pilots a plane in his spare time. That's how he qualifies for membership in the Flying Funeral Directors of America.

Mr. Plaisted owns a little farm there, too. Which is how he qualifies for membership in the Flying Farmers of America.

Like other members in good standing, he pays his dues and flies to the meetings. In 1978, he was elected president of the Flying Funeral Directors. Now that his term is over, he still flies to the fly-ins and sits in on the seminars.

Millions of Americans belong to associations. Nobody knows exactly how many associations exist or the precise total of their ranks. The 1980 edition of the Encyclopedia of Associations lists 14,019 of them—including, in no particular order of significance, the New England Knitted Outerwear Association, the American Producers of Italian-type Cheese Association and the American Miniature Schnauzer Club (whose members are the owners, not the schnauzers). But the encyclopedia makes no pretense of being complete. It excludes many smaller and more localized groups, such as the Society of Native Oregon Born (SNOB).

Specialized Special Interests

Associations of every ilk are nothing new. But their numbers grow every year and seem to be making a strong spurt nowadays as special interests get more specialized. The trend has even spawned a new mini-industry: professional management companies that run associations.

"We do everything an association would do if it had its own management people, office equipment and space," explains Robert Kellen of Atlanta. His company (which bears his name) manages the Association for Dressings and Sauces, the Processed Apples Institute, the International Jelly and Preserve Association, plus a few others. Each group gets its own stationery and staff person. To save time, Mr. Kellen's switchboard operator answers the phone with an all-purpose hello: "Association headquarters."

One pioneer of the association-management business is Smith Bucklin & Associates, a Chicago-based company that runs no fewer than 70 associations, ranging from the National Fisheries Institute to the Popcorn Institute. Smith Bucklin's staff of nearly 200 workers includes 50 lobbyists in Washington, D.C. "It's the wave of the future," says chairman William C. Smith. Without the cost-sharing advantages of outfits like his, he asserts, "associations just won't be able to survive."

Prepared for Disasters

Some groups get along quite nicely without such help. The Flying Funeral Directors, for example, took off about 10 years ago during a meeting of the National Association of Funeral Directors. "Of course, we modeled it a little after the Flying Farmers of America," Mr. Plaisted concedes. Now the group boasts 235 members, holds an annual meeting and banquet and maintains a network of contacts "in case of an air disaster, so we can get right to the scene," Mr. Plaisted says. So far, though, the group hasn't converged on any major disasters.

And some associations provide their members with personal services they couldn't get elsewhere. Many amputees, for example, might not know they can avail themselves of the Amputee Shoe & Glove Exchange. Richard Wainerdi, a Houston businessman whose wife is an amputee, started the group several years ago when he discovered another amputee with the same shoe size as his wife's but with the other foot. The women agreed to swap spares.

So far, the association's business has been rather limited — only 10 to 20 shoe-swaps a year. But the Wainerdis say the card file of amputees keeps growing.

Not all associations have such goals. Some attack other down-to-earth problems. Like bugs. Among those groups is the National Association of Insect Electrocutor Manufacturers. This $7.5 million industry serves paper mills, restaurants and other businesses that have a tough time coping with or killing insects. It's also an industry that feels misunderstood. Thus, an association.

"Our main objective is to have more honest advertising," says Gustav Detjen, the association's president and the boss at Detjen Corp. in Clinton Corners, N.Y., which makes lanterns, wire screens and other electrical bug-killing devices. He complains that some disreputable manufacturers keep consumers from knowing about (and buying) effective electrocutors. To promote the growing field, the association sponsors "Insect Electrocutor Week" and "Filthy Fly Month."

Most folks know what they would do with an insect electrocutor. But that's not quite so for a tapered steel transmission pole. Which is why the Tapered Steel Transmission Pole Institute was formed.

The tapered steel transmission pole, the institute spokesman proclaims, is "an idea whose time has come." The pole is much like a wooden transmission pole—the kind you see lining highways and crisscrossing farms, holding up the wires that deliver electricity to America. But the steel pole is more expensive than the wooden one.

The price and other problems have made steel poles unpopular in some camps. Utilities don't get excited about them because wooden ones have worked just fine. And regulators don't adore them because they cost consumers too much. Such views are based on misconceptions, the institute protests. In the long run, the group argues, steel poles will be cheaper because they're more durable.

Many Americans who don't happen to make or sell things like tapered poles join groups just to pursue an avocation. People who are interested in William Morris, for example, are apt to join the William Morris Society. Mr. Morrris was a poet, writer, designer and printer who lived in England from 1834 to 1896.The society, based in England, works to widen his following by promoting his writings to libraries and educators. The group, which holds seminars in cooperation with the Modern Language Association, claims 200 members scattered across North America.

"Some Associations bestow awards and honors on members. If you are the daughter of a member of the National Pork Council (and there are 97,000 of these daughters), then you have a chance in March to be named National Pork Queen.

Political-Action Units At Firms Are Assailed By Some Over Tactics

Managers Claim Their Bosses 'Coerce' Them for Funds, But Companies Deny It

Who's Naughty & Who's Nice

By STEPHEN J. SANSWEET
Staff Reporter of THE WALL STREET JOURNAL

Federal, state and local candidates in this election year are receiving millions of dollars in campaign contributions from an increasingly lucrative source: corporate political-action committees.

Some middle and senior managers at the 900 or more companies with the so-called PACs, meantime, are increasingly feeling pressured to cough up part of their paychecks to support "our way of life," as one solicitation letter puts it.

"I know it isn't mandatory to give," says an employe of a Litton Industries unit. "But the word around the water cooler is that if you don't give or if you give less than the amount expected based on your salary, you're liable to be called in for a pep talk from the divisional president."

Pressure tactics are denied by Litton and other PAC operators. "We always make it clear that a person's career isn't affected one way or the other," says Leon K. Thorsness, Litton's director of civic affairs. "We're 100% serious about avoiding pressure."

Growth of the Animal

Whatever the tactics, business-related PAC's have burgeoned in the past few years. They have been around for decades, nearly as long as the labor-union political-action committees. But it wasn't until a series of election-law changes in the 1970s that business PACs became a growing force in campaign financing.

In 1977-78, the latest period for which statistics are available, company executives and managers coughed up $17.7 million for the corporate PAC contributions to candidates for office.

That still trailed the $19.8 million that labor PACs brought in. Membership and health groups solicited an additional $25.2 million, and miscellaneous PACs raised $17.8 million. Of the total of $80.5 million raised by nearly 2,000 PACs, $35 million went to candidates for national office. (The rest presumably went to state and local candidates or was undistributed in the 1977-78 period, but the PACs aren't required to disclose that information to federal election authorities.)

Of the $35 million contributed to national candidates, 56% went to Democrats and 44% to Republicans. Contributions through labor-union PACs went to Democrats by nearly a nine-to-one margin. Corporate PACs supported Republican candidates by about two to one. The limit is $5,000 per election for any candidate.

Like the corporate PACs, labor committees have been accused of pressuring union members to contribute. Under a court ruling, for example, the National Education Association last year abandoned a system under which automatic deductions from teachers' paychecks were used for political contributions.

Federal Prohibitions

Federal election law forbids PACs to make any contributions obtained through "physical force, job discrimination, financial reprisals" or through threats of such action. Contributions of hourly paid workers to PACs must be kept confidential, but that rule doesn't apply to "executive and administrative personnel." Most corporate PACs, in fact, solicit only managerial and professional employes.

But with their growing influence have come the recent charges of coercion for contributions. "A lot of corporations go out of their way to avoid the appearance of pressuring executives to contribute, and it's terribly hard to document, but I'm sure that it happens," says Xandra Kayden, a political scientist who was a researcher for a study published last year by Harvard University's Institute of Politics. PAC managers, she adds, were surprised how easy it was to get contributions.

PAC contributions undoubtedly are still a low-priority, take-it-or-leave-it proposition for the vast majority of companies that have PACs. The low level of individual and total PAC contributions at even some of the largest U.S. corporations attests to that. "I don't believe that PACs are effective, and I'm not a giver or joiner anyway," says an executive who recently left Union Oil Co. of California. "I just tossed the first appeal in the wastebasket, and I never heard another thing."

Is Career Affected?

Officials at some other companies with active public-affairs programs say they don't feel under any great duress. "We were propagandized heavily, and it really ticked me off," says a middle manager for Security Pacific Corp., a bank-holding company. "But I ignored the whole thing, and it certainly hasn't affected my career."

But others say that managers often contribute just to be sure that their careers don't suffer, and in some cases that course of action seems especially appropriate. Those familiar with corporate PACs frequently cite Dart Industries Inc. as a company where, they say, pressure to contribute has been applied.

Justin Dart, the company's chairman and a longtime Republican Party power, has been called the Johnny Appleseed of the corporate PAC movement, because he travels around the country urging other executives to start or strengthen corporate PACs

"He pushes PACs so aggressively," says one executive who has attended some of the sessions with Mr. Dart, that some of his tactics of keeping after people to contribute have been "questionable."

In the four years that "Dartpac" has been soliciting contributions from about 800 executives, Dart Industries has sent out dozens of letters, pamphlets, reports and excerpts of speeches by Mr. Dart. Meetings are held between Dartpac officials and those being asked to give. Dart, like about half the companies with PACs, offers a suggested guideline for giving ranging from $25 at an annual salary of $15,000 to 1% of salary above $100,000. Mr. Dart lets executives know he gives the limit of $5,000 a year.

Mr. Dart has said that if his fellow executives don't give after receiving all the Dartpac mailings, "they get a sell" directly from him.

"I don't do that anymore," he now says. "We've laid so much groundwork that I don't have to. They all know where I stand." Dartpac officials say they have stopped circulating lists of employe names and suggested contributions to division presidents and also have ended the practice of having immediate supervisors solicit contributions from subordinates.

"Peer and other pressures are possible but aren't probable," Mr. Dart says. "I'd be a liar if I said that back scratching doesn't exist. I'm pretty well respected around this joint, and it isn't unnatural for others to pick up on my deep-seated beliefs. There isn't a damn thing wrong with that." Mr. Dart says the fact that only about 20% of those solicited have contributed indicates a lack of pressure. "We could get that up to 50% if we wanted to push," he adds.

Last fall, the politically active International Association of Machinists filed a 45-page complaint with the Federal Election Commission charging, among other things, that corporate PACs use coercive methods to raise funds. The accusations are leveled at corporate PACs in general and at some of the largest in particular (those of Dart Industries, Eaton Corp., General Electric, General Motors, Grumman, International Paper, Union Camp, Union Oil of California, United Technologies and Winn-Dixie).

IAM Pursues Case

The election commission dismissed the complaint, but the IAM challenged the dismissal in a federal court in Washington, D.C. The IAM charges that management employes are often solicited by their supervisors and that the employes are vulnerable because their "advancement is entirely dependent upon maintaining the good will of the employer." In the court papers, the corporations respond that the union's own PAC "demonstrates to an even greater extent the same characteristics" that the IAM suit criticizes in corporate PACs.

Corporate PAC supporters, moreover, say employes have never complained about any coercion to contribute. "Coercion doesn't exist except in the minds of union officials who would like to see corporate PACs dispensed with entirely," says Nathan J. Muller, editor of Political Action Report, a PAC newsletter. To lessen the possibility of pressure, a small number of PACs have taken special measures, such as having banks that don't do business with the company act as PAC trustees.

About 20% of the PACs also permit employes to designate the recipients of their contributions. In most cases, however, disbursements of PAC funds are at the discretion of the trustees, who usually are executives of the companies involved. In practice, incumbent officeholders seeking reelection in areas where the companies have facilities often get the largest contributions.

"Most companies are quite concerned that their PACs survive the fishbowl test, especially in light of the illegal corporate contributions that surfaced with Watergate," says Edwin M. Epstein, professor of business administration at the University of California at Berkeley and an authority on PACs. "The IAM complaint reinstated the fear of God in them. They know they're being closely watched." Prof. Epstein says he is convinced that most corporate PACs are "whistle-clean" but that there is pressuring at others. "Upper-level business and labor officials still face subtle peer pressures and psychological arm-twisting," he says, although statutory safeguards tend to protect lower-level workers.

A former manager at a General Electric facility on the East Coast tells of pressure he felt. "I knew that people in my department who decided they wouldn't give were subject to 'consultations,' " he says. "I didn't give as much as they suggested, but I did contribute so there wouldn't be any hassles."

A GE spokesman replies that he can state unequivocally that "there isn't any pressure, direct or subtle, by peers or supervisors." Solicitation is never done by anyone at a level higher than the person being asked to give, and only PAC officers know who gives or how much is given, the spokesman adds.

A rather blatant push assertedly came from a former vice president of American Family Corp., a Columbus, Ga., insurance-holding company whose PAC is one of the largest in terms of funds raised and distributed. One manager says he was told by the vice president, "If you aren't giving, you need to be. And tell your subordinates to give, too; it doesn't matter how much. 'Cause they're making a list and checking it twice . . .' "

The manager adds, "It wasn't Christmas, but I know the next line of that song and I didn't want to be considered 'naughty.' So the next day, I had a meeting with my people and told them to give. I quoted the guy word for word."

Lapel-Pin Pressure

Other subtle pressures to join American Family's PAC have also existed, the manager says. At annual conventions of top agents and managers, the company used to display red, white and blue certificates with the names of PAC members. Lapel pins were presented to members who contributed a certain amount, the manager adds.

"Those who wore the pins were obviously the hale fellows, well met, and part of the team," the manager says. "The new guys wanted to know how to get theirs. I've contributed to the PAC because I've felt it's important to my job, to stay in the good graces of management. I know others who feel the same way."

A random check of five other past and present American Family Corp. managers finds four who say they have never been subjected to any pressure. "No one says you have to give," says the fifth manager. "But when the chief executive is politically involved and they keep hyping the PAC as much as they do, you're made to feel that if you want to be part of the team, then you contribute."

In reply, Lee Parker, vice president for investor relations of American Family, says, "It's possible that some official in the field got a little overzealous and made a pitch stronger than the head office wanted. But I've never seen one instance of coercion. Sure, there tends to be a kind of cheer-leading for the PAC at conventions, but that's because the company believes in it strongly."

In a series of articles in the St. Louis Post-Dispatch a few years ago, several executives of Monsanto Co. were quoted as saying they were pressured to join the company's PAC. One executive was told the contribution should be considered a "cost of employment," the story said. Monsanto responded that the stories exaggerated any problems, although it conceded that "a few supervisors may have been overly zealous." And now, "any pressure that used to exist has disappeared," a Monsanto manager says. An executive at another company says, "Hell, the United Way fund drives are more coercive" than the PAC.

But Fred Wertheimer, senior vice president of Common Cause, the public-affairs lobby, argues that simply by analyzing their own situations, employes can wind up feeling an obligation to contribute to PACs regardless of what company officials say. "There's implicit pressure in the system to begin with," he says. "When you have people working their way up the ladder and their boss asks for contributions to the PAC, many will conclude that this is an expected activity."

———

Opulent Opposition

Liberal Incumbents Are Main Targets of TV Ads As Political-Action Groups Exploit Court Ruling

By JAMES M. PERRY
Staff Reporter of THE WALL STREET JOURNAL

The 30-second television commercial opens with a picture of a large baloney surrounded on a cutting board by other meats. Suddenly a cleaver slices through the baloney and a voice says, "One very big piece of baloney is Birch Bayh telling us he's fighting inflation."

The price tag appears on the sliced baloney, reading $46 billion and the voice says, "That's how much deficit spending Bayh voted for last year alone." Pause. "So, to stop inflation, you'll have to stop Bayh first." And then the kicker: "Because if Bayh wins, you lose."

Ads of a similar nature are appearing now in five states, aimed at liberal Democrats seeking reelection in 1980—Sens. Bayh of Indiana, Alan Cranston of California, Frank Church of Idaho, George McGovern of South Dakota and John Culver of Iowa.

No one has been chosen yet to run against any of these Democrats. These ads aren't *for* anybody. They are against the five Democrats. The ads haven't been approved by any candidate; they are being paid for by the National Conservative Political Action Committee, an independent group in Arlington, Va. NCPAC expects to spend $700,000 in unrelenting attacks on all five Democrats. It has also begun a campaign attacking Sen. Edward Kennedy's presidential candidacy.

Wave of the Future?

The ads represent a new phenomenon in American politics: "the independent expenditure." Some people call it the wave of the future. It will be tested for the first time this election year, especially by so-called political-action committees, or PACs, which collect voluntary donations for political activities.

Federal legislation passed in 1974 limits such committees to contributing $5,000 to a candidate for federal office in a primary election and another $5,000 in the general election. But there is a loophole.

The Supreme Court ruled in 1976 that individuals or committees can't be restrained from spending independently all they want in support of or in opposition to any candidate for federal office. Those are legal independent expenditures, not given directly to any candidate, and the sky's the limit. It is the opening through which NCPAC and others to follow are running.

Generally, the campaigns will be in support of conservatives or in opposition to liberals. Labor unions' PACs haven't any plans to mount independent-expenditure campaigns. They concentrate on helping their friends directly.

In Chicago, the grandfather of all the political-action committees, the giant AMPAC run by the American Medical Association, is completing plans to become deeply involved in independent expenditures for the first time. AMPAC is big business in political spending. In 1978, it laid out $1,879,164 to help its friends and to defeat its enemies in House and Senate races. AMPAC officials hope to collect $2 million for the 1980 elections.

AMPAC's problem is that it collects more money from its participating physician members than it can legally deliver directly to candidates. So Peter Lauer, AMPAC's political-action director, says he wouldn't be surprised if his committee hires media experts and produces independent TV commercials supporting some of the AMA's friends in Congress.

"Without even telling the candidate, we could hire a camera crew and tag along with the guy," Mr. Lauer says. "It would be legal as long as we didn't talk to him or to any of his people. What we'll do is get a list of 100 people or so and put out the word that no one—not any of us here at AMPAC, not our lobbyists in Washington, no one—can talk to these candidates or anyone connected with them because we may go independent expenditure with them. In the end, probably we'll go with 25 candidates this way."

This election, Mr. Lauer says, all of AMPAC's independent spending will be positive—for, not against, a candidate. He concedes, though, that his committee might begin experimenting with "negative stuff" during the 1982 congressional elections.

The negative stuff seems to worry people the most. "It tends to be schlock from what I've seen." Mr. Lauer says, "and we aren't yet convinced it does any good." He is afraid the negative material now being aired against the five liberal Democrats may give independent expenditures "a bad name."

Terry Dolan, NCPAC's executive director and the man chiefly responsible for the "negative stuff," isn't at all apologetic. "There is no question our stuff is strident," he says. "We're as popular out there (in those five states) with the general voters as the plague. But our polls show we have made these liberal Democrats vulnerable, and some people didn't think that was possible."

Aiming at Sen. McGovern

The No. 1 target for Mr. Dolan and the other conservative groups is Sen. George McGovern of South Dakota. So many groups are running independent-expenditure campaigns against Mr. McGovern, says the Senator's aide, George Cunningham, that "it's like Emmett Kelly was orchestrating the whole business" for a three-ring circus.

NCPAC has been running commercials attacking Mr. McGovern as a "globetrotter" who "was touring Cuba with Fidel Castro while the energy crisis was brewing." In a newspaper ad, Mr. McGovern is charged with selling out both Taiwan and the United States.

NCPAC likes some of the ads so much it runs them, with minor changes, against a couple of candidates. The "Globetrotter" ad used against Sen. McGovern is also used with appropriate changes, against Sen. Culver. One 30-second TV spot begins with an announcer saying. "Globetrotter is a great name for a basketball team. But it's a terrible name for a Senator." The ad used against Sen. Culver says he "took four extensive junkets visiting countries all around the world" while the energy crisis was brewing.

Another favorite is a radio commercial called "rating game." In one version of the ad, used against Sen. Cranston, Mrs. Verna Smith of Sacramento is asked how she thinks the National Taxpayers Union rates her Senator on the question of protecting her dollar. "One hundred percent!" she replies. "I'm sorry," the announcer replies. "You lose." The Senator's rating, he says, is a miserable 8%.

Mrs. Smith Loses Again

In another version, used against Sen. Bayh, the same Mrs. Smith is living in Indianapolis. And she is as naive as ever. She loses all three guesses—on how her Indiana Senator stands on protecting her dollar, farm issues and national security. "That's three failing grades," Mrs. Smith says. "I never knew Birch Bayh voted like that." In Sacramento, she says the same thing about Sen. Cranston.

The baloney ad is used against Sen. Cranston and Sen. Bayh. Mr. Cranston, like Sen. Bayh, voted for $46 billion in deficit spending, the ad says. The five Democratic Senators say the charges made against them in the various independent ads are baloney.

In Idaho, so many committees are running anti-Frank Church advertising that it's hard to sort them out.

NCPAC was first with a commercial showing a Republican state legislator standing in front of an empty missile silo to dramatize the allegation that "Senator Church has almost always opposed a strong national defense."

But the missing missile was an early Titan, withdrawn from service when the more sophisticated Minuteman missiles were deployed. "He said we filmed the commercial in front of the wrong missile," Mr. Dolan says. "We don't think that's important. What we want to do is talk about his record, and we're right about that."

NCPAC Connection?

NCPAC is running other ads against Sen. Church, and Mr. Dolan says they are working. Mr. Church's press secretary, Cleve Corlett, says there is a connection between NCPAC and the man who will oppose the Senator, conservative Republican Rep. Steve Symms. "Symms in on the board of a lot of these committees operated by Richard Viguerie, of which NCPAC is just one," Mr. Corlett says.

Mr. Viguerie, a direct-mail specialist, handles the fund raising for Mr. Dolan's committee and for several others interested in "New Right" political causes. Mr. Symms is a member of the board of several "New Right" political groups associates with Mr. Viguerie, but not NCPAC itself.

Buddy Bishop, a veteran Republican political consultant with offices in Washington, D.C., has been at work in Idaho too, developing anti-Church commercials for the Idaho Committee for a Positive Change. Mr. Bishop's commercials also have been criticized, especially one that attacked Sen. Church's record on the Vietnam war. One newspaperman, David Morrissey of the Twin Falls Times-News, said the wording was similar to a John Birch Society attack on Mr. Church published in 1974. Mr. Bishop doesn't deny some of the people on his committee may be Birchers. "In Idaho," he says, "there's no reason to expect anyting else."

Other groups working independently to defeat Sen. Church in Idaho are Stop the Baby Killers, the National Right to Life Committee, and the Citizens Committee for the Right to Keep and Bear Arms.

Kennedy Becomes Target

Neither NCPAC nor AMPAC usually get involved in presidential politics, but the decision by Sen. Edward Kennedy of Massachusetts to seek the Democratic nomination for President was too much for NCPAC to resist. It ran $23,000 of advertising in the Washington Post and the Boston Globe attacking the Senator's record and produced a radio commercial. Soon it will dispatch a "truth squad" to follow Mr. Kennedy. All of the money being spent will be reported as independent expenditures.

AMPAC officials say they won't become involved. But they add that the presidential run by Mr. Kennedy, the leading backer of national health insurance, might encourage their member physicians to open their wallets at all political levels.

Critics of political-action committees contend such groups already have too much influence on political campaigns and politicians. Of the 435 members of the House of Representatives, a study by Common Cause discloses, 320 have received AMA money. Common Cause, the self-styled citizens group, suggests a cause-and-effect relationship in the Nov. 15 vote on an AMA-supported amendment to gut the administration's hospital cost-containment legislation. Of the 234 House members who voted with the AMA, 202 had taken AMA money. "AMA," says Fred Wetheimer, executive vice president of Common Cause, "has put together the biggest and the most successful coalition in Congress."

But in states where conservative groups are mounting independent campaigns attacking liberal Democrats, the problem is getting tough candidates to run against the Democrats.

McGovern Opponents

So far, the only candidate opposing Sen. McGovern is 29-year-old Republican Dale Bell, a former NCPAC employe, who has been running his own anti-McGovern commercials. One of them, introduced on Memorial Day, pictured Mr. Bell standing in a cemetery and attacking Mr. McGovern for wanting to send American boys to Cambodia. (Mr. McGovern says he was talking about sending American troops in conjunction with troops from other countries, to make sure the starving Cambodians got food.)

It didn't help conservatives in South Dakota when two likely Republican opponents for Mr. McGovern, Attorney General Mark Meierhenry and State Treasurer David Volk, were discovered playing blackjack for money in a saloon in Winner, a small town in south-central South Dakota famous for its wide-open gambling during pheasant season.

When two investigative reporters walked up to the two state officials, the attorney general asked them if their visit was official or unofficial. When they said it was official and that they were preparing a news story, he laid down his hand. He had 20, the dealer 19. Then he closed up the bar.

The conventional wisdom in South Dakota is that neither he nor his friend, the treasurer, can beat Mr. McGovern.

Teacher Group's Clout on Carter's Behalf Is New Brand of Special-Interest Politics

By ROBERT W. MERRY
Staff Reporter of THE WALL STREET JOURNAL

NEW YORK—The National Education Association's political clout, wielded in behalf of President Carter at the Democratic National Convention here, reflects a new brand of sophisticated special-interest politics.

With 302 delegates and 162 alternates, the once-sleepy but now politically energized teachers' group represents the largest and most tightly controlled bloc of interest-group convention votes here. Among the states, only California has more delegates, and 24 of those are NEA members.

The organization, representing 1.8 million educators, endorsed a presidential candidate—Jimmy Carter—for the first time four years ago, and jumped on the President's reelection bandwagon with full force last year. In the years between those two campaigns, the NEA won, with intense White House support, its most sought-after prize—a new Department of Education.

Mondale's Statements Cited

The nature of the Carter-NEA symbolists is reflected in two statements by Vice President Mondale when he stopped by to address one of the group's convention caucus sessions.

The first: "I've learned that if you want to go somewhere in national politics these days, you better get the NEA behind you."

The second: "Nothing is more important to this administration than putting education at the top of the priority list."

Indeed, in addition to getting its Education Department, the group also has enjoyed White House support for large increases in federal spending for education and administration opposition to legislation to give federal tuition-tax credits to parents whose children attend private schools.

And working for a second Carter term is particularly important to NEA leaders in light of Republican candidate Ronald Reagan's threat to abolish the Education De-

partment if he's elected. In addition, the group is poised to push for federal legislation guaranteeing collective-bargaining rights for public employes, as well as further increases in federal spending for education.

NEA officials seem to relish their role as political protector of their friend, Jimmy Carter. At Madison Square Garden, they put together a sophisticated system to keep their delegates in line and maximize their clout. Each state had an NEA contact, who reported to six regional whips charged with preventing defections from the official line.

The group activated its whip system on several of yesterday's platform votes, when most of organized labor — including the pro-Carter unions—supported the more liberal economic planks offered by the Kennedy forces. But not the NEA, which generated considerable anger among some labor colleagues by sticking with the President.

But NEA delegates broke with the President to back the volatile plank barring party funds to support candidates who oppose the Equal Rights Amendment. That reflected the group's consistently liberal stands on social issues.

Earlier, NEA leaders sought to keep their delegates behind Mr. Carter's position that delegates must vote for the candidate they supported when chosen. Although the group's recent national convention hadn't taken any position on the "open convention" rules dispute, there were few, if any, defections from the leadership's position.

That generated some bitter, but futile, protests from the small minority in the delegation committed to Sen. Edward Kennedy's candidacy. "There was a lot of pressure on the rule" from NEA leaders, complains David Somsky of Sioux City, Iowa. "And we never had any opportunity to debate the matter in caucus."

The story of how the NEA brought to this convention an overwhelmingly pro-Carter delegation—269 Carter delegates compared with 28 for Sen. Kennedy and five uncom-

mitted—goes back to last fall, when Mr. Kennedy's emerging candidacy began picking up steam nationwide.

Sen. Kennedy looked like a winner then, and to head off prospects that teacher support for him would become uncontrollable, NEA leaders rushed through the group's policy council a Carter endorsement. "Our concern," says Terry Herndon, NEA executive director, "was that, if we let it drift to spring, our members would become hopelessly divided, never to be reconciled again."

That led to a sustained NEA effort to get members into the long delegate-selection process, preferably as Carter partisans. The group's success reflects the new "reform" politics, in which convention delegates congregate as partisans rather than as power brokers.

Under the old system, the greatest clout usually went to those who remained uncommitted the longest, until a delegate bloc became crucial to the outcome. In the new system, those who don't commit themselves early most likely will be left behind; to get the convention to wield clout such as the NEA's requires choosing a bandwagon early.

Punishment Also Posssible

But the NEA's Mr. Herndon emphasizes that the group's philosophy of political rewards carries an implied possibility of political punishment. "The threshold question," he says, "is this: Does the incumbent deserve our support? Actually, rallying support for an incumbent is more difficult than rallying hostility for an incumbent."

Rallying hostility, he says, might well entail a "multicandidate strategy"—getting NEA members to the convention committed to anyone but the incumbent, then trying to rally them in support of a candidate more supportive of NEA goals who has a chance to win.

Either way, it's clear that the NEA has become a force to be reckoned with in the era of "reform" politics. As the group's president, Willard McGuire, told his delegation this week: "The reform rules have helped us meet our goals, and therefore we support them and will continue to support them."

40

Who Are Those to Know in Town? Capital's Lobbyists Have Answer

By James M. Perry

Staff Reporter of The Wall Street Journal

WASHINGTON—New members of Congress attending briefings sponsored by conservative organizations here were told last week that industry lobbyists are the finest people in town. They were told that mainly by some of the lobbyists.

"Don't believe all that talk about three-martini lunches and envelopes stuffed with cash," said Margo Carlisle, a veteran Capitol Hill aide and now director of the Senate Steering Committee. "Lobbyists will be among your most valued allies."

"The bulk of lobbyists in this town are great people," said Warren Richardson, a successful lobbyist here and a favorite to run President-elect Ronald Reagan's congressional office. "A good lobbyist," said Mr. Richardson, "is an extension of your staff. Look at it in that light. Be a creative user of our talents. Use us to perform tasks. All you can do is vote Yea or Nay. We can provide service."

Pushing Appliances

"Lobbying is simply human relations," explained Tom Korologos, another well-known lobbyist who works with William Timmons, a principal adviser to Mr. Reagan. "I was lobbied to come to this meeting. My wife is lobbying me to buy a certain washing machine."

Mr. Korologos, who also is under consideration to head Mr. Reagan's congressional office, told the new Senate and House members they should turn to oil-industry representatives when they need to know something about oil. "Who'd be better?" he asked.

Lobbyists, he said, never give lawmakers bad data. "They'd only do it once," he said. "Thereafter, they'd be finished in this town."

But, one politician in the audience wanted to know, how do you deal with lobbyists who represent "the Other Side?" How, he wanted to know, do you deal with an organization like Common Cause?

Engaging in Battle

"Treat them courteously," Mr. Richardson said. "Listen to their pitch. If you want to engage in a verbal battle—say you're a lawyer—that's up to you."

How do you make sure you get reelected, one of the new members wanted to know. "You've got to satisfy your district," said Mr. Korologos. "It's the lost Social Security check that counts. The Panama Canal treaties, SALT II, they can take care of themselves."

Mr. Korologos explained: "If I were from a district with three oil refineries, I'd sure get close to the oil guys. You get involved in something else outside your district, and you're in trouble."

Mr. Korologos said it wouldn't hurt to support the White House "on an issue that doesn't affect your district."

41

The Year Ahead: A Periscope On Reagan's Chances

James Q. Wilson, Henry Lee Shattuck professor of government at Harvard University and once my very own teacher there, is a full-fledged instructor in scuba diving. This is no small matter. Prof. Wilson is well known. Many people would agree with the proposition that today he is this country's most lucid and insightful observer of American politics and public policy, in the academy or out. But all this dryland stuff means nothing to me. It is because of this native Californian's prowess underwater that when Wilson talks, as he has recently about the Reagan administration's prospects, I listen.

It is his job, after all, to take huddled bunches of frightened and foolhardy people down into some utterly foreign, bizarrely dangerous underwater environment and keep them from killing themselves. Over the years he and I have had several conversations on the subject. I describe the horror of that amplified rasping sound your own breathing makes in your ears underwater; he responds reasonably enough that under the circumstances, it's considerably better than the alternative.

I ask how he copes with the panic that can turn any one of his charges into a wild

---

Capitol Chronicle

by Suzanne Garment

---

man without a moment's notice. "Fetishism," he explains the principle lucidly. "You have to train them to do exactly as you do, down to the most minute detail." He gazes into middle distance, bemused by the implications. "I have left behind me a trail of men and women adjusting their regulators the way I do, winding their watches the way I do, scratching their heads the way I do."

This is self-evidently a man who understands the operational meaning of management and leadership. He came to Washington the other day, bearing a paper to be delivered at the American Enterprise Institute, and in it he told people like me exactly what we should and should not expect from a new Reagan administration that has been plunged into the current sea of American politics equipped with little more than its bare skin and a set of tanks, mask and flippers.

The new administration takes office with a mandate and a desire to wreak a fair amount of change on public policy. But, says Prof. Wilson as he lays out the ground for us, it is going to be up against the most important trend in American politics for the last half century.

Americans have always been at base a cantankerous and adversarial political culture, preoccupied with individual rights and mistrustful of institutions of authority. We used to have countervailing devices like strong state political parties and tightly held congressional leadership, but the country has always viewed these "bosses" and "deals" as not quite legitimate. When challenged, whether by early progressives or latter-day McGovernite reformers, these structures and power centers have gone belly-up with amazing ease in recent years.

We are not likely to see the return of such power-aggregating devices, especially because of another basic trend in our politics. Mass college education in America has been teaching more and more of the citizenry to be moved in their political choices not just by economic interests but by ideas—especially the contradictory notions that we both need government to regulate ever more areas of society and at the same time must make our politics ever more sensitive to individuals' needs for self-expression. These ideas combined have "demanded more and more of institutions," Mr. Wilson puts it, "while making it harder and harder for any institution to function." And the incoming Reagan administration is stuck with them.

This means there are a lot of things the new administration is very likely just not going to be able to do. In particular it is going to have a lot of trouble with what Mr. Wilson calls "line" enterprises—those activities that don't involve just a single choice at a single time but require a government to put together organizational resources and co-ordinate many individual decisions over a considerable period. "I see no means to reassemble the institutional bits and pieces" necessary to such tasks, he says; so we should not be surprised if the Reagan folks find it difficult to improve the readiness of the armed forces, restructure tax and energy laws or improve welfare programs.

But then there remain what Mr. Wilson calls the "point" decisions: the places where an administration can fight for a choice that by itself represents a real commitment. Shaping and ratifying major treaties, raising or lowering military budget ceilings—these are places where the initial decision looms larger than the problems of co-ordination that follow.

In these areas, it is not so much organizational resources as the battle over ideas that counts. But the Reagan people cannot have such victories except by expounding a persuasive government philosophy and showing an intuition for where to tap the residual energy that can overcome the inertial drag of the country's fragmentation. This is the place where we can look for and legitimately demand administration success.

Up close, parts of the transition in Washington these days are acquiring that

slightly gamey smell that rises when applicants and their handlers really start elbowing each other over those sub-Cabinet jobs. It requires effort to remember that this is democracy in action, and to keep that thought pressed to your brain like the scented handkerchiefs people once carried to protect their noses when they roamed the streets during the plague years.

This is the moment when you really need that long view of how we should and should not judge the government in the months ahead. Prof. Wilson has adjusted his regulator and pointed the way to the clear light of the surface; I am going to give him the OK sign and, as I've done so many times, swim right along behind him.

<hr>

Frustration in the House of Labor . . .

By Robert S. Greenberger

WASHINGTON — "Frustration," says Thomas Donahue, the AFL-CIO's secretary-treasurer and second in command, "isn't always a bad thing, especially when it makes you even more determined to get things done."

Seven months into the Reagan administration, there is plenty of frustration to go around within the house of labor. Labor leaders have stood by shocked as Mr. Reagan's blitzkrieg budget attack rolled over many social, health and safety programs that organized labor fought for and helped nurture for many years. The frustration has been mixed with anger and disappointment with historical allies, and soul-searching over labor's own failure to mobilize promptly to protect itself.

"We should have been flooding congressional offices with our positions on issues. They might have given us a better break on the budget cuts," says Fred Kroll, outspoken president of the Railway Clerks union and member of the AFL-CIO's executive council. "But labor wasn't ready. We weren't organized. We were sitting on our duffs."

Assessing the Battle Damage

But now some labor officials, in their first assessment of the battle damage, are agreeing with Mr. Donahue's view that the frustration and adversity of the past six months may galvanize the labor movement. Already, there are faint signals of a

change of course that could bring organized labor more in touch with its members. "Ronald Reagan and his ilk are probably the best organizers we have right now," says William Winpisinger, president of the Machinists union.

But Mr. Reagan isn't the cause of organized labor's current problems. Labor over the years had become used to the protection of the Democratic Party, which dominated the federal government. "We've grown so accustomed to getting things

tional tide of conservatism. "Where the hell is the Democratic leadership?" asks Mr. Kroll. "They're making a big fuss over the tax issue, but they rolled over and played dead on budget cuts."

But emerging from this debacle is the growing awareness of many labor leaders that the end of the old relationships calls for new strategies. The near unanimous view of labor leaders is that Mr. Reagan's budget cuts will produce an adverse public reaction once they are translated into

Labor leaders have stood by shocked as Mr. Reagan's blitzkrieg budget attack rolled over many social, health and safety programs labor fought for.

from the federal government, that we forgot how to get things on our own," asserts an official with one of the AFL-CIO's major departments. And, he adds, labor leaders weren't ready to launch a major budget counteroffensive because their privileged position made them lose sight of the importance of grass-roots organizing and mobilizing.

Labor's special relationship with the government ended abruptly when the Republicans captured the White House and Senate. At the same time, labor leaders have become bitter over the wholesale desertions by many Democratic former allies who have been caught up in the rising na-

losses of services in local communities. As a result, says one labor official: "We have to go back to rebuilding the labor movement. Not from the top down, but from the bottom up."

Characteristically, the early steps of this process have been cautious ones. The AFL-CIO is a cumbersome bureaucracy, made up of more than 100 unions held together by the glue of consensus. And its president, Lane Kirkland, is a cautious technocrat, more comfortable appointing committees than making dramatic gestures.

Moreover, labor begins this task in an uncertain mood because it is playing an unfamiliar role. Mr. Donahue speaks of the need to learn to use "outsider tactics," such as protests and demonstrations. At the same time, he says, labor must protect its flanks because the administration has adopted a "deal-around-the-AFL-CIO attitude" in an effort to divide and conquer. He notes that 14 unions supporting the President's economic program have been courted at the White House, and that about 80 others have been invited individually for special economic briefings. Meanwhile, he says, the upper reaches of the federation's hierarchy have been all but ignored.

What some labor leaders are beginning to understand is that building support from the ground up is important because Mr. Reagan remains popular with many of their members. "The rank and file keeps saying give Reagan a chance. It's a constant theme I've picked up," says a major union official who travels frequently outside of Washington. He says his union urged its members—who are on the low end of the union wage scale—to write to Congress to complain about budget cuts. "We even supplied stationery, stamps and addressed envelopes. We got at most a 20% response," he says gloomily.

So it was significant when Mr. Kirkland and other top officials for the first time traveled this spring to seven regional meetings across the country to listen to the suggestions and complaints of local labor leaders. Although they insist they are in tune with their members—a statement not borne out by Mr. Reagan's strong blue-collar support—top federation officials say the sessions were informative.

Mr. Donahue says, "To most members, cutting the budget meant reducing welfare and government giveaways" – and they support such cuts. "We have to translate this into worker issues. Aid to dependent children (welfare) is an important issue, but we know we can't use it as the centerpiece to take to the workers."

Mr. Donahue concedes there is a gap between the views of members and some of labor's leaders. "They appear to be not following us because we haven't given them the message," he says.

To send the message, the AFL-CIO has quietly begun a pilot program in about 10 states. Daily information about key legislative issues is transmitted by telecopier to state labor officials, who can then get the word out to their locals. These "legislative alerts" tell when the House or Senate will vote, outline labor's position and ask local labor groups to contact their Senators and Representatives.

"It's easy to be critical and say that they're finally getting around to this, and that's true. But what's important is at least they're doing it," says Paul Quirk, AFL-CIO secretary-treasurer in Massachusetts, one of the states in the program.

Still, some labor leaders are impatient with what they see as the federation's glacial pace. Commenting on the AFL-CIO's plan to hold a huge protest rally in the capital Sept. 19, Mr. Kroll of the Railway Clerks asks: "The fall is kind of late, isn't it?"

Shut Down This Country

Mr. Kroll and some others want bolder actions. Referring to the Polish union Soli-

darity, Mr. Kroll says, "We should emulate our Polish brothers. We should shut this country down for a day or two with some militant acts. That's the way to bring the message home." But for now, the federation has rejected such actions.

Some individual unions have moved aggressively and creatively to combat Mr. Reagan's economic programs. The most notable example is the American Federation of State, County and Municipal Employes, which spent about $600,000 to broadcast an "issues" commercial in selected markets. The commercial showed a cake being cut into thick slices for the rich, leaving a slim piece for workers. The union plans two more commercials.

"Just using rallies by themselves can be a disaster, because a lot of people are with Reagan," says an AFSCME staff member. "There isn't any great sense of outrage on the part of our members yet. That's why you have to educate people the way we're trying to do with our TV ads."

Slowly, this idea is taking root within the AFL-CIO's white marble headquarters. Says one top federation official: "We're going to get more into the public relations business. There will be a greater effort to educate our people as to their interests. We're learning that you can't be a leader if you don't have followers."

Mr. Greenberger, a member of the Journal's Washington bureau, covers labor issues.

The New Right Campaigns for Its Social Issues

By JAMES M. PERRY

DALLAS—"It's a hot summer night," Phyllis Schlafly notes, in explanation why barely 6,000 new-right conservatives have turned out for a heavily publicized right-to-life rally in an auditorium here that can accommodate 10,000 persons. Besides, says Edward McAteer of the Religious Roundtable, sponsor of the rally, folks are leaving town for the Labor Day weekend.

Veterans of the old right would scoff at such excuses. I can remember when 40,000 crowded into Dodger Stadium in Los Angeles to hear Barry Goldwater on a night the Dodgers were on the road—and on TV. Or the time the Draft Goldwater Committee rented the armory in the District of Columbia on a July Fourth and filled it to the rafters, while Mr. Goldwater was 2,000 miles away riding a palomino horse in a rodeo parade in Prescott, Ariz.

These new-right conservatives are giving zealotry a bad name.

The trouble, new-right leaders note, is that their people thought the battle was all over when they helped to put Ronald Reagan in the White House. For the old right, it was enough just to win the Republican nomination.

For the new right, though, ultimate victory is still elusive. The man who steps into that Oval Office tends to be a politician first and a zealot second (or third, or fourth, or not at all). Mr. Reagan is a politician, a disillusioning fact just beginning to dawn on these fundamentalist folks. And so some of the fire seems to be going out of them.

Paul Weyrich, who runs the Committee for the Survival of a Free Congress and who is one of the new right's most realistic thinkers, cautions that "we did not achieve

a political revolution in 1980. What we earned . . . was only the right to fight for the social-issue agenda."

Mr. Weyrich admits the new right underestimated what happens to people when they go to Washington. It's a city, he says, where people are made to feel "socially uncomfortable" when they oppose abortion or support school prayers or say creation should be taught in the schools along with evolution. "We underestimated the entrenchment of the secular humanist mentality in Washington," he says.

He calls on the foot soldiers of the new right to be tolerant and patient and responsible. He says sometimes new-right people are too "strident."

But the people at this rally in Dallas are in no mood for that kind of talk. Even Rev. Jerry Falwell of the Moral Majority seems out of step when he says he wants to hear what Sandra Day O'Connor, the President's Supreme Court nominee, has to say at her confirmation hearings, now under way, before taking a position.

The foot soldiers already have taken a position. They have decided Mrs. O'Connor is pro-abortion, pro-ERA and even in favor of women serving in combat. "We have a moral obligation to oppose her," says the Religious Roundtable's Mr. McAteer.

The foot soldiers are deeply disillusioned by Mr. Reagan's appointment. They can barely believe the contents of a letter under his name that went to one of their own people. In it, the President declared that most of the talk against Mrs. O'Connor was stirred up by "one person in Arizona" with a record of being "vindictive." The foot soldiers presume Mr. Reagan is talking about Dr. Carolyn Gerster, a former Arizona state senator (serving with Mrs. O'Connor) and a former president of the National Right to Life Committee.

The language at the rally becomes increasingly strident.

Peter Gamma, executive director of the National Pro-Life Political Action Committee, says Mrs. O'Connor's appointment is a "betrayal" and an "insult" to the pro-life, new-right people. Mr. McAteer, in his keynote address, said, "The 20th Century is the century of Auschwitz—of Cambodia—of the Supreme Court of the United States; it is the century of the intellectual barbarians."

A baroque "Declaration of the People of America," which is supposed to be nailed to every federal judge's door, is read to the crowd. The declaration attacks judges as "ayatollahs of paganism" who are "fawned upon by a cowardly, purchased press."

The answer, both the declaration and Mrs. Schlafly agree, is to end lifetime tenure for federal judges. It would require a constitutional amendment, Mrs. Schlafly says. She would favor a six-year term, after which Supreme Court Justices would run nationally and circuit and district judges would run in the areas in which they serve. It is the only way, she says, to avoid having another Justice William Douglas, who served 36 years on the court, during which time he was married to four women. "We were locked in an embrace with him almost till death do us part," she says. She notes Mrs. O'Connor might serve almost as long.

Of course, it isn't only the new-right folks who are strident. A. Bartlett Giamatti, Yale University's president, told his freshman class that the new-right spirit "sends hate mail, paints swastikas on walls, burns crosses, bans books (and) vandalizes minds."

But these conservative foot soldiers aren't Klansmen or Nazis. Mr. Weyrich argues most of them are lower middle-class Americans who have not participated in the political process before. They are, he says, motivated by principles, and they are not convinced Mr. Reagan is the embodiment of those principles.

In his address Yale's Mr. Giamatti glossed over what many of these conservatives see as excesses of the liberal "spirit" that they hold responsible for abortion, drugs, premarital sex and homosexuality. They see these things all around them— Mr. Giamatti called it cultural pluralism— and they look to the White House, the Congress and the Supreme Court to put things back the way they remember they once were.

Mr. Weyrich is afraid there are high-ranking people in the White House who don't share the new right's conviction that the government can make a difference on such social issues. He says some White House aides believe the new right is "trying to shove their values down other people's throats." He says some Reagan aides think his people are "kooks."

There are such people in the White House. And there are important Republican strategists who will say that while the country is becoming more conservative on economic questions, there is no evidence it is turning to the right on these social issues. And there is, finally, the President himself, an open, worldly man, a Hollywood man, hardly the sort of fellow to tune in Jerry Falwell's Old-Time Gospel Hour.

And so the doubts begin to grow; the romance begins to cool.

"Suppose," says Connaught Marshner, chairman of the National Pro-Family Coalition, "that you are a working-class person . . . You want your children to grow up knowing right from wrong. . . . You know that many schools have real problems with drug users and violent youths, and you believe with your whole heart that the schools would be better off if a prayer were said at the beginning of the day. . . . And along comes a candidate who promises you that he feels that same way. And nearly a year later, you haven't heard anything about it. . . . A note of cynicism creeps in, and you think that this President is no different from any other, and maybe you'll go back to voting Democratic next year after all."

The Mass Media and Politics

          September 12, 1980

Covering Reagan: Boys on the Bus Seem a Bit Tired

By Suzanne Garment

We are hurtling along in a press bus, the police having blocked off every cross street whose traffic might impede the progress of the Reagan motorcade through Kokomo, Ind. There's a surprise stop: The governor is going to drop in on the children at a local schoolhouse. He gets out; we unload and puff along after him. By the time we've reached the building he's already in his limo and on his way again. We swivel and chug right back to the bus, breathing hard. The little kids from the school run along the fence that separates us, squealing in excitement. They think they have never seen such loony people. They are right.

This has been a first time to ride the campaign plane and see if all those stories are true about the manipulation and cynicism of campaign reporting. On this Reagan trip—to Philadelphia, Kokomo, Chicago, Milwaukee, Cleveland and Buffalo—there was plenty of both. But what struck an outsider even more was how settled the rules of the game seem to have become and with what weariness both camps wage their wars.

The Reagan staff had quite obviously geared up for Phase Two of the campaign, designed to shut off those Reagan-the-Mouth stories once and for all. They did this quite effectively by simply cutting the press off from contact with the candidate.

We watched him from a distance. Making speeches. Dancing a decorous two-step with Mrs. Reagan for an audience of the elderly in front of the art museum steps in Philadelphia where the film hero Rocky once ran with such abandon. Even the pool reporters allowed to follow him at nearer range didn't get much to bring back to their comrades. The news hounds who tagged along on Mr. Reagan's visit to Cardinal Krol in Philadelphia duly reported, "on exit there was a smiling small-talk session, mostly inaudible, but eagle ears did detect Reagan saying, 'Well thank you. It was very nice.' "

* * *

The Reagan staffers were perfectly prepared to tell you what they were doing in all this. Press Secretary Lyn Nofziger, chief bearer of the burden, shouldered it manfully. "I asked Nofziger," one journalist reported, "whether there would be time to see Reagan. And he said, 'Not if I can help it.' "

Mr. Nofziger could be seen from time to time along the way standing in some hotel lobby or other, in the middle of a crowd of journalists, speaking some variation of "No, no, no," shaking his head and smiling wearily, polite, apologizing for nothing, conceding nothing. There was no reason for him to behave otherwise. The rules of the new politics not only permit such calculating behavior but savagely penalize its absence. And the camp of Ronald Reagan, in particular, has no reason to try to placate a press corps that is never going to give him the slightest break. The reporters took Mr. Nofziger's rulings quietly.

But they engaged in traditional forms of guerrilla warfare. There were the creature-comfort clashes—a minor revolt over how early in the morning the press would have to present themselves for baggage call, a TV personality exploding over the gaffes of a befuddled volunteer press aide and booming, "It would be too much to expect lucidity from these twits!"

Then there was the search after the lost theme. The press had just gotten rolling on the story of the Reagan blunders; manipulation or no, they weren't about to let it go without something of a fight. So in Philadelphia, when Mr. Reagan made a remark about SALT and a slam at the Department of Education, one reporter listening up on the press podium muttered excitedly, "He's done it again."

Done it again? Done what? But there they were on the press bus after the speech, ears pressed to tape recorders to see whether there had been a juicy bungle. The next day they were still demanding: What had Reagan meant specifically when he said the Education Department was no friend of private education? Was Reagan in error when he called it a "state" Department of Education?

They couldn't find the fatal error; for the time, at least, the Reagan strategy was working. The reporters retreated to the traditional journalistic theme of politics as trench warfare: Reagan on the Defensive. Reagan Attacks. Reagan Surrenders Previous Positions. Reagan Camp Imposes Information Blackout.

* * *

One of the best of the reporters, who knew exactly the limitations of pressing a political day into one of those small boxes, thought that it was nevertheless the honest way of dealing with a campaign. "Their ideas," he said, "aren't meant as anything but weapons," and have to be treated as such. It was near inevitable that the Reagan people would respond to press antagonism with manipulation, and just as inevitable that the press would respond with more cynicism.

It must be counted a character flaw to stay fond of campaign trips for the occasional glimpses you catch of political power, but you may be forgiven if you stick around for the view you get of America. Indiana was very beautiful this week with its hot September sun warming the cornfields and the Chrysler plant alike. And the Lithuanian ladies in Chicago who dressed themselves up on a Monday afternoon and turned out on their clean street to greet Mr. Reagan—well, it is not a bad thing to be reminded from time to time of the hopes that our politics are still capable of enlisting.

But it is not so inspiring to be assaulted three times or so every campaign day by the contrast between the redemptive enthusiasm that some citizens can still summon for our political contests and the dispiriting ballet that the prevailing incentive system has made of the press coverage. It is no wonder that some of the boys on the bus seem to be getting a little tired.

Suzanne Gannent is an Associate Editor of the Journal editorial page, based in Washington.

The Odd Couple

Evans, Novak Still Rile Readers After 18 Years Of Right-Wing Purity

Column Goes Past Reporting To Press Strident Views, Promote Jobs for Friends

Hot Feet and Genteel Parties

By JAMES M. PERRY

Staff Reporter of THE WALL STREET JOURNAL

WASHINGTON—Evans is the slender, debonair one with the sleek, bullet-shaped head. After he spent a year at Yale sleeping all day and playing bridge all night, his father shipped him off to Chicago to work for the railroad. Novak is the short, rumpled one, sometimes called "the prince of darkness." He once managed to set his own shoelaces on fire.

Together they are (Rowland) Evans and (Robert) Novak, journalism's oddest couple, who have somehow shared a byline for 18 years and who have now become the most controversial and talked-about columnists in town.

"I'm fed up with them!" says a prominent politician who has known them both socially and professionally for years. "They've come to believe they're the keepers of the world."

"They do seem to have gotten a little apoplectic," says their old friend and fellow columnist Jack Germond.

What they have been doing—in their column that appears in 223 newspapers, in their newsletter that goes to almost 2,000 subscribers, in their nightly commentary on Ted Turner's cable-TV network and in the more than 50 lectures they deliver each year—is try to hold the Reagan administration's feet to the pure flame of their own increasingly strident brand of conservatism.

They seem to believe that the nation may not survive unless an undiluted supply-side economic program is developed at home and a tougher defense and foreign-policy position to contain the Russians is put in place around the world.

"We don't have much time left," says Mr. Evans, reflecting the doom and despair that permeate the team's reporting.

It's the old journalistic conundrum: Should reporters—and Evans and Novak pride themselves on being shirt-sleeve reporters writing an "inside" column—actually come down out of the press box and take part in the game?

"Dark Foreboding"

"That's what has happened to these two guys," says the editor of a big-city daily who has dropped their column. "They're out there on the field, blocking and tackling and telling the coach what plays to call. I don't need that kind of stuff in my newspaper."

The most recent complaints generally go to their reporting during the transition and the early weeks of the new administration, when they were openly plugging their friends and opposing their enemies for top jobs in the government.

Typical was their report that the administration's failure to name political scientist Donald Devine as the civil-service chief "transformed what should have been a weekend of celebration (for hard-line Reagan supporters) into dark foreboding." (Three weeks later Mr. Devine got the job.) In the same vein, they said "a test of the Reagan revolution's tenacity and future prospects" hinged on dumping Alice Rivlin as director of the congressional budget office. (She is still there.)

During the entire period, they tub-thumped for New York businessman Lewis

Rowland Evans and Robert Novak

Lehrman, a leading supply-side theoretician. After their first choice for Treasury Secretary, former Treasury chief William Simon, was "stabbed," they plugged Mr. Lehrman for the job. Then, when that hope faded, they plugged him for the No. 2 Treasury job. When that went glimmering, they recommended him for chairman of the President's Council of Economic Advisers. And when that didn't pan out, they pushed him for council membership.

Panic in the Defense Community

Martin Anderson, Mr. Reagan's domestic-affairs adviser, told a colleague that the administration was under "tremendous pressure" to put Mr. Lehrman on the CEA. "Pressure from where?" the colleague asked. "Evans and Novak," Mr. Anderson replied.

So far, though, Mr. Lehrman is still in New York.

Mr. Evans, who is 59, and Mr. Novak, 50, were just as eager to see hard-liners—they don't object to the description—placed in the top foreign-policy and national-security positions.

They were disappointed there, too, never more so than in their Jan. 7 column, in which they said "unease" within what they call the "defense community" had "blossomed into panic" over the way Defense Secretary-designate Caspar Weinberger "has booted out 'Reaganaut' military advisers, trashed their recommendations and at least opened the door for soft-liners."

This is the kind of strident reporting some editors deplore. Others see nothing wrong with it. "They're coming from a certain direction and projecting certain values," says Edwin Roberts, editorial-page editor of the Detroit News. "Readers aren't stupid. They know where Evans and Novak stand."

Evans and Novak themselves make no apologies.

Part of the problem, Mr. Novak believes, is the lingering idea that the columnists once were liberals or, at least, moderates. He thinks that goes back to 1964, when they opposed Barry Goldwater's nomination by the Republicans (they didn't think he could win the election). Some people suggest it may go back to the 1964 convention, when Mr. Novak floored a conservative Young Republican with a single punch. The young man hadn't agreed with Mr. Novak's reporting.

The fact is, Mr. Novak says, that he and Mr. Evans have been out on the field, blocking and tackling, for years. "We caught a lot of flak when we were writing about left-wing subversion of the civil-rights movement back in 1964 and 1965," Mr. Novak notes.

"We got the same treatment over our coverage of the war in Vietnam," adds Mr. Evans. "I don't suppose we ever said, 'Let's unleash the generals,' but there was no way readers couldn't conclude we supported the military effort there."

"And we were never bashful in advising how the war ought to be fought," says Mr. Novak.

Mr. Novak, who is more outspoken and aggressive than Mr. Evans, has another explanation. He says criticism of the column has been sharper in recent weeks because "we are running against the grain of the conventional wisdom within the journalistic community." This, he thinks, is especially true in their economic reporting. "Most journalists find it hard to abandon the viewpoints they have held for years. If supply-side economics works, it will be the death knell for much of the system this establishment has built up over the last 50 years."

Evans and Novak have been together for 18 years, the longest-running double byline in journalistic history, they contend. The first column appeared in the old New York Herald Tribune and 44 other papers served by that newspaper's syndicate on May 15, 1963. In it, they said Mr. Goldwater had a chance to win the GOP nomination.

The column was Mr. Evans's idea. He had been badgering his editor at the Tribune for years for a column, finally getting a real taste for it by writing some columns for Joseph Alsop, something of a mentor for Mr. Evans. He was finally told to strike out on his own—six times a week. "No one man could do that," says Mr. Evans. So he went out and recruited a partner.

"The single most brilliant thing Rowly Evans ever did in his entire life was take on Bob Novak," says an old colleague of both reporters.

At the time, Mr. Novak was a 32-year-old congressional correspondent for The Wall Street Journal. He was already something of a legend, not so much for his reporting skill (which was considerable) but for some of his personal habits (which were deplorable).

Smoldering Shoelaces

There is the story, for example, of the time he set his own shoelaces on fire. In those days, Mr. Novak smoked four packs of cigarets a day, never extinguishing them when he was finished but simply dropping them or flipping them over his shoulder. He never tied his shoelaces, either, and one day he managed to drop a cigaret on one of his shoes. The laces began to smolder, then burst into flames.

Another time, he put a lighted cigaret in his pocket before entering the Senate press gallery, where smoking isn't permitted. He became engrossed in the action on the floor and forgot about the cigaret — until his jacket burst into flames.

There are stories, too, about the suits and the food packages his parents would send him from their home in Joliet, Ill. He would throw all of them under his desk, and they would remain there until strange things began crawling around the floor.

"He is still the worst-dressed journalist in Washington," says Art Buchwald, the humorist, whose office is across the hall from the incredibly cluttered quarters of Mr. Evans and Mr. Novak. "I worried about Novak when I heard President Reagan was going to impose a dress code," says Mr. Buchwald. "He could put Novak out of business." (Mr. Buchwald also contends that Mr. Novak's salary is paid out of CETA funds. He thinks either Mr. Evans or Mr. Novak should quit so the other could make really big money.)

Mr. Novak also has a sense of humor, of sorts.

Typical of his wit is the story told by columnist Jules Witcover, another old friend and colleague. Mr. Witcover had just completed his most successful diet—a stern regimen of orange juice, black coffee and tennis—when he encountered Mr. Novak on a downtown street corner. "You've lost a lot of weight," Mr. Novak commented. Mr. Witcover agreed, simpering with pleasure that someone had noticed, and went on to describe how he had lost so many pounds. "I think you got cancer," said the prince of darkness.

He's No Pangloss

John Lindsay, a Newsweek reporter, christened Mr. Novak with that nickname and it has stuck. Mr. Lindsay thinks it goes back to the time Mr. Novak buried himself in the works of Spinoza, arriving at the conclusion—which hasn't changed much since—that things were never going to get better.

Outside of his column, Mr. Novak's main passion is sports. He is a fan of the Washington Redskins football team and the Washington Bullets professional basketball team. His 15-year-old daughter, Zelda, is the Bullets' official ball girl.

But mostly he is a University of Maryland sports fanatic. The terrapin is Maryland's mascot, and Mr. Novak is a "Diamondback Terrapin," which means he contributes at least $1,200 a year to the school's athletic-scholarship fund.

Maryland basketball comes first. Mr. Novak travels with the coach, Lefty Driesell, on recruiting trips. He takes players into his office as interns (a recent intern was the Maryland star Albert King). He rarely misses a game, home or away.

He usually travels with John Heise, a local lawyer and another Terrapin fanatic. Mr. Heise remembers the time they flew to Charlotte, N.C., to make a connection to Clemson, S.C., for a basketball game. But the weather was so bad the connecting flight was canceled.

"Robert prevailed on some contacts and chartered a small plane," Mr. Heise recalls. "We landed at Clemson at night, with no lights on the runway, and Robert had a cab waiting there to take us to the arena. We arrived just as they were playing the national anthem."

A More Exalted Level

For all of Mr. Novak's grumbling about the liberalism and elitism of his colleagues, he is a popular figure with most of them. Mr. Evans, on the other hand, seems to move on a slightly more exalted level. Mr. Evans and his wife, Kay, live in fashionable Georgetown. Mr. Novak and his wife, Geraldine, live in Rockville, an unfashionable Maryland suburb. Socially, the twain rarely meet.

Mr. Evans is a Main Line Philadelphian who breakfasts almost every morning with a source at the Metropolitan Club. He went to a boarding school and briefly to Yale (Mr. Novak holds the pair's only degree, from the University of Illinois). Mr. Evans and his wife entertain with Main Line dignity at their Georgetown home. Greg Schneiders, a former Carter aide, recalls that when he was working in the White House, he was invited to the Evanses for dinner. But Mr. Evans had a preliminary question: Was Mrs. Schneiders "presentable"?

Mr. Schneiders says it was a lovely party. "Henry Kissinger was there, along with the required member of the Senate and the required member of the Supreme Court."

Mr. Evans's friends take exception to the idea that he is something of a dilettante. After all, they say, he was a sergeant in the Marines, while Mr. Novak was a lieutenant in the Army.

Philip Geyelin, the former editor of the Washington Post's editorial page and one of Mr. Evans's oldest friends, recalls the time the two of them hopped a helicopter to go up to War Zone C in Vietnam and observe some of the action. "Rowly took the seat next to the open door—with no strap to hold him in. Suddenly we were in the middle of an air strike, with Phantom jets all around us. The helicopter was swerving all over the place. I don't know how Rowly held on. I had such a case of vertigo I didn't dare look."

The conventional wisdom is that Mr. Novak does most of the work and Mr. Evans takes most of the credit. Although it is true that Mr. Novak is more passionate and excitable than Mr. Evans, it is also true that they pretty much divide the work evenly.

They have been writing the column together for so long that no one can tell which one wrote what. When they look at old columns, they can't tell themselves. And, whatever people may think of the merits of it, the column and its spinoffs pay off. Each man earns something in excess of $200,000 annually.

During the fading days of the presidential election campaign last year, a young reporter from a local newspaper sidled up to Mr. Novak, who was listening to Mr. Reagan's standard speech, and asked him whether he ever got bored.

"Never," he said. "God help me, I love it."

Equal Opportunity?

Minority Journalists Are in Meager Supply In Nation's Newsrooms

Few Seem to Apply for Jobs, But Hiring Practices Are Also Called Into Question

Gripes About the 'Taco Beat'

By Ann Hughey
Staff Reporter of The Wall Street Journal

Earlier this year, Jonathan Maye, a 27-year-old police-beat reporter for the Atlanta Journal, took part in a panel discussion sponsored by the National Association for the Advancement of Colored People. When he introduced himself to one of the NAACP officials, an older black woman, she recognized his newspaper byline.

"She said, 'I didn't know you were black. You wrote so well I thought you were white,'" Mr. Maye recalls, adding: "She didn't mean any harm. She thought it was a compliment."

It was a bizarre, isolated incident, as was the case of Washington Post reporter Janet Cooke, who fabricated her Pulitzer Prize-winning story, "Jimmy's World," about an eight-year-old heroin addict. Though unrelated, the two incidents have a common thread. The NAACP official gave voice to a bias that, while seldom discussed, is still shared by some of the nation's editors. Largely because of such biases, black journalists found the Janet Cooke debacle particularly disturbing. "It wasn't just a reporter who had done something wrong—it was a black," says Saundra Smokes, a young black reporter for the Syracuse Herald-Journal who fears the affair will only reinforce "negative viewpoints" about blacks.

Lack of Minority Journalists

To suggest that Janet Cooke faked her story because she is black is, of course, absurd. (Indeed, since her Pulitzer was rescinded, the credibility of two white journalists—one from the New York Daily News and another from the Village Voice—has also been called into question.) But Janet Cooke's hoax touched off unprecedented soul-searching among journalists, and raised broad questions about how the nation's predominantly white editors recruit, train and evaluate their minority employes and how those editors view the minority communities their papers cover.

No look at the current status of minority journalists can ignore their scarcity. The number of daily newspapers without a minority reporter or editor in their employ has increased—to 63% of the total from 60% last year, according to a survey by Jay T. Harris, assistant dean of Northwestern University's Medill School of Journalism. At the 37% of the newspapers where minorities are employed, editors complain they are locked in competition with other news organizations for a small pool of qualified minority applicants.

For even this select pool, the newsroom experience is seldom without its tensions. Self-generated pressure to excel is intense, if only to dispel entrenched biases. Moreover, some minority newsmen complain editors tend to stereotype them—assigning blacks to cover the black community or Hispanics to what one Hispanic reporter terms "the taco beat"—rather than treat them as professionals in their own right. Others feel demeaned by the special training programs, special treatment and lowered expectations they sometimes encounter.

A Scramble to Hire

If white editors are sometimes naive or heavy-handed in their dealings with minority reporters, it may stem from the days when newsrooms were lily-white and routine coverage of blacks was all but nonexistent. Medill's Mr. Harris recalls a time "not too many years ago" when newspapers refused to print photographs of black brides and one leading Southern newspaper had a policy of "no photos of Negroes or snakes."

Most of today's senior black journalists were hired during the 1960s—partly because of the civil-rights movement, partly because the urban riots of the mid-1960s precipitated a scramble to hire blacks to cover the turmoil. One black journalist, Claude Lewis, associate editor of the Philadelphia Bulletin, wryly credits H. Rap Brown, Huey Newton and other black militants of the period with having accelerated black hiring by urging blacks not to talk to white reporters.

(In 1968, Benjamin Bradlee, now the Washington Post's executive editor, defended his paper's account of a Washington racial incident against a conflicting report by saying, "We had trained Negro reporters present, and they're absolutely convinced.")

"White Press" Criticized

Even by 1968, there were only about 400 minority journalists, working at about 20% of the nation's newspapers, according to Medill's Mr. Harris. That year, President Johnson's National Advisory Commission on Civil Disorders criticized the "white press" for its "failure to report adequately on race relations and ghetto problems." The commission found the news media "shockingly backward in seeking out, hiring, training and promoting Negroes."

Today, according to Mr. Harris, about 5.3%, or 2,400, of the 45,500 daily newspaper journalists in the country are members of a minority race. (This compares with 13% of the nation's chemists, 18.5% of its social workers and nearly 8% of its secondary-school teachers.) Almost half the minority journalists work for big-circulation, big-city newspapers, rather than the smaller papers that offer most of the jobs.

Though professional associations such as the American Society of Newspaper Editors are committed to lofty minority-hiring goals, "the effort to increase the number of minority journalists simply never has had broad-based backing among editors and publishers," says Thomas Winship, editor of the Boston Globe and former ASNE president. (About 7% of the Globe's news staff of 375 are minorities.)

Besides being "the right thing to do," as one editor puts it, proponents of increased minority hiring argue that the greater the diversity of a newspaper's staff, the more informative its news coverage. Mr. Winship further argues that minority readers constitute an untapped source of circulation and advertising revenue for newspapers.

Why, then, are so few blacks and other minorities employed in daily journalism? One answer is that few seem to apply. William Connolly, managing editor of the Virginian-Pilot, a 126,000-circulation daily in Norfolk, says that at his paper black applicants "are like hen's teeth. An over-the-transom resume is almost unheard-of from a black if he's even remotely qualified for the job." Robert Maynard, editor of the Oakland Tribune and a black, says "there's no question that we do not get our share of the top black talent coming out of graduate school."

Editors say this top talent tends to regard newspaper work as offering little chance for promotion or financial reward. "You can count the number of top-ranking minority editors on one hand," says the Globe's Mr. Winship. Mr. Lewis of the Bulletin observes that neither blacks nor whites "get into this business to get rich." But he adds, "If you can't become an editor, you get what the union wins for you."

Moreover, he says, the field's traditional inhospitality to blacks has left many young blacks uncertain of their welcome. White applicants, he says, are generally "more confident and assertive and are more apt to be self-starters," while black candidates tend to hold back, wondering, "Gee, do they want a black?" Nor does it help, Mr. Lewis says, that some white editors have "lower expectations of what blacks can produce." Such attitudes, he says, stem from the assumption that blacks "haven't had opportunity, haven't had education."

Kenneth Field, a black former newsman who now has a public-information job with the government, says that in journalism, "I didn't see a chance for advancement at all." By leaving, he says, "I thought I could better myself financially."

Recruitment Problems

Few blacks apply to The Wall Street Journal, according to managing editor Laurence O'Donnell. Slightly more than 8% of the Journal's 280 newsroom professionals are members of racial minorities. When managers and nonprofessionals are counted, the percentage is close to 10%. "But some of that is phony," Mr. O'Donnell says. "Fred Taylor (the executive editor) counts because he has a little bit of American Indian in him."

In Mr. O'Donnell's view, the Journal may be missing promising black candidates by paying "too much attention to successful blacks," or those who have established themselves at other publications, rather than recruiting on black campuses or catching young journalists early in their careers.

Pamela Hollie, a black who was recently assigned to open a New York Times bureau in Manila, agrees that newspapers neglect talent on small papers. "They're always scouting," she says, "but they don't scout the farm teams."

Smaller papers, however, complain of losing good black reporters to bigger papers—and at a faster rate than they do talented white reporters. Medill's Mr. Harris estimates that as many as 700 minority journalists, or 29% of the total, moved from one newspaper to another last year, compared with an industry-wide turnover rate he estimates to be 10%.

Value of Black Editors

In the campaign to get—and keep—black talent, a newspaper's greatest asset can be a top black editor, says Craig Ammerman, executive editor of the Philadelphia Bulletin. A large urban daily recently failed to hire a black reporter away from the Bulletin, even though it offered her $100 more a week. "She knew she was being hired as a number," Mr. Ammerman says. Moreover, he says, the Bulletin's Mr. Lewis met with her and her family for dinner "and made her see the light." With editors like Mr. Lewis on the staff, Mr. Ammerman says, black reporters "can see evidence that they can move onward and upward at the paper."

The perception that opportunities are limited in journalism has meant that fewer blacks have qualified themselves for the work, according to Larry Allison, editor of the Long Beach (Calif.) Independent Press-Telegram and president of the Associated Press Managing Editors Association. Some blacks who have grown up speaking street argot may have difficulty with standard English skills, he says, though he adds: "I'm generalizing. I'm not speaking from specific experience."

Don Marsh, editor of the Charleston (W.Va.) Gazette, says that given two equally good candidates—one white and one black—he would hire the black. But, he says, when he compares job candidates, "the average black just does not compete with the average white." A recent black applicant to the 56,000-circulation daily impressed him initially, he says, "but there were 14 words on the spelling test and she missed 11. I don't have the time and staff to teach and train people on the job." (The Gazette currently employs two black newsmen.)

Many editors voiced concern over the general lack of verbal skills demonstrated by young job applicants, whether white or black. "They don't seem to have had to learn grammar, much less style," says Michael O'Neill, editor of the New York Daily News.

Hiring More Selectively

At some papers, minority hiring is stymied by the "if you hire them, you can't fire them" syndrome. Some blacks hired in the first big wave a decade or so ago proved incompetent but, either to avoid charges of racism or to bolster minority-hiring statistics, were kept on the payroll. "Some editors hired indiscriminately 10 years ago and got burned, and now they're overly cautious," says Richard Gray, director of Indiana University's school of journalism. Today, suggests the Bulletin's Mr. Lewis, editors are both more selective in hiring blacks and less reluctant to fire them, a change he views as healthy. "If they don't produce, they should be fired," he says.

For blacks who do choose a career in journalism, being thrust into a predominantly white newsroom can be an unsettling experience. "It doesn't bother me because I assimilate well," says Mr. Maye of the Atlanta Journal. "But I know a lot of black reporters who feel like there's this giant pencil being stuck in their backs." Robert Haiman, editor of the St. Petersburg Times, says black reporters sometimes are needled by other blacks who expect the reporter to espouse a cause or who take the attitude, "What are you doing down there working for the Man?"

With most of the active recruitment and hiring being done by large urban papers, many young minority reporters miss the early years of apprenticeship on the smaller papers that have traditionally been the profession's training ground. Thus rocketed prematurely into the big leagues, some falter. The Virginian-Pilot's Mr. Connolly says editors may be "doing minorities a disservice by pushing them too far, too fast before they're ready."

Some on-the-job stress, Medill's Mr. Harris says, can result from faulty management affecting whites and blacks alike. Trivial assignments and insensitive editing are indignities suffered by most reporters at one time or another. But some blacks, Mr. Harris says, may see them as "racially based."

One black reporter agrees that bigotry is sometimes hard to distinguish from "a normal newsroom personality clash." But he contends that if blacks perceive a racial problem, "it's just as important" as if one exists. A frequent complaint is that white editors are inexperienced in dealing with blacks and thus fall back on simplistic stereotypes. A young Hispanic journalism student who recalls being patronized with comments like, "My, have you pulled yourself up!" adds: "I'm about as American as you can get. I was even a Brownie."

The same young woman, a student at Northwestern, says a professor once advised her "not to get internships on my own." She says he told her that "there were special programs for minorities, special treatment and stuff. It was an incredible insult."

Such simplistic thinking can distort a paper's news coverage, some minority journalists say. Mr. Field, the former newsman-turned-government employe, says "There's a tendency to cover only the seamy side of black life." He recalls once working for a paper that deemed crimes by blacks against blacks unworthy of coverage. In a column he wrote about the Janet Cooke episode, the Bulletin's Mr. Lewis described the Washington Post's editors as having been "victimized by their own innocence." Miss Cooke succeeded in her hoax, he wrote, "because she fed Washington Post editors a story based firmly on their own awful assumptions."

As part of his current assignment on the Atlanta Journal, Mr. Maye interviews families of the city's murdered black children. It is both a "black" story and a big national story. Mr. Maye, observing that "a lot of reporters don't want to be labeled a 'black reporter,' " says that in Atlanta, "black is big-time. It's big news down here."

Elsewhere, news about blacks and other minorities seldom makes the front page. The Syracuse Herald-Journal's Miss Smokes, while stressing that her paper tries to avoid typecasting black reporters, says she sometimes initiates a story on blacks because "if I didn't do it, it wouldn't get covered." She adds: "I sort of feel a responsibility. There's a perception that newspapers just don't care about minorities. It's not always racism. It may just be ignorance."

The President

November 20, 1980

The End of an Era?

By Arthur Schlesinger Jr.

Authoritative voices assure us that the 1980 election brings an era to an end. The apocalypts are an impressive lot—The Wall Street Journal, Walter Dean Burnham, Max Lerner, Richard Whalen, David Broder and so on. Perhaps they are right.

But the more venerable among us will remember that the so-called New Deal era has ended at least twice before—and therefore view the apocalyptic interpretation of the 1980 election with a certain reserve. The besetting sin of punditry is reading more significance into events than they have. As Emerson said, "In analyzing history, do not be too profound, for often the causes are quite superficial."

The first time the New Deal era came to an end was in 1952, when Eisenhower beat Stevenson with 55% of the popular vote. The second time was in 1972, when Nixon beat McGovern with 61%. Each of those elections pitted a liberal against a conservative and could be taken as a legitimate test. It is hard to see how 1980, when Reagan got a bare 51% against a candidate who stood for nothing but himself, represented a test of anything. On the face of it, this third end-of-an-era is a good deal less emphatic than the first two—and obviously the first two did not stick, if a third is necessary.

It is hard to see how liberalism was an issue at all in 1980. Liberal policies haven't prevailed in Washington since 1966, when Lyndon Johnson decided to sacrifice the Great Society to the Vietnam war. That was 14 years ago. Since then, we have had Nixon, Ford and Carter—the last of whom, though an alleged Democrat, won the presidency with demagogic attacks on the horrible federal bureaucracy and as President made clear in the most explicit way his rejection of the Roosevelt-Truman-Kennedy-Johnson idea of affirmative government.

Voters' Repudiation

The exit polls show inflation and employment to have been the decisive issues. In this area particularly, Mr. Carter followed the same line as his predecessor, Gerald Ford—recession and unemployment as the remedy for inflation. What the voters repudiated in 1980 was not liberalism but the miserable result of the conservative economic policies of the last half dozen years. "The evidence indicates," as George Gallup wrote after the election, "that there is no strong movement to the political right" and that both candidates "rated lower on personal appeal than any

---

Board of Contributors

It is hard to see how 1980, when Reagan got a bare 51% against a candidate who stood for nothing but himself, represented a test of anything.

---

other presidential candidates whose appeal we have measured during the last three decades."

The vote represented, in short, the rejection of a failed presidency. This does not by itself invalidate the end-of-an-era thesis—only the heavy verdicts handed down by the pundits. For in one respect 1980 is like 1932. Mr. Reagan now, like Roosevelt then, was elected on a negative vote. Mr. Reagan now, like Roosevelt then, received, not a mandate, but an opportunity. It was what Roosevelt did with his opportunity that ended the Republican era. It will be what

Mr. Reagan does with his opportunity that will determine whether 1980 will be seen as an "earthquake election" like 1932—or as a passing tremor.

It all depends on whether Mr. Reagan's policies will work. While I deeply regret the defeat of several of my best friends in the Senate, still a Republican Senate and a House dominated by the old coalition of Republicans and conservative Democrats offer compensating advantages. At least we can have a full and fair test, conducted without easy alibis, of hallowed conservative propositions—that government is the root of all evil, and that our problems will promptly solve themselves once that ol' debbil gets off our backs. If the free-market therapy works, fine. If it fails, then at least the country has got that out of its system, and can move on to something else.

My guess is that it will not work, that inflation, interest rates and unemployment will rise, that Mr. Reagan in two years will be in as much trouble as Mrs. Thatcher today, and that by 1984 his telling campaign question "Are you better off than you were four years ago?" will return to haunt the Republicans. As to why the Reagan policies will fail, I cannot improve upon the excellent statement by James Wieghart of the New York Daily News: "The problems facing the country and the world—the energy crisis, pollution, overpopulation, structural unemployment, pervasive inflation and much more—simply do not lend themselves to solution by a weak central government which is subservient to an unfettered private sector."

In the meantime, what about the Democrats? Defeat gives them an opportunity too—an opportunity, long needed, to start thinking hard and anew about the problems that afflict the nation. I hope my party keeps this in mind when it chooses a new national chairman. The best Democratic national chairman in my lifetime was Paul Butler in the late 1950s. He cared about issues, argued them incisively on national television and fostered serious thought about them in an instrumentality he created for the occasion, the Democratic Advisory Council. A party in opposition needs not just a nuts-and-bolts expert, but someone who will see as his main business the priming of the party's intellectual pump. Like the Republicans, the Democrats will stand or fall on the strength of their ideas.

For the New Deal era is of course over —simply because the problems of the 1980s are vastly different from the problems of the 1930s. The commanding domestic issues of our time—chronic inflation and the passing of the age of low-cost energy—are novel issues and demand novel remedies. In the same way the New Deal faced novel problems in its own time—problems of depression and mass unemployment—that Theodore Roosevelt and Woodrow Wilson had never had to face.

Yet a continuity remained, stretching from Theodore Roosevelt to Lyndon Johnson—the belief in the use of the national government as a means of promoting the general welfare. The question confronting the Democratic Party is whether this tradition is now useless in face of the problems caused by inflation and high-cost energy. A "neo-liberal" school forthrightly joins the clamor against affirmative government. Alas, its members are less forthright when it comes to disclosing their own remedies.

Profound Silence

Take as an example Sen. Paul Tsongas of Massachusetts, who has been overflowing with speeches and interviews about the dangers of big-government liberalism. Mr. Tsongas has sensible things to say about the need for liberals to meet the preoccupations of a new generation of voters. But he falls into a profound silence when asked about alternatives. After his much publicized speech last June before the Americans for Democratic Action, I wrote him expressing my regret that departure from Massachusetts had deprived me of the opportunity to vote for him and my hope that he might vouchsafe "some remedies for inflation, unemployment and the energy stringency that do not call on affirmative government and intelligent public purpose." Receiving no answer, I wrote him again a month later, enclosing my original letter and begging once again for specifics. Still no answer; and after another month I wrote, "Your refusal to offer even the courtesy of an acknowledgment leaves the inevitable conclusion that your neo-liberalism is so empty that you have nothing at all to say in explanation of it." Continued silence from the Tsongas office would seem to confirm this melancholy conclusion.

Obviously some aspects of affirmative government have become irrelevant. There is no point in calling for reruns of failed federal programs, as in housing and urban renewal, or in defending idiotic regulations promulgated by one or another federal agency, or in supposing that federal spending is the answer to every perplexity. These are not the issues. Happily not everyone is so bashful as Sen. Tsongas about possible ways out.

For a genuinely fresh and valuable analysis of current problems, take a look at Felix Rohatyn's recent speech in Houston, reprinted in the New York Review of Books (Dec. 4). Mr. Rohatyn hardly shares the neo-liberal disdain for government. This is the real issue: whether we want to confide our future in an age of shrinking resources to a private market dominated by great corporations, or whether we are a purposeful society using government as one of the means by which to recapture control of our destiny.

____

Mr. Schlesinger is the Albert Schweitzer Professor of the Humanities at the City University of New York, winner of Pulitzer Prizes in history and biography and a member of the Journal's Board of Contributors.

Restoring Control: Ronald Reagan's Electoral Mandate

By MORTON M. KONDRACKE

It's interesting and, I think, important that the two rhetorical high points of the 1980 presidential campaign were both evocations of America's past and declarations that its glories could be recaptured.

One was Edward Kennedy's Democratic convention speech, recalling the greatness of the liberal tradition—"to speak for those who have no voice, to remember those who are forgotten . . . the cause endures, the hope still lives and the dream shall never die." The second, far less remarked upon, was Ronald Reagan's election eve television address, in which he recalled that on Americans' return from World War II, "we built a grand prosperity and hoped—from our own success and plenty—to help others less fortunate. Our peace was a tense and bitter one, but in those days the center seemed to hold. Then came the hard years —riots and assassinations, domestic strife over the Vietnam war and in the last four years, drift and disaster in Washington. . . ."

According to Mr. Reagan, "The question before us tonight (is) does history still have a place for America, for her people, for her great ideals?" Some, he said, say no, that the country's energy is spent. But Mr. Reagan, of course, disagreed, and with a tear in his eye and a choke in his voice recalled the statement of a dying John Wayne: "Just give the American people a good cause, and there's nothing they can't lick."

What was important about these two speeches was their shared critique of the status quo. Both Mr. Kennedy and Mr. Reagan challenged Jimmy Carter on the theme that things had gotten out of control in America and the world, but that the greatness of the past could be restored. Jimmy Carter replied, sometimes explicitly, that this was impossible. He said it was simplistic and misleading to promise a return to the country's postwar security and comfort because the conditions on which they were based are gone, especially the U.S. nuclear monopoly, an abundance of cheap energy and U.S. dominance of the world economy.

* * *

Democratic primary voters sustained Mr. Carter against Mr. Kennedy, but I think the meaning of Mr. Reagan's big victory is that the American people in general want to regain their lost sense of control. They are upset by runaway inflation, the loss of jobs to foreigners, a weakening of traditional social values and government's simultaneous costliness, high-handedness and impotence. They are also worried and angered by the uncontained growth of Soviet power and by the accelerating disrespect shown to the U.S. by assorted world barbarians. They want their President to make the center hold again.

In his post-election press conference, for example, Mr. Carter said he thought Governor Reagan "will do the very best he can to carry out his campaign commitments, which are deeply held by him, I'm sure, to restore as much as possible our nation's pre-eminence in some areas where we have not been able to exert our will to dominate others."

In electing Ronald Reagan and a Republican Senate with him, the country has decided to try recapturing control by turning to basic American devices, John Wayne devices—private enterprise, individualism, the free market, military strength and interventionism overseas. But, decisive as the Republican victory was at the top, it was not complete down to the House, governorship and state legislative levels, suggesting that this was a 1932-style election—a tentative choice, a tryout —rather than a 1936, a massive political conclusion. If the Republicans fail to deliver a restoration of control, or at least the appearance of control, I think the people well may turn the other way—you could call it the Kennedy way—toward wage and price controls, protectionism and government planning at home and a self-preoccupied, European-style nationalism in foreign policy.

* * *

I consider myself a liberal, but I still hope the Reagan way works. I would rather see the economy prosper by free market decisions than by government direction. I would rather secure American jobs by improving productivity than by barring imports. I would rather help the poor with private sector jobs than with welfare. I'd rather have my taxes cut than raised. I'd rather order the Russians out of Afghanistan than worry about where they might go next.

If Mr. Reagan can make the center hold again, he deserves the political success of FDR. But there are reasons to think he can't. One is that the market simply isn't free anymore, but significantly controlled by cartels, conglomerates and labor unions, all requiring government regulation. Another is that corporate executives may be so wedded to short-term profit-seeking that they need government to help them plan for the long term. A third is that the Reaganites (despite present assurances) will prove indifferent or punitive toward minorities and the poor, causing a national social crisis. A fourth is that Mr. Reagan's anti-inflationary tax cuts will prove hyperinflationary, creating demands for wage-price controls. And a fifth is that Mr. Reagan might embark on some foreign adventure to demonstrate "will" and find himself in a quagmire.

Still another possibility is that conspiratorialists in the Reagan entourage might launch witch-hunts, mole-chases and loyalty probes, bogging the administration down in replays of the McCarthy era.

Or, Ronald Reagan might not be smart enough for the hard tasks at hand, or a bad strategist or an inept manager. If he can't recapture control, I don't think the country will settle for Jimmy Carter's excuse—that nothing can be done—but will search for control another way. Even John Wayne would understand that.

Mr. Kondracke is executive editor of The New Republic magazine.

Let Mr. Reagan Remember the Alamo

Here we are, only days away from the moment when Ronald Reagan in his $1,150 morning suit (thrift cometh in the evening with the white tie and merely retrofitted tails) will place his hand on an emblem of the currently fashionable Judeo-Christian heritage and launch off on his term. It seems a miracle he has got this far.

I must say I thought the jig was up back before Christmas when Reps. David Stockman and Jack Kemp urged him to declare an economic Dunkirk. To someone like myself, brought up on the other side of the Atlantic this seemed a counsel of madness. Mention of Dunkirk by British politi-

Viewpoint

by Alexander Cockburn

cians, from Churchill through almost every subsequent prime minister, has been a certain sign that not only does catastrophe loom but no solution is in prospect, beyond intense suffering by the electorate and its unstinting support for the government.

Hence the usual concomitant allusions to the "Dunkirk spirit" (things are bad), "blood, sweat and tears" (they'll get worse) and fighting "on the beaches" (we're calling the IMF).

The fact that some historians suggest that Hitler let the British Expeditionary Force flee Dunkirk only the better to spread appeasing despair on the other side of the Channel further reduces the appeal of this particular historical reference. If he must, let Mr. Reagan remember the Alamo and leave it at that.

But quite aside from the worrisome Dunkirk incident, has there ever been such a commotion of excited rhetoric, of fierce talk about "radical solutions," of knives plunging deeper, ever deeper, into this or that part of the budget's distended anatomy (always excepting defense) and hacking furiously at regulation?

To judge from the querulously vindictive abuse heaped on their heads by conservatives pre- and post-November 4, it seems surprising that a refugee column is not already fleeing for Mexico, headed by the fellows of the Institute for Policy Studies and trailed by every "McGovernite" strong enough to walk. As they crossed the border they would have the added discomfiture of seeing Latin American generals rushing the other way for their aid packages from an administration more understanding of the difference between our dictators and theirs.

Though adherents of a philosophy presumably supportive of restrained behavior, conservatives do seem addicted to a vocabulary of extreme violence or death. We had George Will, noted pundit of the right, remarking in the first post-election spasm that "the massacre of incumbents was a catharsis for the electorate, a clean sweep with a strong broom." We had William Buckley, presumably an opponent of the practice when inflicted on humans, urging "euthanasia for government programs."

Along the same lines, the very day after Christmas, an editorial axman here at The Wall Street Journal said sternly, "As to Chrysler, it is not a question of shooting horses, but of disconnecting a life-support system we can ill afford."

I know we won't see the right-to-lifers rallying around government bailout programs just on grounds of linguistic etiquette, but the verbal violence does seem to me to reflect a violence of thought and a violence to thought which have become more common and more intense on the rightward end of the political spectrum in the past few years.

Much of it has had to do with the threat of inflation that accompanied the latest phase of the arms race, the war against SALT II and the Soviet menace in all its innumerable incarnations. If you start with the preposterous assumption, devoutly believed by conservatives, that the Soviet Union is meditating a preemptive first strike on the land based missiles of the continental United States, and conclude with a preposterous *roman a clef* ("The Spike") widely read by conservatives, suggesting that the Vice President of the United States is in some manner a pawn of the KGB, froth will surely gather at the corners of the mouth, and you will fall upon the rug and start chewing.

Irrationalism about Moscow has been paralleled by irrationalism about Washington until, listening to him during the campaign, I was sometimes uncertain which of the two Big Governments Reagan disliked more; a Cruise missile on Brezhnev's breakfast table or Stockman's ax to the budget (fat, not bone, naturally) should maintain parity here.

Say long enough, loudly enough, that the Russian tanks in Kabul presage their imminent arrival in Paris, and the Clean Air Act paves the road to ruin, and then the agitators for bigger defense budgets will start to believe their own propaganda and conceive that their opponents are not only deluded but—presaging the reviving Senate subcommittee on subversion—traitors to the American way. "Extremists" is the current term used to exclude such opponents from political discourse, as in Reagan's dismissal of the environmentalists protesting his nominee for Secretary of the Interior.

The Wall Street Journal editorial page, I'm glad to say, remains relatively sanguine. Its year-end editorial on December 31— possibly written by someone cheerier in disposition than the Chrysler-killer—concluded that the American electorate, while lately understandably distressed with its leadership over the last decades, remains "fundamentally sound." The word "fundamentally" is a little grudging, but it is good to know this. "Sound," eh? Phew!

So with the fundamentally sound electorate all agog and expectant, Dunkirk avoided, and—though they still have a few days to change their minds—no preemptive Soviet first strike, we have almost made it through the transition period, beyond which time President Reagan will have to live well below the expectations of his supporters if the rudiments of social tranquility are to be preserved. All oppositions are prisoners of their own propaganda. They come to believe that things are what they have all this time been saying they are. The danger comes when these delusions are carried into power.

Alexander Cockburn, a 39-year-old Irish citizen born in Scotland, settled in New York in 1973, since which time he has written weekly columns on the press and—with James Ridgeway—on politics for the Village Voice. He is also a contributor to the New York Review of Books and to Harper's. He will be writing a monthly column for the Journal in this space.

Pledges to 'Lighten Tax Burden'

Reagan Takes Oath, Making Economy First Priority And Putting 'Strict Freeze' on Federal Civilian Hiring

By Timothy D. Schellhardt
Staff Reporter of The Wall Street Journal

WASHINGTON—Asking Americans to begin "an era of national renewal," Ronald Wilson Reagan pledged an immediate start in restoring "a healthy, vigorous, growing economy."

His first priorities, he declared in assuming office as the nation's 40th President on a bright, balmy day, are "to reawaken this industrial giant, to get government back within its means, and to lighten our punitive tax burden."

Progress toward these objectives, he acknowledged, "may be slow—measured in inches and feet, not miles." But, he promised, "we will make progress." Almost immediately, in his first presidential act, Mr. Reagan ordered a "strict freeze" on the hiring of federal civilian employes, who currently number 2,154,000. The action, he maintained, "begins the process of restoring our economic strength and returning the nation to prosperity."

Alludes to Hostages

The tone of his 19-minute inaugural speech reflected his familiar sunny optimism and the themes of his presidential campaign. In it, the President didn't specifically mention the 52 U.S. hostages in Iran, who, as he spoke, were departing the country where they had been held captive for 444 days. Mr. Reagan did allude to the hostage situation, however. He said his administration will call on the "will and moral courage" of the American people to defend the national interest. "Let that be understood by those who practice terrorism and prey upon their neighbors," he asserted.

Jimmy Carter, denied his dream of announcing personally that the hostages had been freed, spent most of his final hours as President unsnarling problems that had developed over the transfer of funds required by the hostage accord. Those problems were untangled early yesterday morning, but hostages weren't freed until about 12:25 p.m. EST.

After his successor's swearing-in, Mr. Carter flew to Plains, Ga., his hometown. Today, he is to fly to West Germany to greet the hostages as an official U.S. envoy of President Reagan.

President Reagan's inaugural ceremonies contrasted sharply with those of Mr. Carter four years ago. Then, Mr. Carter discarded much of the traditional pomp of such ceremonies. He wore a business suit, walked —rather than rode—in his parade, and promised in his inaugural address a presidency of "humility" and closeness to the people.

The man who defeated him overwhelmingly last November restored the familiar inaugural pomp, complete with a 21-gun salute. Mr. Reagan took the 35-word oath of office wearing formal morning dress. And he rode with Mrs. Reagan in the presidential limousine in their parade.

At age 69 (he'll turn 70 in 16 days), Mr. Reagan is the oldest man to assume the presidency. The former movie actor, the son of a shoe salesman, didn't start campaigning for public office until he was 55. Yet throughout his political career, first as California's governor and then during his presidential quest, the conservative Republican has advocated several familiar and unchanging positions.

His crusade, Mr. Reagan has asserted repeatedly, is to "take government off the backs of the great people of this country" and to restore the nation's military strength and clear superiority.

Samples of Address

Those were clear messages of his inaugural speech, as was the upbeat view that Americans can conquer their problems. Here are some samples, with Mr. Reagan saying:

—"It is time to check and reverse the growth of government which shows signs of having grown beyond the consent of the governed."

—"In the days ahead, I will propose removing a number of the roadblocks that have slowed our economy and reduced productivity."

—"When action is required to preserve our national security, we will act. We will maintain sufficient strength to prevail if need be, knowing that if we do so we have the best chance of never having to use that strength."

References to patriotism and its symbols also predominated in the President's address. Yesterday, for the first time, a President was sworn in on the West Front of the Capitol, enabling Mr. Reagan to speak facing this city's monuments to Presidents Lincoln, Jefferson and Washington and to Arlington National Cemetery. That picturesque backdrop allowed him to pay tribute to Americans who had died in battle, including a World War I casualty, Martin Treptow.

His voice filled with emotion, Mr. Reagan recalled the diary of the soldier, which included a pledge the small-town barber had written. "America must win this war," Mr. Treptow wrote. "Therefore, I will work, I will save, I will sacrifice, I will endure, I will fight cheerfully and do my utmost, as if the issue of the whole struggle depended on me alone."

Remedying the nation's economic ills, which Mr. Reagan termed an "affliction of great proportions," won't require the kind of sacrifice that Mr. Treptow made, the President said. It will require, he said, "our best effort and our willingness to believe in ourselves and in our capacity to perform great deeds." Concluding his speech, he asked, "Why shouldn't we believe that? After all—we are Americans."

Mr. Reagan lost little time in moving to keep his campaign pledge to curb the size of the federal government. His action to freeze government hiring could reduce federal civilian employment by 151,200 individuals in a year, given the normal 7% turnover rate among the federal work force.

Reagan aides concede, however, that it will be difficult to trim employment by 150,000 or so. For one thing, a number of top government officials and political appointees aren't affected by the freeze. For another, the President intends to exempt those delivering "essential services," likely including air-traffic controllers.

In addition, experts say the normal attrition rate drops during a hiring freeze. Although President Carter placed a partial freeze on hiring permanent, full-time employes, total federal employment rose 41,844 during his term. Alan Campbell, who headed the Office of Personnel Management under Mr. Carter, says that in the past, hiring freezes died after a few months because "the exceptions become the rule, largely in order to get the work of government done."

President Reagan is expected to take several other steps soon aimed at fulfilling campaign pledges to reduce government interference and to bolster the economy. Among other things, he plans to stop new government regulations from going into effect until all pending ones are examined by his administration. He also intends to send Congress his economic proposals in the near future, his aides say.

---

51 ⎯⎯⎯⎯⎯⎯⎯⎯⎯⎯⎯⎯⎯⎯⎯⎯⎯⎯⎯⎯⎯⎯⎯⎯⎯⎯⎯⎯⎯⎯⎯⎯⎯ *February 11, 1981*

Before Ronald Reagan Chooses, Edwin Meese Sorts Out the Choices

Aide Extoled as Calm, Loyal; But Some Say His Office Is Becoming a Bottleneck

A Passion for Flow Charts

By Timothy D. Schellhardt

Staff Reporter of The Wall Street Journal

WASHINGTON — As Ronald Reagan's chief of staff during his California governorship, Edwin Meese gained the unofficial title of "assistant governor."

As President Reagan's chief counselor, Mr. Meese already has acquired the label "assistant President."

The label fits, say his friends and critics alike. This is the man Mr. Reagan says he would turn to first in a crisis. In terms of personal influence and proximity to Ronald Reagan, the soft-spoken, affable, unflappable lawyer outranks everyone but First Lady Nancy Reagan.

That close relationship, which has spanned 12 years, has begun to spawn jokes suggesting that Mr. Reagan is a figurehead Chief Executive and that his trusted aide actually pulls the strings. "The real question we should be asking ourselves," quips political satirist Mark Russell, "is, Just what kind of President will Ed Meese make?"

Actually, the serious question developing is, Just what kind of presidential counselor will Ed Meese make?"

He will unquestionably be a powerful one. As the President's chief counselor, with Cabinet rank, he coordinates development of both domestic and foreign policy and oversees the strengthened system of Cabinet government that Mr. Reagan insists can best manage the nation's affairs. Just now, Mr. Meese is helping decide on the remaining sub-Cabinet appointments and helping shape the high-priority package of tax and budget cuts soon to be delivered to Congress.

To his many friends and supporters, he is the consummate public servant and presidential confidant. "Undauntedly loyal," says one. "Stills rather than stirs the water," says another. "Possesses a razor-sharp, tidy mind that condenses complicated issues for the boss's quick analysis," adds a third. Helene von Damm, Mr. Reagan's longtime personal secretary, declares: "Ed Meese has never let Ronald Reagan down."

The Other Side

But, say his detractors, Ed Meese's failings could prove Ronald Reagan's undoing. They consider the 49-year-old adviser a bottleneck, and they worry that he will slow critical economic and foreign-policy decisions the President needs to make soon. "It's already becoming a problem," a White House associate says. "He's scheduling too many Cabinet meetings, and we've been considering some things without proper staffing."

His critics maintain that Mr. Meese takes on too much, doesn't manage his time well despite working 13-hour days, procrastinates in making decisions, shuns confrontation and lacks political savvy. That last shortcoming, some say, shows up in what they consider an insensitivity to the need to recruit minorities and women for high administration posts.

To further support their complaints, some Meese critics point to the recent presidential transition office that he headed—a $3 million, budget-busting operation that hired hundreds of people but missed time-tables for choosing top-level officials for the new administration. These transition problems, some insist, have kept the President from starting at the quick pace he promised. "If that was an example of the lean, streamlined government the President long has advocated, then he and we are in big trouble," declares one prominent conservative Reagan supporter.

Contrast With Reagan

Even Mr. Meese's friends and family acknowledge some of the criticism is fair. "It's the story of his life: He does too much," says a longtime associate. Mr. Meese's wife, Ursula, says: "One of the things he'll have to learn on the job is to get his priorities in order so he doesn't spread himself too thin."

Right now he is spread rather thin. He often works from 7 a.m. to 10 p.m., yet amid the pressures of a newly organized White House he manages to stay calm—and cautious. His style is a distinct contrast to the President's: Mr. Reagan is decisive, short-tempered at times and accustomed to keeping nine-to-six working hours.

Different though the two men are, their relationship works—as it has worked for so long. Early last year, Mr. Meese joined the Reagan presidential campaign to oversee policy development and research. Later he became chief of staff after surviving an intense power struggle with political strategist John Sears. (Mr. Sears wanted Mr. Meese ousted but got the boot himself instead.) During the recent 3½-month transition period, Mr. Meese not only directed the vast operation but also served as its chief spokesman.

Mr. Meese thinks his relationship with Ronald Reagan has thrived because the President "has confidence I'll do my best to provide him with objective advice and a wide range of viewpoints and observations. Mrs. Meese believes the two work well together because they "think very much alike. Also, Ed sees through to the nitty-gritty."

The two men share the same basic conservative philosophy. And while there have been differences on some issues, they generally see eye to eye on pivotal matters, Mr. Meese says. He won't specify where they have disagreed, although Mrs. Meese says her husband's view on abortion isn't as severe as the President's. "The President is for no abortions; Ed can see the necessity of abortions in some circumstances," she says.

Mr. Meese suggests his new job will free him of the administrative chores that apparently bogged him down during the campaign and the transition. Most of those responsibilities — from overseeing political appointments to directing other Reagan aides—have been delegated to James Baker, the White House chief of staff and a former aide to President Ford. "Baker's the manager, Meese the synthesizer," says one top White House official.

"Part of the President's concept of my job was to design it so I could spend a lot of time with him," says Mr. Meese. His wife notes that when they discussed going to Washington, "We never considered his being chief of staff again. He had done that, and in that job it's easy to get burned out on a lot of personnel matters and the daily routine."

Charting a Course

The counselor's post has allowed Mr. Meese to pursue a favorite pastime; devising organization charts. A criminal-justice specialist, he used to collect and study charts of police departments across the country. He has spent hours studying the Executive Branch flow charts of former Presidents and designing one for President Reagan. According to one aide, a delay developed in naming a U.S. representative for foreign-trade negotiations because Mr. Meese found the trade negotiator's box dangling untidily on the flow chart.

The relationship between Mr. Meese's job and that of his near-equal James Baker is so unusual—and so awkward, contend some observers—that Mr. Baker insisted their respective assignments be put on paper and agreed to in writing. Both men insist they don't expect problems to develop in their relationship. "I don't think it ever will" fall apart, says Mr. Meese.

If nothing else, a cultural-social bond of sorts may help them get along together. Mr. Baker notes that he graduated from Princeton University in 1952 and Mr. Meese graduated from Yale the next year. "We found we had a lot of mutual friends," Mr. Baker says.

But Verne Orr, a longtime associate of Mr. Meese and President Reagan's Air Force secretary, believes his friend will have to make some adjustments. "It's going to take some work: Ed's most difficult job will be to give up territory," he says.

His style of management, Mr. Meese says, is that of the college football coach. "You take the players you have and mold a team, as opposed to the quick-hire/quick-fire or the management-by-fear approach," he says. "Teamwork" is the key word in the Reagan White House, and Mr. Meese says he expects the staff to avoid the divisive public quarrels that characterized the Carter administration.

"The President's staff should have a zeal for work and a passion for anonymity," he says. Some prospective presidential appointees think they got scratched from consideration because Mr. Meese didn't believe they would be good team players. Former Treasury Secretary William Simon has told friends as much.

In part, this "team-player" approach reflects Mr. Meese's own low-key, unassuming style. During the presidential campaign, he never upstaged his boss even though reporters frequently sought him out to explain a terse and incomplete statement by the candidate. For instance, when Mr. Reagan sharply attacked the Carter administration's initial loan guarantee for the ailing Chrysler Corp., Mr. Meese assured reporters that Mr. Reagan believed there were several choices between government bailout and Chrysler bankruptcy.

Affable Ed

The "affable" description of Mr. Meese, which caught on then, has stuck. During the campaign, reporters referred to him so often as "affable Ed" that, says one, "We began to say his first name was 'Affable.'" E. Pendleton James, the White House personnel chief and a longtime Meese friend, recalls: "Once when I mentioned that a magazine had referred to him as an 'affable bear of a man,' he turned on me rather sharply and said, "Pen, what's wrong with being affable?'"

Personality aside, Mr. Meese's penchant for scheduling early-morning and late-evening meetings doesn't please some associates. One top transition planner says he found such early-morning meetings unproductive. At the White House, Mr. Meese's day includes many such meetings; he believes they provide the opportunity for everyone to get his or her view across on an issue. While conducting them, Mr. Meese takes pages of notes in ring-binder notebooks, using pens of different colors.

Though there was never much doubt he would become the President's chief policy adviser, Mr. Meese has told several friends he would really have liked to be Army secretary. "It would be fun to manage an organization like that," says this recently retired lieutenant colonel in the Army Reserve.

Other friends believe he would like to head the Federal Bureau of Investigation someday. He is a former Alameda County (Calif.) deputy district attorney who gained a reputation for tough enforcement of drug laws. He attracted then Gov. Reagan's attention in the mid-1960s by his efforts to deal with campus disturbances, and the governor later chose him as his extradition and clemency secretary.

Today Mr. Meese maintains a deep interest in criminal justice and in police work particularly. (To mock those who call the police names, he has a collection of pigs.) The presidential counselor expecially enjoys the technology of law enforcement. At his home in La Mesa, Calif., he used to spend hours listening to his police radio.

Tuning In

Mr. James recalls that when the two men were driving once along a Los Angeles freeway, Mr. Meese's eyes riveted on a passing highway-patrol car. "I asked him if he was interested in the weighty subject we were discussing. 'You know, Pen,' he said, 'I'm more interested in that new antenna. It means the police have a new communications system.'"

Mr. Meese's new prominence is requiring some adjustment for his family. "Suddenly we've become a household word," says his wife with a certain resignation. Their youngest son, Scott, who graduated from high school last month, dropped the idea of coming to Washington with his parents. "All I'll be known there as is Ed Meese's son," he told his parents.

Mr. Meese says he doesn't expect the heady White House atmosphere to change his quiet, gentle approach. "I don't have any compulsion to work. I'll leave if I have to," he says.

And he bristles at the notion that he is the master pulling President Reagan's strings.

"It's totally untrue," he asserts, his face acquiring a redness that Helene von Damm says is the only way she can tell he's angry. "What people don't understand is that Ronald Reagan is probably one of the best executives in this country. He has a natural ability to handle work and handle people well. He's able to delegate a certain amount of responsibility and reserve time for thinking and making decisions."

'Worst Mess Since Great Depression'

Reagan Urges Congress to Lower Taxes and Spending To Fight Inflation and Prevent 'Economic Calamity'

By Kenneth H. Bacon
And Timothy D. Schellhardt
Staff Reporters of The Wall Street Journal

WASHINGTON — President Reagan warned that the nation faces "an economic calamity of tremendous proportions" unless Congress takes stern measures to curb inflation.

In his first televised address from the Oval Office, Mr. Reagan sought to mobilize broad public and congressional support for the substantial tax and budget cuts he will propose Feb. 18. He promised his program would spur growth and reduce inflation.

The President didn't present any new details about his economic proposals. Instead, he concentrated on explaining the results of an economic "audit" that he said shows the nation is "in the worst economic mess since the Great Depression." Inflation, which he blamed on big government deficits, has destroyed incentives to save and to invest, and high taxes have eroded the rewards of working, he lamented.

Mr. Reagan used an array of figures and charts to help make his case. At one point, he compared a dollar bill to a quarter, a dime and a penny, saying that since 1960 inflation has reduced the value of a dollar to 36 cents today.

"When we measure how harshly these years of inflation, lower productivity and uncontrolled government growth have affected our lives, we know we must act, and act now," Mr. Reagan said. "We must not be timid."

Although he warned that there's "no quick fix" to the nation's economic problems, he said: "We can't delay in implementing an economic program aimed at both reducing tax rates to stimulate productivity and reducing the growth in government spending to reduce unemployment and inflation."

Mr. Reagan said the plan he will present to Congress in a State of the Union message Feb. 18 will call for three annual 10% across-the-board reductions of individual income tax rates, starting this year, plus accelerated business depreciation write-offs for new investment.

In addition, Mr. Reagan promised budget cuts in "virtually every department of government" to help slow the increase of federal spending. "The federal budget is out of control and we face runaway deficits of almost $80 billion for this budget year, that ends Sept. 30," he said. His figure referred to the total Treasury borrowing necessary to cover the actual revenue deficit of $55 billion plus borrowing necessary to finance a variety of "off-budget" federal loans to finance housing, rural development and other programs.

Other Announcements Expected

In his Feb. 18 address, Mr. Reagan is also expected to announce that he plans to pare $13 billion to $14 billion in spending from the current fiscal year's budget, and a hefty $35 billion to $40 billion in fiscal 1982.

The President's advisers already are circulating on Capitol Hill a 150-page "hit list" of federal programs whose budgets can be reduced. Mr. Reagan's aides, however, insist the president hasn't made any final decisions on his budget cuts.

The suggested reductions hit many domestic social programs, including Medicaid, education aid, food stamps, certain Social Security benefits, urban-development grants and job-training funds. In addition, there are proposals to limit lending by the Federal Financing Bank and the Export-Import Bank, to share spending for the Space Shuttle program and Amtrak, and to reduce substantially the synthetic-fuels program.

Disclosures of the suggested cutbacks already have triggered howls from many lawmakers and from interest groups that would be affected.

Reassuring Public

A prime purpose of the speech was to undercut such opposition, in part by seeking to reassure the public that he won't undo necessary social programs. "Our spending cuts will not be at the expense of the truly needy," the President promised. But he said the administration will "seek to eliminate benefits to those who aren't really qualified by reason of need."

He also noted that his plans will merely slow the increase in government spending, rather than reduce outlays from one year to the next. "Government revenue will increase as the economy grows, but the burden will be lighter for each individual" taxpayer, he pledged.

The President and his top staff already have done quite a bit of lobbying with influential lawmakers in an effort to convince them the administration's program offers the best solution to the country's economic problems. White House officials believe their talks on Capitol Hill before his State of the Union address are crucial to lay the groundwork for congressional passage of the tax and spending cuts.

They believe President Carter in early 1977 failed to do that early groundwork for his energy programs. As a result, they note, the Carter energy proposals were changed drastically and didn't get passed until 18 months after they were sent to Congress.

The President said he's "found a real willingness to cooperate" from both Democrats and Republicans in Congress. He also appealed to business and labor for support. "The only special interest we will serve is the interest of the people," he promised.

Examples of Distress

In building his case for economic change, Mr. Reagan cited several examples of economic distress, many of which he used throughout his presidential campaign. Last night, he again focused on the high cost of government regulation, declining U.S. productivity and the difficulty of competing in world markets, the rising tax burden on workers and the high cost of buying a home.

Many economists doubt that the Reagan prescription of lower taxes, slowed spending and a tight credit policy by the Federal Reserve Board will work. They say, for instance, that cutting taxes before spending is under control will fuel, rather than cool, inflation.

But Mr. Reagan declared that traditional economic nostrums—waiting to cut taxes until spending is under control or alternating government policy between belt-tightening to fight inflation and pump-priming to cure unemployment—have failed.

"We don't have to choose between inflation and unemployment. They go hand in hand," Mr. Reagan said. "It's time to try something different, and that's what we're going to do."

Perennial Battle
War on Federal Waste Is Easy to Declare But Difficult to Win, Experience Indicates

By Burt Schorr

Staff Reporter of The Wall Street Journal

WASHINGTON—Get ready for another war on waste, fraud and abuse in federal spending.

Billions of dollars can be saved. President Reagan and his budget director, former Rep. David Stockman of Michigan, are convinced of that. They are talking about initially trimming $13 billion in waste from federal spending. One Stockman target is the supposed fat in the $3 billion that Uncle Sam shells out yearly for travel expenses of federal civilian employes and military personnel. Abuses in the food-stamp, disability, housing-assistance and other government programs offer further opportunities for corrective actions, Mr. Stockman believes.

Mr. Reagan got off to a fast start after being sworn in, by ordering a 15% cut in government travel, a 5% reduction in consulting contracts and a halt to certain equipment purchases. He also fired the 15 departmental inspectors general, whose job is to fight waste; he plans to fill the posts with choices who are "meaner than a junkyard dog," as one Reagan aide put it.

But battle-scarred veterans of past skirmishes in the fiscal foxholes warn that finding waste is a lot easier than stopping it. Uncle Sam's accountants already have a long list of targets, including: the $16 billion or so that could be recovered on overdue or defaulted debts owed the government; the nearly $7 billion spent on unnecessary operation of nonmilitary aircraft; the more than $4 billion lost annually through Medicare and Medicaid errors and abuses and wasteful health-care practices.

Carter Campaign

Indeed, Washington in some ways has been fighting waste all along. President Carter launched *his* war to save federal dollars back in 1977. Some members of Congress have been at it even longer. But trying to penetrate the bureaucratic bunkers to get at the problems has produced mostly frustration.

"The scandals are lying around like rubble, yet nobody removes the people responsible," complains Sen. Max Baucus. The Montana Democrat headed a Judiciary subcommittee in the last Congress that investigated such abuses as unjustified grants to small rural colleges and millionaires who benefited from a federal contracting program supposed to aid disadvantaged small-business people.

Republicans are convinced, of course, that they will do a better job of ferreting out misuse of federal cash. But there is a lesson for them in the experiences of their predecessors: Seepage of wasted dollars from the federal budget is much like the seepage from an ancient water system; stopping it is often tedious work that can be prohibitively expensive.

Consider welfare payments. Over the past six years, New York City has employed tougher eligibility procedures and computer cross-checking of clients to slash improper disbursements of welfare funds by almost three-fourths. Nevertheless, the tighter controls didn't prevent a 45-year-old Brooklyn housewife from being cleared in December 1979 to receive $544 a month in so-called aid to families with dependent children, half paid with federal funds.

Nine months later, when New York State auditors included the woman in a sampling of welfare clients selected for intensive review, they found that she never should have received city approval. Some of the evidence was in state income-tax records that are off-limits to city welfare workers. It showed that an $870-a-month hospital aide had filed a joint tax return with the woman from her address. The auditors concluded that they are husband and wife living under the same roof, and thus the woman isn't eligible for the payments for the three children.

Many Other Cases

Thousands of similar cases around the country suggest that, despite Washington's threat to cut funds of poor performers, states may not be able to improve much on the improper-payments rate of 8%, or about $550 million, in aid to families with dependent children.

Such gaps in the federal money machine may account for the loss of 5% or more of the $650 billion that Washington expects to spend in the current fiscal year, some here estimate.

Part of the blame can be placed on federal statutes, like the welfare law, that assign states the primary supervision of spending without ensuring that they maintain maximum vigilance against abuses. Officials who attempt to plug leaks, moreover, often find themselves hampered by conflicts and ambiguities in state and federal laws. But too often, federal bureaucrats lack the motivation to attack wasteful uses of government money, critics contend.

"All the incentives for federal officials are rigged to reward those who push money out the door, not those who try to collect money owed the government," says Wayne Granquist, a Carter appointee in the White House Office of Management and Budget who directed a study that uncovered numerous shortcomings in the way agencies handle debts owed to Uncle Sam.

As the following glimpses of waste and abuse of federal funds suggest, change won't come easily.

Uncle Sam, an Easy Touch

When the Office of Management and Budget looked into debt-collection practices at 24 federal agencies last year, officials were shocked by the findings. Of $175 billion owed Uncle Sam by all his debtors, some $25 billion represented loans that were delinquent or in default. The agency suspects that an additional $7 billion to $8 billion would be listed in those categories if the Small Business Administration and other lending agencies hadn't chosen to "reschedule" debts as an accommodation to borrowers.

"The entire system, from the time we extend credit to the time we try to collect on it, is in a state of collapse," says one staffer who worked on the survey.

The problem at the Internal Revenue Service, for example, is sheer volume; the agency finds itself overwhelmed these days by two million delinquent accounts representing $13 billion in owed taxes. Although it already has about 10,000 employes assigned to collection of back taxes, the IRS figures it would need an additional 1,500 workers to overtake the backlog.

The Department of Housing and Urban Development has another problem. Because of its inability to develop a centralized accounting procedure, despite nearly five years of effort, the headquarters frequently can't keep track of more than 2,000 HUD-guaranteed apartment-house mortgages that the department has taken over from original lenders. As of Sept. 30, 1979, 1,442 of the mortgages were delinquent, with about $500 million of principal and interest overdue, the General Accounting Office reported to Congress last year.

Checking delinquent mortgages in the files of HUD's New York regional office, the GAO found that five of them represented individual apartment buildings in Delano Village, a Harlem project. Even though Axelrod Management Co., the manager of the project, hadn't been meeting payments on the mortgages, it had withdrawn $2.7 million of rental revenues for other purposes, the GAO discovered.

Axelrod hadn't concealed its actions. Its audit reports to HUD made clear that the funds in question had been lent to Axelrod and to the estate of a partner in the projects. The independent accountant for Axelrod even noted that the handling of the funds was contrary to HUD regulations. To which the management firm replied: "This procedure facilitates the maintenance of proper books and records."

Jobless Benefits

Labor Department officials asked about abuse of unemployment payments have said that there is very little. Year after year, desk-bound federal analysts used state-supplied figures to calculate that less than 1.5% of such disbursements to unemployed workers represented overpayments due to fraud, error and other causes.

The figures would be reassuring, because states this fiscal year will pay out about $16.5 billion in basic unemployment funds mostly collected from employers, and Washington will kick in another $2.2 billion to cover 50% of supplemental claims beyond the initial 26 weeks of joblessness. But now the Labor Department has doubts about the low estimate of abuse.

A government-sponsored study of unemployed workers in Buffalo, N.Y., New York City's borough of Queens, Pittsburgh, Oklahoma City, Phoenix and Salt Lake City last year found far higher overpayment rates than Washington had suspected. The average for the six cities was 12.6%, and the figure ranged as high as 22% in one area. (The specific city results weren't disclosed.)

In well over a fourth of the overpayment cases, recipients weren't conducting "the active job search" most states require. The amount of fraud, including cases where workers on unemployment also had paying jobs, was much smaller, but it still was several times greater than the government had suspected.

If the data are confirmed by current studies, getting rid of the abuses won't be easy, officials say. "We could perfect better work-search plans (for clients) and do telephone follow-ups," Henry Haas, Arizona's unemployment administrator, concedes. However, Washington, which currently pays about $1.5 billion annually to states for the administrative costs of their unemployment programs, has been notoriously stingy with money for such purposes, Mr. Haas complains.

The Hospital-Planning Muddle

When a hospital adds beds or expensive equipment that the local community doesn't need, much of the extra cost is shouldered by federal taxpayers through hospital charges to Medicare and Medicaid patients.

So, in 1974, Congress authorized the creation of local citizen review boards to pass on such capital investments. A board rejection generally means a hospital can't get the necessary state permit to proceed with its plans.

Some boards have used their power effectively. But the system has raised blood pressure in the health-care industry by generating mountains of paper work and causing expensive delays in hospital projects. Congress probably will seek an alternative to the boards and their related health-services agencies next year when the legislation comes up for renewal.

Meantime, boards continue to struggle with decisions like the one reached last year on plans of Atlanta's Scottish Rite Hospital for Crippled Children to add a wing with 62 beds and other facilities at a cost of $11 million.

A survey conducted by the staff of the North Central Georgia Health Services Agency found pediatric beds almost 40% vacant at other area hospitals—a situation that ordinarily would call for rejection of the proposal. However, many of the Scottish Rite Masons around Georgia inundated the 25-member local board with telephone calls and letters, and some 250 showed up for the hearing on the hospital's application. Although the justification was "strained," according to one hospital planner involved in the proceedings, the board voted in favor of the proposed wing "due to the uniqueness of the applicant's facility and role."

Stockman's Hour

Reagan's Budget Aide Shaped Economic Plan With Firmness, Skill

---

Administration's Efficiency Shows It Taking Control, But Dissension May Rise

---

Easy on the Brash Brilliance

By ALBERT R. HUNT
Staff Reporter of THE WALL STREET JOURNAL
WASHINGTON—When David Stockman returned to his office last Sunday, he discovered that $4 billion had vanished since he had gone home at about 1 a.m. that day.

More precisely, Mr. Stockman, the director of the Office of Management and Budget, learned that new estimates put the savings from Ronald Reagan's budget cuts $4 billion lower than had been anticipated. He quickly went to work, finding additional savings in places as diverse as federal hiring levels and exaggerated Pentagon outlays; by day's end he had recouped almost all the $4 billion.

That's the way President Reagan's economic plan was fashioned: with determination and at times frenetic effort.

The President formally unveiled the program in an address to a joint session of Congress last night. It includes $41.4 billion in cuts from President Carter's fiscal-1982 budget, affecting dozens of major programs and requiring changes in some of the nation's most important domestic laws. It also calls for a supply-side tax cut that would reduce individual income taxes 10% a year for three years and give business more liberal depreciation write-offs.

The package was assembled with amazing speed and skill. The chief architect was Mr. Stockman, until recently a Michigan Congressman and now, working 19 hours a day, the 34-year-old *Wunderkind* of the Reagan administration.

Congressional Battle Ahead

Although the critical battle to win congressional approval lies ahead, the way the economic package was put together provides an insight into the early workings of the Reagan administration. In some ways, it suggests that this administration is better prepared than most to grab the reins of power; at the same time, there are signals of internal troubles ahead. The preliminary readings:

—Unmistakable evidence that Mr. Reagan is committed to his economic plan and willing to stand some political heat. With rare exceptions, the President stuck with the budget-cut proposals during last week's final review sessions; a few times, he even made deeper cuts.

—Indications that Mr. Stockman combines his unquestioned ability on issues with more political sensitivity and flexibility than critics expected. Some top officials, however, resent Mr. Stockman's pivotal role; when the young budget chief was late for the official Cabinet portrait, the air was full of gallows humor about his absence.

—A serious doubt about how well-equipped the Treasury is to do its part in the coming economic-policy struggle. Treasury Secretary Donald Regan is unversed in the ways of Washington.

—The emergence among the Reagan economic advisers of three distinct factions: the supply-side tax cutters; the monetarists, who stress money-supply control, and the more orthodox conservatives.

Shortly after he was named OMB director in mid-December, Mr. Stockman, taking his cue from Mr. Reagan, decided he must assail a wide range of politically sensitive programs. These included certain benefits paid through Social Security, food stamps, trade adjustment assistance and unemployment compensation. It was decided, though, to spare important sacred cows —general Social Security cost-of-living increases, Medicare and veterans' benefits—for fear of storms of protest from huge constituencies.

The planners made a calculated effort to avoid the appearance that fiscal frugality was focused on the poor. Thus, a few hours before Rep. Jack Kemp of New York went on the "Meet the Press" TV interview show, Mr. Stockman called to urge his friend to emphasize the cutbacks in benefits to business, such as synthetic-fuels subsidies and Export-Import Bank loans; the lawmaker made this point. It's true that a Stockman proposal to go after a few tax "loopholes," such as the oil-depletion allowance, was vetoed by the President. The budget chief did, however, push through substantial increases in users' fees, including a proposal to more than double fees paid by corporate jets.

The "Dunkirk Memo"

The initial working papers included the much-publicized "Dunkirk memo" of Messrs. Stockman and Kemp, lists of possible budget cuts drawn up by Caspar Weinberger (now Defense Secretary), and recommendations from Senate Budget Committee Chairman Pete Domenici of New Mexico.

By the turn of the year, Mr. Stockman, longtime Reagan adviser Martin Anderson and Alan Greenspan, chief economic adviser under President Ford, were shaping specific spending and tax cuts. They, along with presidential aides Edwin Meese and James Baker and Treasury Secretary-designee Regan, met with the President-elect in Washington on Jan. 7 and were given the green light to keep cutting.

At first Mr. Stockman envisioned a blitz in which the economic package would be tied to the needed early increase in the national-debt ceiling. But in a strategy session at Senate Majority Leader Howard Baker's Washington home, Sen. Baker warned against the Stockman idea: "You'll pick up all the enemies of (increasing) the debt ceiling without gaining any new friends." And the White House decided to hold off until mid-February.

The meeting at Sen. Baker's house was the first of a half-dozen planning sessions involving Mr. Stockman, other top administration figures, the Senate leader and other influential GOP Senators, including Finance Committee Chairman Robert Dole of Kansas and Sen. Domenici. At these meetings the emerging proposals were aired throughly, giving the lawmakers a genuine sense of participation. For example, Sen. Dole helped persuade Mr. Stockman to shrink the food-stamp cut for fiscal 1982 to about $1.8 billion from the more than $2.5 billion originally planned.

Mr. Stockman, whose brash brilliance often rankled his senior colleagues in the House, displayed political sensitivity in his dealings with Sen. Baker. One project he decided not to tackle was the Clinch River breeder reactor in Tennessee. "Howard Baker's active support is essential," he told associates. "If he doesn't lead with gusto and conviction, this won't work."

And Mr. Stockman made a special trip to the majority leader's office to inform him of a proposal to curb the Tennessee Valley Authority's loan activities. The Tennessee Republican replied, "I'm willing to listen but I'm not prepared yet to agree." But he was impressed with the young budget director's knowledge and forthrightness.

Mr. Stockman also took care to consult New York's Rep. Barber Conable, the ranking Republican on the House Ways and Means Committee. Nor did the budget chief ignore Democrats; some of the House Democratic leaders, who oppose many budget cuts, were impressed when Mr. Stockman, without the usual cadre of aides, came to give them a detailed budget briefing a few weeks ago.

"I'm Looking for $50 Billion"

In late January the budget planners began meeting with each Cabinet member. Each Secretary would sit on one side of the green-covered oblong table in the OMB conference room, with the budget working group on the other. Mr. Stockman set the tone for each session: "I'm looking for $50

billion of savings in fiscal 1982 and up to $100 billion by fiscal 1986," he said. "I can't do that without your help."

The Cabinet officers often were overwhelmed by the case for cutbacks. When Energy Secretary James Edwards insisted that the department's direct aid for synthetic-fuels projects was necessary to counter the OPEC oil cartel, Mr. Anderson and chief presidential economic adviser Murray Weidenbaum ridiculed that argument; a ruffled Mr. Edwards had to concede. Similarly, when Commerce Secretary Malcolm Baldrige fought the Stockman proposal to slash Export-Import Bank loans and subsidies, Deputy Treasury Secretary Tim McNamar tossed out a sheet of paper showing that last year more than two-thirds of the benefits went to seven large corporations, with Boeing Co. alone getting 27%. (Another supporter of this cutback was Mr. Weidenbaum, who used to be Boeing's chief economist.)

Mr. Stockman lost some battles, however. He supported a plan to assign the strategic petroleum reserve to a government corporation that would issue oil bonds. But that was beaten back when the Treasury complained it would be a "gimmick."

Health and Human Services Secretary Richard Schweiker staved off both proposed cuts for the National Institutes of Health and suggestions to change the early-retirement option in the Social Security program. And Transportation Secretary Drew Lewis averted planned reductions in subsidies for Northeast rail service when he warned, "If we do this, a freight train is going to collide with an Amtrak passenger train someday and 350 people will be killed."

Both these department heads, however, did take big cuts—Mr. Schweiker in Medicaid and Mr. Lewis in subsidies for mass transit and funds for highway construction.

Staged "Table Pounding"

The most controversial session was with the State Department, which had leaked Mr. Stockman's proposal to slice $2.6 billion from the Carter foreign-aid budget in an attempt to block the cuts. Both sides were braced for a major confrontation Jan. 31, but Secretary of State Alexander Haig and Mr. Stockman met beforehand and agreed they would try to settle the dispute later—although each could "pound on the table" to placate his constituency at that day's meeting.

The bargaining then began, with the State Department making two offers and the budget office coming back with three counteroffers. In the end they agreed on a cut of $1.8 billion from the proposed fiscal-1982 budget.

The final sessions with the President went surprisingly well, participants say. White House Counselor Meese and Chief of Staff James Baker offered support for the Stockman plans. One of the very few cuts the President rejected was in merchant-marine subsidies, vetoed on national-security grounds.

At the same time, a few compromises were made. Housing and Urban Development Secretary Samuel Pierce, with Mr. Meese's support and over Mr. Stockman's objections, won milder cuts in Urban Development Action Grants but was thwarted in an effort to get back $300 million for public-housing modernization.

In a few areas, Mr. Reagan applied the knife a little more deeply. Under the Stockman proposal, some 40 social- and health-services grants were to be combined and financed at 80% of the level proposed by Mr. Carter; President Reagan cut this to 75%. And he agreed to a proposal to save money by calculating federal retirees' cost-of-living benefits only once a year, abandoning a campaign pledge to continue calculating them twice a year.

"We won't leave you out there alone, Dave," the President jested at the end of the long sessions. "We'll all come to the hanging."

The assembling of the tax part of the package didn't go as smoothly. But it provided insights into Mr. Reagan's philosophy and method. The President never wavered from his commitment to the 30% individual tax cut, and only reluctantly agreed, at Mr. Stockman's urgings, to postponing the effective date to July 1. Philosophically, he was attracted to the proposal to lower the maximum tax on "unearned," or investment, income to 50% from 70%, but his political advisers warned it would look like a giveaway to the rich. When Mr. Anderson, the presidential aide, said Mr. Reagan had never discussed the idea during the campaign, the President decided against it.

When Mr. Stockman suggested that it might be politically advantageous to slash a few tax preferences for the wealthy, such as the oil-depletion allowance, the President vehemently dissented. But he easily accepted ideas increasing user taxes on barges and corporate jets. Such levies, the President remarked, are "the most ideal tax available."

One of the most important struggles arose over whether to send Congress one tax bill or two. Budget Director Stockman and GOP congressional tax-writers Dole and Conable argued for one major bill; otherwise, they contended, the Democrats would seize the initiative by loading up the first bill with such popular measures as ending the tax penalty on married couples that have two incomes—and the Republicans would be on the defensive.

But the Treasury fought hard for first sending up one slimmed-down bill, consisting only of the 30% individual income-tax cuts and liberalized depreciation for business. It was essential, the argument went, to "highlight" these supply-side tax cuts; other tax-relief measures would be included in a second Reagan bill. Last week Rep. Conable went to the Treasury to try to persuade Secretary Regan to change his two-bill strategy; he was unsuccessful, but he then argued, with some success, "at least then spell out what's going to be in the second bill."

A Major Error?

With Mr. Stockman preoccupied with other fights, the Treasury won the two-bill approach. It's almost certain, however, that congressional tax-writers will push one bigger bill instead. Some Reagan strategists fear they may have made a major tactical error.

Perhaps the most heated struggle of all was fought over the administration's economic assumptions. The supply-siders, led by Treasury Under Secretary Norman Ture, forcefully argued that the Reagan package would result in strong economic expansion and sharply lower inflation. The monetarists, led by Treasury Under Secretary Beryl Sprinkel, advocate more moderate money-supply growth and thus a lower projection for total national output.

In the middle were Mr. Weidenbaum and Alan Greenspan, an increasingly important outside adviser who sat through several high-level sessions. They argued that the economic goals had to be credible. "If the debate focuses on the economic assumptions," Mr. Greenspan contended, "then we've taken attention away from the budget fight and lost the war."

The economic strategists held no fewer than four "final" meetings on the economic assumptions, and the debates were sharp. "It's like two football coaches for the same team," Mr. Stockman noted at one stage. "One favors a high-scoring offense and the other a low-scoring defense."

When the supply-side economic model Mr. Stockman brought in from Claremont College cranked out a picture of rapid growth and inflation of less than 4% by 1985, Mr. Ture was delighted. But Mr. Weidenbaum, who would have to defend the projections, balked. A further complication arose during one session when Treasury Secretary Regan complained that his deputies hadn't informed him of the estimates. Finally, on Feb. 7 Mr. Stockman and Mr. Weidenbaum made a "dictatorial decision": If the Reagan program is enacted, there will be steady growth and inflation will drop to 5.2% by 1985. The others were given two hours to sign on; they did so, but some ill feeling lingered.

Mr. Stockman is drawing fire on other counts. Some supply-siders think their old ally hasn't been sufficiently vigorous in emphasizing tax cuts. "I was a budget-cutter before I was a tax-cutter," he tells them. And some Cabinet members privately complain about what one sarcastically calls "The David Stockman Show."

But, at least for now, the young budget director appears to rate high with Mr. Reagan. "The President really is enraptured by Stockman's brains and energy," says one Reagan confidant. After last week's budget reviews, a top presidential aide joked to his boss, "Mr. President, Stockman is out-Reaganing Reagan." The President smiled approvingly.

Top Reagan Talent Scout Discovers Political Factor in Selection Process

By Timothy D. Schellhardt

Staff Reporter of The Wall Street Journal

WASHINGTON — E. Pendleton James, Ronald Reagan's chief talent scout, was eating breakfast in the White House mess recently when presidential political adviser Lyn Nofziger rushed in.

"Why are you considering this guy?" Mr. Nofziger yelled, waving a personnel clearance paper. "He's a Democrat!"

"That's why I ran it by you in the first place," Mr. James answered matter-of-factly. "To find out about these things."

So one prospective Reagan appointment fell through. For Pen James, it was yet another lesson in the difference between executive head-hunting for business and public-service screening in the White House. Mr. James, 50 years old, a professional executive recruiter more at home in his old job than in his new one, acknowledges that the political leanings of potential presidential appointees weigh much heavier than the politics of business job-seekers. But even having the "right" politics doesn't guarantee admission to high government rank.

No to Carter Man

For example, Mr. James had expected no trouble with his choice for a top sub-Cabinet post. Although the candidate had held a job in the Carter administration, he shared President Reagan's conservative philosophy and had strong recommendations from several influential Reagan advisers. But the President himself ruled out the Carter holdover, and Mr. James had to come up with another candidate.

Mr. James still has headaches in trying to finish filling 200 top jobs in the adminis-

E. Pendleton James

tration and then in selecting a larger batch of lower-level political appointees. Although the top spots are almost all filled—17 people were nominated on Tuesday and a few more yesterday—he has yet to make a lot of progress in middle-management jobs, such as deputy assistant secretaries and regional administrators.

His critics contend that Mr. James has favored candidates with Ivy League credentials, overlooked women and minorities, and moved too slowly in filling jobs. "You can count on Pen to dot every i and cross every t to make sure an appointee's papers are in order, and that's fine in the private sector," an administration official says. "But we've got to get this administration rolling, and he's just taking too long."

Mr. James says that in his Los Angeles firm of Pen James Associates Inc. he often did take three months or longer to fill positions in private business. But he says that "you don't have that luxury in government. The time constraint on filling senior-level executive spots is much narrower." To hire faster, Mr. James has employed a staff of 50. He and his staff rely on five main criteria in evaluating candidates: philosophical commitment to the President's policy, integrity, competence, "toughness," and team spirit.

The Trent Case

Technical skills and knowledge, though often important in business, are less important in some government jobs, Mr. James says. As an example, he cites the case of Darrell Trent, deputy secretary of transportation, who lacks any special experience in that field. Mr. Trent seems to seek political power as much as anything else.

The Republican from Kansas served in the Nixon administration, and then worked at Stanford University's Hoover Institution on War, Revolution and Peace, a conservative think-tank, while waiting for a Reagan rise to power. Mr. Trent also worked in the 1980 campaign. His business experience years ago consisted mainly of property management and development.

"Darrell probably doesn't know any more about the highway system than I do," Mr. James says. But he says Mr. Trent has "a proven ability to develop strategy and to conceptualize, and he's very knowledgeable about the President's objectives and philosophy. As a result, he's the No. 2 guy at transportation."

The exercise of power and the chance to influence policy appear to attract candidates as much as anything else, although Mr. James puts it more delicately. He talks about "the satisfaction that you work in an administration you believe in" and calls government service a "broadening, stretching opportunity" that offers insights into "how government works compared to how you thought it works."

Otherwise, he says, government jobs offer little. "There are no perks you can offer," he says. "All you can promise are long hours, lots of frustrations, tension, and pressures."

For those reasons or others, some candidates have turned down administration jobs. Agriculture Secretary John Block and President Reagan himself tried to persuade a 35-year-old black executive to take an important sub-Cabinet job, but the candidate said he just couldn't leave his own business.

White House counsel Fred Fielding says others have turned down offers because of ethics-in-government law. One prospect rejected a job because to take it would have jeopardized a business partnership; restrictions prohibit a government official from continuing such an outside business arrangement. A wealthy candidate for another job turned it down because he feared that financial disclosure might tempt kidnappers, Mr. Fielding says.

Two-career married couples create problems, too. Mr. James has been trying to recruit a female executive, but she has asked him to find a job for her husband in Washington, too. Mr. James is trying.

Mr. James, who also served as a personnel recruiter in the Nixon administration, dismisses complaints that he's overlooked women and minorities. "It's unfair to compare our record after one month with Jimmy Carter's after four years," he says. "After six months, look at the footprints we're leaving. If there isn't a fair representation of blacks, women and minorities by then, we're not doing our jobs."

Thinking Things Over
——By Vermont Royster——

Press Conferences

President Reagan is a bold man indeed. Never mind that he's whacking away at the government's budget and its octopus arms. Now he's trying to reshape White House press conferences.

Mr. Reagan wants them to be less like free-for-alls in a Roman arena. So he's experimenting with various schemes, including even a lottery, to have an orderly way for reporters to put their questions. At the very least he'd like a little decorum at these media rites.

I wish him luck. Something needs to be done if White House press conferences are to serve a purpose other than displaying a President's grace under pressure, or lack of it, before a mob. That has its uses but it isn't what a press conference ought to be, an occasion for press and Presidents to have an orderly two-way communication so that people are better informed about their government.

* * *

Some nostalgia, I must confess, fathers my wish. My first presidential press conference was back in 1936, in a different time and clime, when I was a young reporter for The Wall Street Journal. I was there mainly out of brash curiosity since the conference was actually covered by Bernard Kilgore, then chief of our Washington bureau.

But I remember there were only about 30 reporters present and the conference itself could be held in the Oval Office, the reporters gathering around President Roosevelt's desk. I remember too that as I entered the West Wing there was just a tiny press room to the right, and to the left two small offices, one for Steve Early, the press secretary, the other for Marvin McIntyre, appointments secretary and general factotum. That was all there was to the President's Executive Office. Or to the press corps assembly.

There were no radio mikes, no winking TV cameras to make everyone feel "on stage." When the President spoke, his words were not beyond recall or correction since he couldn't be quoted directly. As for the questions, reporters were unidentified, and without pride in authorship one could follow up another's question. It was like a conversation in a living room.

This informality didn't alter the fact that, then as now, there was fencing between President and press, the one trying to yield no more information than he intended, the other probing for ways to break through the shield. But it was all done quietly, and politely.

I needn't tell the reader all is different today. A President no longer sits behind his desk; he needs a podium to face a hall jammed with reporters. Mikes and cameras abound. The press conference has become a show-biz spectacular.

If there's a gain in that people can see their President in action, there's a loss in his freedom to speak frankly. When words once spoken are irretrievable, he must live in constant fear of a slip-of-the-tongue and be tempted to say no more than could as well be put in a press release. That loss of freedom is a loss to the President, to the press and ultimately to the public.

The worst of the change though, at least to me, has been the loss of civility, of simple good manners.

With so many voices clamoring for the President's attention (and a chance to be glimpsed on TV) recent press conferences have often degenerated into shouting matches that make me cringe. Because the loudest voice doesn't necessarily belong to the most intelligent questioner, many questions are trivial or even stupid. And in this setting there's no defense against stupidity. On camera reporters won't quietly tell a colleague to shut up; a President won't suggest, as FDR didn't hesitate to do, that a dumb questioner go sit in the dunce corner.

* * *

Much of this change is unavoidable. The sheer size of the Washington press corps today carries its own imperative; intimacy between the President and the press is forever lost. Some of it lies in the residue of aggressiveness bordering on arrogance within the press that came with Vietnam and Watergate.

But some of it, I think, is the fault of recent Presidents. Like teachers in unruly classrooms they've lacked the presence— or the courage — to maintain decorum. They've also erred, perhaps out of fright, by holding too few press conferences.

When the conferences are separated by weeks the pressure of unanswered questions builds up and reporters feel they must seize the day. With two each week, FDR's custom until the war, they become routine. Pressure for both attendance and questions drops. If nothing else, the atmosphere becomes less tense.

It's not possible to go backwards, to shrink the size of the press corps, to banish the mikes and cameras. The television spectacular is here to stay. There ought to be some way, though, to make the conferences more orderly so they can fulfill their prime function of providing a public and civilized discussion with a President on public questions.

President Reagan seems at least brave enough to try. So far the press has at least accepted his efforts with good humor. How long that will last, I don't know.

Few of us in the press are over-endowed with humility. All are competitive by nature and many have a low flash point. Good manners aren't required by the Constitution. It may not be long before the press grows restive under the restrictions of a lottery as to who can question or of being asked to sit like schoolchildren raising their hands, and not their voices, to gain attention.

But it isn't nostalgia alone that makes me hope for more civility between Presidents and the press. We profit nothing from the want of it.

---

57   *July 14, 1981*

Rating Reagan

For First Six Months, President Gets A-Plus For Economic Efforts

But a Global Strategy Fails To Emerge, and Cabinet Posts a Spotty Record

Focus: One Ball at a Time

WASHINGTON—When the talk at White House meetings turns to his economic package, President Reagan listens closely, often interrupting to offer observations or suggestions. "He's in the thick of things," declares a presidential assistant.

But when the talk turns to foreign policy, "Well . . . ah . . . he often yawns," discloses another lieutenant.

The striking contrast tells a lot about Ronald Reagan's first half-year in office. As

> *This article was prepared by Wall Street Journal staff reporters Timothy D. Schellhardt, Albert R. Hunt and Gerald F. Seib.*

the administration approaches its six-month birthday next Monday, the President is on the verge of receiving handsome gifts: Final congressional approval of his far-reaching budget cutbacks is almost certain, and acceptance of most of his tax-cut proposals is likely.

Thus, in evaluating the administration's record, friend and foe alike credit the White House with extraordinary success on the economic front. "We're ahead of schedule," gloats presidential counselor Edwin Meese. "I have to admit it," acknowledges liberal Rep. Don Edwards, a California Democrat. "He's certainly been very skillful so far."

Even top Reagan aides, however, turn defensive when it comes to foreign policy—explaining why they haven't spelled out their objectives. "We purposely haven't hyped our foreign policy," contends Mr. Meese. "We didn't want to take a lot of public attention away from our economic package."

Lacking a Global Strategy

In contrast to Mr. Reagan's clear-cut goals in domestic economic policy, a comprehensive global strategy still appears to be lacking. The Reagan foreign-policy team continues to suffer from incessant infighting, with Secretary of State Alexander Haig usually at the center of controversy, and it has produced a series of contradictory or ill-defined policy pronouncements. Other than demonstrating a desire to check Soviet expansion, this administration mainly has reacted, often in a confusing fashion, to world events.

"You don't sense any Reagan objectives in foreign policy other than to contain the Communist horde," maintains Edwin Hargrove, a University of North Carolina specialist on the presidency. And a pro-Reagan Republican Senator muses, "We all can be thankful there hasn't been any real foreign-policy crisis yet."

Still, the Reaganites believe this problem isn't clearly perceived yet by the public or the politicians. So, with all the success on the economic front, they are delighted with the President's first half-year. "We'll certainly take another six months like the first six," exclaims James Baker, the White House chief of staff.

The Achievements

The achievements, they say, go beyond the tax and spending areas. Administration officials feel they have started a sweeping cutback of federal regulations and have at least laid the groundwork for turning back a lot of responsibilities to state and local governments.

And despite a slow start in filling high posts, the President's people generally are pleased with his appointments. They feel they got a clear plus with last week's nomination of Arizona Judge Sandra O'Connor to be the first woman on the Supreme Court. Although this selection has been criticized by some right-wingers and anti-abortionists, it has won wide praise, and Mrs. O'Connor is expected to be confirmed easily. "This is a politically brilliant choice," declares the Senate Democratic whip, Alan Cranston of California.

Moreover, the administration's political skill and the President's strong personal appeal still win many favorable comparisons with the record of Jimmy Carter. The likeable 70-year-old Chief Executive, polls show, is far more popular than many of his programs; a major source of this strength, many politicians believe, was his remarkable behavior and speedy recovery from the March 30 assassination attempt. "He came across as so courageous and warm," notes one liberal Senate Democrat. "If it weren't for that, the President would be in a lot more trouble now."

The Troika at Work

Another important plus is that, by all accounts, the troika of top White House aides—Messrs. Baker and Meese and the deputy chief of staff, Michael Deaver—are working remarkably well together. "I'm still not sure how long it can last," says another White House aide, "but so far there has been very little friction at the top."

All the accomplishments have camouflaged what some administration stalwarts and may outsiders believe are serious weaknesses in the Reagan operation. Although no one doubts that the top team performs smoothly when focusing on one basic issue like the economy, the White House often stumbles when other matters arise.

For instance, even top Reagan aides acknowledge that the administration's proposed cutbacks on Social Security benefits were ill-conceived and hastily presented; pollsters say this misstep has cost the President politically. And no one is pleased with the clumsy manner in which the administration has handled its plan to sell sophisticated AWACS radar planes to Saudi Arabia.

"The problem with Jimmy Carter was that he always had about 27 balls in the air at once and couldn't pick priorities," says one veteran Washington politician. "This group has learned that lesson. But they only seem to be able to focus on one ball at a time. Unfortunately, you usually don't have that sort of luxury, and as time goes on, this is going to be an increasing problem for them."

Already, Mr. Reagan's much-touted system of Cabinet government appears to be falling short. A few Cabinet members get high grades, but the total performance is spotty, White House aides concede. Thus, more and more major decisions end up in the White House.

But, except for David Stockman's solid budget office, the White House team hasn't yet got its act together to deal effectively with the agenda ahead. Or so fear observers both inside and outside. The domestic-policy staff, headed by longtime Reagan adviser Martin Anderson, is considered weak and disorganized. Mr. Anderson isn't interested "in process, just access," one colleague says. Similarly, the national-security staff gets low ratings; critics charge that Richard Allen, its chief, is a poor administrator and may be in over his head.

The President's "failure to understand the machinery of government and to staff up to master it (may) bring down his administration," argues political scientist Walter Williams, a public-policy and management expert at the University of Washington. Mr. Williams praises budget chief Stockman's office but contends that the national-security staff is "extremely weak" and the domestic-policy outfit "almost as grim."

These two groups will be severely tested in the months ahead. On the national-security side, the President soon must decide on how to base the MX missile, whether to build a B1 bomber and what to do about nuclear nonproliferation. But the diciest item of all may be how to win congressional clearance for selling the radar planes to the Saudis; already, a majority of both houses have expressed opposition to any such sale.

On the domestic side, the Reagan White House faces difficult choices on social issues—abortion, private-school aid, public-school prayer—pressed by the Moral Majority. In addition, hard decisions must be made on topics as diverse as extension of the Voting Rights Act, revision of the Clean Air Act, and policies on telecommunications and immigration.

President Reagan's dealings with Congress win praise from lawmakers, but some think the effectiveness may be exaggerated. Much of the President's success is attributable to his personal charm, a commodity that may be stretched thin as more issues pile up. And although top Reagan lobbyist Max Friedersdorf looks good compared with President Carter's man, Frank Moore, the Reagan lobbying team has been slow to react to trouble spots, such as congressional protests against Social Security cuts and the nomination of Ernest Lefever as human-rights chief. (Mr. Lefever withdrew after being overwhelmingly rejected by the Senate Foreign Relations Committee.)

Furthermore, the President's influence on Capitol Hill may diminish when the remarkable string of budget cutbacks he is pushing through takes effect. Some critics already see the stirrings of a backlash among affected interest groups. "He's beginning to lose one segment after another—the elderly with his Medicare and Social Security cuts, Hispanics and blacks, educators and even scientists," asserts Democratic Rep. Edwards.

Foreign Policy

Even a number of congressional Republicans fear the cutbacks may produce a sharp anti-Reagan turn. The key may be whether the economy shows gradual improvement—further easing of inflation, a drop in interest rates and a renewed increase in employment. "As long as things generally are going well economically, the country will tolerate small imperfections," argues John Sears, Mr. Reagan's former campaign manager and one of the capital's shrewdest political analysts. "But change the perception that things aren't going well in the economy, and it's a different ball game entirely."

Even if the economy holds up, though, the administration has to straighten out its foreign-policy act, some Reagan loyalists concede. Contradictions abound: The President doesn't like the Soviets, but he lifted the grain embargo; he emphasizes his friendship for Taiwan but took the historic step of offering to sell arms to Communist China; the administration once played up the Communist-inspired threat to El Salvador, but then played it down amid complaints that all the talk was interfering with its economic goals and that many of the claims were exaggerated.

Most of all, critics say, Mr. Reagan hasn't shown a coherent view of the world. On some issues he has avoided clarifying his views by postponing decisions. The administration put off a resumption of the Middle East peace-seeking process until after the Israeli elections last month. New strategic arms-limitation talks with Russia won't begin before next year.

In other instances, the administration merely has responded to events. It sent Philip Habib to the Middle East to mediate a threatened war over the Syrian missiles in Lebanon and agreed to open talks on European nuclear arms in response to intense pressure from U.S. allies.

Personal conflicts haven't helped matters. Secretary of State Haig has alienated White House aides with his abrasive style and has disagreed frequently on tactics with Mr. Reagan's longtime friend, Defense Secretary Caspar Weinberger. As a result, the administration that promised to speak with one voice on foreign affairs often speaks in confusing and even contradictory voices. Rumors persist that Mr. Haig will be out by the end of the year (the hottest rumored replacement is United Nations Ambassador Jeane Kirkpatrick), but White House aides repeatedly deny any such plan.

A Foreign-Policy Speech

Sensitive to charges that the President lacks a comprehensive view of the world, aides insist he has broader ideas that will become clearer, perhaps in an oft-postponed foreign-policy speech in the next few months.

In any event, Mr. Reagan is going to have to start devoting more of his attention to foreign policy. Immediately ahead are the seven-nation economic summit in Canada next week, meetings here with Anwar Sadat of Egypt next month and with Israel's Menachem Begin in September, and a North-South meeting in Mexico in October.

Even if he can improve his showing in the international sphere, the President may find himself with less than heroic standing in the public's eyes. Although polls show that hard-core support for Mr. Reagan and his programs is more solid than that enjoyed by his predecessor, it is also true that four years ago today President Carter's ratings in the polls and the public's general optimism about the nation's future were slightly higher than comparable showings for the Reagan administration now.

"President Reagan has become a 'mortal' versus an 'immortal' President," says Democratic polltaker Peter Hart. "And that's a big difference" from several months ago.

The Congress

Running Scared

Democratic Chiefs Are GOP's Prime Targets In Congressional Races

Ullman, Udall in Jeopardy, Wright Is Hard-Pressed; AMA Angers a Surgeon

Is God on Brademas's Side?

By DENNIS FARNEY
Staff Reporter of THE WALL STREET JOURNAL

FORT WORTH, Texas—"My plea is that of the well-known woodsman who was treed by a bruin. 'Lord, if you can't help *me,* just please don't help that bear.' "

Thus ended a plaintive letter last month from Jim Wright, the second-ranking House Democrat, to business-oriented campaign contributors supporting his Republican opponent. The letter showed how seriously the powerful Texan is taking his reelection race, his toughest in 26 years in Congress.

For if Majority Leader Wright hasn't exactly been treed, he has certainly been jolted this fall by a made-in-Washington Republican strategy with an unusual twist. Its targets are the House Democrats who theoretically ought to be the least vulnerable to defeat on Nov. 4: House leaders and longtime committee chairmen.

"Republicans are practicing, in a little more subtle form, the same thing that Abbie Hoffman practiced on the streets in 1968," fumes Mr. Wright, speaking both of the effort to unseat him and of increasing Republican obstructionism on the House floor in Washington. "It's the politics of disruption—guerrilla warfare."

Republicans, who have recruited attractive, well-financed challengers to a dozen senior Democrats,

Rep. Jim Wright

see things differently, of course. "If congressional leaders aren't responsible for the shape we're in, then who the hell is?" demands Georgia Rep. Newt Gingrich, a young fire-breather. The GOP is gambling a bundle that voters feel the same way. It is pouring $8.5 million into a national TV ad campaign directed against Democratic domination of Congress and particularly against the congressional leadership.

"Leaders may be easier to defeat than followers," reasons Michigan Rep. Guy Vander Jagt, chairman of the National Republican Congressional Committee. "Incumbent Democrats are geniuses at running against their own record and their own Congress, but it's easier to hang Congress around leaders' necks."

Some May Fall

Aiding the GOP effort are ultraconservative New Right groups, which aim to sow confusion in Democratic ranks and to intimidate younger Democratic Congressmen by toppling their leaders. "Damaging the leadership of the House is one of our top priorities this year," says Paul Weyrich, director of the Washington-based Committee for the Survival of a Free Congress. "Jim Wright, for example, has played an incredibly important role in keeping moderate and conservative Democrats in line. Defeating him would free up a lot of Democrats to go their own way."

Majority Leader Wright, whose position makes him the odds-on favorite to become Speaker of the House when Thomas P. O'Neill retires, is expected to survive his challenge from the GOP's Jim Bradshaw, a former mayor pro tem of Fort Worth. But his majority will surely be much narrower than the 68% he rolled up against a weaker opponent in 1978.

Other top Democrats may not be so fortunate. Given the scope of the GOP effort and the closeness of many of these races, it is almost certain that at least a few of the most powerful Democrats in the House will go down on Nov. 4.

Rep. John Brademas

One of the most vulnerable is the Democrats' third-ranking House leader, Majority Whip John Brademas of Indiana. Mr. Brademas, an 11-term liberal from the South Bend area, is locked in a tight race with John Hiler, 27, a conservative businessman making his first try for elective office. Republican polls show Mr. Hiler pulling ahead; Brademas supporters concede that the race is extremely close. "Three weeks ago things looked bad, very bad, but now I think John's ahead, just a fraction," says one.

Democrat Brademas is bedeviled by unemployment ranging between 10% and 15% in the counties of his marginally Democratic district, which has been hurt by the slumping market for automotive parts and recreational vehicles. But the Congressman concedes that another liability is his leadership position, which makes him a lightning rod for public dissatisfaction with Congress generally.

"Politically, I made a big decision being whip," he told the South Bend Rotary Club the other day. "I could have stayed in my committee, done my constituent work and come back every two years and complained about the rest of Congress. Well, I decided to take on the responsibility, although it often meant more political negatives than pluses."

Similarly, a committee chairmanship, once a near-guarantee of reelection, has become a mixed blessing today, for chairmen are often compelled to support "national" measures that aren't popular in their own districts. This fall, six House chairmen are embroiled in close races that could go either way.

The most vulnerable appears to be California's Harold Johnson, who heads the Public Works Committee. At 72, an unflamboyant product of an earlier political era, Rep. Johnson may have grown dangerously complacent. This year, Republican challenger Eugene Chappie is giving him his first tough race in a decade or more, and Democrats fear he may go under.

Support for "national" controversial measures has hurt three better-known and more prestigious chairmen. Republicans, waging aggressive campaigns against all three, would score a major coup by unseating even one.

On paper, the most vulnerable of the three is Interior Committee Chairman Morris Udall, a liberal environmentalist in a Tucson, Ariz., district that is growing more conservative. Mr. Udall, who was hurt in the district by his 1976 presidential campaign, won with less than 53% of the vote in 1978. Now he's trying to survive a full-dress attack by developer Richard Huff. The Republican has raised some of his $500,000 campaign war chest from far-off Alaskans enraged by Mr. Udall's sponsorship of the Alaska parkland bill that would bar development of millions of acres.

"It's ironic," muses Mr. Udall. "The Congressional Fellows Association gives me an award as 'Legislator of the Year,' my colleagues (in a magazine poll) call me the second-most-respected guy in the House. And here I am, in trouble." By hitting back hard at his opponent, Mr. Udall has opened up better than a 10-point lead according to his own polls. But the race has been complicated by his surprise disclosure last week that he suffers from a mild case of Parkinson's disease, a nerve disorder.

In Oregon, Ways and Means Committee Chairman Al Ullman, hurt by his suggestion (since retracted) that Congress might study imposing a kind of national sales tax, is pressed hard by Republican Denny Smith, a newspaper publisher. Mr. Ullman leads in the polls, but his camp worries about a huge undecided vote, unusual for so late in the campaign. And in Washington state, Agriculture Committee Chairman Thomas Foley, whose eastern Washington district is the state's most conservative, leads GOP challenger John Sonneland by 10 points in Sonneland polls.

Abscam Troubles

More vulnerable, Republican strategists think, are two chairmen indicted in the congressional Abscam scandal. They are New York's John Murphy, who heads the Merchant Marine Committee, and New Jersey's Frank Thompson, an ally of organized labor who heads the House Administration Committee.

Finally, Republicans have high hopes of unseating three senior Democrats who wield great influence on House legislation.

In California, 20-year veteran James Corman, a staunch liberal and the House's foremost advocate of national health insurance, is in the fight of his life against Republican Bobbi Fiedler, an anti-busing activist in a district roiled by busing. In Texas, Bob Eckhardt, a seven-term veteran and foe of the oil companies, may be in trouble against Republican Jack Fields, who is heavily outspending him. And in normally Democratic Toledo, Ohio, Republicans insist they have a chance of upsetting Thomas Ashley, a 13-term authority on urban and energy policies.

This fall's attack on entrenched Democratic leaders represents a decided change in strategy for Republicans, still trying to recover from a disastrous 43-seat loss in the post-Watergate election of 1974. In 1976, the GOP strove mightily to defeat the freshman "Watergate babies," but managed to beat only two of the 78 seeking reelection. In 1978, Republicans focused more on "open seats"—those being vacated by departing incumbents—but the results were still disappointing: a net gain of only 11 seats.

This year, only the most optimistic Republican strategists expect the party to return to its pre-Watergate House strength, which would require a net gain of 33 seats. (A more typical projection is 25 seats; Democrats concede they'll likely lose 20 seats or more.) But unseating some big-name Democratic leaders would give the party plenty to cheer about—and make Democratic followers more cautious in the next Congress.

For all the vulnerabilities that the leaders have, however, running against them isn't easy.

Most of the Democrats facing serious challenges are superb campaigners. Arizona's Mo Udall, a man with a Will Rogers brand of humor, "comes back here, strokes his chin, tells funny stories and quotes Abraham Lincoln," grouses opponent Richard Huff. "It's hard to get people to focus on his voting record."

Moreover, the veteran incumbents all have friends in high places—in the case of Indiana Rep. Brademas maybe the highest place of all. At a Brademas fund-raising event earlier this year, Notre Dame's president, Father Theodore Hesburgh, carefully pointed out that he never endorses political candidates. But then, noted the South Bend Tribune, "in a special prayer (he) specifically asked God to help Brademas."

Mistakes of Inexperience

In Washington state, Agriculture Committee Chairman Foley, a moderate, was recently endorsed by the American Medical Association—a development that stunned opponent Sonneland, who is a surgeon. "I'll never send the AMA another check," he vows. (Mr. Foley voted against President Carter's hospital-cost-control proposal, which the AMA opposed.)

Two days after the AMA endorsement, the White House announced that the Chinese may soon be buying millions of tons of Washington state wheat—and Mr. Foley cheerfully showed up on local television to reap some of the credit.

The Republican challengers are mostly political neophytes. Although they all get a lot of coaching from Rep. Vander Jagt's campaign committee in Washington—their campaigns sound so similar that Democrats label them "Vander Jagt's clones"—they're still prone to the mistakes of inexperience.

In Indiana, Brademas opponent Hiler erred tactically by saying he's "happy" that Indiana ranks at the bottom of the 50 states in federal aid per capita. That statement was tailor-made for Rep. Brademas, who repeatedly brags about a new gasohol plant and an assortment of grants he has helped to land for the district.

And somehow, doors do seem to open more easily for the powerful incumbents. Here in Fort Worth, Majority Leader Wright recently got some good television footage by roaring off into the stratosphere in a new two-seat F16 fighter, produced by General Dynamics Corp. here. Asked about his teeth-rattling ride, which had the plane shooting straight up at one point, he replied mildly: "I fully expect to serve for several more years in Congress and to vote for a strong defense, including the F16."

Republican Jim Bradshaw, eager for that kind of publicity, asked for a ride in the F16 too. He's still waiting.

59

Reagan Sweep Could Topple Congress's Liberal Era; Power Balance Shifts in Key Panels of Senate, House

Conservative Swing Already Had Begun as Democrats Sensed Rightward Drift

By DENNIS FARNEY
Staff Reporter of THE WALL STREET JOURNAL

WASHINGTON—Ronald Reagan's landslide may signal the end of the liberal era in Congress.

At the very least, the election results put President-elect Reagan in the congressional driver's seat. Congress was growing more conservative even before the election, as Democrats, sensing the country's rightward drift, began abandoning legislation backed by labor, consumers and public-interest lobbies. The next Congress, with Republicans controlling the Senate for the first time since 1954 and House Republicans back to their pre-Watergate strength, will accelerate those trends.

"We're in a position to govern," says Reagan campaign aide Roger Stone.

Many Democrats agree. The heart of the liberal lineup in the Senate has been swept away, along with some of the House's most influential liberals. The liberals who remain —"soldiers with the shellfire still echoing in their ears," one top House aide described them yesterday—almost certainly will try to redefine their political philosophy.

"Locked in Our Own Dogma"

"What happened Tuesday was inevitable," says Massachusetts Sen. Paul Tsongas, a freshman who has been arguing that liberals must redefine their goals and purpose. (Sen. Tsongas, elected in 1978, won't have to run again until 1984.) "We Democrats have been locked in our own dogma for a long time," he says. "To the extent that the dogma didn't correspond to reality, a comeuppance was inevitable."

"There's no way the next Congress is going to resemble the last," says Rep. Guy Vander Jagt of Michigan, who headed an unprecedented GOP drive to defeat seemingly entrenched Democrats in the House. "Democratic leaders who managed to survive had the bejesus scared out of them."

The Republican landslide toppled seven of the Senate's leading liberals, replacing most of them with extremely conservative Republicans. All told, assuming that GOP Sen. Barry Goldwater of Arizona and Democratic Sen. Patrick Leahy of Vermont retain narrow leads, Republicans gained 12 Senate seats. Democrats dropped from a 59-to-41 Senate majority to a 47-to-53 minority.

Gain of 33 Seats in House

The GOP gain in the House—at least 33 seats with a possibility of one or two more—was the best Republicans have done there since picking up 47 seats in 1966. The 1966 election put the brakes on Lyndon Johnson's Great Society; Democrats fear the 1980 election could mark the beginning of an effort to roll back Great Society programs.

Foremost among Democratic Senate casualties were four staunch liberals targeted, not only by the GOP, but by a host of conservative single-issue groups.

In South Dakota, Sen. George McGovern, the party's 1972 presidential candidate, lost to Rep. James Abdnor. Indiana's Sen. Birch Bayh, a three-term veteran, lost to Republican Rep. Dan Quayle. Idaho's Sen. Frank Church, the Foreign Relations Committee chairman, was defeated by Rep. Steven Symms. And in Iowa, Sen. John Culver—who, almost alone among endangered liberals this year, refused to back off his liberal record—lost to Rep. Charles Grassley.

Others Who Were Defeated

The Reagan landslide also uprooted Wisconsin Sen. Gaylord Nelson, a three-term liberal environmentalist and watchdog of the drug manufacturers; Washington's six-term Sen. Warren G. Magnuson, chairman of the Appropriations Committee, and New Hampshire's John Durkin, a populist foe of the oil companies. The new GOP Senators, respectively, are conservative Robert Kasten and moderates Slade Gorton and Warren Rudman.

In addition, Republican Mack Mattingly upset Senate Agriculture Committee Chairman Herman Talmadge in Georgia and Republican John East upset Democratic Sen. Robert Morgan in North Carolina. And Republicans picked up Democratic Senate seats in Alabama, Florida and Alaska, three states where Democratic incumbents lost their party's primary. The new Senators, respectively, are Jeremiah Denton, a retired admiral and former Vietnam prisoner of war; Paula Hawkins, a former Florida public service commissioner, and Frank Murkowski, a former Fairbanks, Alaska, bank president.

Democrats had hoped to take Republican-held seats in New York, Pennsylvania and Oklahoma. But they lost all three bids.

In New York, liberal GOP Sen. Jacob Javits and liberal Democrat Elizabeth Holtzman split the liberal vote, handing victory to conservative Alfonse D'Amato. In Pennsylvania, where GOP Sen. Richard Schweiker is retiring, Republican Arlen Specter beat Democrat Pete Flaherty. In Oklahoma, conservative Republican Don Nickles held the seat of retiring GOP Sen. Henry Bellmon.

Liberals Who Survived

The Senate returns weren't completely bleak for the Democrats. Two other liberals targeted for defeat, California's Alan Cranston and Missouri's Thomas Eagleton, survived rather easily. Colorado Sen. Gary Hart engineered a come-from-behind victory, and in Connecticut, Rep. Christopher Dodd held the seat of retiring Sen. Abraham Ribicoff.

The Senate upheaval gives Republicans control of committees, throwing a small army of Democratic staffers out of work and relegating Sen. Robert Byrd (D., W.Va.) to Minority Leader. The leading contender for Republican Majority Leader is Tennessee's Sen. Howard Baker, who yesterday claimed pledges of 40 of the 53 GOP votes and the support of Nevada Sen. Paul Laxalt, Ronald Reagan's closest friend in the Senate.

Republicans didn't do quite as well in the House, but took enough liberal scalps to reinforce a growing conservative trend there. Democrats, who have a 276-to-159 majority in the present House, seem likely to drop to a 243-to-192 edge in the new one.

Brademas a Top Victim

The top Democratic victim was the House's third-ranking leader, Majority Whip John Brademas of Indiana. Rep. Brademas, an 11-term veteran, fell to GOP challenger John Hiler, 27, a businessman. A possible successor in the whip post, an appointive position, is Chicago Democrat Dan Rostenkowski, a product of the old Mayor Daley machine. But because Republicans defeated another big-name Democrat, Ways and Means Committee Chairman Al Ullman, Mr. Rostenkowski also is in line to chair that powerful committee. He'll have to choose, and if he chooses the committee chairmanship, one possible contender for the whip position would be Washington's Thomas Foley.

Other House Democratic casualties included California's Harold Johnson, Public Works Committee chairman; California's James Corman, the House's strongest advocate of national health insurance; Texas's Bob Eckhardt, a foe of the oil companies, and Ohio Rep. Thomas Ashley, an authority on energy and urban policy.

Several big-name House Democrats survived an all-out Republican effort to defeat them. Majority Leader Jim Wright of Texas, who is in line to become House Speaker some day, easily turned back a challenge from Republican Jim Bradshaw. Arizona's Morris Udall, the Interior Committee chairman, who was a 1976 candidate for the Democratic nomination for President, won the race of his life against challenger Richard Huff. And Washington's Mr. Foley, who chairs the Agriculture Committee, apparently beat Republican John Sonneland. (Mr. Sonneland would have to win a lion's share of the absentee ballots to overcome Rep. Foley's lead.)

Top GOP Boon Seen in Tax Policy as Both Finance Units Get New Chairmen

By Robert W. Merry

Staff Reporter of The Wall Street Journal

WASHINGTON — The Republican surge that struck the government with such force Tuesday left a profound impact on congressional committees, those repositories of legislative power.

With the Republicans taking control of all Senate committees, and with four Democratic House committee chairmen going down to defeat, the Republican agenda is expected to get a warmer congressional reception than at any time in more than two decades.

The Republican takeover of the Senate was a particularly valuable development for President-elect Ronald Reagan because it wipes away the hostility that would have greeted some of his programs and appointments in such key committee panels as Judiciary, Labor and Budget.

But the biggest boon was seen in tax policy, probably Mr. Reagan's top legislative priority. Both the tax-writing House Ways and Means Committee and its Senate counterpart, the Finance Committee, will get new chairmen.

Most experts agree that the elevation of Republican Sen. Robert Dole of Kansas to the chairmanship of the Senate Finance Committee will stengthen moves for large individual tax cuts next year, a centerpiece of the Reagan domestic program. Similarly, the defeat of Ways and Means Chairman Al Ullman of Oregon could bolster such tax-cut efforts in the House, although the situation there is a little more murky.

The strengthened position for Republican tax cutters in the Senate doesn't stem from any broad differences in outlook between Republican Sen. Dole and the current chairman, Louisiana's Democratic Sen. Russell Long. Sen. Long, one of Congress's shrewdest legislators, already had embraced the idea of deep individual tax-rate cuts and had steered his committee to near unanimity in favor of such a bill last summer.

But Sen. Long naturally was more concerned about considering the views of the more liberal members of his party than the new Republican leadership will be. And the changed makeup of the committee, to reflect the Republicans' overall Senate gains, will give the new majority party a chance to add panel members who support the party's official doctrine of deep tax cuts.

Sen. Dole's elevation will have a "critical bearing" on next year's tax legislation, predicts economist Michael Evans. He says he expects passage of a "modified" version of the so-called Kemp-Roth tax bill, which calls for 10% across-the-board cuts in individual tax rates for three consecutive years.

On the Ways and Means Committee, attention is focused on Rep. Dan Rostenkowski of Illinois, next in line to succeed Chairman Ullman. He is a bright and tough-minded legislative infighter who would be expected to tighten control over the committee, which has been in drift under Mr. Ullman.

But Rep. Rostenkowski is described as undecided on whether to take the job or move into the position of Democratic whip, left vacant by the defeat of Rep. John Brademas of Indiana. That would put Mr. Rostenkowski in position to rise eventually to Majority leader or even Speaker.

"His real ambition is to be Speaker," says one top Democratic House aide. "The Ways and Means job doesn't strike him as much fun."

Next in line after Mr. Rostenkowski would be Rep. Sam Gibbons of Florida, a maverick legislator whose possible elevation causes jitters among some Democratic leaders. Thus, top House Democrats are expected to urge Mr. Rostenkowski to take the job.

If he does, most committee watchers expect him to work more closely with House Democratic leaders than Rep. Ullman has. "His past history indicates he would be more partisan than Ullman," says one of his committee colleagues. That could mean tough conference-committee battles between Mr. Rostenkowski, aligned with the House Democratic leadership, and Sen. Dole, aligned with the Republican Senate and the new President.

But some experts believe the Republican surge and the changed makeup of the committee could blunt any Democratic inclinations to fight for more traditional Democratic solutions. "I think Dan would move the committee in the direction that makes it work," says his committee colleague.

Mr. Gibbons, on the other hand, already is predisposed to large tax-cut programs and likely would steer the committee more in the direction of the Senate Finance Committee.

Among the chairmanship turnovers in the Senate, probably the most dramatic is the Judiciary Committee, where South Carolina's conservative Republican Sen. Strom Thurmond will replace the liberal Democrat Edward Kennedy of Massachusetts. Mr. Thurmond's elevation could enhance the new President's ability to get his favored nominees to the federal bench, including the Supreme Court.

And pet Reagan programs likely will be greeted warmly by Senate committees that would have been hostile if the Democrats had maintained control. An example is Mr. Reagan's proposal for a "sub-minimum" wage for teen-agers, which will get an enthusiastic hearing from the Labor Committee's new chairman, expected to be Sen. Orrin Hatch (R., Utah).

In addition, Mr. Reagan's call for cutting "waste and fraud" from the federal budget is likely to be taken quite seriously by the Budget Committee's new chairman, Sen. Pete Domenici (R., N.M.), an earnest foe of what he considers bloated federal programs.

The Republican surge also could influence the race for the chairmanship of the House Budget Committee, where two traditional Democratic liberals, Reps. Paul Simon of Illinois and David Obey of Wisconsin, are competing with the more conservative and budget-conscious Rep. James Jones of Oklahoma. Some observers believe the voters' hostility toward Democratic liberals may help tilt the race toward Mr. Jones.

"I think it improves—and maybe guarantees—Jones's chances," says one top congressional staff aide.

Such Good Friends: Policy and Society In the Capital

By Albert R. Hunt

WASHINGTON—Amid all the discussion about the policies and personnel of the Reagan administration, this town is abuzz with talk about a sharp change in the social atmosphere here.

Most in the social set are delighted that the Reagans are coming and the Carters are leaving. Liquor will return to the White House, and the Reagans and their friends like Betsy Bloomingdale—honestly, that's her name—will reactivate the dinner-party hostesses in fashionable Georgetown and Cleveland Park.

Some pundits, who were shut out socially during the Carter years, talk of this almost as a seminal change. In Time magazine, Hugh Sidey writes of a "new meaning" coming to Washington, where "fun could come back in style and class would return to social events." Syndicated columnist Joseph Kraft holds forth about a "touch of class being brought to the White House instead of blue jeans."

The "blue jeans set" understandably isn't very happy about being held up to scorn. "If I had come to Washington with independent means, with half a million bucks to spend on a house, I still wouldn't have chosen to socialize with that bunch," White House Press Secretary Jody Powell, who actually favors three-piece suits over jeans, complained to the Boston Globe.

The shame of this debate is that it purports—but fails—to address a serious subject: the desirable style to govern successfully in Washington.

The widespread notion that glittering dinner parties and embassy bashes are the focal point of power in Washington is nonsense. Such things may have mattered decades ago, but today the social scene is of only peripheral importance to those who govern.

That's the view of Richard Cheney, a Wyoming Congressman who was President Ford's chief of staff. "Social Washington, the people who do the benefits and balls, tend to be very nice people but they don't play any role in setting policy," he says. When he was in the White House, he remembers being "inundated with invitations for embassy dinners and Georgetown parties. You accept a few but they are of very limited utility."

* * *

A survey of Embassy Row functions or stuffy Georgetown dinner parties rarely would turn up Tip O'Neill, Orrin Hatch, Charis Walker or Kenneth Young. Mr. O'Neill is the Speaker of the House; Sen. Hatch is the incoming chairman of the Senate Labor and Human Resources Committee; Mr. Walker is one of the city's most influential business lobbyists; Mr. Young is a top aide to AFL-CIO President Lane Kirkland. All appreciate the use of power here and all exercise their influence while shunning the social circuit.

These are the sort of people whom any administration should cultivate. Rather than at fancy parties, however, this can better be done over lunch, at a ball game, a small, simple dinner party or, in some cases, at church or neighborhood outings.

This is a distinction the Carter people never understood. They came to Washington believing the "social scene" was some sort of homogeneous entity; they failed to appreciate the difference between the important lawmaker and the vacuous social climber. This misunderstanding was evident in a revealing interview that top Carter aide Hamilton Jordan gave last week to the Washington Post's Meg Greenfield. "Maybe if I had it all to do over again, I'd become a socialite here in Washington, but I don't think so," Mr. Jordan said. "I mean, it's just not my nature. I recognize that there are benefits to being part of the social scene, wining and dining; but I came here to work and to think."

It's unfortuante that Mr. Jordan even today seems to believe that working and thinking are somehow separate from really understanding the ways of Washington. He didn't need to attend embassy parties. But he could have had dinner periodically with, say, Dan Rostenkowski, the influential Chicago Democrat on the House Ways and Means Committee. And he didn't have to alienate Tip O'Neill so thoroughly that the Speaker privately called him "Hannibal Jerkin."

There are, of course, many reasons for the Carter administration's failures. The problems it faced were enormous, some of its policies were misdirected and the political mood of America was moving the wrong way for the Carter people. But surely they would have found governing a little easier if they hadn't been so intent on remaining "outsiders." Like it or not, when you're in the White House you're an insider.

While there, Dick Cheney notes, "it's important to form professional friendships. Politically, social contacts are most useful with someone else involved in making policy—members of Congress, key staff people on Capitol Hill and a few of the more important lobbyists."

These are the contacts the incoming Reaganites should try to develop. Our form of governing often is a very personal process and in recent times most successful officeholders, from Franklin Roosevelt to Senate Republican leader Howard Baker, have realized this; they have won friends and influenced people.

There are some encouraging signs that the Reagan people know what they must do to exercise influence in Washington. Edwin Meese is the President-elect's top policy aide and he served in that function when Mr. Reagan was governor of California. John Burton is a very liberal Democratic Congressman from California and served in the state legislature during the Reagan years. He and the conservative Mr. Meese rarely agreed on any issues. "Ed Meese would arrest you for spitting on the sidewalk," says Mr. Burton. "But he's also a guy you can talk to. He'll listen and occasionally change. I like him."

What the Carter White House needed was not its version of Betsy Bloomingdale but more Washington hands who felt that way about Hamilton Jordan and his colleagues.

Mr. Hunt, a member of the Journal's Washington bureau, covers politics.

Leader Michel Strives to Keep GOP in Line

By Dennis Farney
Staff Reporter of The Wall Street Journal

WASHINGTON — Capital cynics think Ronald Reagan's Republican friends may cause him more agony than his Democratic enemies.

They say it could be a replay of that old refrain, "Been Down So Long It Looks Like Up to Me." Congressional Republicans are so accustomed to opposing a President, they've forgotten how to support one, the theory goes.

It's the job of Robert Michel, the new House Republican leader, to prove the cynics wrong. The success of the President's economic program will depend heavily upon the ability of this avuncular man from Peoria to shake his Republican troops out of their knee-jerk responses.

"I'd like to see our senior members, particularly, think beyond the ends of their noses," he says.

Off and Running

He's off to an impressive start. Last week, in the first test of his leadership, he persuaded 150 of 186 voting Republicans to support a $50 billion increase in the national debt limit. The last time House Republicans supported a debt-limit increase, a distasteful but necessary task if the government is to continue operating, was in 1973.

But last week's vote doesn't necessarily signal clear sailing, even among Republicans, for the coming Reagan proposals to reduce taxes and spending. Those proposals will strike hardest at Democratic programs. Yet many will be painful for Republican leg-islators to accept, and Bob Michel will have his hands full holding his troops in line.

"We've got to support the Reagan cuts as a package, not start fighting over the pieces," says Rep. Richard Cheney of Wyoming, who is part of the GOP House leadership. "If we start down that road, the alligators will eat us alive."

This will be harder than it looks at first glance. Cuts in the food stamp program, for example, might appear to be easy for Republicans to support. But Midwestern Republicans have habitually voted for food stamps, in exchange for urban support of farm subsidies. Similarly, cutting the new "synfuels" program will force Republicans to confront some of the nation's largest corporations. Efforts to scale back loans for college students will alienate the suburban middle class. Nor are House Republicans united in support of the 30%, three-year Kemp-Roth tax cut. Some fear it could backfire by increasing inflation.

A Difference in Style

A look at the way Rep. Michel rounded up support for the debt-ceiling increase suggests how he'll approach these coming legislative tests. Although hardly novel, his approach differs significantly from that of his predecessor, John Rhodes.

First, he is more forceful than Mr. Rhodes. After a preliminary vote count on the debt-ceiling issue found more than half of the House Republicans leaning against the President, Mr. Michel delivered a rousing appeal in a closed meeting. "John Rhodes was very effective, one-on-one," says a GOP aide who knows both men. "But he could never have rallied a group like that."

Second, Mr. Michel worked with the White House to shape the President's proposal. "Be credible," he told Mr. Reagan's staff; don't make the mistake of asking for an unrealistically small increase that would require another increase before long. Later, when some House Republicans suggested "sweetening" the proposal by tying it to a package of spending cuts, he insisted on keeping the issue simple. "One man's sweetener is another man's poison," he argued.

Finally, Rep. Michel stayed in touch with his troops. In contrast to Rep. Rhodes, often criticized for remaining remote from the House floor, Mr. Michel patrolled the aisles, vote count in his pocket, cajoling and listening. Thus he could alert White House lobbyists to wavering Republicans.

On the Links

Mr. Michel also has links to the majority House Democrats that John Rhodes never had. (For one thing, he's a frequent golf partner of Speaker Thomas P. O'Neill.) "I've had more contact with Bob Michel in a month than I had with John Rhodes in the last two years," says an aide to the Speaker. Although a sharp bargainer in private, the Illinois Republican operates with a light touch.

"He postures . . . but with a wink," says the Speaker's man.

Rep. Michel himself talks of "building a network that stretches to the other side of the aisle." Democrats outnumber Republicans 243 to 191 (there's one vacant seat) in the newly elected House, meaning that as few as 26 Democratic defectors could tip the balance in favor of White House budget cuts. Finding these defectors shouldn't be difficult; the Democratic lineup includes at least 60 conservative-leaning members.

"I'm convinced there are 35 or 40 members on the other side who'll be with us on many issues," says the House GOP leader.

But his biggest challenge will be in holding down defections from his own party in the tough votes ahead. To govern is to choose. With a Democrat in the White House, congressional Republicans were required neither to govern nor to face up to unpleasant policy choices. Now they must do both.

Rostenkowski and the Tax Bill

By Robert W. Merry

WASHINGTON — In less than three months as chairman of the House Ways and Means Committee, Rep. Dan Rostenkowski has quickly acquired the kind of control over the tax-writing panel that his great political patron, the late Mayor Rich-ard Daley, once held over Chicago. The result is that even his adversaries in the administration have acquired a healthy respect for his political skills.

"The guy is really good," says an admiring Treasury Department official. "He's in complete control of that commit-tee. He knows what he wants to do, and he plans to do it."

Mr. Rostenkowski brings to the job some obvious characteristics and some not-so-obvious ones. Outwardly, the Illinois Democrat is a man of imposing size who sports a Sunny Jim smile, a penchant for friendly banter and a passion for give-and-take politics. One aide describes his political style by saying, "Danny leans into the job."

But behind that friendly exterior is a steely-cold political operator. Mr. Rostenkowski sees legislative politics as endless trading of interest and influence backed up by careful distribution of rewards and punishments. A congressional aide once watched Mr. Rostenkowski take elaborate pains in a conference committee to sabotage a pet measure of Abraham Ribicoff, then a Democratic Senator from Connecticut. Inquiring about the motive, the aide learned it went back nearly a decade to the emotion-charged 1968 Democratic Convention in Chicago. At the convention, Sen. Ribicoff had publicly blasted Mr. Rostenkowski's friend Mayor Daley.

Final Vote on a Pet Bill

A Ways and Means colleague remembers standing on the House floor during the final vote on a pet bill Mr. Rostenkowski had helped shepherd through Congress as part of an earlier agreement between the two Congressmen. A House page walked up with a note that reminded the Congressman: "I always keep my promises — Danny."

Underlying Mr. Rostenkowski's style is an instinct for political combat. That instinct was evident this week when he declared President Reagan's proposal for a 30% reduction in individual income-tax rates all but dead. Mr. Rostenkowski challenged Republicans on his committee to accept the proposal's demise and get down to the business  of hammering out a "consensus" tax bill "that the whole committee can be proud of."

In essence, the chairman was admonishing Republicans to drop their insistence that the President's individual tax-cut plan, the so-called Kemp-Roth measure, be put to a vote in committee and on the House floor. The Republicans didn't bite.

This initial face-off provided a hint of the political forces converging on the committee in this season of political jockeying. Basically, there are three central forces—the White House; the House Ways and Means Committee's Republicans; and the panel's Democrats, dominated by Chairman Rostenkowski.

The White House refuses to waver from its commitment to a "clean bill" with only two components: across-the-board tax-rate cuts for individuals and faster depreciation write-offs for business. President Reagan doesn't want his main goal—firing up the economy—complicated by efforts, however laudable, to end perceived tax inequities or by wrangling over how to "target" the tax cuts for best economic results.

In fact the administration is so committed to the clean-bill approach that some officials wouldn't mind seeing House Democrats completely rewrite the tax bill along old-style liberal lines. Their reasoning: House Republicans would stick with the President in opposition to such a bill, and this Republican unity would enhance the White House's chances of getting a clean bill from the Republican-controlled Senate. Then the final product could be forged in a House-Senate conference committee.

Democrats view the current maneuvering much differently. For them the aim is extricating themselves from their predicament born of last November's election. Their challenge in these times of Republican muscle-flexing is to preserve their

---

Mr. Rostenkowski's style is an instinct for political combat. That instinct was evident this week when he declared President Reagan's proposal for a 30% reduction in individual income-tax rates all but dead.

---

party identity while protecting themselves from the voter wrath of the last two elections. It won't be easy.

Preserving the Democrats' identity means a powerful opposition to the three-year Kemp-Roth plan. Democrats despise the idea of such a sharp cut, in part because Republicans have campaigned on it so assiduously—and sometimes effectively—in recent elections. It's also unlikely that House Democrats will accept a three-year program; more likely they will seek a one-year tax cut.

At the same time, avoiding the voters' wrath requires some accommodation to what the voters seemed to be saying last November and some compromise with a President who is perceived as very popular. That's why Mr. Rostenkowski has been insisting of late that he "would like very much to work a consensus out of the committee." The panel's Republicans, once skeptical, are beginning to believe his words are sincere.

But the committee Republicans have their own problems. They aren't exactly pleased with the administration's clean-bill approach, but they're stuck with it—for now. Many of these committee Republicans developed ideas for tax changes that have bounced around the committee in recent years—measures to end the extra tax on two-income married couples, to provide tax relief for Americans working overseas, to increase incentives for savings. Naturally, they won't like opposing some of their own ideas should the Democrats propose them.

But that's what the White House persuaded them to do, however reluctantly, on the ground that they don't wield serious clout in the committee. Although Republicans made sizable House gains in the last election, the Democrats are still in control and retain a two-thirds majority on the Ways and Means Committee. The result: Committee Republicans lack power to bargain effectively with the Democrats. Rep. Barber Conable of New York, the committee's ranking Republican, says, "I told Danny that he robbed me of my independence. So I've got to go with the administration to have any impact."

Moreover, while most of the committee's GOP members question the economic merits of the Kemp-Roth formula, nearly half the Republicans in the full House campaigned—and won—on the issue. The White House argues that these pro-Kemp-Roth Republicans shouldn't be ignored simply because committee Republicans tend to have more traditional economic views.

Carefully surveying all this is Rep. Rostenkowski. He has the power to get just about anything he wants through his committee. But to foster his aims of preserving a Democratic identity and protecting the party from voter anger, he must split off committee Republicans from the White House and get them to join him on his "consensus" bill. The question: How far can the Democrats' tax bill depart from the Reagan proposal and still garner support from House Republicans?

A couple of recent developments provide the beginnings of an answer. Consider, for example, the idea of dropping the top rate on "unearned," or investment, income to 50% from 70%. Supply-side economists in the administration say that's probably the single most important tax change for renewing economic activity and growth. But White House political advisers successfully argued against including it in the President's package on the ground it would backfire politically because it helps the rich. The administration's plan would drop the investment-income rate down to 50% only after three years.

A "Young Turk"

But now comes a "Young Turk" liberal Democrat on the Ways and Means Committee, Rep. William Brodhead of Michigan, with a bill to drop the rate down to 50% immediately. Republicans naturally perked up when that bill went into the hopper.

Then there is the plan to offset this year's Social Security tax increase with an income-tax credit. Liberals generally have liked the tax-credit idea, which would reduce taxes only on the first $30,000 of annual income of any taxpayer who earned more than that. Republicans have opposed the credit on the ground that it wouldn't provide the incentives for savings, investment and work effort that they contend across-the-board tax cuts would supply.

Although some committee liberals had been working to generate a political head of steam for the tax-credit idea, it now appears doomed. "That plan," says Rep. Conable, "is pretty well dead."

Offsetting Social Security taxes with an income-tax credit appears to be too great a departure. As Rep. Willis Gradison, a committee Republican, says, "There's about as much Republican support for that plan as there is Democratic support for Kemp-Roth." Hence the plan appears dead.

For much the same reason, the idea of dropping the top tax rate on investment income to 50% appears very much alive. Asked whether the Democrats' bill will contain that provision, Mr. Rostenkowski breaks into a sly grin. "I guess it would be pretty hard for Republicans to vote against that, wouldn't it?" he says, or, as Rep. Gradison expresses it, "If Danny goes with that, he'll just steal the ball and make a basket."

Dan Rostenkowski is a politican who likes to steal the ball and make baskets—even if it means placing political accommodation over ideological purity. And that's what it seems to mean in these early days of the Reagan presidency. "I have confidence," says Rep. Conable, "that Danny will put together a package with a good deal of appeal to conservatives."

Mr. Merry, a member of the Journal's Washington bureau, covers tax legislation. An editorial discussing Mr. Rostenkowski's tax plan appears today.

Republicans Reflect on What They've Wrought

By Dennis Farney

WASHINGTON—Republican Congressman Newt Gingrich surveys politics from an Olympian perch, as befits a former professor of European history. And these days find the brash, cocky Georgian almost euphoric over the sweeping vista opening up before President Reagan and the Republican Party.

"We have a chance," he says, "to bring about a half-century of right-of-center government."

Newt Gingrich's elation stems from more than the President's smashing victories on tax and budget cuts—or growing evidence of liberal exhaustion in Congress. What excites him most is the unified, unshakable support congressional Republicans have given Mr. Reagan so far. That, and the possibility that the well-disciplined Republicans just might stick together to enact the rest of what the White House calls "the Reagan revolution."

The Congressman believes the extraordinary GOP support so far may reflect more than just a Reagan honeymoon; it may signal the beginnings of congressional politics akin to those of the British Parliament, where the disciplined majority party can be expected to support the prime minister, come what may.

President Reagan has the opportunity to "create a de facto parliamentary system of government here," declares Mr. Gingrich. The Congressman has just sent Mr. Reagan a letter suggesting that he sharply limit legislative objectives for the rest of this year, while he refines grand strategy with GOP congressional leaders.

The President may not pay much attention to this advice from a second-term Congressman, but the question the letter raises is fundamental. Will congressional Republicans remain a disciplined phalanx, the instrument of sweeping change—or will they soon revert to the parochial behavior that congressional Democrats displayed under the hapless President Carter?

The best guess is that Republicans, much more homogeneous than Democrats, will always give Mr. Reagan more support than the fractious Democrats gave Mr. Carter. An overwhelming majority will continue to back the Reagan economic program — unless it comes a cropper — although some have qualms about it even now. Still, we may have already seen the high-water mark in GOP support of the President. Congressional Republicans are unlikely to remain a rubber-stamping "parliament" for much longer, especially when the agenda turns to such highly devisive social issues as abortion, prayer in public schools and civil rights.

Margaret Thatcher could hardly improve upon the level of party support President Reagan has received so far. On the tax vote and the two most crucial budget votes, House Republicans backed him 190 to 1, 190 to 0 and 188 to 1; on similar votes, Senate Republicans supported him 52 to 1, 50 to 2 and 52 to 0. The net result, here as in Britain, has been a spectacular leap into the dark—a colossal gamble on a novel economic theory.

This is the nature of parliaments, and of American congresses on those rare occasions when they behave like parliaments. They don't check the power of the Executive; they amplify it. They shun the messy compromise for the bold stroke. Having shunned compromise, Republicans now are living with the decisive choice they have made.

"There were two weddings last week," says Rep. Ralph Regula of Ohio, a respected Republican member of the Budget Committee. "Prince Charles married Lady Diana and the Republican Party married the economic issue. For better or worse, it's our economy now."

No doubt House and Senate Republicans would make the same fateful choice again. Even so, it's obvious that some have qualms about the marriage they have made.

Senate Majority Leader Howard Baker calls Reaganomics a "riverboat gamble." Asked to rate the chance, on a zero-to-10 scale, that Reaganomics will succeed, Republican Rep. Carl Pursell of Michigan concludes: "Seven or eight. I'm not as optimistic as Jack Kemp (the indefatigable supply-sider)," he says.

The marvelously outspoken grande dame of the House, New Jersey Rep. Millicent Fenwick, probably expresses the feelings of many. A reporter asked how she felt after voting for the budget and tax cuts. Exhilarated? Exuberant, perhaps? The tall, aristocratic Congresswoman lit her ever-present pipe.

"Want me (puff, puff) to tell you the truth?" she replied. "I thought to myself—well, victory. I just pray to God that we're right. What else can you do but pray?"

Republicans feel more comfortable about their deep budget cuts than about the tax reductions; the spending cuts, after all, delivered on a pledge the party has been making since the New Deal.

Still, at least a few Republicans worry that they have cut too deep, too fast. The worriers are mostly limited to about two dozen Representatives from the Northeast and Midwest, regions of ailing industries, struggling cities and high unemployment. One such member is Rep. Silvio Conte, a moderate-to-liberal Republican from Massachusetts.

Last May, on the day of the House's first showdown budget vote, Mr. Conte grumpily told a conservative colleague, "You guys don't know how much trouble you'll be in a year from now." Yet despite such misgivings, Mr. Conte voted for the Reagan budget cuts.

The unanswered question is how long skeptical Republicans like Millicent Fenwick and Silvio Conte will continue going down the line for Mr. Reagan. How long, in other words, will congressional Republicans continue voting like members of a parliament instead of representatives of their individual districts?

Recent history suggests that parliamentary outbreaks are shortlived. Perhaps the last time Congress acted like a parliament, enacting a sweeping presidential program in one sustained push, was in 1965-66, when disciplined Democrats passed Lyndon Johnson's Great Society. It is one of the ironies of history that the present Congress has begun dismantling much of what that one put together.

The conventional wisdom holds that Republican discipline will soon begin eroding as Congress turns to volatile social issues and constituents react to painful budget cuts. But congressional Republicans are different from Democrats—more homogeneous, more philosophically united, less inclined to fight among themselves. So it's possible that, given skillful coordination from the White House, congressional Republicans will remain a parliament for a good while longer.

————

Mr. Farney, a member of the Journal's Washington Bureau, covers the House

————

64

The Democrats Now Search for Solutions

By JAMES M. PERRY

WASHINGTON—When the new team moved into the headquarters of the Democratic National Committee after Jimmy Carter's humiliating defeat, it found 15 IBM Selectric typewriters—but only three "elements" (those little round typing balls) to operate them.

That was pretty much the story of the country's oldest political party in the aftermath of Ronald Reagan's landslide: The elements were missing.

They're still missing, of course. The personally popular Mr. Reagan is in the White House, the Republicans control the Senate and they seem to be able to pick up enough conservative Democrats in the House to win the big ones.

But it would be premature to dismiss the Democrats. It is *always* premature to write off either the Democrats or the Republicans. The Whigs and the Barnburners may have folded, but the two current parties hang in there, decade after decade. And there are signs that the Democrats, slowly and tentatively, are drawing some lessons from their defeat.

Querulous Ideologues

Perhaps the best indication of that is the absence at most Democratic gatherings these days of those folks we remember from the '60s and the '70s—those querulous ideologues, wearing Greek fisherman's caps, nattering hour after hour about quotas, gay rights and decriminalization of marijuana.

There was hardly a fisherman's cap in the room early in June when the Democratic National Committee, meeting in Denver, voted to limit participation in the party's mid-term conference, probably to be held in June 1982 in Philadelphia, to 950 people. Last time the Democrats did this sort of thing, they had 2,400 delegates.

"This is going to be a leadership conference," says the new party chairman, Charles T. Manatt. The party that once wanted to establish quotas for almost every conceivable minority is going to invite what passes these days for the likes of Mayor Richard Daley.

Chairman Manatt talks a little like Ray Bliss, the old Republican chairman, who preached "nuts and bolts" politics to his party during some of its darkest days. "I'm here to do business," Mr. Manatt says. "I'm here to bring this party, organizationally and technically, into the 20th Century."

Thus, Mr. Manatt is introducing Democrats to the computer. It will be used in the party's first mass direct-mail program, just getting under way. In recent years, it has been something of an embarrassment to the Democrats that they collected thousands from large contributors, while the Republicans collected millions in small donations.

Mr. Manatt will help other Democrats seeking office—from mayors to Senators. There hasn't been much money around in recent years to do that sort of thing.

"The only way we will ever exert party discipline," says Eugene Eidenberg, the national committee's executive director, "is by electing Democrats who have been helped in important ways by something the national party has done for them."

There's some payoff already. The national Democrats put time and money into the party's most striking recent success—the election of liberal Democrat Wayne Dowdy to what had been a Republican House seat in Mississippi. The national party gnashed its teeth at its inability to play a similar role in another special House election—in Ohio, where the Democrat, Dale Locker, lost by only 378 votes to the Republican, Michael Oxley, in what had been a heavily Republican district. The national Democrats couldn't help Mr. Locker because he opposed the Equal Rights Amendment and the last party convention (at which there were still a number of fisherman's caps) established a rule against helping anti-ERA candidates.

It is, of course, one thing to introduce Democrats to the computer; it is another to introduce them to new ideas.

The national committee won't play much of a role in that. The emphasis will be on mechanics, even though new advisory councils on issues—defense, the envi-

————

It would be premature to dismiss the Democratic Party. The Whigs and the Barnburners may have folded, but our two parties hang in, decade after decade.

————

ronment, economic development, for starters—will go to work in the fall.

Democrats can always fall back on wishful thinking that they won't need to work up new ideas because the Reagan Republicans will self-destruct eventually.

The standard Democratic refrain one hears now is something of a replay of an old Republican favorite: We can cut the budget better. Or, perhaps: We can do it more mercifully.

The refrain is being played most prominently by the party's two foremost contenders for the presidential nomination in 1984—Sen. Edward Kennedy and former Vice President Walter Mondale.

Mr. Mondale has it down pat. "Progressives," he says (there are no more self-styled liberals), "have learned some lessons. . . . Where we overregulated, we should cut back. Where we fueled inflation, we should restrain our deficits. Where we overtaxed, we should push for tax relief. Where government has been clumsy or intrusive, we should make government better."

The Reagan administration, in other words, is on to something. But, the Democrats say, the execution is all wrong. "When you make drastic cuts in child nutrition and immunization," says Mr. Mondale, you don't do much for America. "And when you turn us into the only major Western democracy without a legal aid program—you do not toughen the faith that people have in our system, you sap it."

Sen. Kennedy concedes less and talks tougher. "We are told, and it is surely cor-

rect, that we cannot solve our problems simply by throwing money at them," he says. But he goes from there to attack the Reagan budget cuts and to describe the administration's economic program as "pop sociology."

"We have only just begun to fight," says Sen. Kennedy. But the question may be: Have the Democrats begun to think? Some of the new party leaders don't seem to believe they have. Mr. Manatt, for example, says it's not enough for Democrats to say they can govern better. They must demonstrate it.

And so, in some corners of the party, there is skepticism about both Mr. Mondale and Sen. Kennedy, for, like it or not, they are part of the fisherman's cap tradition.

Younger Democrats would like to see men of their own age and experience considered for 1984. Names often mentioned are Govs. James Hunt of North Carolina and Bruce Babbitt of Arizona and Sen. Gary Hart of Colorado. These, at least, are the kinds of Democrats who seem to be demonstrating how to get along in the politics of the 1980s.

Down to Basics

Sen. Hart is interesting because he started out in politics as campaign director in the 1972 presidential campaign of George McGovern, when the fisherman's-cap syndrome hit its peak. Now he's beyond all that sort of thing. He won't discuss gun control or gay rights or those other favorites out of his past. "I don't hear any of that talk any more. We're down to basics

now. We can't afford not to be. We're talking about major reform of taxes and welfare and about new ideas on how government should work. And we're talking about a quality defense."

Defense has been Sen. Hart's special field of expertise for some time. He doesn't necessarily oppose increased spending for the military; he argues we should be thinking more about what we're getting for all those billions. And, as he goes along, he's picking up followers, both liberal Democrats and conservative Republicans.

He concedes the Democrats haven't come up with an issue as dramatic as the Republicans' supply-side economics. But he thinks something will evolve as these younger Democrats come into power. As for himself, he's pushing a proposal that would use the tax system to give workers and corporations direct financial incentives to hold down wages and prices voluntarily. He says both liberal and conservative economists are interested in the idea.

Finally, there is some evidence an important missing element in the way Democrats behave is being rediscovered — a sense of humor. It's time to poke some fun at the Republicans, suggests Barney Frank, the 41-year-old freshman Democrat from Massachusetts. Who else, he asks, but Republicans would seriously propose bringing the battleships out of mothballs.

"I won't vote for a weapon that's older than I am," he says.

Mr. Perry, a member of the Journal's Washington bureau, covers politics.

House Keeper
Jim Wright, Activist Yet Reflective, Strives To Rally Democrats

Majority Leader Gets Bolder As He Counters Reagan And Eyes Job of Speaker

Honeyed Voice, Hot Temper

By Dennis Farney
Staff Reporter of The Wall Street Journal

Oct. 25, 1979:
I've seldom felt quite so despondent about this job. I seriously—truly more se-

riously than ever before—contemplate retiring from this well-nigh impossible task . . . . What does this say . . . of my tensile strength? Of my basic motivations? . . . Is it an insatiable thirst for approval that drives me?

Later that day:
Well, all right. Suppose I did retire? What would I do? Where else would I find . . . the sense of its mattering?

—Excerpts from the journal of
House Majority Leader James R. Wright.

WASHINGTON—Politicians are human too—only more so, with larger-than-life emotions and ambitions. As a case in point, consider Jim Wright, the proud and driven Texan who could be the next Speaker of the House.

The House majority leader, second-in-command to Speaker Thomas P. O'Neill, is a man with a honeyed voice and a hot temper. A former Golden Gloves boxer, he nearly came to blows on the House floor a few years ago with a fellow Democrat, California's Fortney "Pete" Stark.

"I remember thinking, 'I'm about to get

hit in the face and I think it's going to hurt a lot,' " says the breezy Mr. Stark, who stresses that the whole thing was his fault. But, characteristically, Mr. Wright's anger evaporated as quickly as it had flared.

His mellifluous, stem-winding oratorical style — effective on the House floor, less so on television— harks back to the 19th Century stump speaker. But he saves his innermost thoughts for this private journal. There, in entries scribbled during airplane flights and during predawn bouts with insomnia, the 58-year-old Texan has been conducting a private debate with himself over the past two years. Is the "crazy" political game he's playing worth the effort?

It appears Rep. Wright has resolved that

debate—in favor of playing even harder. For he's increasingly asserting himself in the House, taking a bigger part in Democratic legislative strategy. One objective apparently is to strengthen his claim on the Speaker's chair when the 68-year-old Tip O'Neill eventually retires. Majority leaders customarily have moved up to the speakership, and, as one old friend puts it, "There isn't any question that he wants to be speaker."

Synfuels Showdown

The results of Jim Wright's activism have been mixed. Despite fervent pleas, he failed to prevent the heavy defections of Southern Democrats that clinched President Reagan's smashing budget-cutting victories in the House. Another Wright initiative backfired spectacularly. Late last year he urged that two fellow Texas Democrats, Reps. Phil Gramm and Kent Hance, be named to the Budget and Ways and Means committees, respectively. Once on those prestigious committees, the two men promptly defected to President Reagan's side.

But other initiatives have fared better—at the least, increasing Mr. Wright's visibility among his Democratic colleagues.

When House Democrats held a weekend strategy retreat at a local hotel early this year, he took the lead in organizing it. When Budget Director David Stockman contemplated deep cuts in the infant synthetic-fuels program, which Rep. Wright helped launch in 1979, the Texan quickly rounded up dozens of senior House Democrats who warned Mr. Stockman to back off. The petition was ridiculed by editorialists who thought the Democrats' first priority should have been the poor; "let them eat synfuels," said a sarcastic New York Times. But so far, the heart of the synfuels program has survived.

"He's Looked Forceful"

In an apparent gesture to conservative Democrats that upset Speaker O'Neill, Rep. Wright joined GOP minority whip Trent Lott in endorsing a formula for tightening up the congressional budget process. And when House Democratic leaders haggled over the tax cut in a White House meeting with President Reagan, Rep. Wright just happened to have his own personal compromise proposal, written on a paper he handed the President.

Such activity, although criticized as opportunistic by some colleagues, has helped Rep. Wright strengthen what began as a weak claim on the speakership. He won his majority leader's job in 1976 by only one vote, and that on the third ballot—hardly a mandate. But "this year, he's looked forceful at a time when we're all groping for leadership," says one House Democrat.

That's the way Jim Wright likes to be perceived. He's a big-play man, a lover of the long pass, the bold stroke. He's a man who, in a journal entry last New Year's eve,

summed up Jimmy Carter's defeat in four words: ". . . He thought too small." Mr. Wright's proudest moment in the House may well have come in June 1979, when he quarterbacked the drive to an overwhelming vote that launched the $20 billion synthetic-fuels program. "It was sweet!" he exulted in his journal that night.

He's also a can-do man. Pessimists annoy him. Two years ago he questioned whether reporters haven't become unwitting "enemies of government" who contribute to public cynicism by being too cynical themselves. "I hate it when there seems to be a continuous gabble of gripes, an uninterrupted dirge of despondency," he said.

He remains a "national Democrat," a moderate who generally supports New Deal and Great Society economic and social programs. He has a streak of populism that shows up in an antipathy to high interest rates and the Federal Reserve policies that lead to them.

Yet the majority leader is openly disdainful of the House's most liberal Democrats, particularly those he sees as advocating "no-growth" economic policies. "Jim's a liberal of the 1950s variety: Help the poor, end discrimination, minimum wage, education," says Craig Raupe, a former Wright staffer and manager of his 1980 congressional campaign. "But Jim parted company with the liberals" on some divisive issues of the 1960s.

Mr. Wright remained hawkish on the Vietnam war long after many liberals declared against it, for example. He has never been an ardent environmentalist; friends say he still hasn't quite given up on a costly scheme to channelize the Trinity River, opening Dallas-Fort Worth to barge traffic from the Gulf of Mexico. Although he is less friendly to the oil industry than many Texas legislators are—he voted for President Carter's "windfall profits" tax after losing on an amendment to soften it—some liberals nevertheless think he's too friendly.

Still, the majority leader gradually has earned the grudging respect of some colleagues who voted against him in 1976. "He's willing to listen, he's willing to be educated," says Connecticut Rep. Anthony "Toby" Moffett, who backed Californian Phillip Burton for the majority-leader job. "That says a lot to me."

There are two schools of thought about being House majority leader. One holds that the post is prestigious in its own right and a short step away from the speakership. ". . . The majority leader—i.e., the future speaker—knows in that green glade where the ego blooms that he shall leave behind a well-marked grave," author Larry L. King (who once worked for Mr. Wright) has observed.

Maybe. Yet there are times when the job seems considerably less than it's cracked up to be. "I know that I've been mostly unhappy since I've become majority leader," Rep. Wright wrote in his journal in 1979.

Carl Albert once complained bitterly

when he was majority leader that, in the eyes of the White House, even freshman Senators counted for more than he did. That's the nature of the job; it doesn't exactly bowl Washington over. "Only the President and the Vice President outrank the speaker on the protocol list," observes Rep. Thomas Foley of Washington, the third-ranking house Democratic leader "but everybody and his brother outrank the majority leader."

Hurdles to Leap

Despite the place he has reached, several hurdles stand between Mr. Wright and the speaker's chair. The most obvious, of course, is that Republicans could win the House in November 1982, or come close enough to persuade conservative Democrats to join with them to elect a conservative speaker when the next Congress organizes. Democrats now control the House 243 to 190; there are two vacancies.

A second complication is uncertainty over when Tip O'Neill will retire. The speaker says he'll run again in 1982, despite earlier rumors that he would quit at the end of this session. "My feeling is that time doesn't work in Wright's favor," says one well-placed House observer. In this view, there's a generation gap, a psychological divide, between Rep. Wright and the younger, post-Watergate Democrats.

A possible liability is the Texan's personal finances, which have raised questions in the past. The Congressman disclosed, for example, that he converted $98,501 in 1976 campaign contributions to payment of "personal and political debts" and to taxes on the conversion; such conversions are legal but have often drawn political fire. And his part interest, with a group of Fort Worth oil men, in a Texas gas-well drilling venture became an issue in his 1980 campaign.

Battling Reagan

Finally, other powerful Democrats may also be eyeing the speaker's chair. One man thought to harbor that ambition is Ways and Means Committee Chairman Dan Rostenkowski, a canny vote-counter whose influence among House Democrats will rise if he can defeat President Reagan in the coming tax-cut showdown. Rep. Rostenkowski is thought more likely to seek the majority leader's post if Speaker O'Neill retires. But his decision obviously will depend upon Mr. Wright's standing in the House—which will depend on his performance as majority leader in the face of the President's general domination of Congress.

The popularity of Ronald Reagan and his budget-cutting drive has buffeted and baffled Jim Wright almost as much as it has Tip O'Neill. Last February he wrote, "It is just now becoming clear to me that Reagan himself and most of those he has chosen . . . actually believe . . . that all will be well . . . if only we reduce government spending." But Mr. Wright thinks the controversial proposals to cut Social Security benefits have begun to erode the President's popularity. He argues that House Democrats have at least an outside chance of beating the Reagan forces in the tax-cut vote.

"Stay with us, don't commit yourself too early," he has been urging conservative Southern Democrats lately. "You don't want to be in the position of giving $6.5 billion to the super-rich (through the Reagan tax cut) while taking $7 billion from Social Security recipients."

The majority leader doesn't know whether such arguments will prevail. But he firmly disagrees with fellow Democrats who contend that the best course would be to support the President now—then sit back and confidently wait for his policies to fail. "I can't develop any enthusiasm for the vision of a resurgent Democratic party arising from the ashes of economic collapse," he says.

"I don't want to lose," he declares. "I want to win. It's more than a gaudy game for me."

66

Man on the Right

Despite Courtly Ways, Sen. Jesse Helms Is One Shrewd Operator

North Carolina Republican Raises Millions to Push Causes of Conservatives

Too Big for His Britches?

By ALBERT R. HUNT and JAMES M. PERRY
Staff Reporters of THE WALL STREET JOURNAL

WASHINGTON—The attractive woman who answers the door at 325 Constitution Ave., in the shadow of the Capitol, is wearing a red dress with a plunging neckline. She says her name is Darlene Dove.

She invites her visitors to step inside the three-story, red-brick town house. The living room is furnished with a handsome antique desk, comfortable couches and an expensive stereo set, upon which sits a bottle of medium-quality Bordeaux. There are bedrooms upstairs.

This is the headquarters of the Institute of American Relations, just one of the increasingly significant, and well-financed, outposts of a growing political empire run by, or in the interest of, Sen. Jesse Helms, the staunchly conservative Republican from North Carolina.

"Jesse Helms is unique," says Herbert Alexander, a leading expert on money and politics. "No one else raises so much money; no one else is so deep into political high technology. It is the wave of the future."

This Senator, who many believe is the second most powerful conservative in the country, and his cause are a study in paradox. While the hero of the Moral Majority crowd is as strait-laced as they come, Jesse Helms is surrounded by a staff that churns and bubbles with bizarre ideas, clashing egos— and sometimes with plain good spirits.

Sen. Helms himself carefully cultivates the courtly country-boy image. But he is one of the shrewdest and toughest operators in American politics, even to the point of downright meanness, especially on racial matters.

Some of the 59-year-old North Carolinian's power is rooted in the Senate. He is the chairman of the Agriculture Committee, a senior member of the Foreign Relations Committee and the chairman of the Western Hemisphere Subcommittee. He also heads the GOP steering committee, a group of about two dozen activist conservative Senators.

Formidable Fund-Raiser

But Sen. Helms's power has much wider roots. Operating out of North Carolina's capital, Raleigh, in his behalf is the Congressional Club, probably the most potent independent political operation in the country. It raised more than $7 million for the Senator's 1978 reelection and raised another $8 million last year to help Ronald Reagan and a number of other conservative candidates. The club has more than 300,000 contributors, 45 full-time or part-time employes and its own sophisticated computer.

In addition, Sen. Helms's top staffers have created four foundations including the IAR—an organization that does research and publishes studies on foreign affairs. Other foundations back "pro-family" positions and a return to the gold standard. All but one are tax-exempt. They provide information for the Senator and his staff and pick up the tab for their foreign travels. Last year these foundations raised more than $2 million; no other office on Capitol Hill has anything comparable.

This political conglomerate is widely suspected of being a Helms machine for a run at the White House some day. The Senator dismisses that suggestion. "Cross my heart and hope to die, I've got no idea, no interest and no plan for running for President," he says.

Jesse Helms is a longtime Ronald Reagan supporter. Yet it's clear the Helms forces view the Reagan presidency as only a transition to what they see as real conservatism. Asked whether he agrees with his aides' assertion that conservatives aren't in charge in the Reagan administration, Sen. Helms says, "There is some evidence that pragmatism is being given more emphasis than it should be." He has voted against four Reagan nominees including Defense Secretary Caspar Weinberger; no GOP Senator has voted against more.

Powerful Coalition

Both Helms lieutenants and conservative activists suggest that if Ronald Reagan doesn't run in 1984, when he will be 73 years old, Jesse Helms might. "Without Reagan, the top two contenders would be George Bush and Jesse Helms," says Richard Viguerie, the New Right direct-mail expert who works closely with the Helms empire. The Senator, he says, easily could raise a record $20 million for the primaries and put together "a powerful, powerful coalition—the lion's share of the pro-life groups, all the New Right and the religious right."

As he has moved from the status of fringe figure to national power—leading fights against food stamps, abortion and school busing and defending right-wing regimes around the world—the Senator stirs as many passions as anyone in American politics.

"If there were an indispensable man," says Howard Phillips, the head of the Conservative Caucus, "Jesse Helms would qualify for the title without any close competition."

But to Senate Democratic Whip Alan Cranston, Jesse Helms "has introduced more meanness than I've seen in the Senate before." The Californian suggests Mr. Helms may be the "most dangerous" figure in the Senate since the late Joseph McCarthy.

It isn't just the liberals who are complaining. "I don't like the central issues, such as abortion, that Jesse Helms and his Moral Majority followers are pushing," says Sen. Barry Goldwater, the godfather of modern American conservatism. He says Sen. Helms isn't a "real conservative" in the Goldwater tradition and warns: "If Jesse and his followers continue to operate this way, we're going to see conservatism right back in the same fix we were in when I ran for President."

Many Senators, liberal and conservative, complain Mr. Helms doesn't play by the rules. They say he introduces extraneous amendments and then uses the ensuing votes in election campaigns against Senate colleagues he wants to defeat.

The critics also point to the way he ran roughshod over Sen. Charles Percy, the chairman of the Senate Foreign Relations Committee, in holding up some of Mr. Reagan's State Department appointments. They say he brushed aside Senate Majority Leader Howard Baker's plan to postpone consideration of divisive social issues until the President's economic plan is enacted, after first privately promising to abide by that timetable.

Maybe, some think, Sen. Helms is getting too big for his britches. Perhaps a backlash is developing. Sen. Helms, his critics point out, could muster only six colleagues to vote with him against Chester Crocker as assistant secretary of state for African affairs and three colleagues to vote with him against Myer Rashish as under secretary of state for economic affairs. Now he seems to be backing away from leading a challenge against Judge Sandra O'Connor, President Reagan's nominee for the Supreme Court, after being upbraided by Sen. Goldwater and others.

Still, Sen. Helms dismisses the sniping. For one thing, he explains, he is merely following the principles he believes in. For another, he says his opponents are simply "upset because finally conservatives are winning. As long as we were getting clobbered, I was just a courtly nuisance. Now that we're winning, I'm mean."

But Jesse Helms has always been tough.

The Meanest Campaign

The first campaign he participated in—31 years ago—was the meanest in North Carolina's history. It pitted Frank Graham, the president of the University of North Carolina, against Willis Smith, the chairman of Duke University's trustees. In the final hours of the campaign, the state was flooded with pamphlets suggesting Mr. Graham was pro-Negro. The headline said, "White People Wake Up."

Mr. Helms claims he didn't play a major part in the Smith campaign, but others insist he was a chief architect of Mr. Smith's

strategy. In any case, Mr. Smith won and brought Mr. Helms to Washington as his administrative assistant. Mr. Helms subsequently returned to North Carolina to be executive director of the state bankers' association and then, for 12 years, to be the conservative editiorial voice of Raleigh TV station WRAL.

He ran for the Senate in 1972, the year the Democrats nominated George McGovern for President. Mr. Helms won by opposing busing to achieve racial balance in the schools and by plastering the state with billboards linking his opponent to Mr. McGovern.

That campaign led to the founding of the Congressional Club. After the campaign, says Tom Ellis, who had been the campaign manager and who now is director of the club, "we were about $150,000 in debt. So we organized the club to pay off the debt. And we been plowing along ever since."

The club's big year was 1978, when Sen. Helms was running for reelection against Democrat John Ingram. That year, the club went "prospecting" across the country for contributors—and found more than 300,000 of them. Mr. Helms raised $7.5 million and defeated Mr. Ingram, who spent $264,000, by 100,000 votes.

Going National

In 1980, its computer bulging with the names of contributors, the club went national. It contributed $65,000 to conservative candidates around the country, it paid for the Senator's campaign swings, it laid out close to $4 million as an "independent expenditure" for Mr. Reagan's campaign and it ran three statewide campaigns of its own in North Carolina. It spent $8 million altogether.

Its biggest success was the election of John East, a little-known North Carolina college professor, to the Senate, upsetting the incumbent Democrat, Robert Morgan.

To manage Mr. East's campaign and the ultimately losing campaigns of Republican candidates for governor and lieutenant governor, the club, on the advice of a prominent Washington law firm, reorganized itself as a corporation. That way, it avoided legal limits on the amount of money and services it could provide its candidates.

The club, camouflaged as a corporation, attacked Sen. Morgan's voting record in an effort to portray him as a liberal. Sen. Morgan, who had carefully built a moderately conservative image, was apoplectic, issuing a long, detailed "white paper" to rebut the allegations.

One of the charges leveled against the incumbent Senator was that he voted to allow "union bosses" to use "forced dues" for political purposes. Actually, Sen. Morgan voted against a Helms amendment that would have barred unions, but not corporations, from using treasury funds to communicate with their members on political matters. The opposition also sought to link Sen. Morgan with Sen. Edward Kennedy and

George McGovern as being weak on national defense, citing a vote against the B1 bomber. Actually, Sen. Morgan was a hardliner on defense issues and consistently supported the B1, except on one meaningless vote in which he was joined by most other Senate hawks.

The actualities didn't matter. Sen. Morgan lost, Mr. East won—and Jesse Helms became a man to reckon with.

The Senator insists he shouldn't be given any credit; he says he knows little or nothing about the club, which really isn't his "personal possession." But Mr. Ellis, his friend and closest adviser, says the Senator is the club's "titular head and political saint." Mr. Helms's photograph appears on almost every wall and on every desk in the club's headquarters, which occupies an entire floor in an office building in Raleigh.

This year, with the money still accumulating, the club has run a series of ads throughout the country supporting Mr. Reagan's economic program and mounted a campaign in North Carolina against Democratic Gov. James Hunt's proposal to raise the gasoline tax three cents a gallon to replenish the state highway fund. The ads attacked the program and, by implication, Gov. Hunt. Democrats don't think that's accidental, for politicians widely believe Gov. Hunt will challenge Mr. Helms for his Senate seat in 1984.

The club's ads attacked the governor's "cronies" for such alleged indescretions as throwing their weight around to prevent state bulldozers from destroying two treasured magnolia trees. But the governor fought back with his own TV ads, singling out the Congressional Club for spending so much money on TV ads when money was needed for filling potholes. And the governor won; the gas tax was enacted. "We beat the hell out of them," exults Gary Pearce, Mr. Hunt's press secretary.

In Washington, some of the Senator's aides weren't all that disappointed by the news from North Carolina. They see the club as a rival to their own activities, some of which are just as innovative.

That handsome town house on Constitution Avenue is the home of both the Institute of American Relations and the Foreign Affairs Council, each of which raised an estimated $800,000 last year. Other Helms operations include the Institute of Money and Inflation, run by economic aide Howard Segermark and wholly dedicated to putting the country back on the gold standard. And then there's the American Family Institute, which promotes conservative pro-family positions and was run by Helms aide Carl Anderson until he landed a job at the Health and Human Services Department.

Aide Among Aides

The Senator's aide among aides is 47-year-old Jim Lucier, described by Mr. Helms as a "brilliant young man, a deep thinker, a scholar." Mr. Lucier is active in the two foreign-policy foundations.

Also active in these foundations—and a founder of the Family Institute—is the Peck's Bad Boy of the staff, fun-loving, roly-poly John Carbaugh, who can often be seen at expensive downtown restaurants whispering inside stuff to reporters. The Senator says he has cautioned the 35-year-old Mr. Carbaugh against drinking champagne in the middle of the day and absenting himself too frequently from his "lovely wife and children." Mr. Carbaugh's hideaway is in the town house; he concedes the bottle of French wine on the stereo is his.

Mr. Lucier and Mr. Carbaugh travel abroad frequently, often to countries in South America and to South Africa. A serious flap occurred on a trip to London in 1979 during the negotiations on the future of Rhodesia. British Foreign Minister Lord Carrington indignantly complained to then-Secretary of State Cyrus Vance that Mr. Lucier and Mr. Carbaugh were trying to sabotage the delicate negotiations. The two Helms aides deny it, but Mr. Carbaugh likes to recall a meeting they had then with the white Rhodesian leader, Ian Smith, who talked with them in his hotel room, in his bathrobe.

The third foreign-policy expert on the Senator's staff is Richard McCormack, who is not fun-loving. A rigidly disciplined man, he doesn't get along with Mr. Carbaugh at all. He has told associates that Mr. Carbaugh tried to talk the Reagan administration out of giving him a State Department job. Mr. Carbaugh says he did no such thing.

The staff philosophers are Mr. Lucier and Mr. Segermark; both sometimes wander off conversationally into very deep waters. Mr. Lucier, for example, is developing a thesis involving "rationalist" and "normative" politicians. A rationalist, he says, is one who uses reason as the sole guide to his behavior, while a normative politician never veers from the path of "traditional Judeo-Christian values." Thomas Jefferson, he says, was a rationalist; his own particular hero, Patrick Henry, was normative. And Jesse Helms even if he doesn't know it, is normative, too.

Mr. Segermark, even while he works to take the country back to the gold standard, muses about "anarchical economics." That would be "an orderly society without government." Theoretically, he says, "you can make a case for it." The courts, he believes, could be operated by a private business.

Others on the staff aren't so solemn. During the campaign last year, about a dozen Helms aides paid their way into an Edward Kennedy fund-raising fete to listen to the music. Featured, they say, were black groups playing "beach" music.

Mr. Chairman

Sen. Robert Dole Plays Major Role in Future Of Reagan Tax Bill

As Finance Committee Chief, He Stresses Compromise, Sheds Tough-Guy Image

A Big Appetite for Publicity

By ROBERT W. MERRY

Staff Reporter of THE WALL STREET JOURNAL

WASHINGTON—A few weeks ago, when his Senate Finance Committee was in the middle of writing a major tax bill, Chairman Robert Dole of Kansas spent a long day in bill-writing sessions and then flew up to Philadelphia to deliver a speech. After that, he caught a late-night flight back to Washington.

The next morning he rose in time for a 7:15 breakfast with magazine editors, met with the nation's governors at 8:40 a.m. and resumed committee action at 9:30. Grabbing a candy bar for lunch, he headed down to the Senate floor for a budget debate that stretched to midnight. Dinner was a bowl of soup at 9 o'clock.

Despite such a frenetic pace—or perhaps because of it—the 57-year-old Sen. Dole is having fun in his new role as chairman of the tax-writing Finance Committee, where 11 votes can redirect multibillion-dollar flows of capital. Five years after he ran for Vice President and collected a reputation as a partisan Republican bruiser, a year after he ran for President and promptly fell to the back of the pack, the smooth-faced, sharp-tongued Sen.

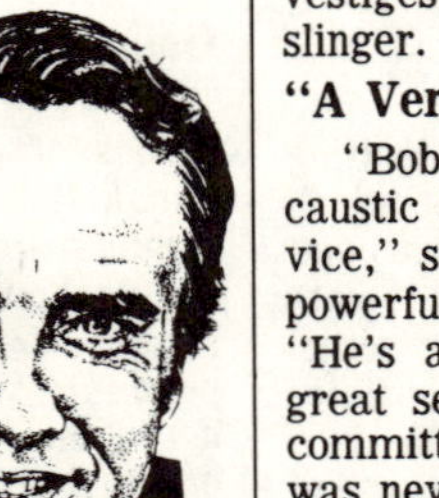

Robert Dole

Dole is gaining a new reputation as a wily, effective legislator.

That fledgling reputation will be tested starting today when the tax bill Sen. Dole shepherded through his committee three weeks ago goes to the Senate floor for several days of debate—and innumerable efforts to reshape it. To preserve the bill, the chairman will have to demonstrate anew the legislative acumen he showed in committee. There he maneuvered members to approval —on a 19-to-1 vote—of a bill that is close to what President Reagan wanted and even closer to what Bob Dole wanted.

"It was as deft a piece of legislating as I've seen in a hell of a long time," says Sen. Malcolm Wallop of Wyoming, a Finance Committee Republican.

What's more, the new chairman managed to preserve the bipartisan atmosphere that had prevailed in the committee through the almost legendary chairmanship of Louisiana's Democratic Sen. Russell Long. Thus, Sen. Dole's performance should help dispel vestiges of his reputation as a partisan gunslinger.

"A Very Compassionate Man"

"Bob Dole's press image as a tough, caustic hardliner does him a great disservice," says Sen. Lloyd Bentsen of Texas, a powerful Finance Committee Democrat. "He's a very compassionate man with a great sense of fairness." Referring to the committee's tax bill, Sen. Wallop adds, "He was never arrogant or devious, and nobody felt outmaneuvered."

A Senate floor defeat this week on any major amendment could serve to unravel the chairman's control of the issue and lead to a transformation of the bill—and a serious setback for the President. Particularly troubling are efforts to expand tax breaks for charitable giving and to trim back a provision in the bill to end tax-avoidance schemes called commodity straddles. An unraveling of the Senate committee's bill would hearten House Democrats struggling to produce their own alternative because it would give them more bargaining room in a House-Senate conference committee.

But duplication of the chairman's Finance Committee performance would produce a nice victory for the President as well as for Sen. Dole, who is probably more responsible for the shape of the current bill than any other single individual. His stamp on the measure is a product of a series of deft, well-timed moves designed to steer events toward the kind of compromise package his committee eventually produced.

Adding Some Fat

In the early days of the Reagan administration, Sen. Dole's strategy was to remain noncommittal on the President's tax proposal in order to keep his options open and require that other players move toward him. "He could be very frustrating," says an administration official. "He sent out conflicting signals; we never knew for sure where he was coming from."

The Senator's aim was to soften the President's insistence on a lean bill containing only individual tax cuts and faster depreciation write-offs for business. That wasn't feasible, he felt, because there were too many other tax ideas with too much congressional support.

"He definitely wanted to remind us," says a Treasury Department official, "that he was the chairman, and . . . we were going to have to make accommodations to him." At one point, Sen. Dole invited a group of Treasury officials to hear the views of Finance Committee Republicans, who accepted the three-year tax-cut concept but flatly rejected the lean-bill approach.

Later, in a series of interviews, the Senator said the president's 30% tax-cut proposal lacked enough votes to get through his committee. Still, he publicly advised the administration against compromise—at that time. "We interpreted that," says the Treasury official, "as saying it's time for us to start thinking compromise—but only with Dole. Those in the administration who wanted to hold out for the full 30% in the Senate were undermined."

The chairman's next move came in late May at a breakfast with reporters, when he unveiled a compromise plan calling for a 25% cut in individual tax rates, the accelerated-depreciation plan and a series of other tax revisions designed to spur savings and investment or redress certain perceived inequities.

That proposal, similar to proposals floated earlier by conservative Democrats in the House, eventually became the framework for the compromise bill embraced by the President in early June—and approved, with slight modification, by the Finance Committee three weeks later.

Sen. Dole quickly steered the panel to endorsement of the total size of the compromise package and the 25% cuts in personal taxes so dear to the President. But the chairman also supported a few fine-tuning suggestions from members as a way of keeping them happy and preserving the committee's bipartisan tenor. Again, that exasperated administration officials, who felt, as one expressed it, that Sen. Dole "was harder on us than on his members."

In fact, it isn't unusual for Sen. Dole to exasperate administration officials, some of whom think he's sometimes unreasonable in expecting recognition of his position as Senator. An example is the Senator's fight to get a former aide named to an Agriculture Department post that the White House would rather give to someone else. "He just won't let go" on the issue, complains a White House aide.

Some see a relationship between this tenacity on such matters and the Senator's appetite for publicity, which one former aide terms "insatiable." The former aide, a Dole admirer, quickly adds: "But he never wants publicity so much that he will resort to gimmicks. . . . He wants press, but only if it's linked to issues and actual performance."

This staffer echoes the expressed perceptions of many other Dole associates, who consider the Senator a complex man, full of apparent paradoxes. Always a rock-ribbed Republican, he nevertheless has championed a number of causes generally considered liberal, including help for the handicapped, food stamps (naturally a help to the Kansas farm economy) and a national health program to provide catastrophic-illness coverage for all families.

He is considered a kind man, and other Senators' aides say Sen. Dole treats them with a generosity of spirit that is rare on Capitol Hill. Yet turnover in his own office is high; one former top assistant, then new at his job, went to a meeting of senatorial administrative aides to find them organizing a pool on the question of how long he would stay on the job. "The shortest was six weeks; the longest was five months," he says. "I lasted seven months."

Then there's the well-known Dole wit. This hard-driving politician leavens his purposefulness with an ability to cast a detached eye at the often-ludicrous machinations of politics and capture them in a quip. Referring to Ronald Reagan's age during last year's Republican primaries, he said the former governor's opponents wouldn't dream of making an issue of it; quite the contrary, he said, they would like to sponsor a big birthday party for him on national television.

But some critics believe Sen. Dole too frequently falls back on quips. Says a Republican colleague in the Senate, "I think he relies too much on his wit and not enough on substance."

In any event, those who know Sen. Dole well suspect that the seeming paradoxes in his approach to politics and people may be related to his experiences during World War II, when he fought in Italy with the 10th Mountain Division and was nearly blown apart by mortar and machine-gun fire. He was left for dead on a Po Valley battlefield for 24 hours, then spent more than three years in hospitals recovering from his wounds. At one point he was paralyzed from the neck down, and even today he has no use of his right arm.

A Wife's View

"I'm not a psychologist, but I should think that contributed to Bob's unusual strength and backbone," says his wife, Elizabeth, herself a power in Washington as President Reagan's public-liaison chief. "Things don't get him down; he puts things in perspective."

No doubt that sense of perspective contributes to his sense of whimsy. But others attribute other Bob Dole traits to those harsh wartime events of the past. One former aide lists his ever-present inclination to drive himself toward completion of tasks, as well as his "soft spot for social programs."

And some even link the battle experience and its aftermath with the high turnover on his personal staff, which they attribute to a deep reluctance to delegate responsibility. "What's the key to the kind of rehabilitation Dole faced after the war?" asks the former assistant who outlasted the pool predictions. His answer: "Self-reliance. Bob Dole is the most self-reliant person I know."

Mrs. Dole marvels at her husband's self-reliance. After the national campaigns of 1976 and 1980 ended in failure, she says, "I never heard him complain. . . . He just picked up and moved forward."

The Senator himself recalls feeling some sadness after the 1976 campaign, when he was assigned the role of playing campaign hardball and emerged with a reputation as something of a political hatchet man "who couldn't sell beer on a troopship," as some critics put it, resurrecting an old political adversary's line.

Depressing Time

The most depressing time, the Senator recalls, "was the night after the 1976 election. I was exhausted, had caught a cold, and Barbara Walters had the temerity to ask me on national television if I thought I had cost Jerry Ford the election. I felt pretty bad about that for a while."

These days, the Senator is in a far brighter mood. He seems especially pleased about his success in guiding his committee to what he calls "a bipartisan bill." He says: "Everyone was satisfied with the process; nobody felt rushed."

But maintaining a bipartisan atmosphere on the committee wasn't easy. Because just about every member had a pet amendment to push, it was necessary for the chairman to forge a new opposition coalition on every vote, picking up allies who had opposed him on the last one.

But even when he lost he managed to salvage something. An example was an amendment by Sen. Max Baucus of Montana to provide tax breaks to trucking firms hurt by last year's trucking deregulation bill. The Montana Democrat carried the committee by a single vote.

Sen. Dole later picked up another vote and, brandishing it, he offered Sen. Baucus a choice: He could accept a compromise designed to lessen his amendment's budget impact or stick with his original measure and take the risk of having it overturned in a new committee vote. Sen Baucus took the deal.

But a Treasury official watching the session closely says he wasn't sure the chairman could have carried a second vote. Trucking lobbyists were working the committee feverishly, he says, and the situation was pretty fluid. "We were just as pleased that Baucus took the deal," he says.

As Wyoming's Sen. Wallop, an admirer of the chairman's legislative wiles, puts it, "I'd hate to play poker with Bob Dole."

Justice Douglas: His Politics Were His Law

By Robert H. Bork

One reads William O. Douglas's account of his 36 years on the Supreme Court with growing discomfort and frustration. Discomfort because of the careless writing and organization. This is less a book than a melange of anecdotes about, and evaluations of, Presidents, Justices, politicians, lawyers, friends and enemies, with cursory summaries of Mr. Douglas's thoughts about particular fields of law. Discomfort, again and to a greater degree, because Mr. Douglas's swift evaluations of people and events are often savage, frequently wildly unfair, and in some instances, obviously untrue.

It must be said in fairness that Mr. Douglas's reactions are not entirely partisan. He is often remarkably generous to those with whom he disagreed most profoundly, men such as Felix Frankfurter

---

The Bookshelf

"The Court Years 1939-1975"
By William O. Douglas, Random House. 434 pages. $16.95.

---

and Stanley Reed. I know this admirable quality of the man first-hand, for during a particularly stressful time in government, Justice Douglas, with whom I had never exchanged a word except across the bench and who knew my unfavorable estimate of his judicial performance, went well out of his way to express personal support.

The man behind the book seemed an enigma, therefore, until, at the very end, there came a sudden illumination. Mr. Douglas writes that from his earliest days his mother drummed into his ears Sir Walter Scott's lines: "And darest thou, then,/ To beard the lion in his den,/ The Douglas in his hall."

She was convinced that through the Douglas blood "we had acquired an indomitable will and capacity for achievement." This sudden vision of William O. Douglas as a turbulent, implacable Scottish chieftain makes somehow more comprehensible his embattled life, the anger and ferocity apparent in the book, the strong loyalties he gave and received and his bursts of warmth even toward those whom he regarded as philosophical and political ene-

mies. These personal characteristics are important to an understanding of his judicial career. Those strands of intuition about the limits of judicial capacities and the requirements of democratic theory, which add up to the "philosophy" of "judicial restraint," are likely to prove too tenuous a web to constrain a man of such passion and energy for long. His sympathies went straight and undiluted into his view of politics and society, and that view, in turn, went, with precious little dilution, into his reading of the Constitution and laws.

That Justice Douglas' politics were those of the Democratic left is made plain here. He saw American ideals threatened on all sides, indeed in imminent danger of destruction, by an evil and omnipotent "Establishment." Universities, he wrote, were "corrupted" by the CIA and the Pentagon, faculties becoming "more and more defenders of the status quo" and walking more and more "in goose step to the tunes of the Establishment."

The "all-powerful military-industrial complex now commands our lives," and by the 1960s and 1970s "the corporation dominated American life. Its lobbies ran Washington, D.C., the power behind almost all of the federal agencies." Moreover, "the military were so strong in our society [in President Kennedy's time] that probably no President could stand against them." If the Establishment consists of persons and institutions who have special ability to influence the direction of the nation, then, by any reasonable definition, Justice Douglas and the court he helped create were very powerful parts of it. Many of those to whom he attributes such malign power will read his book wistfully.

It is impossible to determine from the two volumes of his autobiography the source of Mr. Douglas's skewed vision of reality. Perhaps it has something to do with the extreme hardship of his youth, the sympathy he acquired early for working men, hoboes and Wobblies (the fact that he rode boxcars with such people is mentioned frequently), or his law school faculty and New Deal associations. Whatever the source, Mr. Douglas acquired an unprogrammatic radicalism (he disapproved of socialism because of the bureaucracies it inevitably creates) which he never abandoned.

Mr. Douglas's urge, which became the

dominant theme of the Warren Court, was the redistribution of society's wealth, prestige and political power. He, as part of a court majority, accomplished: school desegregation; legislative reapportionment on a rigid one-man, one-vote formula; the destruction of laws controlling obscenity, birth control, abortion and residency requirements for voting and welfare benefits; an end even to racially non-discriminatory poll taxes; and limitations on the death penalty. He routinely voted against business litigants whatever the legal context.

Mr. Douglas himself was often in dissent because he wished to do more and go further. Most observers, even those who approve, found it difficult not to conclude that Justice Douglas's politics were also his law. Though he frequently claims merely to construe the law literally, at one point he admits to almost complete subjectivity as a judge. He reports that he learned the truth of Chief Justice Hughes's remark to him, "At the constitutional level where we work, ninety percent of any decision is emotional. The rational part of us supplies the reasons for supporting our predilections." Mr. Douglas states he found this "shattering" because he had "thought of the law in the terms of Moses—principles chiseled in granite."

Whatever Mr. Hughes may have meant, Mr. Douglas cannot be "shattered." He had identified himself at Columbia and Yale with sociological jurisprudence and legal realism, with professors who taught that judging is largely political. Judges before Mr. Douglas had been legislative but rarely so frequently or so openly. He and the Warren Court demolished a restraining tradition and it is questionable whether it can be restored.

The book frustrates because it does not deal at all with this transformation of our legal culture. Some word of explanation, some outline of a judicial philosophy, is necessary from a man who labored so long and so single-mindedly to accomplish a revolution in the relations of our institutions of government.

It is difficult to see how a legislative judiciary and the premises of constitutional democracy can be reconciled, particularly when the judiciary's power rests upon the widespread misapprehension that it is not legislating. It is this problem, central to his entire career on the bench, that one wishes

Justice Douglas had addressed. This is not a case of merely complaining that the author should have chosen a different subject. When William O. Douglas writes an autobiography called "The Court Years" and fails to address the legitimacy of the enormous expansion of judicial authority which he helped create, it is a little as if Omar Bradley's autobiography had skipped over World War II.

Mr. Bork, the Alexander M. Bickel Professor of Public Law at Yale Law School, was U.S. Solicitor General from 1973 to 1977.

First Woman Chosen

Sandra O'Connor, Arizona Judge, Nominated for the Supreme Court

WASHINGTON — President Reagan picked Arizona Court of Appeals Judge Sandra Day O'Connor for the Supreme Court, a selection that may bring about more of a symbolic than a philosophical change on the court.

If, as seems likely, she is confirmed as the 102nd Justice in the 191-year history of

> *This article was prepared by Stephen Wermiel, Robert E. Taylor and Monica Langley.*

the Supreme Court, Mrs. O'Connor will become its first woman member.

While her nomination holds a symbolic importance for women, the philosophical impact is less certain and it may be several years before the effect is fully realized. The 51-year-old Phoenix Republican is described by Arizona lawyers as moderate to conservative, with much of the independence and judicial restraint that marked her predecessor on the high court.

"It's going to be Potter Stewart all over again," says John Frank, a Phoenix attorney and longtime Supreme Court watcher.

Classmate of Rehnquist

Those who know her say she is less fixed in ideology than Justice William Rehnquist, the court's most hard-and-fast conservative, who was a classmate at Stanford University Law School and with whom she has remained in contact. Charles Ares, a University of Arizona law professor, says she isn't "a right-wing ideologue. I guess that means she'll be in the middle."

On some specific issues, her views appear to be consistent with the President's, according to administration aides and others. As a state senator, she helped draft death penalty legislation and as a trial judge she imposed the death sentence. She also favors increased use of state courts and limited access to federal courts, according to a recent speech she made. She has been reluctant to exclude police evidence on the ground that it was obtained through unconstitutional means.

Questions concerning Mrs. O'Connor's degree of commitment to some conservative issues may present the major obstacle to her confirmation. The Moral Majority and the National Right-to-Life Committee quickly announced opposition to her nomination, saying that as an Arizona state senator she had backed the Equal Rights Amendment and on several occasions opposed curbs abortion.

Sandra O'Connor

Dr. J. C. Willke, president of the National Right-to-Life Committee, called the nomination "a direct contradiction of the Republican platform," which calls for the appointment of judges who "respect traditional family values and the sanctity of innocent human life."

But at the White House, Deputy Press Secretary Larry Speakes said her votes as a state legislator were being misrepresented. He said that Mrs. O'Connor had assured President Reagan last week that she finds abortion "abhorrent" and believes its use can be restricted by law.

Although conservative Senators, such as Sen. Jesse Helms (R., N.C.), may rally some votes against her and delay confirmation by a simple majority, it seems unlikely that they can defeat Mrs. O'Connor's appointment.

No Review by ABA

The American Bar Association may question whether the state appeals court judge has sufficient exposure to federal law, federal court procedure and constitutional issues to be on the Supreme Court. But the legal association's view may carry limited weight. The White House chose to announce the nomination without giving the association a chance to review Mrs. O'Connor's record, a departure from the procedure adhered to with many previous Supreme Court vacancies.

In choosing Mrs. O'Connor, President Reagan fulfilled a campaign pledge to put the first woman on the high court. The choice came at a time when women's groups have been unhappy with the Reagan administration on providing jobs for women.

Mrs. O'Connor was born to a prominent ranching family. She practiced law for a very short time in Arizona after returning from Stanford, where she was an editor of the law review. After four years as an assistant state attorney general, she was elected to the state senate in 1969. She served until 1974, becoming Arizona's first woman majority leader. She was elected a superior court trial judge in Phoenix in 1974 and held that position until 1979, when she was nominated to the state appeals court by Gov. Bruce Babbitt, a Democrat.

She has long been active in Arizona Republican politics. In 1972, she was organizer of the state Committee to Reelect President Nixon. In 1978, she was urged to run for Governor but chose to remain a judge. As recently as last month, her name was again being mentioned as a candidate for governor.

Mrs. O'Connor has also had Arizona business connections. She was on the board of First National Bank of Arizona in Phoenix from 1971 to 1974 and was on the board of Blue Cross-Blue Shield of Arizona from 1975 to 1979.

She is married to a Phoenix lawyer, John O'Connor, and they have three children.

Last Appointment in 1975

In making the first nomination to the high court since 1975, President Reagan and top aides said they were looking for a "strict constructionist" who would interpret federal laws and the constitution rather than make new laws or substitute the court's judgment for the legislature's.

They think they have found just that in Mrs. O'Connor. "She has a strong sense of judicial restraint," says Kenneth Starr, counselor to Attorney General William French Smith. "She tends in her opinions not to attempt to substitute her view for the trial judge below . . . or for the state legislature or state agencies." Mr. Starr said one of Mrs. O'Connor's "most commendable qualities" was her legislative experience.

Among specific views that appealed to the White House was Mrs. O'Connor's belief in narrowing access to federal courts. In a January speech to a conference on state and federal courts in Williamsburg, Va., Judge O'Connor said state courts should be given more opportunity to consider federal constitutional issues. She said it would be a "step in the right direction to defer" to state courts on federal issues. She also called for curbing the use of federal courts to sue state and local officials for violating a person's civil rights. Such suits, under an 1871 federal civil rights law, should be filed only after all state court channels are pursued, she said.

Supportive of Police

In the criminal justice area, Mrs. O'Connor's opinions show "she doesn't reach to strike down police conduct," Mr. Starr said. She shows a strong "presumption of validity" toward police behavior, he added.

In such criminal justice matters and in narrowing access to federal courts, liberals may find her less acceptable than they found 66-year-old Justice Stewart.

But the Reagan administration's expectations notwithstanding, observers say it is difficult to predict how any nominee will vote once on the high court. Moreover, as a judge Mrs. O'Connor hasn't had much exposure to most of the issues that will confront her on the Supreme Court.

If her "moderate to conservative" reputation holds true, her voting may make few material changes in the court's decisions. President Reagan may have to wait to see if he gets another chance to fill a Supreme Court vacancy before he can make a strong philosophical imprint on the high court. Five justices are 72 or older, although none has indicated any plan to retire.

Lawyers who know Judge O'Connor say she won't have any trouble getting along at the high court or holding her own with her new colleagues. They universally praise her intellect and say she is a friendly, open and congenial person who frequently sports a big smile.

Women's groups were largely pleased with the choice. Although she hasn't been an ardent feminist, she has supported the ERA. And she developed model legislation to let women manage property that they own in common with their husbands. The legislation was passed in Arizona and several other states.

The Senate Judiciary Committee will hold hearings on the nomination but hasn't set a firm date. The White House hopes Judge O'Connor will be confirmed and in place before the Supreme Court returns to the bench Oct. 5.

However, a quick start on the confirmation process may be delayed. As of yesterday, checks of Mrs. O'Connor's background by the Federal Bureau of Investigation hadn't begun, an FBI spokesman said.

                                                    July 8, 1981

REVIEW & OUTLOOK

The Retiring Judiciary

When he announced his intention yesterday to name Sandra O'Connor to the U.S. Supreme Court, President Reagan seems to have fulfilled not one but both of his long-standing commitments on the subject. First, of course, he had promised to search for a qualified woman to fill a vacancy; not surprisingly, it appears he has easily found one. But second, it looks like the nominee meets the ideological test Mr. Reagan said he would apply—not the test of political conservatism, but the test of belief in a philosophy of judicial restraint. Mr. Reagan is fed up with the imperial judiciary. So are a lot of people. So is the Supreme Court itself. The question is whether they are fed up for the right reasons.

About five years ago commentators began to notice that a new kind of judicial activism was abroad in the land. It involved a certain role reversal: The traditionally conservative courts seemed now to be fighting the Executive and Legislature in behalf of the liberal principle of extending government's protective scope.

Moreover, the new activism seemed on its way to becoming entrenched so that it could not be easily reversed by elections or swings of opinion. The courts were operating by expanding the definitions of basic constitutional concepts like standing and due process; such ground once broken is difficult to abandon. The courts also had a seemingly ever-growing field of overall government activity and public interest lawyers to cope with; this, too, seemed a near irreversible trend.

Conservatives didn't like the development because they saw liberals using the courts to protect themselves against the swelling conservative tide in electoral politics. But conservatives said the problem was more general than that. The danger, they argued, was that the courts were reaching for partisan definitions of constitutional rights in order to subvert the legitimate authority of democratic politics.

The Burger Supreme Court had certainly done its share of the judicial colonizing the critics were worried about, but in the decisions it handed

down this term the court showed that it has begun to take the case against the imperial judiciary quite seriously.

There were first of all the big decisions. The Justices upheld the President's power to take U.S. citizens' claims against Iran out of American courts and put them in the hands of an international tribunal. The court similarly upheld the Secretary of State's authority to take away Philip Agee's passport once he had decided that the former CIA agent threatened national security. And the court endorsed the discretionary power of Congress to set up an exclusively male military draft.

There were other such decisions as well: upholding Congress's and OSHA's right to promulgate unreasonable occupational health standards, defending localities' powers to ban topless dancing and keep Hare Krishna proselytizers from wandering around state fair grounds, standing up for state government powers in the imposition of severance taxes. Of course there were qualifications in these opinions, and partial dissents, and the special circumstances of particular cases, and disclaimers by the Justices about how the holdings were really narrower than they might appear. But through the opinions did run the thread of a newly self-conscious deference to Legislative and Executive authority.

On some of these decisions we liked the bottom line and on some we didn't. We think the holding on Iran was a big mistake; in distinct contrast, we are not mourning the obliteration of Philip Agee's passport. But like them or not, we found the majority opinions in the prominent cases sometimes disquiet-ing. On issues from Hare Krishna to the draft, they trotted past free speech, due process or equal protection issues that were not merely lurking in the bushes but standing in the middle of the road waving banners. You don't have to be overly sensitive to think such questions were at least worth a more extended arm wrestle.

There is going to be continuing pressure in the future to deimperialize the Judicial Branch. But maybe along the way it would be well to remember that insofar as the disenchantment with the overreaching judges was more than a partisan complaint, it was not an end in itself. It called for deference to the democratic process, but not an indiscriminate deference: It asked instead that individual rights be both defined with self-discipline and defended with care. It was a plea, in other words, that the judicial concern for individuals not be allowed to fly apart into an incoherent defense of both anarchy and statism.

That, and not a simple passivity, is the kind of restraint we're going to be looking for from Mrs. O'Connor's opinions and from Mr. Reagan's future appointments.

———

The Administrators

71 ____________________ *January 21, 1981*

Commerce Chief, a Government Outsider, Starts Learning Intricacies of Bureaucracy

By Kenneth H. Bacon
Staff Reporter of The Wall Street Journal

WASHINGTON—Malcolm Baldrige has solved one problem he faced on being named Ronald Reagan's Secretary of Commerce. He has found a place to keep his horse and to practice his hobby of roping steers.

But now this 58-year-old member of the Rodeo Cowboys Association and former chairman of Scovill Inc. faces a much larger problem: mastering Washington's bureaucratic ropes in pursuit of his goal to make the Commerce Department a more effective voice for U.S. business.

Unlike other Reagan cabinet members, such as Secretary of State Alexander Haig and Defense Secretary Caspar Weinberger, Mr. Baldrige calls himself "a complete newcomer" to government. But in the weeks he has spent here preparing to run the Commerce Department, he already has learned that most of Washington's ropes are red tape.

"There are a lot of rules," he said after a recent all-day briefing on the mechanics of government for the Reagan cabinet. "A lot of the rules assume that everyone's on the take. You have to remember when you go out to dinner to pick up the tab, or people will think it's a bribe. I just don't think that way."

No Time for Minutiae

Still, Mr. Baldrige left that pre-inaugural meeting of the Reagan cabinet and the White House staff with a feeling of excitement. "Ronald Reagan has a way that makes you feel part of what he's doing, that you'll be consulted and that he'll listen," he says.

At the early meetings, Mr. Reagan stressed that his cabinet will operate as a board of directors, advising the President on ways to slow the growth of government and reduce the financial and regulatory burdens it places on business and consumers. "There isn't going to be a lot of time wasted on minutiae," Mr. Baldrige predicts.

But over the past month, the new secretary, with the help of the Reagan transition office, has concentrated on the details of staffing and running the Commerce Department. Right away he learned that things don't move as quickly in Washington as they did in the Waterbury, Conn., headquarters of Scovill.

On his first trip to the Commerce building, he was depressed by the dark, shabby appearance of the main entrance. He called in the building manager to ask if the lobby could be spruced up, only to learn that the General Services Administration, the government's landlord and a bureaucratic rat's nest in its own right, is responsible for such things.

Lists and Vacancies

Hiring has also been a problem. Within days of the Dec. 11 announcement of his appointment, Mr. Baldrige received from the Reagan personnel office computerized lists of candidates for the 15 sub-cabinet slots at the top of the 30,000-employe department.

Although he has spent more than 50 hours interviewing candidates, none has been formally named. It will take weeks before his top aides complete their Senate confirmation hearings and actually take office, although some will start working as consultants before then.

With very few exceptions, Carter appointees in the government left their jobs yesterday, so Mr. Baldrige will find a lot of empty offices when he reports to work today. Some Carter people complain that their departure before replacements arrive will threaten the continuity of some programs, but Mr. Baldrige says "continuity isn't the main thing." Assembling a good team is the most important consideration, he says.

Between recruiting people and working with other cabinet members on the details of President Reagan's economic programs, Mr. Baldrige has concentrated on learning about his department's grab bag of agencies. Former Secretary Juanita Kreps used to describe the department as "Noah's Ark, but the Commerce Department has only one of each thing."

Its agencies range from the National Fire Prevention and Control Administration to the Census Bureau. The department is responsible for measuring the Gross National Product, forecasting the weather, registering patents and helping to set U.S. foreign-trade policy.

Shortly after the election, a Reagan transition team moved into the Commerce Department to draft a report for the new secretary. "We tried to cull out of all the material those matters the new administration will have to deal with in the first few weeks of its tenure," says Calvin Collier, a Washington lawyer who headed the team.

The report treats a melange of issues, ranging from the future of a Carter administration program to support the U.S. shrimp industry to trade relations with the Soviet Union. Mr. Baldrige says the transition studies shaved three or four months off his learning time.

Improving Productivity

Among other things, Mr. Baldrige plans to concentrate on reducing government regulation of business, improving the productivity of both management and labor, and increasing U.S. exports. He has discovered that many U.S. export regulations are so complex that companies have "to hire a Wall Street law firm" to figure them out. He wants to simplify them to make it easier for small companies to export.

One of Mr. Baldrige's goals is to increase U.S. exports to Japan. "We're a little more than half way there with free trade with Japan," he says. "There's free trade going one way now."

Malcolm Baldrige already has discovered that "there are a lot of rules." Many of them "assume that everyone's on the take," he says. "You have to remember when you go to dinner to pick up the tab, or people will think it's a bribe."

He says he's particularly concerned about the influx of Japanese auto imports at the expense of U.S. car sales. During his Senate confirmation hearing, he said he believes President Reagan should "talk to the Japanese and see if we can't work out something" so the U.S. auto industry "can get back on its feet."

The secretary also expects to help plan other measures to improve the auto industry's health. The Reagan administration is considering steps to relax costly automotive regulations.

Mr. Baldrige says Mr. Reagan "told me specifically that he wants a strong Commerce Department" when Mr. Reagan recruited him the Friday after Thanksgiving. But the new secretary lost his first bureaucratic battle for expanded influence even before he took office. He failed to win a greater role in setting foreign-trade policy at the expense of the U.S. international trade negotiator, a cabinet-rank post now filled by William Brock, a former Senator and chairman of the Republican National Committee.

If he's disappointed by this, Mr. Baldrige doesn't show it. Although he concedes the Commerce Department has a reputation for "weak" participation in setting economic policy, he expresses confidence that in the pro-business Reagan administration, the department will gain new luster.

So far, he says, his biggest problem has been keeping up with Washington's social pace. "It's hard to work 10 or more hours a day and then take in two or three receptions," says the Commerce Secretary, whose sister was once first lady Jacqueline Kennedy's social secretary. "I've been doing it, but I've got to stop. I know it's important to get out and meet people, but I don't know how people do it night after night."

Uncle Sam's Hemorrhage of Senior Managers

By JOANN S. LUBLIN

WASHINGTON—The U.S. government is suffering a serious "brain drain" of its most experienced top managers and Congress could hardly care less.

Thus a promising experiment in improving government efficiency may be in danger of extinction.

The experiment involves the Senior Executive Service, created by the Civil Service Reform Act of 1978. A cadre of top civil servants gave up certain job protections in return for the right to win bonuses for superior performance. These officials oversee 1.7 million workers and a nearly $700 billion budget, so any boost in their productivity could have a vast ripple effect on government efficiency, a much-stated goal of the Reagan administration.

But the lack of any recent pay raises for the 6,700 senior federal executives and the setting of limits on expected bonuses are hurting morale and contributing to an unprecedented wave of resignations and early retirement. More than 45% of nearly 1,000 senior executives polled recently said they may leave the government within the next two years. Many agencies also face increasing difficulty in recruiting qualified replacements from the private sector.

A report released yesterday by the President's Advisory Committee on Federal Pay criticized the widening gap between federal and private-sector salaries. "We're losing a serious investment in people" from the resulting "alarming" executive brain drain, committee Chairman Jerome Rosow told a news conference. "You can always get a warm body" to replace federal managers, he went on. "But what's the long-term impact?"

"The government is losing and the country is losing" from the inevitable employment of inexperienced top managers, says Robert Wiseman, 57, a retiring SES member who has had trouble recruiting top engineering scientists for the Army.

The Reagan administration recognizes

that "the loss of key individuals is going to (have an) impact on the effectiveness of implementing its program," admits George Nesterczuk, an associate director of the Office of Personnel Management, who oversees the SES. He adds a note of hope, however: "It may just be a matter of time before we can turn that whole pay thing around."

"The whole pay thing" affects not only the Senior Executive Service but also 26,300 middle managers in the government. Despite big differences in their duties, all these officials' salaries remain frozen at $50,112 because of Congress's refusal in March to grant raises to them and to itself, the judiciary, the Cabinet and sub-Cabinet. This so-called "pay compression" is "very galling, especially when people who have a great deal of responsibility running an organization bigger than many corporations are getting the same thing as minor functionaries," says Sally Greenberg, Mr. Nesterczuk's predecessor.

Congressional reluctance to invite public outcry over big pay boosts is nothing new. But federal executives' salaries rose only about 35% during the 1970s, compared with an 84% increase for other white-collar federal workers and a 125% rise for private-sector executives, reports the General Accounting Office. The GAO says inflation during the decade eliminated 31% of the federal executives' purchasing power.

Senior U.S. officials would feel less unhappy about their compensation if Congress hadn't also curtailed bonuses. Under the 1978 law, up to half of an agency's SES positions could receive awards of up to $20,000 a year. But last summer Congress cut those eligible to 25% and the OPM knocked down that share to 20% after hearing reports of favoritism and use of the bonuses to sidestep the pay ceiling rather than reward performance.

Now the Reagan administration is fighting renewed congressional support for eliminating the senior executives' bonuses altogether—which the House voted to do last year. "This isn't the kind of cut that's really going to hurt people, like cutting back on food stamps or low-income housing," says Aubrey "Tex" Gunnells, a House Appropriations Subcommittee staffer. "You go out to Podunk and see if you can convince them to give someone in government making $50,000 a $10,000 or $20,000 bonus for doing his job."

Nonetheless, poor prospects for pay raises and bonuses have doubled the usual employe turnover rate to 18% or 20% among SES members at NASA, the Air Force and other agencies. NASA expects to soon lose 30 senior officials who played important technical roles in the recent space shuttle project. "That can have an adverse impact on the continued development of the shuttle," says Carl Grant, NASA personnel director.

Many bonus-winners leaving the government land much better-paying jobs in the private sector. Dr. Robert Levy, 44, is quitting as head of the National Heart, Lung and Blood Institute to become Tufts University's health sciences vice president for twice his $60,000 government salary. After getting a $5,000 bonus last year, he saw little chance of winning another this year because of the restrictions. "But I wasn't so much frustrated with the SES," Dr. Levy says, "as with the fact that I work seven days a week . . . and I'm rapidly moving into debt." Three of his children will attend Ivy League colleges next fall.

Filling Dr. Levy's job and other SES vacancies can't be done easily. The pay ceiling means "you take second best" for top research posts, a National Institutes of Health official says. Five "well-qualified" outside candidates recently rejected offers for one such position.

The Army wanted to consider promoting a middle manager to be a command, personnel director. The man, who had been in an executive training program for two years, decided that a move from San Antonio to Atlanta without a pay raise would be too costly. The Army's civilian personnel director, Fred Newman, says, "We're going to have to go for the less knowledgeable person with less expertise. It's like bringing up someone from a farm team like the Alexandria Dukes to play for the New York Yankees."

These problems are not lost on the Reagan administration. Though the President is committed to reducing the bureaucracy, "We want effective people in there," says Donald Devine, director of the Office of Personnel Management. Without a first-rate civil service, he adds, "You're going to be wasting billions of dollars."

Ms. Lublin, a member of the Journal's Washington bureau, covers labor.

Reagan Men Learn What GOP Women Really Want: Jobs

* * *

Discontent Rises Over Number Of Female Appointees; 'Calling and Raising Cain'

By Monica Langley
Staff Reporter of The Wall Street Journal

WASHINGTON—Wendy Borcherdt is a woman torn between her loyalties.

Long a worker in Ronald Reagan's cause, she is proud to be serving as a presidential personnel assistant in charge of placing women in high administrative and regulatory posts. Dressed in red, white and blue and wearing a pin bearing the presidential seal, she tells how seriously she takes the job: Sometimes she wakes up at night "with my tummy turning because of the realization that I'm helping determine the President's only true resource," his people.

Yet this Reagan loyalist admits she isn't pleased with the number of women selected thus far for policy-making posts. The 45-year-old Californian is deeply disappointed that there are only 41 women among the 390 or so appointees named so far who require Senate confirmation. Mrs. Borcherdt, managing a smile, sighs and says, "But I guess I'll never be satisfied."

Some other women serving in the Reagan administration share her discontent, among them Dorcas Hardy, the assistant secretary for human development in the Health and Human Services Department, and Mary Jarratt, the assistant secretary for food and consumer services in the Agriculture Department. All are loyal to the President and insist his male appointees are capable, but they also feel a loyalty to their sex. Thus Miss Jarratt questions the implication that women are qualified for only about 10% of the President's appointments.

More outspoken are Republican women outside the administration. Even many who side with Mr. Reagan in opposing abortion and the Equal Rights Amendment are discontented—indicating that he is in serious trouble on the issue, according to Sen. Paula Hawkins of Florida, who says she has been "calling and raising Cain."

"Unacceptable Record"

Nancy Chotiner, who handled liaison with women's groups for the Reagan transition team, says the record is "so bad that I don't know how anybody could say anything else." And Betty Heitman, cochair of the Republican National Committee, says: "Surely by now it has dawned on the White House that they have an unacceptable record. I suspect we will, or should, see a more concerted effort to appoint women from here on out.'' And with a seat open on the Supreme Court, these women are urging the President to prove his confidence in their sex by selecting the first female justice.

Male White House aides promise they will try harder to find women for the posts still vacant. Lyn Nofziger, the assistant to the President for political affairs, says Mr. Reagan has urged Cabinet members to appoint more women. About 100 high-level positions remain to be filled, according to Pendleton James, the chief personnel assistant to the President. As the appointment process moves along, the percentage of women picked has been rising slightly.

But Mr. James doesn't consider it unduly low. ''I don't accept the premise that this administration has done poorly on the appointment of women,'' he says. Contending that the number chosen so far is respectable, he asserts: ''I fully expect this administration will have one of the best records in modern times on the appointment of women. Our record will reflect women's increasing role in society.'' Mr. James complains that a false view took root when only one woman got a Cabinet-level post and ''it's been bird-dogging us ever since.''

Resume Blitz

False view or no, women in the administration and outside are taking it upon themselves to work for a more even balance. At the Health and Human Services Department, Miss Hardy is interviewing seven women and only three men for each slot for which she has responsibility. Several women's groups are sponsoring a Coalition for Women's Appointments, and they plan to deluge White House personnel aides with the resumes of Republican women in the next few weeks while the last appointments are being decided.

The appointment process begins in Mr. James's personnel office, where resumes are reviewed, prospects are interviewed and the field of candidates for each post is narrowed to three. Whenever one of them is a woman, she must submit to an additional interview by Mrs. Borcherdt. The resumes and evaluations by the personnel office then go to the President's top aides, Edwin Meese, James Baker and Michael Deaver, before Mr. Reagan makes the final choice.

To survive the process, Miss Hardy says, a woman needs to ''present a bolder resume and squawk a little louder.'' As one rejected female applicant sees it, ''The decision makers know the woman better by the decision time and thus have more factors at their disposal to use as reasons against the appointment.''

This female professional also charges that ''fear of an open conflict with Reagan's views, particularly on ERA and abortion, is the motivation in precluding women when possible. A woman, merely because of her uniqueness in a male power structure, is extremely visible and therefore is likely to be asked for her opinions on such issues.''

Helen Delich Bentley, a former Federal Maritime Commission chief who recently was considered for under secretary of the Navy, says Virginia Republican Sen. John Warner told her the Navy wasn't ready for a woman. Asked about this, the Senator, a former Navy Secretary, says, ''Whether we like it or not, that is a man's world—one that is unlikely to change.''

There is much complaining about the working of so-called old-boy networks in the administration. One active Republican woman who failed to get a top position says she has never seen such a tight clique.

With most of the executive-branch slots already filled and with doubts that the ratio will change much, Mrs. Borcherdt worries that the lack of female appointees in some departments will leave a dearth of superiors to whom women employes can come with their problems. To help provide an outlet for their concerns, she soon will recommend the establishment of an interdepartmental task force on women's issues.

Women's groups also are troubled by the shortage of good contacts in the government. Mary Grefe, who is the president of the American Association of University Women and is a Republican, complains: ''We feel as though we have no voice in this government. Furthermore, some of those few women appointed suffer from the Queen Bee syndrome and are stricken with the 'I made it on my own, let the others' attitude. Consequently, they are more detrimental than helpful.''

Republican women feel that lingering resentment over the appointments will keep many of them from working in next year's congressional election campaigns and even in the next presidential contest. Mrs. Chotiner advises the Reagan administration to listen to its own female party leaders and appointees; their message, she says, is, ''A pat on the head will not suffice, or get ready for a rude awakening the next time around.''

Review & Outlook

No Room for Compromise

With passions in the air controllers' strike rising and local union leaders starting to go to jail for contempt, organized labor is protesting that President Reagan is out to bust the controllers' union.

There's another way of looking at it. By choosing to go head-to-head with the administration and federal law, the Professional Air Traffic Controllers Union (PATCO) has put itself in the position of trying to bust the Reagan administration. And it should be obvious now, if it wasn't before, that the President simply cannot afford to let that happen, for all sorts of far-reaching reasons that have absolutely nothing to do with relations between the Federal Aviation Administration and PATCO.

Mr. Reagan confronted the controllers fairly and forthrightly. As federal employes they had signed an oath agreeing not to strike, in accordance with a federal law that says ''an individual may not accept or hold a position in the government . . . if he participates in a strike against the government.'' In firing the strikers the President was doing exactly what the law requires.

The President yesterday supported this legal requirement with a philosophical principle, saying, ''If ever we feel that our oath of office need not be kept, how long would we have this society?'' When put that way, a small strike by only 15,000 federal workers becomes a big issue. And it seems to us about time American Presidents took such stands more often. Politics is indeed the art of compromise but leadership is the art of espousing solid principles and defending them so that others will have a standard to follow. It is a wise President who knows when to do the one and when to do the other.

Organized labor also is confronted with an issue of principle, the knotty question of how much support to give to an illegal strike. Its main response, in addition to the strike-busting charge, has been to claim that the anti-strike law is unjust to federal workers. The American Civil Liberties Union has picked up that theme as well, but surely the lawyers at the ACLU know that the proper place to argue such a point, when the law is so clearly written, is in the Congress, not in the streets. If the labor movement and the public sector unions who now play such a major role in the AFL-CIO intend to employ civil disobedience as a collective bargaining weapon they might do well to first ask themselves how this will go down with a public and Congress that have become increasingly irritated over their demands.

That is not to say that the task of the administration in dealing with the controllers is not unpleasant and messy. A Virginia federal judge yesterday jailed Steven L. Wallart of PATCO Local 291 in Newport News and Norfolk for contempt, making him the first PATCO official to feel the full power of the courts and thus a potential martyr. William Winpisinger, the left-leaning head of the Machinists, has asked his aircraft maintenance workers not to cross PATCO picket lines. If passions continue to rise, labor may yet choose to try to elevate the controllers struggle into a major contest.

But Lane Kirkland and other cool heads at the AFL-CIO should first give some thought to what the administration has at stake. Mr. Reagan has tried to restore public confidence in presidential policy and repair the erosion that occurred during the zigzags of the Carter administration.

Central to this effort are clarity and constancy of presidential purpose on a whole range of issues with global implications. They include, for example, commitments to rebuild military strength, to restore the dollar to soundness, to cut taxes and regulation, to resist Soviet imperialism, to curb the wild ascent of federal spending. Resisting the demands of a small labor union was not even on the agenda until PATCO chose to try to strong-arm the White House. Now that it has, the symbolism is all too clear.

If the President backs off on what he said he would do—that is to uphold the federal law—both respect for the law and his presidency will suffer. He will be labeled irresolute, unable to stand the heat that labor unions can so effectively apply, another Margaret Thatcher beaten by the public sector in his first year. The underlying fear in this democracy that elected leaders are gradually losing their power to the civil service and the permanent bureaucracy will have another brick of evidence to support it.

The struggle with the controllers may be short or it may be protracted and bitter. But if PATCO is busted as the union leaders fear, its members will have no one to blame but themselves. They have simply chosen to put the President in a position where the losses from compromise would grossly outweigh any gain.

---

75 *October 20, 1981*

Revisionist Regulator

Political Realities Slow Up EPA's Chief, But She Still Manages to Jolt the Agency

By ANDY PASZTOR
Staff Reporter of THE WALL STREET JOURNAL

WASHINGTON—Shortly after Anne Gorsuch took over last May as head of the Environmental Protection Agency, her staff hit upon a bold plan to help President Reagan in his battle against federal regulations.

By quickly scaling back certain hazardous-waste rules and giving states greater authority to control disposal sites, aides figured, Mrs. Gorsuch could establish her credentials as a no-nonsense administrator. But the carefully conceived strategy backfired.

The new EPA chief had to relent on some of her cutbacks after lobbyists for several chemical companies and trade groups protested that the proposed changes would go far beyond what they wanted. Parts of the plan, these business people complained, could create additional delays for licensing new dumps and expose many companies to conflicts among various states' requirements.

"Nobody from the administrator's office bothered to check with all the parties they were trying to help," recalls one industry executive. "We had to convince them to ease up and go a little slower."

The episode illustrates how Anne McGill Gorsuch's effort to bring swift, dramatic changes at the EPA is running into harsh political realities. The former Colorado state legislator was expected to emulate the confrontational style of her political mentor, Interior Secretary James Watt. "She came in like a whirlwind, itching to shake up the agency," says a former EPA official who worked with her until last month. "Now, she's out there trying to test the political winds to see what's possible" to accomplish.

With her determination to make government less of an adversary to business, Mrs. Gorsuch has indeed shaken up the EPA. Dozens of regulations are being scrapped or rewritten, thousands of employes face layoffs, and the agency is spearheading the drive to get Congress to loosen a number of environmental laws. In the process, though, Mrs. Gorsuch has alienated not only environmental groups but also many lawmakers and business leaders who otherwise support the administration's goals.

"A Sense of Lurching"

Mrs. Gorsuch's supporters still praise her knowledge of the issues and her desire to rein in the bureaucracy. But now, barely five months after sweeping into office, the 39-year-old attorney appears increasingly isolated and much of her staff is in turmoil —two of her own top appointees quit abruptly last month. The furor is occurring at a time when the EPA, which regulates everything from multibillion-dollar sewer projects to auto-pollution controls and warning labels on pesticide bottles, is facing a crucial turning point in funding and philosophy.

The EPA administrator and "a close-knit group of aides have developed a white-knuckles approach to running the agency," says a veteran career official who agrees with many of their goals. "There's a sense of lurching from one issue to the next, without much control," he says.

At a hearing last week, Republican Senator Robert Stafford of Vermont, chairman of the Senate Environment Committee, described the EPA as "an agency in agony, with its senior officials under siege." The severe budget cuts under consideration, he contended, "could amount to a de facto repeal of some environmental laws."

Mrs. Gorsuch shrugs off the controversy swirling about her. Confident that the White House supports her, she says she remains committed to making sure that everything the EPA does is "based on sound scientific research. What I am interested in is true regulatory reform." She adds that "unless it's done in a reasoned and balanced way," the new regulations easily can become "part of the very problem we're trying to solve."

The tall, dark-haired Mrs. Gorsuch conceded at last week's hearing that there was "a very serious morale problem" at the agency, but she argued that things would improve dramatically after the final budget numbers were released. The Reagan administration, she maintains, doesn't intend to gut the agency's enforcement efforts as long as they are consistent with the country's "deep grass-roots commitment" to protect-

ing air and water quality while encouraging economic development.

Staff Reflects Attitude

The young, hard-driving staff that Mrs. Gorsuch recruited primarily from private industry reflects her belief in a less activist approach to regulating business. The agency's new leadership, promises Thornton Field, Mrs. Gorsuch's special assistant for hazardous-waste issues, "isn't going to fall into the trap of conducting litigation or enforcement by press release."

Nevertheless, Mrs. Gorsuch's lack of Washington political savvy, many EPA observers agree, has left her vulnerable to attacks by critics. One of the agency's press officers says that "a lot of the staff (that came in with Mrs. Gorsuch) seem to be in way over their heads." The result, this official asserts, is that "people agonize over the politics of some minor decision but often let the big ones slip by."

Even a few White House aides express misgivings about Mrs. Gorsuch's ability to soothe ruffled feathers in Congress and improve the agency's morale while running the day-to-day operations of an agency with more than 10,000 employes and an annual budget of $3 billion. "The crossed signals and little slips have hurt us in some areas," concedes a top administration policy maker.

One big headache for Mrs. Gorsuch was her decision earlier this year to begin preparing legislation that would fundamentally weaken the Clean Air Act. "Everyone (in Congress) jumped all over us" the moment the draft bill leaked out, Vice President George Bush said recently. "Most people, even advocates (of substantial changes in the law), felt it went too far," Mr. Bush recalled.

A Hasty Retreat

Mrs. Gorsuch quickly retreated and promised to work more closely with congressional leaders to fashion a more moderate, bipartisan bill. But the miscalculation lost her important political points and unquestionably wrecked any chance the administration may have had of getting an air-quality measure through Congress this year.

The thorniest problem confronting her now, both inside and outside the agency, is sharp criticism of her proposal to reduce the EPA's work force by nearly 30% over the next two years. Disclosure of the proposed cutbacks earlier this month sent shock waves through the EPA's staff and prompted two congressional committees to launch investigations.

Some EPA insiders contend that the move could "virtually dismantle" entire program offices and signal a basic retreat by the federal government on a wide range of environmental initiatives. Douglas Costle, who ran the agency under the Carter White House, believes that it could take a decade or more for the EPA to recover. "This is not a question of saving money for the budget," Mr. Costle told reporters recently. "This is

a wrecking crew at work." William Drayton, one of Mr. Costle's EPA assistants calls it "a bomb-in-the-basement budget."

What bothers many observers the most, including Sen. Stafford of the Environment Committee, is that Mrs. Gorsuch is planning substantial budget cuts precisely at a time when the agency's responsibilities and its work load are increasing sharply.

Toxic-Chemical Laws

In the next few years, the EPA must carry out a number of complex new laws designed to protect the public from the growing danger of toxic chemicals used by industries. The agency must draw up and enforce regulations to make sure that approximately 40 million tons of industrial wastes are safely disposed of in the U.S. each year. It is also charged with cleaning up the huge backlog of abandoned, leaking chemical dump sites that pose serious public-health hazards for communities in every part of the country.

The proposed budget cuts, according to Mr. Drayton, "guarantee that the agency won't get an effective handle on the toxics problem until the end of the decade." (The EPA has acknowledged that it is nearly half a year behind in getting the cleanup program off the ground, and the General Accounting Office has reported that the agency doesn't have the staff or the procedures for making sure that disposal facilities comply fully with the law.)

Some critics assert that many of the agency's programs and its credibility have already been damaged. They cite last month's abrupt resignations of Frank Shepherd, the agency's top legal officer, and Nolan Clark, Mrs. Gorsuch's handpicked choice for the new post of associate administrator for policy planning. Both men apparently left because they clashed with their boss over policy matters, the extent of the proposed cuts and the way in which reductions were decided. Mr. Clark, according to one senior agency official, decided to leave after Mrs. Gorsuch reportedly told him he was too much "under the influence" of the civil servants in his office.

Topsy and Alice

EPA spokesmen insist that the hefty cuts under consideration won't interfere with the agency's long-term responsibilities because Mrs. Gorsuch intends to concentrate on those programs "that do the most for environmental quality." In the past, the agency "was allowed to grow like Topsy, without any real management control from the top," contends Byron Nelson, Mrs. Gorsuch's chief press aide. "That had to stop."

One White House budget official says that a large chunk of the layoffs is slated to come in the clear-air office because many of its functions properly belong with the states anyway. "It's like Alice in Wonderland," Mrs. Gorsuch argues, "to say that all the things I'm doing (to comply with current clean-air laws) are making the air any cleaner. It's just shuffling paper around."

According to Mrs. Gorsuch, many of her most vocal critics have a vested interest because they either worked for the Carter administration or head environmental groups whose main purpose is fighting with the EPA. "It's important to change the mistaken impression," she says, "that the only people who care about the environment are on the banks of the Potomac."

Still, the hard-charging EPA chief has decided to pull in her horns somewhat and take a closer look at a number of controversial issues. But this, too, has gotten her into hot water with some people.

Recently, for instance, the EPA has come under attack from some business executives who are upset that Mrs. Gorsuch isn't moving to slash regulations and take other actions fast enough to suit their needs. "I know plenty of businessmen who probably agree 110% with every principle she stands for," says one auto-industry official here. "But they say she's inaccessible and keeps everything too close to her chest."

Her aides say Mrs. Gorsuch gives these executives this impression because she is careful not to send possible "wrong signals" to interest groups about future decisions.

Mrs. Gorsuch says she is "certainly not encouraging any new regulations" that would impose additional burdens on industry. But she now readily concedes that rewriting and loosening the hundreds of existing regulations she thinks may be improper is a job that won't be finished in just a few months.

———————

Regulatory Politics and Policies

Business vs. Free Enterprise

As he attempts to disassemble some of the regulatory apparatus of the government, President Reagan probably won't be surprised to find that business isn't always the champion of free enterprise. Many sectors of industry have become accustomed to the protection afforded by U.S. regulations and lobby aggressively to preserve their privileged positions.

Take the television industry. The Federal Communications Commission approved a plan earlier this month to allow hundreds of low-power television stations, which would broadcast with a weaker signal than regular stations and thus cover only a neighborhood, not a region. The decision touched off an angry reaction from commercial and public broadcasters. They got the FCC to extend the deadline for applications for low-power stations, and the commission will likely be flooded by proposals from existing stations and networks. The paperwork could become enormous, delaying the development of low-power broadcasting.

Similar anti-competitive pressure by the railroads has slowed deregulation and stymied efforts to set up coal slurry pipelines. However, despite opposition from railroads and many shippers, the Interstate Commerce Commission last Thursday dropped agreements that allow the railways to meet and set freight rates collectively. Collective pricing, it said, tends to inflate shipping costs and discourages innovation.

Citicorp Chairman Walter B. Wriston, in a speech last Wednesday, criticized businessmen for proclaiming their faith in free enterprise in public but lobbying for regulatory protection in Washington. "Every time one of us tries to tighten the chains around someone else," he said, "he insures that government will eventually do the same to him. It is a losing game for everyone." The railroads, for instance, fell victim to the delusion of protected markets and didn't recognize new forms of competition, he noted. "Our commercial history is filled with examples of companies which failed to change with a changing world, and became tombstones in the corporate graveyard," he added. "It's time we realized there's no social

security for companies in the world marketplace, no seniority rights, no disability pensions."

Airline deregulation, one of the Carter administration's genuine economic policy achievements, is a fine example of how the re-introduction of competition can generate greater efficiency and benefit consumers. There were some initial dislocations and the deregulation process still leaves inadequate competition on some routes, but on the whole, the industry has been rationalizing itself with equipment and schedules better adapted to needs. Despite rising fuel costs and inflation, fares actually have dropped on some highly competitive routes.

Mr. Reagan will find that deregulating industry is not a popular pastime in Washington and that businessmen, labor leaders, and their Congressmen will be on his doorstep demanding continued shelter. But if he wants to revive the economy and benefit all Americans, we can think of few endeavors that offer better possibilities.

Easing Up

Reagan Starts Moving on Deregulation; Some Proposals Face Storm of Opposition

By Stan Crock and Albert R. Karr
Staff Reporters of The Wall Street Journal

WASHINGTON—President Reagan wants government to "stand by our side, not ride on our backs," and his administration is starting to move on a passel of proposals to carry out the heralded dismounting.

If Mr. Reagan's advisers have their way, regulatory burdens will be eased or removed in just about all sectors of the U.S. economy. Companies with noisy factories could buy earplugs for workers instead of being required to install costly sound-covers for machines. Auto makers could put off further cuts in emissions. New York and other cities wouldn't have to shell out millions of dollars to make it easier for the handicapped to use buses and subways.

The administration hasn't yet decided which of these and many other ideas offered by advisers—and pushed by industry—will, or can, be adopted. But the goal is clear. "We should deregulate from top to bottom," declares Commerce Secretary Malcolm Baldrige. "We're overregulated everywhere."

Actually, the movement to reduce regulation started to pick up steam under President Ford and Carter. But the Reagan rhetoric has been far more emphatic.

Oil Controls Off

Mr. Reagan has already moved to follow up on some of his promises. He quickly ended controls on oil prices and imposed a temporary freeze on more than 100 pending regulations by Executive Branch agencies. His administration also has scrapped proposed bilingual-education rules for schools and delayed an auto-safety regulation requiring "passive restraints," such as air bags and automatic seat belts. More regulations will be killed or rolled back, aides vow.

More important, say Reagan advisers and other observers, the new administration will seek a fundamental change in government philosophy by appointing more regulators who don't like regulation and who will pay greater heed to business complaints about excessive rules. President Carter named many "crusaders" to high regulatory posts, says Richard Breault, a vice president of the U.S. Chamber of Commerce. The Reagan regulators, he predicts, will be "very sensitive" to costs of regulation.

A Chance for Nader?

On Tuesday, Mr. Reagan ordered all executive agencies to scrutinize the costs of all their major new regulations and to adopt the least-expensive option. The action goes beyond a Carter-administration order that required agencies to make cost analyses that didn't have to be taken into account when drafting final rules.

Despite the bold talk and early actions, regulatory change may not be so dramatic. One reason: Oil-price decontrol and deregulation of such industries as trucking, airlines and communications already had been started by Congress and the Carter administration. In addition, the new administration seems to be pulling back on some promises. For example, rollbacks of certain environmental restrictions might not be as broad as originally envisioned.

President Reagan's anti-regulation efforts are likely to have wide support in Congress, but they will stir stiff opposition from backers of strong health, safety and environmental rules. "Ralph Nader isn't going to disappear," says one Reagan supporter; in fact, "he has a great opportunity to come back."

The Reagan administration's goal is to try to take quick control of the governmental regulatory machinery that has been built up over the past two decades and to begin dismantling it. Budget Director David Stockman, in his much-publicized "economic Dunkirk" memo, warns of a "ticking regulatory time bomb" set to explode in the next 18 to 40 months. He contends that rules scheduled to take effect during that period will hit companies with more than $100 billion in added costs and that these costs will further spur inflation.

Mr. Stockman cites, among other things, home-appliance efficiency standards and emission rules for heavy-duty trucks. He singles out rules for the disposal of hazardous waste as "a monument to mindless excess." The new budget chief may have indulged in a bit of excess himself: His list of pending rules includes a standard for bumper strength that has been the law for two years, and he hasn't documented his $100 billion cost estimate.

Nevertheless, many of the "ticking" rules are prime targets to be eased, delayed or stopped. At the Environmental Protection

Agency, top candidates include not only the pending rule for hazardous wastes, but also future auto-emission standards and rules aimed at reducing pollution from new small industrial boilers. Other advisers want to roll back costly existing rules, such as Transportation Department requirements to make mass transit more accessible to the handicapped.

ICC, SEC, FDA and FTC

Other proposals by Reagan advisers:

—Further reducing regulation of transportation, perhaps even abolishing the Interstate Commerce Commission. "We don't want the ICC to celebrate its centennial (in 1987)," says one transition adviser. "The slogan is, '99 years is enough.' "

—Sharply cutting back the information that companies must file with the Securities and Exchange Commission when they register securities, plus easing of periodic reporting requirements. The SEC transition team wonders whether investors get protection from publicly available disclosure documents, but it doesn't say which should be eliminated.

—Speeding up Food and Drug Administration approval of new drugs.

—Defining more narrowly the Federal Trade Commission's broad mandate to attack "unfair" trade practices.

Some of these proposals will be pursued, others will be discarded. The primary goal, Reagan administration officials say, will be to change the government's basic approach to regulation. Consider, for example, plans for the agency that some business people consider public enemy No. 1: OSHA, or the Occupational Safety and Health Administration.

The strategy isn't to eliminate OSHA but to transform the Labor Department agency from a cop to a business consultant. Rules for worker health and safety probably would be drafted after closer consultation with business and labor and would allow greater flexibility in meeting standards, aides say. Thus personal-protection equipment could substitute for expensive engineering changes.

When OSHA inspectors arrive at a business site, they will probably be more cooperative. "There will be much greater use of first-time consulting rather than investigative visits," a transition-team source predicts. Under changes being considered, this adviser adds, "inspectors will avoid the $100 Mickey Mouse citations for violations."

Immediate Turnovers

Besides taking control of Executive Branch agencies, Mr. Reagan will be able to put his own people in charge immediately at many independent regulatory agencies, such as the SEC and the Federal Communications Commission. At the FTC, a frequent target of industry criticism, a vacancy may not open up until September. But the FTC, like other agencies, already had begun curbing its regulatory zeal before Mr. Reagan took office.

Much of what the administration would like to do would require congressional approval. In many areas, such approval isn't likely to be a problem. Rep. Newt Gingrich, a Georgia Republican, predicts that "this will be the most deregulatory Congress in the last 30 years." With the Reagan administration's leadership, he says, a conservative Democratic-Republican coalition in the House will join the Senate GOP majority "to substantially reduce regulation in this country."

Even the liberal Democratic House leadership has signaled that it wants to put an ice pack on what politicians and business complain is a swollen regulatory burden. The leadership chose a "regulatory reform" bill as H.R. 1, the first bill to be introduced in the new Congress, to symbolize the importance it attaches to the measure. The bill would force agencies to take a closer look at regulations' costs and would make it easier for courts to overturn regulations. Congress also is expected to consider a legislative veto of agency rules.

Advisers Split

Reagan advisers are divided over the constitutionality and effectiveness of a legislative veto, although Mr. Reagan supported it on the campaign trail. And some advisers aren't sure they want courts to have more leeway to reject agency action now that the Republicans are in power. "I would rather have those calls made by the agencies than by the 250-odd Democratic judges that Jimmy Carter appointed," says Antonin Scalia, a Reagan regulatory-task-force member.

Despite Congress's general sympathy for anti-regulation efforts, some proposals could provoke bruising battles. One is a measure that would require benefits to outweigh costs in rules issued by independent agencies, which aren't covered by President Reagan's executive order of Tuesday. The House Investigations Subcommittee contends that the idea that costs or benefits of rules can be weighed with precision is "simplistic" and "dangerously wrongheaded" because "the state of the art is far too primitive." Mr. Stockman, in the "economic Dunkirk" memo, didn't even discuss the value of any benefits from the proposed rules.

Proposed rollbacks of health, safety and environmental regulations could create a storm of opposition. Betsy Agle of the National Clean Air Coalition, an environmental-health-labor organization, says that the Clean Air Act, which is up for congressional review this year, can be improved, but she predicts a battle if business tries to change the law "from the ground up."

Many Rules Required

Without major changes in laws, though, the Reagan team may have a tough time cutting back on regulations. Many rules are required by laws on the books. That reality sank in during the transition period. "People have stopped talking about uprooting the system" of environmental regulation, says one transition aide who handled environmental matters. "The emphasis is on modifying and changing the system to make it work more smoothly."

And then there's the question of getting the bureaucracy to budge. In Harvard Prof. Richard Neustadt's classic, "Presidential Power," he relates President Truman's musings in mid-1952 on what would happen if Gen. Eisenhower became president. " 'He'll sit here,' Truman would remark (tapping his desk for emphasis), 'and he'll say, "Do this! Do that!" *And nothing will happen.* Poor Ike—it won't be a bit like the Army. He'll find it very frustrating.' "

Many government observers believe that things haven't changed much since then. "For a new President, dealing with a recalcitrant agency can be like fighting an unfamiliar prehistoric monster," says Lewis Engman, president of the Pharmaceutical Manufacturers Association and a former FTC chairman. "He can stab it high and stab it low. But if he doesn't know where its vital organs are, he is likely to wear himself out before he even gets its attention."

Skeptics question whether Mr. Reagan will be able to budge the bureaucracy, but the President's advisers say that the skeptics are wrong. James Miller, a top regulatory official at the White House Office of Management and Budget, warns: "Those in the regulatory agencies who are banking on the fact that the bureaucracy has such inertia of its own are going to be greatly disappointed."

---

78   *March 26, 1980*

Is Airline Deregulation Working?

By James C. Miller III

The success or failure of airline deregulation has become an issue in the current fight over trucking deregulation. The trucking industry points to airline reform as proof that deregulating truckers would be a disaster. Reformers claim just the opposite.

President Carter signed the Airline Deregulation Act in October 1978, thus bolstering and affirming reforms that the Civil Aeronautics Board had begun a year or two earlier. Although the process won't be complete until the CAB goes out of existence in 1984, enough evidence has accumulated to enable a preliminary judgment as to whether airline deregulation has been a success or a failure.

Perhaps the best way to judge the issue is to review the predictions of its major supporters and opponents, and then compare these claims with what actually happened. The evidence so far indicates that airline deregulation has been good for both the industry and its users.

The principal proponents of airline deregulation were the Ford and Carter administrations, the CAB itself, several influential members of Congress (most notably Senators Cannon and Kennedy) and economists in universities and public policy institutes. They argued that deregulation would mean lower fares, more traffic, and reasonable earnings.

Argument Against Deregulation

The principal opponents of deregulation were the major airlines (at least initially) and organized labor. They argued that deregulation would mean substantial losses of service to small communities, unemployment or disruption of airline labor, increased need for subsidies, higher fares (perhaps after a short round of cut-throat competition), plummeting profitability, greater industry concentration, a breakdown in the airline network and perhaps compromises in aircraft safety.

What's the evidence?

Fares: Between 1970 and 1976, the domestic trunk carriers' fare per mile rose by 36% as against a 47% rise in the Consumer Price Index. In 1977, the average fare rose by 5.8%, compared with a CPI rise of 6.5%. In 1978, the average fare actually fell 1.9% in face of a CPI rise of 7.7%. During 1979, however, due largely to a doubling of fuel prices, the average fare rose again—by 5.3% as opposed to a CPI increase of 11.3%. But adjusting for the fuel price increase puts the nominal 1979 fare below that of 1978.

Productivity gains: According to CAB offical Robert Frank, inflation-adjusted unit costs have fallen a whopping 32% because of higher load factors, installation of more seats on aircraft and greater utilization of equipment. During 1977, trunk carrier load factors averaged 55.9%, but rose to 63.2% in 1979. Between fiscal year 1977 and fiscal year 1979, the airlines increased seating some 5.3% on the typical aircraft and the number of hours flown by over 12%. These efficiency gains are rivaled only by the 25% to 30% productivity gains brought on by the introduction of jet aircraft during the late 1950s and early 1960s.

Traffic: Over the period 1970 to 1976, trunk-carrier revenue passenger miles increased at an annual rate of 5.4%. But traffic increased 7.5% in 1977, 16.2% in 1978 and 10.1% in 1979. Of course, the data also reflect recovery from the recession of 1974-75, the recent slow-down in economic activity, and the massive United strike and DC-10 grounding that occurred during 1979.

Profits: Trunk airline profits (defined by the CAB as net income plus interest on long-term debt) averaged $349 million per year between 1970 and 1976, or 5.4% return on investment. For 1977, 1978 and 1979, profits were $634 million, $1,102 million and $564 million respectively, or returns of 9.1%, 12.8% and 5.8%. The 1979 figure, of course, reflects the soaring price of fuel—a situation that makes the outlook for 1980 even more pessimistic. Despite this, Aviation Daily's index of airline stock prices now stands at 53 as compared to 31 at the beginning of 1975, when deregulation received its initial impetus.

Service to small communities: Since 1976, the number of trunk-carrier departures is up 4.0%, and the number of available seat-miles is up 21.4%. But not all cities have benefited equally. Service by the major airlines has increased more at the large, hub airports and less at the smaller airports. Service among hubs has also increased more than between hubs and non-hubs, which has increased more than service among non-hubs. In many instances the major airlines have left small towns to the commuter airlines, continuing a pattern in place before deregulation. In most cases, however, this has meant more frequent service and substantial increases in traffic.

Airline labor: Since 1976, employment in the trunk airline industry has increased approximately 14.1%. To date none of the labor protection provisions requiring federal subsidy incorporated in the deregulation act have been exercised, simply because the adverse impact on airline labor has been insignificant.

Subsidy: The board's program of subsidy to local service carriers has continued under deregulation at virtually the same level of funding—$72.5 million for fiscal year 1976 versus $69.6 million for fiscal

---

Although the process won't be complete until 1984, enough evidence has accumulated to enable a preliminary judgment as to whether airline deregulation has been a success or failure.

---

year 1980. However, to provide assurance to small communities (which were fearful that deregulation would mean a curtailment of service), the deregulation act contained an additional program guaranteeing that all points would continue receiving scheduled service for a period of 10 years. This essential service program will cost an estimated $7 million for fiscal year 1980, and the amount is expected to rise over the next few years. But even including this new program, the inflation-adjusted subsidy bill is now less than before.

Industry concentration: In 1976, the trunk carriers' market share was 90.5% and the regional carriers accounted for another 8.3%. For 1979, the figures were 89.9% and 9.9% respectively. Only one merger of any consequence has been consummated—Pan Am and National—and the CAB conditioned its approval on Pan Am's not absorbing National's only major competitive route, Miami-London. Moreover, several new carriers have appeared, and intrastate carriers now compete in interstate markets. Midway now serves out of Chicago, Southwest serves New Orleans from its Texas base, and Pacific Southwest has finally crossed the California border, serving Reno, Las Vegas, Phoenix, and Salt Lake City.

The airline network: Little, if any, deterioration in the network of service has been observed. The carriers have not only continued to cooperate in transferring passengers, but because of deregulation they have been able to provide direct service to many additional points. From December 1976 to December 1979, the number of pages in the "Official Airline Guide" increased by 25%, a crude indication of the increase in system size and complexity.

Safety: Travel by air is incredibly safe compared to performance of yesteryear and travel by the family automobile. Fatality rates for the major airlines were 0.38 per billion passenger miles in 1977, 0.07 in 1978, and 11.4 in 1979. The 1979 increase, of course, reflects the tragic DC-10 crash in Chicago. But almost no one blames deregulation, since the maintenance program held responsible for the accident was in use well before the act was passed.

Substantial Efficiency Gains

Also of relevance to the question of air passenger deregulation is what happened when air cargo was deregulated in 1977. As Lucile Keyes concludes in a study just published by the American Enterprise Institute, air cargo reform has also led to substantial efficiency gains. Since regulation had held air cargo rates too low, they were bound to rise. But because of efficiency gains they rose by only one-half what the CAB itself had concluded was justified and was prepared to allow. Moreover, with a more rational rate structure, service mushroomed and the rate of traffic growth more than doubled.

No institutional change of the magnitude of airline deregulation is going to please everyone. Some have gained more than others, and some, at least for a time, may actually be worse off. But what is striking about airline deregulation is how limited and localized the adverse effects have been. And no program of publicizing horror stories is going to change that basic fact.

The evidence thus far is overwhelmingly on the side of the proponents of deregulation. By 1984, when the CAB is scheduled for extinction, reasoned judgment may be on the other side. But that would happen only if in the meantime the industry experienced failures of disastrous proportions.

The author is a Resident Scholar at the American Enterprise Institute for Public Policy Research. The views expressed are his own and not the Institute's.

Truck Deregulation Has Cut Rising Costs, Improved Service in a Year, Shippers Say

By John D. Williams
Staff Reporter of The Wall Street Journal

Despite dire warnings, shippers say deregulation of the trucking industry has spurred some favorable changes for them.

Here are a few of the results since deregulation became effective a year ago tomorrow with the Motor Carrier Act of 1980: discounted rates, more truckers, improved service, service innovations and more Teamsters union concessions on work rules.

Big truckers, who had fought deregulation, had warned of small towns stranded from truck freight service, of truck rigs falling into disrepair and of overall chaos. But that hasn't occurred, major shippers and analysts say.

"The changes are very healthful and we're saving money," says Fred M. Zitto, International Paper Co.'s manager of U.S. distribution operations. A quarter of the motor carriers he uses are new to International Paper.

Beating the Railroads

Both he and Richard Haupt, Ford Motor Co.'s director of transportation and traffic, believe that truckers, despite their opposition, are winning an increasing share of intercity traffic from railroads because they have adapted faster. Railroads, which favored fewer federal controls, have had them since October but have done little with them, analysts say.

Harbridge House Inc., a Boston management consulting firm, surveyed 2,200 of the nation's largest manufacturers and, from the 10% responding, found that 65% were getting lower truck rates. Only 23% of the respondents won lower rail rates since deregulation.

Specific Discounts

The manufacturers, with average 1980 sales of $1.2 billion, favor trucking deregulation three-to-one. Their savings in the past 12 months have averaged $1.8 million of their $23.7 million truck-freight bills.

Trucking rates in the past 12 months have risen about 17%, but discounting by certain leading carriers cut the overall rise to 12%, estimates William M. Legg, an analyst with Alex. Brown & Sons, the Baltimore securities house.

Because of inflation, the discounting hasn't shown itself at the supermarket, but it's clear prices could have been higher without such discounts. John F. Throckmorton, vice president and director of Carrier Consulting Services for A.T. Kearney Inc., a Chicago management consulting concern, figures general for-hire motor carriers would have had up to 4% more revenue in the past year save for their rate discounts.

Overnite Transportation Co., a Richmond, Va.-based trucker that serves 16,000 points today, up from 13,400 a year ago, cut its rates 10% and hired 20 more salesmen for its expanded territory.

Another leading carrier, Yellow Freight System Inc., Shawnee Mission, Kan., began March 30 offering rate discounts of 3% to 20% on certain types of shipments. Consolidated Freightways Inc., based in San Francisco, started offering 6% discounts on certain volume shipments in December.

"It's like walking into a candy store," says R.G. Stanley, manager of motor carrier transportation for Union Carbide Co., which buys about $165 million of trucking services annually. Many special bargains are being offered under deregulation.

Gauging the effect of deregulation is difficult, however, because of the impact of the nation's sluggish economy. Trucking tonnages have been off or flat, except for a small rise in April, ever since deregulation began.

In the 1973-1974 recession, truckers didn't offer special rate discounts. Now they do.

Shippers themselves—taking advantage of an expanded list of truckers—are creating ways to get more for their trucking dollar. (There are about 18,000 general for-hire truckers, up from 17,000 a year ago despite several hundred carriers that folded.)

For example, J.C. Penney & Co. recently asked motor carriers to submit proposals on rates they would charge to haul certain tonnages on specific runs. Penney is currently analyzing the proposals.

The transportation manager of a big electrical-equipment company is offering truckers from 10% to 200% more freight if it gets, in return, 5% to 24% rate discounts. Thus far, the company has 22 new agreements with truckers that were after larger slices of its annual $200 million trucking business.

Other Changes

There are a host of other changes occurring because of trucking deregulation. For example, most of the new truckers entering the industry are nonunionized, making it tougher for unionized middle-sized and small truckers to compete. Some of the unionized companies are currently seeking pay cuts from Teamsters.

Yellow Freight recently won "flexible workweeks" from Teamster locals at its expanded number of terminals. Under the new set-up, five-day workweeks can begin on Saturday or Sunday, with no overtime for such days.

Some truckers are diversifying to stay strong. Consolidated Freightways and others are forming units to specialize in handling containers for ships; Roadway Express of Akron is test marketing an air-express service.

"A dramatic shakeout is under way in trucking, just like the one that started in the securities industry in 1975," says Andras Petery, an analyst with Morgan Stanley & Co., New York.

The Panic Over Inflation

By IRVING KRISTOL

Austria is a small nation with practically no natural resources, and with an overblown, expensive welfare state that produces regular, annual budgetary deficits. It also has the lowest inflation rate in Europe. Why this should be the case, I have no idea—I know very little else about Austria. But the facts are right, and I call attention to them only as a reminder that, though the principles of economic theory are simple and clear enough, successful economic policy-making in specific contexts is never a simple matter. Indeed, the greatest single danger in economic policy-making is over-simplification—in focussing on one factor to the exclusion of others, in looking at short-term effects at the expense of intermediate-term or longer-term effects, or of confusing these various effects and their root causes.

In a sense, making economic policy can usefully be compared to a perpetual game of three-dimensional chess, where new players replace old ones at regular intervals, and where there is a lot of background noise that drowns out all communication between them. Under these circumstances, you don't fully understand why your situation is as it is, and you have only an imperfect sense of its risks and possibilities. But you do know—or ought to know—that the very worst thing you can do is to panic.

Yet this is what the Carter administration, and much of the business community and media too, have done in the face of our inflation. They have panicked. Astute financiers have called for credit, price and wage controls—i.e., political magic as a cure for economic distress. The media, meanwhile, keep focussing on isolated symptoms in such a way as to create a climate of hysteria. Won't tight money, which is supposed to cure inflation, send interest rates higher and thereby increase the cost of living? The answer to that question is "Yes, but . . .," at which point the media turn off their hearing aid and rush out to announce the apocalypse, an apocalypse being the most interesting of all possible media happenings.

Quick Maneuvering

As for the Carter administration, it has engaged in some quick maneuvering that is, at best, pointless. It has cut 1981 spending, increased taxes and triumphantly announces a "balanced budget" for that year. The question one ought to be asking oneself is: In an economy of our magnitude, how much real difference can a cut in expenditures of a few billion make? And the answer is that, in itself, it is of no economic significance at all—any more than an increase of several billion in expenditures for military purposes, say, would have, in itself, any economic significance. If the world's financial markets had sufficient confidence in the basic thrust of our economic policies, they would lend us that kind of money without blinking an eye. As it is, the financial markets, both here and abroad, seem quite unimpressed by Mr. Carter's balanced budget.

The tax increase, however, is bad economic news. Withholding taxes on interest and dividends is merely a method of increasing those taxes, and this is no way to spur savings and capital formation. As for the tax on gasoline—well, that is a tax, and it will inevitably have the effect of discouraging all economic activity in which gasoline plays a role. For some reason, the idea of a tax on gasoline meets with the enthusiastic approval of all sorts of people

---

Board of Contributors

Astute financiers have called for credit, price and wage controls — political magic as a cure for economic distress. The media, meanwhile, keeps focussing on isolated symptoms in such a way as to create a climate of hysteria.

---

who would otherwise agree that, at this time, a tax increase is what we really don't need. Perhaps there is a kind of homeopathic fetishism at work—because the increase in oil costs is so painful, we'll proceed to stick pins into ourselves by increasing those costs still more, and that will make us spiritually superior to those nasty OPEC nations, while teaching the gasoline itself a lesson. Or whatever—I really do not understand how one can be in favor of an increased sales tax on gasoline while disapproving of an increased tax on, say, clothing or TV advertising. What is so special about gasoline? There isn't even a "balance of payments" issue here, since we now have such a balance in our external accounts.

So what should we be doing about inflation? Well, the first thing to do is to distinguish between the illness, its symptoms, and the pains associated with its cure.

The disarray in the credit and financial market, resulting from Mr. Voicker's efforts to correct the very loose monetary policy of the past decade, is certainly painful enough. But the plain truth is that it is an absolutely unavoidable and curative "credit crunch" we are going through. The further plain truth is that those financial institutions that have been making a lot of money because of the Fed's generous lending policies ought to have realized that a day of reckoning would come, and should have positioned themselves to cope with it better than they are.

It is truly astonishing how many banks will urge upon you the importance of saving for a rainy day, while themselves playing the grasshopper rather than the ant. And it is equally astonishing how many intelligent business executives persuaded themselves that it made sense to go ever more deeply into debt, because inflation would eventually bail one out. In the end, however, inflation reaches a point where it mangles—if in different ways—both over enthusiastic creditors and overenthusiastic debtors.

There is little argument among economists as to whether Volcker is or is not on the right track. His is, in fact, the only track that leads us out of the spiraling maze of inflation. There is, however, debate over whether he is moving fast enough. Some conservative economists insist that he cut monetary growth radically and quickly, regardless of consequence, because this is the only way to break inflationary expectations.

Others, notably Milton Friedman, are more fearful of those consequences, and are for a gradualist policy. On political grounds alone, it does seem to me that Friedman and Volcker are correct. Whether Friedman is also correct in asserting that a very gradual squeeze on the money supply, however discomforting, will avoid the agony of a deep recession, remains to be seen. But the growth of the money supply just has to be slowed down, and if a temporary "credit crunch," as well as temporarily sky-high interest rates, are the prices to be paid, they will have to be paid. If we don't pay them now, we'll pay a much higher price later.

The surge in the cost of living, about which the government is being urged to "do something," is no less painful—only this is a symptom for which we have no treatment. Here too, the plain truth is that government, in the shorter term, is absolutely powerless to do anything—except perhaps make matters worse.

To some degree, the perceived increase in the cost of living is a statistical illusion. The distortions inherent in the Consumer Price Index are by now widely recognized. This index includes various taxes, which is ridiculous—no government that imposes indirect taxes (e.g., a sales tax) can have as its goal the maintenance of after-tax price stability. It notoriously exaggerates the cost of housing. It includes energy costs, a good portion of which ought simply to be regarded as an OPEC sales tax. All of these do result is a more expensive consumer basket. But so does a drought that sends meat and bread prices higher—yet no one regards such a situation as "inflation."

The true rate of inflation—i.e., an increase in the price level for which one can reasonably hold governmental policies to be responsible—is probably about 10% to 11%. That is high enough, Lord knows, and cause enough for concern. But not for panic, especially since (a) the monetary policy needed to reduce inflation might actually tilt the cost of living upwards for a while (via the diffusion of higher interest costs); and (b) most people do reshape their consumption habits to minimize their costs—a fact the Consumer Price Index blandly ignores.

Three-Pronged Strategy

To cope with inflation itself, as the cause of this and other symptoms, a three-pronged strategy would seem to be called for. First, we have to gain credibility for our efforts to slow down the rate of growth of government spending, so that it doesn't look like a one-shot affair. Second, as already indicated, we have to slow down the rate of growth of the money supply. Third, we need a successive series of tax cuts—especially on investments, savings, and business enterprise—that will encourage economic activity on "the supply side," stimulate economic growth, and lessen the pain of the transition to a non-inflationary economy. And when one starts thinking about such tax cuts, there is no point in being chintzy. After all, as Karl Brunner has pointed out, just to bring our average tax burden down to the 1976 level would require an $88 billion tax cut.

For such a tax policy to be instituted, however, we would need less immediate concern about a balanced budget—though no less concern about government spending. An unbalanced budget does not of itself cause inflation, as the case of Austria shows. It all depends on why and how it is unbalanced, as well as on the context established for it by other economic policies. A deficit resulting from a tax cut and a deficit resulting from increased government spending can be two quite different economic phenomena, even if they result in an identical number. It is the difference between a young man incurring debt because he is living beyond his means and a young man who incurs the identical debt in order to go to medical school.

Needless to say, none of these policies can be effective overnight, nor can we entirely avoid the pain today resulting from yesteryear's follies. We shall need some patience and fortitude. It would be nice if we could all be candid with ourselves, and our statesmen with us, about this. Absent such candor, panic will do us all in.

Mr. Kristol is Professor of Social Thought at the NYU Graduate School of Business, a Senior Fellow of the American Enterprise Institute and a member of the Journal's Board of Contributors.

81

Fed Urged to Let Money Supply Increase Faster

Treasury Chief, Citing 'Flat' Period, Wants a Rise in Growth Closer to Target

---

By KENNETH H. BACON
Staff Reporter of THE WALL STREET JOURNAL

WASHINGTON—The Reagan administration, increasingly worried that the economy may be slipping into a recession, wants the Federal Reserve system to let the nation's money supply grow slightly faster.

"They have to be very careful not to undershoot" their monetary growth targets this year, Treasury Secretary Donald Regan said in an interview during the weekend. "Since we're in a flat period" of economic activity "which ultimately may be called a recession," the Fed has to go against the cycle and relax its restraint enough to enable more economic growth, he said.

The Treasury chief stressed that he is advocating only a "subtle" adjustment in the central bank's operations to bring the growth of M1-B into the "lower end" or "middle" of the Fed's target range for the year. M1-B, which includes cash and money in checking accounts, is the most closely watched measure of the nation's money supply. It has grown 1.7% from the fourth quarter of 1980 through August, far below the Fed's target range of 3.5% to 6% growth for this year.

Earlier in the year, Reagan administration officials worried that the Fed wouldn't slow money-supply growth enough to produce a steady cooling of inflation. After months of tight money and faster than anticipated progress in the fight against inflation, the administration now is becoming more concerned that continued high interest rates may delay the economic upturn it expects from its tax cuts. Economic growth that is slower than the White House anticipates would hold down tax receipts and hinder President Reagan's efforts to reduce the budget deficit.

The administration's latest expression of concern about monetary growth came after the central bank reported that M1-B fell $1.9 billion in the week ended Sept. 23. Last week the government also reported that unemployment rose in September and that construction spending and factory orders fell in August, providing new evidence that the economy is slumping under the burden of high interest rates.

Treasury officials are anxious to avoid giving the impression that the administration wants the Fed to allow an inflationary boom in the money supply or the impression of a confrontation with the central bank. "We haven't changed our basic stance," stressed Beryl Sprinkel, Treasury Under Secretary for monetary affairs. "We want a gradual decline in the monetary growth." But, he said, "our major concern" is that money-supply growth "might get weaker and weaker" as the economy slows. He fears this could increase pressures on the Fed to fight recession by pumping up the money supply too quickly, fueling more inflation. "We're saying let's maintain stable monetary growth" that's neither too low nor too high, Mr. Sprinkel said.

Reaganomics: Is That All There Is?

By WALTER W. HELLER

When Mr. Reagan pins his hopes for lowering interest rates and calming Wall Street's nerves on further budget cuts, one has to ask: Is that all there is? Do we have options other than relentless budget slashing to lead us out of the wilderness of towering interest rates?

"High interest rates are killing us" is the cry of borrowers everywhere, especially in housing, savings institutions, farming, small business, and state and local government. Their cries reflect the escalating costs of containing inflation through tight money:

Economic slack and slow growth: The most obvious impact is the suppression of economic expansion. The White House, as such, has no anti-inflationary program (leaving aside long-run effects of deregulation and investment stimulus) other than to say to the Fed: "sic'em." In fact, by running a pro-inflationary fiscal program, it makes the Fed's job harder.

Retarded investment: Here, the conflict between loose fiscal and tight money policy is particularly evident. The most generous tax breaks for savings and investment in U.S. history show no signs of being able to overcome the stultifying effect of high interest rates. Recent Commerce Department and Conference Board surveys show business fixed investment flat in real terms for 1981-82.

Low Housing Starts

Housing and autos: They are gasping. Only twice in the past 35 years have housing starts fallen as low as August's annual rate of 937,000 units.

Small business, savings institutions and state-local government: A rising tide of small-business bankruptcies, forced mergers of savings and loans and the withering impact of 14% and 15% interest rates on state-local borrowing reveal severe economic strain.

Cost-push inflation: As money costs soar into the 15%-25% range, Federal Reserve efforts to curb demand inflation generate more cost inflation. Mortgage costs, now above 18%, are an obvious case. Less obvious is the sharply rising burden of net interest costs of non-financial corporations. From an average of $40 billion a year in 1976-79, that burden rose to $56 billion in 1980 and ran at a rate of $62 billion in the first half of 1981. Insidiously, this tends to give business a vested interest in inflation—a sharp drop in price advances in the face of these soaring fixed charges on business debt would put a big squeeze on profit

margins. We are witnessing a transfer of the risks of inflation from lender to borrower.

Pressure on foreign economies: Our high interest rates are forcing restrictive policies on our trading partners that account in significant part for their stagnant economies. Less developed economies are also finding the refinancing of their dollar debts a burden.

Pressure on the federal budget: Interest costs are the fastest-rising and least-controllable major component of the federal budget. The budget is caught in a vicious circle of ballooning deficits that soak up credit and thus generate still higher interest rates, resulting in still higher deficits. In the past decade, the budget as a whole has risen at an .1% annual rate while interest rates have risen at a 19% annual clip. Since March, the federal tab for interest-related costs in 1982 has been raised by over $15 billion—$10.3 billion from March to July and another $5 billion or $6 billion since the Mid-Session Review.

These costs dominate the Reagan

ised to deliver robust growth, ebbing inflation and interest rates and balanced budgets. No hard choices, no tough trade-offs in this economic wonderland that zealous supply siders and monetarists—united in shotgun marriage — offered the Reagan White House. It was, and is, unreal.

In reality, unswerving pursuit of present policies offers huge deficits, suffocating interest rates and a fits-and-starts economy. How can we find some relief from the sky-high interest rates of Reaganomics?

Much of the answer lies in taking some of the excessive burden of fighting inflation off the shoulders of the Federal Reserve by budget cuts and courageous tax action. But part of the answer lies in the Fed's own hands. If it insists on a monetarist target, a sensible first step would be to change cleanly to M1-B, the best index of transaction funds, as its money supply gauge. With M1-B running below the Fed's targets, with the economy sputtering and with favorable breaks on the inflation front, a letup in credit stringency makes sense. It would not relieve us of the inherent contra-

---

Board of Contributors

Mr. Reagan has back-tracked gracefully on Social Security and school-lunch cutbacks. Why not on tax cuts?

"budget creep" from the $695 billion level promised in March to $726 billion today (prior to new cuts).

Eroded asset values: Fears of flying at high-altitude deficit levels for years to come have played the major role in chopping some $200 billion off stock values and $300 billion off fixed-interest security values since June.

Inequities: High interest rates shift burdens from the strong to the weak. Businesses and individuals in high-income brackets have an automatic shield against the full impact of high interest costs. Those with little or no income have no such shield. Lower-income groups suffer triple exposure: as net debtors or as would-be debtors who can't afford to buy a car or house; as targets of further budget cuts to offset the unanticipated rise in interest on the public debt; and as the ones most likely to lose jobs as tight money squeezes the economy.

It was all supposed to have been so easy. The "new faith" Reaganomics prom-

diction in Reaganomics, but it would allow some short-run trimming of interest rates.

A second step would be for the Fed to provide some informal credit guidance, a few words to the wise in the banking community asking them to conserve the limited supply of credit, to guide it into the most productive channels. It would not take a very heavy hand to dissuade bankers from pumping money into corporate takeovers, commodity speculation and excessive foreign loans in order to give higher priority to plant and equipment investment, farming, small business, residential construction and the like.

This guidance or "credit conservation" would be a logical counterpart to the tax guidance so liberally practiced by the White House and Congress in the Economic Recovery Act of 1981. For example, savings are guided—almost bludgeoned—into All-Savers Certificates. Business funds are lured into buildings, refineries and long-lived equipment by 15-10-5-3 depreciation and so forth.

Funds are nudged into public utilities through tax-free dividend reinvestment. Moribund companies are given succor through juicy tax-sheltered leasing arrangements. For the Fed to guide lendable funds into constructive and productive uses is surely no greater interference with private markets than the powerful tax guidance encoded in the 1981 act.

In tightening fiscal policy, the name of the Reagan game is to slash social programs. Surely careful pruning of the defense budget could save more than $13 billion, or 2% of the $667 billion of defense spending, in the next three years. Such targets as uneconomic river and harbor projects, overindexing of Social Security, unwarranted tobacco, maritime and peanut subsidies and overgenerous hospital benefits for veterans have hardly been touched. But political and economic limits will stop budget-cutters far short of a balanced budget by 1984.

Mr. Reagan has to recognize that massive tax cuts lie at the heart of the country's deficit jitters. Tax cuts that will cost $150 billion in 1984, $200 billion in 1985 and a staggering $267 billion in 1986—roughly 4½% of projected GNP—are widely viewed as fiscally irresponsible.

A Courageous Tax Policy

The most important step that should be taken to inject fiscal prudence into Reaganomics lies in a courageous tax policy. Mr. Reagan has back-tracked gracefully on Social Security and school-lunch cutbacks. Why not on tax cuts? Why not roll back the recent tax cut, as Sen. Hollings proposes, or make the third-stage 10% tax cut contingent on the outlook for deficits and inflation? Tax indexing, adopted in haste and without hearings, should be put in cold storage. If such logical moves are beyond the political pale, there will be growing pressure for the value-added tax or some other form of consumption tax in a few years.

Significant tax action need not wait on such major moves. The President has already opened a tiny crack with his proposed $3 billion of tax tightening. Indeed removal of some unwarranted income tax preferences or "tax expenditures" should have high priority. Eliminating the deduction of interest on consumer debt could bring in $6 billion a year. Putting a $5,000 lid on deduction of mortgage interest would add $4 billion more. Including half of Social Security benefit payments in taxable incomes for taxpayers with incomes above $15,000 would yield $4.5 billion a year. One might also limit the exemption of contributions to employer health plans; apply withholding to interest and dividends; eliminate deductions for retail sales taxes; and give the IRS funds to bring the underground economy above ground for tax purposes.

The revenue agenda should include not just higher user fees for commercial aviation, waterways, irrigation projects and boating, but boosts in excises on liquor, tobacco and gasoline and extension of the windfall profits tax to deregulated natural gas. One could put together a $30 billion to $40 billion revenue program without touching the 1981 cuts.

Mr. Reagan's new economics of "gains without pains" won't work. If he would open his mind to a balanced approach embracing not just budget cuts. but tax increases and credit guidance (with some White House appeals for wage-price restraint thrown in for good measure), he could quickly improve the economic climate with a minimum of pain.

Mr. Heller is regents' professor of economics at the University of Minnesota, former chairman of the Council of Economic Advisers under Presidents Kennedy and Johnson and a member of the Journal's Board of Contributors.

Taxing and Spending

Understanding the Deficit Problem

BY PHIL GRAMM

At the beginning of the congressional budget debate it appeared as if all the political conditions necessary for balancing the budget existed this year. A clear majority of the people recognized that federal deficit spending is inflationary and favored a balanced budget. A substantial number of conscientious and influential legislators knew what the people wanted and committed themselves to spending cuts which would not have jeopardized national security or imposed unreasonable costs on the poor, sick or elderly.

Six months later, Congress passed a budget reconciliation bill which mandated $5.7 billion of reductions in a budget that had grown by 15.3% over the comparable 1980 budget figure. The fiscal 1980 deficit had grown from $29 billion to $63 billion and the projected 1981 deficit had exceeded $35 billion. Recognizing the political implications of admitting that the deficit would exceed $35 billion only three months after trumpeting a balanced budget, the leadership of the Congress put off final consideration of the budget until after the November election. Ultimately, the failure of Congress to respond to such a clear public mandate to balance the budget reveals a weakness in our political system much more fundamental than the cliche of failed leadership would suggest.

The public mandate to balance the budget was frustrated by the legislative process itself. The piecemeal way in which the Congress creates and funds federal programs strongly prejudices the outcome of congressional decisions toward higher spending. The standard program established by Congress provides a substantial amount of benefits to a small, well-defined group and imposes negligible costs on the average taxpayer. As a result, it is almost impossible to defeat a bill increasing federal spending unless there is considerable opposition to the program on the ground that it is a bad idea, rather than that we can't afford it.

Congressional committees that write the laws, like the bureaucracies that administer them, almost invariably become captives of their special constituencies. Seldom does a testimonial for a retiring committee chairman contain praise for what he did for the taxpayer. Bouquets are given for being a friend of the poor, the old, the veteran, the farmer, the scientist, ad infinitum.

Looking Over His Shoulder

When a vote on reducing an existing federal program does come to the floor, the member finds that the beneficiaries of the program are looking over one of his shoulders, but the people who pay for the program in the form of higher taxes and inflation are seldom looking over his other one.

A recent House vote on the twice-a-year inflation adjustment in federal retirement pensions is a good example. The budget had contained a hard-won spending cut which changed the inflation adjustment from twice a year to once a year. The proposed amendment, which put back the bi-annual inflation adjustment, eliminated one of the few real spending cuts in the budget resolution. My office received over 900 letters, phone calls and personal visits from constituents and lobbyists urging me to reinstate the twice-yearly inflation adjustment by supporting the amendment.

Not one person contacted me to voice opposition to the amendment. The reason is that federal retirees, like everyone else who is entitled to a monthly check from the Treasury, are far more vocal and active politically than the average person who will pay a minuscule share of the higher cost of the program in taxes and inflation.

The irony of these situations is that the labels liberal and conservative are no longer a good guide as to whether members will favor or oppose higher federal spending. The amendment to retain the bi-annual inflation adjustment in federal retirement pensions will cost the taxpayers $700 million a year and is very difficult to justify on policy grounds—no other form of direct payment by the government to individuals is so adjusted and 97% of private pension benefits are not tied to inflation at all. Yet the amendment was offered by Rep. Bob Bauman of Maryland, chairman of the American Conservative Union and nationally known, with great justification, as an ardent opponent of big government.

Under existing procedures, Congress is institutionally incapable of achieving meaningful reductions in federal spending on an issue-by-issue basis. The only solution to the problem is the adoption of some form of constraint on congressional spending decisions that will force special interests to compete with each other, rather than against the taxpayer, for the limited amount of the nation's scarce resources that we can afford to let the government distribute each year. By imposing a limit on public-sector dollars, we will force the proponent of a new initiative to prove not only that his idea is good, but that it is better than anyone else's.

A clear indication of how a mandatory restriction on the federal spending can force spending interests to compete occurred July 2. Members were anxious to

---

The failure of Congress to respond to a clear public mandate to balance the budget reveals a fundamental weakness in our political system.

---

complete action on the fiscal 1980 appropriations bill so they could go home for the holiday. Early in the evening, after a passionate appeal by the Speaker, the House passed an amendment sponsored by Clarence Long of Maryland. that added $528 million in foreign aid money to the bill. Unbeknownst to Mr. Long and most other members, his amendment also raised the amount of funds in the bill above the ceiling imposed by the most recent budget resolution. The chairman of the Appropriations Committee rose to offer an amendment rescinding revenue-sharing payments to the states for the fourth quarter of fiscal 1980, noting that unless the House approved the rescission or reversed itself on the Long amendment, Congress would have to pass a new budget resolution before it could aprove the appropriation bill. Confronted with a limit on what they could spend imposed by the Budget Act and the need to pass the legislation before adjourning, members quickly ordered their priorities and repealed the Long amendment.

I believe that a general constraint can be successful where individual cuts have failed.

A Piece of the Pie

It is perfectly consistent behavior for an individual to fight for a piece of the public pie and at the same time be willing to accept a smaller slice if everyone is forced to do so. The average citizen seeks specific benefits from government because what he gains far exceeds what he loses. He receives benefits from a particular program, but, as one of 95 million taxpayers and 220 million consumers, he pays only a minute part of the cost of his benefits in higher taxes and inflation. At the same time, although he may stand to lose a portion of his benefits if his program is cut due to the imposition of an overall limitation on federal spending, he also stands to gain substantially as a taxpayer and as a consumer.

Congressional leaders are aware of the strong public support for a general limitation on federal spending. The leadership has been forced to bottle up spending-limitation proposals in committee and to use procedural tactics to prevent the House and Senate from having the opportunity to vote on them.

The high water mark of the spending limitation effort in the 96th Congress came last year when the House failed by two votes to strike down a rule that prevented Congressmen Jim Jones, Trent Lott, and me from offering an amendment requiring a balanced budget beginning in fiscal 1981. Had the vote occurred on our proposal rather than on the procedural issue, which was not likely to be understood by the public or trigger political reprisals, the amendment would have passed by a substantial margin.

Entrenched liberals in Congress will oppose any broad limitation on federal spending. They understand that forcing members to order their priorities within an agreed-upon constraint will mean a reduction in the growth of many social welfare programs and with it the destruction of a political power base. Since these liberals now control Congress, passage of a budget constraint will require the building of a political base capable not only of mustering a majority in both houses but capable of forcing the issue to a vote as well. If the people understand what is at stake, I believe the effort can succeed.

Mr. Gramm, a Democratic Congressman from Texas, is a former economics professor at Texas A&M University.

Can Federal Spending Be Reduced?

By Martin Feldstein

The most difficult challenge facing the Reagan administration and the Congress is to reduce the growth of federal nondefense spending. Such spending in fiscal 1981 is expected to top $500 billion, or nearly 18% of GNP. By contrast, a decade ago, nondefense spending was $136 billion, or about 13% of GNP. And only 15 years ago, nondefense spending was just a bit more than 10% of GNP. The growth looks out of control.

Some opponents of substantial budget cuts assert that although small economies might be achieved by eliminating managerial waste and inefficiency, the level of spending cannot be significantly reduced without serious injury to the nation's well-being. Perhaps the simplest antidote to that view is looking at the spending level of a decade ago. Even if interest payments on the national debt are excluded, the per capita level of nondefense spending was then $1,250 at today's prices; this year it will be $1,880.

The innovations and expansions of nondefense spending in the past decade have added $630 per person (at today's prices) to the budget, equal to a total of $140 billion this fiscal year. Would we be significantly worse off if we reversed some of the expansions and innovations of the past decade?

Budget-Cutting Review

One useful way to begin budget-cutting would be to review every addition and expansion of the past decade and to ask whether that additional spending deserves to be continued. If half of the domestic spending increases since 1971 could be eliminated, the budget would be reduced by nearly $70 billion.

Although I have not pursued this approach, I have examined the budget from a different perspective. Budget-cutting is often regarded by its opponents as synonymous with taking benefits from the poor. Or at least it is criticized as a selfish activity, since the tendency of budget-cut advocates is to focus on the government spending that benefits others.

I decided, therefore, to review the budget and to identify major spending programs that benefit *me* and that look like good candidates for a reduction in spending. These expenditures are typically subsidies to something that I buy or subsidies that reduce my state and local taxes by paying part of the cost of the programs of my state and local governments. These subsidies raise the federal tax bill and re-

distribute money to me and others in a haphazard way. More important, by lowering the apparent price of certain goods and services, they distort the way that we spend our money and the way that our state and local governments behave.

Consider the school lunch program that allows my daughter Janet to buy a hot lunch for 75 cents a day. Malnutrition is not a problem among American middle class children and the school lunch room isn't likely to be more efficient or to provide more nutrition than the typical brown bag from home. Why should the federal government spend $4 billion a year subsidizing school lunches?

Or consider the $3 billion airport subsidy that I and other frequent travelers en-

The most common argument of those who claim that government spending cannot be checked is that the major part of government outlays is for "uncontrollable entitlement programs." In an entitlement program like Medicare, Congress from time to time defines the benefits for which individuals are eligible and then each year automatically provides the money to pay for those benefits. This is supposed to contrast with a traditional spending program like defense in which Congress decides how much it wants to spend each year.

This dichotomy is surely false, an excuse for Congress not examining what benefits it wants to provide and at what cost. Congress established Medicare and subsequently enlarged the benefits. Why should

---

Board of Contributors

Why should the federal government spend nearly $5 billion for local sewage treatment? Why should elementary and secondary education... receive nearly $4 billion of federal funds? And why, with state and local governments enjoying a $25 billion surplus in 1979, should the federal government have provided $7 billion in general revenue sharing...?

---

joy. We are hardly a low income group and there is surely no reason to encourage energy-intensive air travel. Why shouldn't the full cost of airports be paid for by the passengers?

Many of the subsidies that I receive come to me indirectly through payments to state and local governments for activities which really should be decided on and paid for at the state or local level without distorting financial incentives from the federal government. Why should the federal government spend nearly $5 billion for local sewage treatment? Why should elementary and secondary education, generally regarded as the exclusive province of the state and local community, receive nearly $4 billion of federal funds? And why, with state and local governments enjoying a $25 billion surplus in 1979 and the federal budget in deficit, should the federal government have provided $7 billion in general revenue sharing, $3 billion in "community development grants," $5 billion for public service employment and a long list of other funds?

Congress not look at the current cost implications and reduce the benefits if it believes these costs unjustified?

What are some of the ways that spending on "entitlement" programs might be reduced? Consider first the disability program. In 1980, about three million individuals who were classified as "disabled workers" received benefits of over $12 billion. Even after adjusting for inflation and the growth of the population, this represented a more than three-fold increase in real per capita disability benefits since 1965. The primary reason for this was that the number of beneficiaries nearly tripled in response to a change in the standard of eligibility.

Moreover, a nearly 50% increase in the average real benefit has made disability status a more attractive option than working for many who could otherwise find only low-wage jobs. A return to the old eligibility rules would probably eliminate one-half to two-thirds of current beneficiaries, saving the program $6 billion to $8 billion. Moreover, many of those individuals would find productive employment and become taxpayers, further reducing the deficit.

Or consider Medicare, which has exploded from $7 billion in 1970 to $34 billion in 1980. Spending on this more than doubled in the last five years.

The simplest method of introducing some discipline in Medicare spending is to require patients to pay a moderate out-of-pocket co-insurance on all hospital and medical bills. Current law limits the co-payment in almost all cases to physicians' services and other outpatient care and allows individuals to buy additional private insurance that eliminates their co-payment. Because retirees are generally a low-income group, the maximum co-payment in a year should be limited by a cap that is related to total income from Social Security and other sources. But if the co-payment averaged even 10% of current hospital benefits and succeeded in discouraging 10% of total Medicare spending, the saving at the 1981 level could easily be $7 billion.

The program of cash benefits for retirees and their dependents is the largest of the transfer programs and probably politically the most difficult to change. There is nevertheless increasing agreement among experts that the future growth of Social Security benefits that is specified in the existing law must be reduced to avoid a rise in the payroll tax rate from the current 13% to more than 20% as the ratio of retirees to workers increases.

Between 1971 and 1980, the average real Social Security benefits paid to retired workers rose more than 30%. The average real wage in private employment, however, fell by 10% before tax and by even more after tax.

The unusually rapid growth of Social Security benefits reflects the windfall for retirees and potential retirees in 1972 when benefits were raised 20% and then tied to the consumer price index. That increase, which caused benefits to depart from the long established relation to earnings, was not the carefully considered choice of Congress but an election year gambit of Ways and Means Committee Chairman Wilbur Mills, who momentarily saw himself as a presidential aspirant.

Modify the Increases

It would surely not have violated any principle of "just entitlement" to have rescinded this 20% increase in 1973 or 1974. After eight years have passed, it would no doubt be too upsetting to eliminate the increase all at once. It would not be unreasonable, however, to modify the annual increases in Social Security benefits for the next five or six years until the 20% increase is eliminated and the old ratio of benefits to average earnings is reestablished. The annual saving from such a change would exceed $20 billion at the 1981 level of benefits.

The federal budget reflects, with a lag, the nation's political consensus. Although the idealistic enthusiasm of the Great Society programs has abated, the spending grows. But now the public wants less spending and lower taxes. If the political process is functioning properly, the budgets of the 1980s will see a substantial contraction of the share of national income devoted to government spending on domestic programs.

Mr. Feldstein is professor of economics at Harvard University, president of the National Bureau of Economic Research and a member of the Journal's Board of Contributors.

The Doubts of Liberal Economists

By Christopher Conte

WASHINGTON—From their new positions on the sidelines, liberal economists are watching the new Reagan economic team with a mixture of disbelief and resignation.

Not surprisingly, the liberals doubt claims by "supply-side" theoreticians that Mr. Reagan will work a miracle with the economy. Inflation and stagnation, these economists say, will probably prove as intractable for the new administration as they were for former President Carter.

But many liberal economists concede that the new conservative leadership may nevertheless produce a significant social transformation. The Reagan administration has a good chance, they say, of replacing traditional Democratic policies that enlarged the public sector and tried to "redistribute" income with a program designed to unleash the private sector and keep government out of the business of distributing income.

"For the moment, the conservative view has captured the mainstream," says Otto Eckstein, president of Data Resources Inc. and formerly an economic adviser to President Johnson. "Four to eight years from now, there will be a new agenda for Democrats and their constituencies. But right now, the coming agenda for social reform is an absolute blank page."

As the liberals see it, Democrats didn't fail because they misunderstood economics. Instead, their failure was that they were unable to maintain their traditional programs while still delivering a rising standard of living to the middle class. As a result, they believe the middle class turned to Mr. Reagan.

Middle Class Is Falling

"When people voted for Mr. Reagan, they weren't saying they had suddenly become more conservative on economic policy. They were saying they wanted a higher standard of living," declares Lester Thurow, a liberal economist at the Massachusetts Institute of Technology. "The traditional Democratic program was designed to keep the lower class up with the middle class," Mr. Thurow continues. "But that doesn't solve today's problem, which is that the middle class is falling."

Mr. Reagan's problem, according to Mr. Thurow and others, is that there isn't any way in the short-run to deliver everybody a better standard of living in a society staggered by increasing oil prices and declining productivity.

To restore price stability and economic growth, they argue that the government first must persuade people to accept a lower standard of living for a while rather than push up wages in a futile effort to maintain buying power. Then the government needs to discourage consumption and encourage investment until the economy can revive itself, they say.

Liberal economists say that it would take some time—perhaps a decade or more, for such a program to work, but they aren't convinced voters would tolerate the wait. "It isn't clear our political process can deal with solutions whose horizon for success might be 10 years away," says Robert Solow, another MIT economist.

Mr. Reagan, of course, calls this an economics of scarcity, which he says voters rejected in the last election.

Liberals believe the Reagan administration has come up with some politically appealing approaches to the problem of perceived scarcity in the short run, but they question whether the proposed solutions solve the nation's basic economic problems.

For example, liberals contend that the President's proposed three-year 30% cut in personal income tax rates is more of a way of bolstering purchasing power than a long-term solution to inflation. Indeed, they argue that the tax cut is very much in the traditional liberal mold of John Maynard Keynes's philosophy that government actions to stimulate consumption, or demand, increase supply. "An across-the-board tax cut is a Keynesian remedy," Mr. Thurow argues. "The only thing President Reagan has done is rehabilitate it by calling it supply-side."

Reagan administration officials strongly disagree. Treasury Secretary Donald Regan boasts that the administration's tax cut differs from past Democratic, demand-oriented proposals because it explicitly avoids "redistributing the wealth." By providing more of the benefits of the tax reduction to people in upper tax brackets,

---

Many liberals believe there is no way in the short run to deliver everybody a better standard of living in a society staggered by increasing oil prices and declining productivity.

Mr. Regan argues, the administration's proposal will have a greater impact on savings and investment than typical Democratic progressive tax measures because the well-to-do tend to save and invest more.

Mr. Regan's argument is supported by supply-side theorists who contend that sharp tax cuts will spur investment and cut inflation. Republican Rep. Jack Kemp of New York, for instance, emphasizes that supply-siders propose reducing all marginal tax rates, while Keynesians, in an "obsession with demand," advocate "steeply graduated income tax rates" in order to "stimulate consumption."

Most liberal economists scoff at that theory, first broached by California economist Arthur Laffer. "There isn't a shred of evidence to support the claim that the reaction will be as strong or as quick as they say," declares Gardner Ackley, a Univer-

sity of Michigan economist who served under Presidents Kennedy and Johnson. Brookings Institution economist Henry Aaron asserts: "Laffer is the Laetrile of economics."

But just as Laetrile has a strong public following because conventional medicine can't cure cancer, liberal economists concede that so-called supply-side cures have won a large political following because orthodox economics hasn't provided many answers. And, ironically, while most liberals question whether Mr. Reagan's tax cut will cure chronic inflation, many support it as a reasonable short-term remedy to continuing economic weakness.

Northwestern University economist Robert Eisner, for instance, believes Mr. Reagan won't be able to cut spending as much as he reduces taxes. As a result, Mr. Eisner argues, the government will wind up pumping more spending power into the economy than it withdraws from it, with the result that demand will increase. That in turn will drive up employment and output, he says. "On balance, I believe the economic policies of the Reagan administration may be better than Carter's—although I don't like their distributive implications," the liberal economist concludes.

Liberal economists are also unenthusiastic about the Reagan administration's heavy emphasis on tight money policy, along with budget cuts, as a means of controlling inflation. Edward Gramlich, a professor at the University of Michigan, agrees with Mr. Eisner that the President's budget and tax policies will stimulate the economy. He says that will conflict with the Federal Reserve's restrictive monetary policies and the result will be continuing high interest rates. And high interest rates, Mr. Gramlich says, will in turn discourage investment, preventing businesses from realizing the productivity gains that are needed to ease inflation. He concludes that it would be better to have a more restrictive fiscal policy so that monetary policies could be relaxed to let interest rates come down.

Liberal economists maintain that there are workable long-term remedies for inflation other than those being pursued by the Reagan administration. But so far, they say, Democratic politicians haven't found a way to rally their constituencies behind these proposals.

An All-Out Attack

These remedies include an all-out attack on what they regard as the sources of

rising costs in the economy—price supports, trade restrictions; excise, payroll and sales taxes; and unnecessarily costly government regulations. "When it comes to disputes over detailed government regulation, there isn't much disagreement between liberals and conservatives," says Northwestern economist Robert Gordon.

Second, liberal economists agree that the economy needs more investment in order to improve productivity. But rather than hoping that personal tax cuts will encourage savings and in turn lead to more investment, they recommend cutting taxes that will directly spur business to modernize. "We need for a time to have 100% of the tax cuts go into investment rather than having most go into consumption," Mr. Thurow says.

Finally, many liberal economists continue to believe, despite repeated setbacks, that the government should try to encourage voluntary moderation in setting prices and wages. The only alternative, they contend, is more of a market alternative that would force restraint by preventing the government from intervening to maintain purchasing power during recessions. In that situation, businesses and unions would have little choice but to cut prices and wages when demand falls because each slump could be long and deep.

"We have broken the discipline of the market in order to give people some discretion," says Barry Bosworth, a Brookings economist and former director of the Council on Wage and Price Stability. "The fundamental question is how do you get people to exercise that discretion with some restraint?"

That question poses a political puzzle that liberals haven't yet solved. Most concede that trying to persuade voters to exercise restraint isn't a very appealing alternative to President Reagan's promise that government will restrain itself while everybody else's lot improves. But skeptical as they are, liberals do have some reason to wish Mr. Reagan well: If the President succeeds in restoring economic growth and price stability, society may again decide that it can afford liberal social programs.

Mr. Conte, a member of the Journal's Washington bureau, covers economic issues.

Uncovering the Underground Economy

By MORTIMER CAPLIN

Collecting taxes from the underground economy may be the surest way to balance the 1981 budget. According to a recent study of the Internal Revenue Service, individuals failed to report as much as $135 billion of taxable income for 1976. This produced a $26 billion federal tax loss for that one year alone. Some estimate this tax gap to be four times as large, even disregarding sizable inflation since 1976.

The IRS study is not comprehensive. Not included is unreported income from bartering, white-collar crime or corporate tax evasion. Nor is there an estimate of the revenue loss from other kinds of tax cheating, such as falsifying exemptions or deductions, or phony tax shelters. The IRS did not develop new data. Rather, it based its estimate on existing sources alone; a sampling of tax returns under its taxpayer compliance measurement program (TCMP); a search for nonfilers; an analysis of moonlighting, tips and other types of "informal incomes" and cash payments to proprietorships and off-the-book workers.

A Significant Study

Despite criticisms by a House subcommittee, the IRS study is highly significant. It documents for the first time the existence and approximate size of the "underground economy"—a convenient term for economic activity wholly or partially unreported to the IRS.

Included are illegal activities, such as sales of narcotics, gambling and prostitution. The greater part, however, is business activity not itself illegal, but which generates income that individuals illegally fail to report.

The breadth of participation of Americans in large-and small-scale tax cheating is alarming — not only because of the amount of direct revenue loss, but also in the suspicion created that voluntary compliance, on which our tax collection system is based, is being seriously threatened:

—A stunning 36% to 40% of all income earned by self-employed people goes unreported. This includes a lot small businesses run as sole proprietorships—Ma and Pa grocers, restaurant and movie theater operators, used-car dealers and even doctors and lawyers—or any business that generates a lot of receipts in cash, often easy to skim-and-forget when tax time comes.

—35% to 50% of all rental and royalty income is not reported. Landlords, free-lance writers, oil well owners and others are the villains here.

—17% to 22% of all capital gains on sales of property is unreported. This can include everyone from the high-rolling wheeler-dealer to the ordinary citizen who buys and sells a few shares of stock, or invests his nest egg in a duplex apartment.

—Eight to 16% of interest and dividend income is unreported. This category potentially includes anybody with a savings account or corporate stock.

The figures are particularly unsettling to those of us just now filing our 1979 income tax returns. If you are like most American taxpayers, you are still careful

---

National defense and other government expenditures must ultimately be met by taxes, and to the extent that some cheat, the rest of us foot the bill.

---

to report every penny of income and claim only those deductions you know you are entitled to. But what about our fellow citizens?

From all signs, this underground economy has been expanding in recent years. Why? While not readily verifiable, several reasons come to mind: (1) the public's continued post-Watergate disrespect for government, (2) the financial pressures exerted by mounting inflation, and (3) the IRS's limited enforcement capabilities.

What can be done to repair the corrosion of our tax system? Strong congressional action on an anti-inflation program is fundamental. Beyond this, I recommend three immediate steps:

—Expand the IRS's enforcement capability, particularly the personnel needed to examine more income tax returns.

—Improve the IRS's capacity to match information returns against individual tax returns.

—Provide for withholding of taxes on dividends and interest payments.

First and foremost, the IRS should be given the resources to examine more tax returns. It is in our collective self-interest that this be done. There is nothing wrong in having your tax return checked for accuracy. We all do it with grocery bills and bank statements. Why shouldn't the government do it for tax bills?

In particular, the IRS needs more examiners—examiners not only well-trained in sophisticated tax audits, but also im-

bued with the philosophy and practice of courtesy, helpfulness and fair-dealing. To handle some 140 million returns of all types, the IRS now has barely 19,000 revenue agents and office auditors. While Congress is loath to have an army of tax collectors scrutinizing all our financial affairs, the number today is clearly insufficient—given the growth of our population and rise in tax return filings. Indeed, examiners are without doubt the best bargain in the federal budget since they collect about five dollars in additional tax for every dollar of additional IRS enforcement budget.

Today very few returns are ever subjected to real scrutiny. Over the last several years, IRS audit coverage—the percentage of tax returns reviewed by IRS examiners—has been below 3%, and falling. In fact, audit coverage of the latest batch of individual income tax returns was only slightly over 2%—1.84 million examinations out of 87.3 million filings.

Although high-bracket returns are more likely to be examined, the long odds against being audited make outright tax cheaters bolder and offer even honest taxpayers an incentive to give themselves the benefit of every conceivable doubt. The IRS simply must cut down the odds of this tax lottery by examining more tax returns and by exacting full civil and criminal penalties from flagrant tax violators.

The IRS, too, still needs to improve its handling of the information returns it receives—a mind-boggling total of nearly 500 million items each year. More than half are on magnetic tape, and these are generally matched against the individual's tax return. In contrast, the information reported on paper documents is matched less than half the time. Even when "matched" on computers, the information is often not available to the IRS examiner at the time he audits the individual's tax return. This is a lamentable waste, in view of the cost—public and private—of collecting the information in the first place.

Mr. Carter's Recent Proposal

Furthermore, compliance by taxpayers can be vastly improved if Congress enacts the President's recent proposal to extend tax withholding to bank account interest and dividends from corporate stock. For those free from tax because of exemptions or deductions, a system of filing exemption certificates will avoid unnecessary witholding.

I have advocated withholding on interest and dividends for many years and believe it is needed now more than ever. Administration estimates show that this proposal will increase revenues by $3.4 billion in the next fiscal year alone—a 20% bite out of the budget deficit, without raising taxes or reducing expenditures. It seems foolhardy to pass up such an opportunity.

Participants in the underground economy place a heavy burden on the overwhelming majority of honest American taxpayers. National defense and other government expenditures must ultimately be met by taxes and, to the extent some cheat, the rest of us foot the bill. Whether the annual tax gap is $26 billion or $100 billion, it contributes mightily to our unbalanced budget and, by doing so, adds fuel to inflation.

We American taxpayers paid over $450 billion in federal taxes last year. This gives us a substantial stake in seeing everyone else pay his or her fair share—and in rooting out subterranean operators by even-handed and thorough enforcement of our tax laws.

———

Mr. Caplin, a Washington attorney, was Commission of Internal Revenue during the Kennedy and Johnson administration.

87

March 4, 1981

Reagan's Budget: A Fundamental Change?

By Paul W. McCracken

It is just possible that the President's economic program and the inexorabilities of developments in recent years will combine actually to produce a fundamental change in the direction and pattern of the economy. This is possible. It is also far from certain—as people in Washington, at the grass roots in the United States and others in Europe and Japan are constantly reminding us.

Fundamental changes in the direction of national policy have not occurred often in our history and that has been a source of political stability and strength. A "change of government" at the White House or on the Hill (or both) has usually meant a change of emphasis between parties, both of which were in pretty solid agreement about the fundamental rules of the larger game.

Ours has not, for example, been the experience of Britain, whose change to a Labor government meant a nationalization of the steel industry, followed by the Tories who de-nationalized it, succeeded by the Labor Party who re-nationalized it—the primary result of it all being a steel industry gasping for survival. Nor have we had to face, as French voters did at the last major election, a coalition of Socialists and Communists as the alternative government.

There are times, however, when a more drastic change of direction is in order. In the middle of the last century (1846 to be precise) an England whose prosperity was increasingly based upon industry and foreign trade finally repealed the Corn Laws. These protectionist measures had been bastions of the nation's economic policy with roots extending back to the 12th Century, but economic developments had outpaced these laws, and they were finally jettisoned.

Cleansing the System

A half-century ago the American strategy of economic policy finally brought us to 1933. The approach of cleansing the banking system of all "unsound" banks and tightening monetary policy to protect the dollar's international position was orthodox enough, but it also had the result that by 1933 40% of the banks had been extinguished, and 25%-30% of the work force was unemployed. A fundamental change in the direction of policy was obviously required, and it occurred. (The Great Depression was, of course, the logical result of the policies we pursued, not a condition inherent in the nature of the economic system.)

The result of last November's election may represent little more than the momentary vexations of a citizenry exasperated by a diverse array of events ranging from Iran to the shortage of oil and peanut butter. Elections have been won and lost before because of such reasons. If so, the pattern of political and economic life may quickly settle back into what has been business as usual.

There are, however, persuasive reasons for thinking that November 1980 was a mandate for a fundamental change of direction.

The poor performance of the economy was itself making the case. An economy which historically had delivered a doubling of the real purchasing power of pay envelopes every 25 to 30 years seems to have lost any capability for gains in real income at all, and the U.S. performance in terms of gains in productivity seems now to be the poorest among major nations in the industrial world.

Our current rate of inflation would double the price level in five years, is two to three times that for Japan or Germany and has been accelerating persistently in recent years—this for an economy whose average rate of inflation in reasonably undisturbed periods (e.g., 1900-29 or 1948-65) has been about 2% per year. And an economy which historically has operated with an average unemployment rate of 4.5% to 5% (4% under Calvin Coolidge) now seems to be stuck with a floor of 6% to 7%.

The President was not engaging in purple rhetoric when he asked: "Can we who man the ship of state deny it is out of control?" The empirical evidence points dramatically to an affirmative answer.

Whether what the President put forward represents precisely the right mix of ingredients is, of course, something about which reasonable people will not completely agree. For an economy suffering from a productive plant that is too small and too old, a tax reduction package with more emphasis on capital formation would have been in order. Conventional depreciation procedures are understating the true current cost of capital currently expiring by close to $30 billion per year, and the extra taxes paid on this fictitious element of profits have been a major deterrent to needed new investment.

The absence of some action to slow

Board of Contributors

———

The time does come when the important thing is to run effectively the play that has been called—rather than to remain forever in the huddle arguing. . . .

---

down the overly rapid expansion of Social Security outlays was also a surprise. These might have taken the form of annual price-level adjustments, use of a price index less prone to exaggerate the true rate of inflation than the CPI or the inclusion of Social Security income (perhaps in excess of a special deductible amount) in taxable income.

The time does come, however, when the important thing is to run effectively the play that has been called—rather than to remain forever in the huddle arguing about the details of what might be the perfect play.

One thing about which there can be no argument is that a projection of the 1976-1980 trends to 1983 would bring us to a change in real growth at a −5% per year rate and a 12% per year rate of inflation (for the GNP price index). The President's program would at least start to point the economy in a more favorable direction. Questions about whether it would really bring us to 4.5% real growth and down to 7% inflation are about as useful as numerological arguments usually are. On this the President cannot be sure—but neither can anyone else.

While the President put forward an integrated program, all elements of which are important, the key to the program is regaining control of the expenditure side of this budget. The projections in President Carter's January Budget Message suggested a rise in federal outlays (including off-budget items) from fiscal 1980 to this fiscal year of $85 billion to $100 billion. With a rise in state and local spending of $25 billion-$30 billion, this implied a rise in total public sector outlays equal to 50% or more of the projected rise in the total national income.

If disinflationary pressure required for the whole economy were to be concentrated only on the private sector, and a public sector absorbing a growing share of the economy's resources were to escape, the pressure and dislocations in the private sector would be severe. This is the clear lesson from Britain's experience in recent years. Then even the results from tax reduction would be disappointing. The Treasury would have to enlarge further its already large share of funds advanced in credit markets (36% in 1980), leaving that much less to finance capital formation, housing and auto sales.

There will be three formidable sets of forces deployed against this crucial effort to constrain the growth in the public sector. First, there are those who have genuinely believed that more and larger government programs would be the route for bringing disadvantaged and lower income people into the mainstream of national life. It is increasingly clear that this strategy leads to disappointing results. Many of these programs have had a pauperizing effect on their own intended beneficiaries and have not been an exit from poverty and an entrance to the mainstream.

Feeding at the Public Trough

Then there are the vested interests of those with not-so-low incomes (in many cases quite fancy incomes) who have a personal and professional stake in persistently enlarging government. These will range from those making a comfortable living running these programs to legal groups feeding at the public trough to some members of Congress who enjoy the additional power from dispensing yet more public funds and having jurisdiction over yet more government agencies.

The rhetoric will be the liturgical lament about what spending constraints would do to the poor. Their real concern will be the usual reluctance to see changes adverse to themselves. They in this modern drama will, therefore, be the true establishmentarians—even the reactionaries.

Finally, we will be assured that the program will not really work. After the President's speech on February 18, for example, a Japanese newspaper carried an American comment that our economy is now simply mature and must be expected to grow more slowly. This may be true. It does, however, bear a striking resemblance to the mature-economy thesis of a few decades ago when we were also assured that investment would be weak because in a mature economy profitable opportunities had already been exploited—when, in fact, we were then heading into an investment boom. Whether capital formation is vigorous or stagnant depends heavily on the policies we pursue, and that should be kept in mind as we plan for the 1980s.

In spite of the impediments, the basic direction of national policy may still begin to undergo a fundamental change for the better. The President, like Truman, may find that no one supports him—except the people.

———

Mr. McCracken is Edmund Ezra Day University Professor of Business Administration at the University of Michigan, former chairman of the Council of Economic Advisers under President Nixon and a member of the Journal's Board of Contributors.

Uncertain Outlook

Tax-Cut Picture Clears, But Effect on Economy Remains Very Cloudy

Some Economists See a Surge; Others See Stagnation, Inflation, Credit Crunch

Are Reaganites Too Upbeat?

A WALL STREET JOURNAL *News Roundup*

Uncertainty over precisely what sort of tax-cut measure would gain congressional approval has nearly ended, but the fog obscuring the long-term economic and social outlook seems as dense as ever.

Although some economists are predicting a resurgence in the American economy, others see such dangers as more inflation, a period of stagnation and perhaps a credit crunch lurking ahead. And as the White House savors President Reagan's tax-cut victory, even some administration officials worry that the President's economic program presents substantial economic and political risks.

The administration's bold combination of sweeping tax cuts, budget reductions and less government regulation, along with slower money-supply growth by the Federal Reserve Board, is designed to shrink the government's role in the economy and to spur a business boom by increasing private incentives to produce, save and invest.

So far, Congress has given Mr. Reagan about what he wants. The White House package of personal and business tax cuts will reduce federal revenues from previously expected levels by $732.8 billion between now and fiscal 1986, which begins Oct. 1, 1985. In addition, the administration has won the first phase of a budget-reduction package designed to reduce the rate of growth of federal spending to 4.7% a year through 1984 from an average annual increase of 13.6% over the past three years.

"Enormous" Conflicts

But one Cabinet official worries that the new program could produce "enormous" conflicts for the Reagan administration as it seeks to achieve a balanced federal budget in fiscal 1984 while cutting taxes. As a result, he fears that the administration may be forced to scale back its proposed defense buildup if it plans to honor its promise for a balanced budget and reduced federal borrowing.

"The only way they can reach their objective is with very high growth and low inflation," notes Joseph Pechman of Washington's Brookings Institution.

This is precisely what the Reagan administration predicts. The White House forecasts that its programs will propel the economy out of its current "stagflation"—the debilitating combination of high inflation and slow growth—to an era of sustained high growth and lower inflation and interest rates.

Reaganite Projections

Last year, inflation, as measured by the consumer price index, was 13.5% and "real" gross national product, the nation's output of goods and services after adjustment for inflation, fell 0.2%; the average interest rate of 91-day Treasury bills was 11.5%. But for 1983, the administration projects inflation of 6.2%, real GNP growth of 5% and Treasury-bill rates averaging 7.5%.

This is more optimistic than most private forecasts. For example, Chase Econometric Associates Inc. projected, shortly before the congressional action this week, inflation of 8% in 1983, real growth of 4.1% and Treasury-bill rates of 11.6%. As a result of the congressional voting Wednesday, Lawrence Chimerine, Chase Econometrics' chief economist, now is just a bit more sanguine. He expects "a little higher rate" of economic growth in the second half of 1983 than he predicted earlier. He explains that "the final 10% of the tax cut turned out to be effective in July 1983, or six months earlier than we originally expected."

The administration believes that its policies, combined with slower monetary growth, will rapidly reduce inflation and interest rates. But many private economists see a slower unwinding of inflation, as well as conflicts between tight monetary policy, on the one hand, and the stimulus of the administration's high defense spending and lower taxes, on the other.

Continued Sluggishness

"I don't foresee catastrophe in the economy, but the net result is going to be continued economic sluggishness" that will prevent output from growing as quickly as the administration projects, says Charles Schultze, who was the chairman of President Carter's Council of Economic Advisers and currently is with the Brookings Institution.

The Federal Reserve Board also questions the administration's economic projections. "If I have one argument with the administration's economic program, it's that it has been presented in too upbeat a fashion," says the Fed's vice chairman, Frederick Schultz. He sees a combination of tax cuts and defense-spending increases heating up the economy late this year and early next year and keeping inflation and interest rates high.

William Niskanen, a member of Mr. Reagan's Council of Economic Advisers, concedes that "there's some experimentation involved" in the administration's program. But he believes it's "possible" that the combination of policies will achieve the high growth and slower inflation that the administration projects.

Not surprisingly, the uncertainty suggested by Mr. Niskanen's comments is reflected in the disparate views of private analysts.

Albert H. Cox Jr., the chief economist at Merrill Lynch & Co., calls the tax bill "terrific. We can look forward now with confidence to expanding economic activity, declining inflation and declining unemployment all the way out to 1984"—which is as far as Mr. Cox's radar reaches.

In contrast, Sam I. Nakagama, the chief economist at Kidder, Peabody & Co., an investment firm based in New York, says: "It's absolutely the wrong kind of tax cut. It will bring a prolonged period of stagnation, and it raises the possibility of a credit crunch and some sort of financial accident, maybe in the second half of next year. Congress muffed a great opportunity; they've done too much to stimulate consumption and not nearly enough to spur business investment."

Between these two extreme forecasts, most private economists seem to tilt a bit more toward Mr. Cox's optimism than toward Mr. Nakagama's pessimism. In any event, the consensus is that this tax bill is a good deal better than no tax cut at all, and probably somewhat better than what the House Democrats unsuccessfully pushed. In addition, many economists are simply relieved that the suspense is over.

"If we hadn't had a tax cut," remarks Leif H. Olsen, chief economist at New York's Citibank, "I would have to assume that expenditure restraints would have begun to disintegrate; that probably would have meant we would have had more inflation."

Also feeling relieved is Morris Cohen, an economic consultant based in New York. Not only doesn't he expect any recession this year—in contrast to the near-term forecasts of many analysts—but also he anticipates that "1982 will be strong—the tax bill will deliver the goods" and will stir "a wave of spending (on plant and equipment), now that the details are all available."

Wall Street's Reaction

But despite the general optimism, the Reagan program is failing to produce the anticipated results on Wall Street. The White House expected the stock market to boom and interest rates to fall as it put its program in place. Instead, the stock market has fallen and interest rates have climbed over the past few months even as the administration has won its legislative victories.

The financial markets remain skeptical that the administration will be able to deliver on its promise to reduce spending enough to offset the tax cuts and produce a balanced budget by fiscal 1984. The Office of Management and Budget projects a deficit of $55.6 billion this year and a surplus of $500 million in fiscal 1984.

"We're in the rare position of having delivered on all our promises so far," says Lawrence Kudlow, the chief economist at the Office of Management and Budget. "At some point, observers will start to have to give us high marks for credibility."

Nevertheless, he concedes that the Reagan administration's biggest "challenge" is to show that it can control the budget and "substantially reduce federal credit demands." This will "reduce inefficient resource allocation, which has inhibited economic growth; reduce pressure on interest rates, and eliminate interference with monetary policy," he says.

Curb on Spending

But administration officials say the tax cuts will force Congress to hold spending down. "Inexorably, the revenue numbers are going to require budget restraint," one official says. "This is the biggest freeze on new programs in the history of this government."

Mr. Pechman of the Brookings Institution agrees that new programs won't be possible. "What the Congress and the administration are saying is don't expect anything (more) from the federal government for the next decade—in fact, expect less," he says. The Reagan program intends to reduce federal spending as a percentage of GNP to 19% in 1984 from 23% this year.

According to White House economists, the share of GNP that the government is giving up will go into business investment, financing an extensive modernization of business plant and equipment and increasing productivity. And because defense spending is expected to rise to 33% of the federal budget in 1984 from 25% this year, the Reagan program means a substantial reduction in federal spending on social and other programs.

"If you could get a relatively sustainable economic boom, the social problems the cuts will generate will be fairly minimal," Mr. Schultze says.

However, Mr. Schultze notes administration economic projections showing that through 1984 the tax cut will leave the government $125 billion short of meeting projected government spending, including the increased military outlays envisioned by the President. The much-publicized round of budget cuts that Congress is just completing will narrow that gap only by $55 billion, leaving the administration facing the need to make $70 billion in additional cuts to balance its budgets.

Hard on the Poor?

Assuming that the administration doesn't change its mind about increasing military spending and that the politically sensitive Social Security system can't be trimmed much, Mr. Schultze sees the possibility of either continuing large federal deficits, inflation and high interest rates, or an even deeper round of cuts in social programs. Either way, he contends, the poor stand to suffer more than the well-off.

The administration, of course, argues that it has retained a "safety net" of social programs to help the truly needy and that the poor will benefit from the economic expansion that the Reaganites hope to create. But antipoverty lobbyists reply that, even if jobs do become plentiful, the really poor don't have the skills to take them. ,

Says Vernon Jordan, the president of the National Urban League: " 'A rising tide lifts all the boats' is no answer. A rising tide lifts only those boats in the water . . . and we know we will be stranded on dry land."

Mr. Jordan, in a speech to the league's recent annual meeting, said the combination of the administration's tax and spending cuts amounts to "a massive transfer of resources from the poor to the rich. We agree with them that inflation must be curbed," he said. "We agree with them that blacks do better when the economy is better. We agree with them that America must produce more and create more jobs in the private sector. But . . . what are black and poor people supposed to do in the meantime?"

Indexing Provision

However, it is precisely the long-term implications of the tax-cut bill that intrigue some economists. Allan H. Meltzer, an economist at Pittsburgh's Carnegie-Mellon University, says, "For the first time, we're writing a long-term fiscal policy into law. It stretches out past 1983, because of the indexing provision"—the provision that would offset the upward creep of income-tax brackets caused merely by inflation.

Yet, not all economists are happy about the long-term aspects of the bill. Herbert E. Neill Jr., the chief economist at Harris Trust & Savings Bank in Chicago, says: "The first significant tax cut doesn't come until July 1982. The economy probably will be pretty weak then, so it's not likely to cause much trouble. But 1983 and 1984 may be another story," because, he says, "a big tax cut may mean more inflation" at that time.

Moreover, Mr. Neill dislikes tax-indexing because its effect, he suggests, may be to "cut government spending by denying the government money, but I wonder whether that will really slow the upward push of military spending."

And another huge imponderable that will remain even after the tax bill becomes law concerns monetary policy. W. Lee Hoskins, an economist at Pittsburgh National Bank, shares a widespread worry that big budget deficits may accompany the tax cuts. He believes that "there's no necessary relationship between the size of deficits and inflation or interest rates," but cautions that whether a large deficit proves to be inflationary "all depends on the Federal Reserve."

89

New Economics

Supply-Side Theories Became Federal Policy With Unusual Speed

---

Politicians and Journalists, Rather Than Academics, Played a Crucial Role

---

Is a Gold Standard Needed?

By Paul Blustein
Staff Reporter of The Wall Street Journal

NEW YORK—Interest rates are hanging high. The federal deficit is looming large. And the Reagan administration's critics are chortling that these things weren't supposed to happen, at least not according to "supply-side economics," the theory behind the recently enacted tax-cut program.

The supply-siders think that there have been some misunderstandings.

According to Arthur B. Laffer, a professor at the University of Southern California, the economy's problems could be solved if the dollar was restored to a gold standard. Mr. Laffer has long been associated in the public mind with the supply-side notion of cutting taxes to spur production, but he says the recent tax cut was less than half the battle. "Gold has always been the most important issue in my mind," he declares.

The problem, retorts another leading supply-sider, Treasury Under Secretary Norman B. Ture, is that zealots such as Mr. Laffer exaggerated and oversold supply-side theory in the first place. Mr. Ture, who opposes a gold standard, says all that's needed is time for the Reagan program to work. "I would say that it really is asking a bit much for the economy to have attained a state of perfect grace" so quickly, Mr. Ture says.

Startling Revolution

How did supply-side theory, with all its forecasts of economic resurgence, come to the fore? A half-dozen years ago, the term "supply-side economics" hadn't even been coined; last Aug. 13, the theory became enshrined in national economic policy when President Reagan signed a three-year, 25% cut in personal income tax rates. A look back at this remarkable revolution shows that much of its driving force came from outside traditional channels of economic thought.

Many of the people behind the supply-side movement, notes Herbert Stein, a professor of economics at the University of Virginia, aren't trained economists but rather "politicians and journalists." Mr. Stein, who was the chairman of the Council of Economic Advisers during the Nixon administration, also believes that some supply-siders who are trained economists "were people who felt they weren't getting recognition in the profession and wanted to make a splash."

Mr. Stein and other economists insist that this criticism isn't based on professional snobbery. They do complain that supply-siders have submitted little academically respectable evidence to show that lower marginal income-tax rates will lead Americans to work, save and invest far more than they do now. But they admit that it's hardly any wonder that politicians and voters want to try tax cuts, given the profession's dismal record of fighting stagflation. They also concede that the effects of taxes on incentives to produce and invest had long been woefully neglected.

Some Real Problems

The rise of supply-side thought, says Rudolph Penner of the American Enterprise Institute, "wasn't all public relations. There was an enormous amount of substance behind it. Inflation had distorted our tax system horribly"—especially, he says, for upper- and middle-income families being pushed into higher and higher tax brackets.

"There's been a whole shift in the profession to look at the effects of taxes on incentives," Mr. Penner says. But most economists, he adds, "wouldn't agree that the responses are as large as the Laffers of the world say they are."

The 41-year-old Mr. Laffer has been described in the media as the supply-side movement's "guru" and "eminence grise," although "grise" hardly seems appropriate for his glib speech, boyish face and effervescent personality. Nor do all supply-siders consider him their guru; such assertions irk Mr. Ture, for one.

But nobody disputes Mr. Laffer's important role in the supply-side movement. His work "gained public attention to the idea that there was an alternative to John Maynard Keynes," Mr. Ture acknowledges.

A Fast Start

As a faculty member at the University of Chicago business school in the late 1960s, Mr. Laffer was something of a *Wunderkind*, obtaining a tenured position at the age of 28. He became a disciple of Robert Mundell, a highly respected expert on international monetary theory. Mr. Mundell, a Canadian now teaching at Columbia University, espouses the now-unorthodox view that foreign-exchange rates must be fixed, and currencies convertible into gold, for the world economy to stabilize.

In 1970, Mr. Laffer took a leave of absence to become the chief economist in President Nixon's Office of Management and Budget under another distinguished Chicagoan, George Shultz. But then Mr. Laffer's career began faltering. He made a forecast concerning gross national product that was ridiculed in the financial press as too optimistic and in the economics profession for having been based on a too-simplistic model. "To Chicago, I was an enormous source of embarrassment," Mr. Laffer says.

Matters worsened when some of his faculty colleagues learned that he hadn't quite finished his Ph.D. requirements at Stanford. A committee was formed to investigate charges that he had misled his promotion panel. University officials and professors decline comment on the findings, but Mr. Laffer says that he was innocent of misleading anybody and that the committee "didn't come up with anything" to justify action against him. In 1972, he received his Stanford doctorate after completing the remaining requirements.

But on returning to Chicago in 1972 after his stint at OMB, Mr. Laffer says, "I was never invited to parties, and 90% of the faculty wouldn't talk to me in the halls. They believed in their heart of hearts that I *had* misled them." Despite his popularity with Chicago's students, Mr. Laffer says, he didn't get a salary increase for the rest of his career there (he left in 1976 for USC). He felt sure that his academic research wouldn't be published because of the tight-knit academic community's prejudice against him.

"It was horrible," Mr. Laffer says emotionally. "I knew there was no way on God's earth that I could make it in the profession. So I went other routes—the press, the political process, consulting."

While still at OMB, Mr. Laffer met Jude Wanniski, then a columnist for the now-defunct National Observer (which was owned by Dow Jones & Co., publisher of The Wall Street Journal). The intense, flamboyant Mr. Wanniski soon became a close friend. The pair kept in touch by phone almost every day, long after both had left Washington in 1972—Mr. Laffer for Chicago and Mr. Wanniski for New York, where he wrote editorials on politics and defense for the Journal.

"Art was the only economist I knew who would answer silly questions about economics," says Mr. Wanniski, whose college major had been in political science. One of Mr. Wanniski's first questions was: "Who is the greatest economist alive today?" Mr. Laffer's reply: Robert Mundell.

Crucial Address

After studying Mr. Mundell's teachings on international economics, Mr. Wanniski argued at the Journal for editorials advocating fixed exchange rates and a gold standard, but he didn't get anywhere. Then, in 1974, Mr. Mundell gave an address at a conference in Washington.

Defying conventional economic wisdom, Mr. Mundell argued for a tax cut, rather than a tax increase, following the surge in world oil prices in 1973. The oil-price shock would cause a recession, he predicted (accurately) and thus, he said, should be combated with a stimulative tax cut. The inflationary effects of high oil prices could be checked by a tight monetary policy. To objections that tight money would clash with a loose fiscal policy, Mr. Mundell replied that monetary and fiscal policy had different effects, that tax rates could influence both demand and supply by influencing decisions of people and businesses to produce.

Mr. Laffer, who was in the audience, listened raptly. "It just set me off," he says. He eventually worked out a theory elaborating on Mr. Mundell's idea. The income tax, he decided, was stifling economic incentives so much that a broad-based tax cut needn't merely increase consumer spending — as "demand-side" models showed. If properly structured, a tax cut could ignite such an explosion in productive effort, he held, that the loss in Treasury revenues would be more than offset.

The Famous Curve

It was over cocktails at a Washington restaurant with a top Ford administration aide, according to Mr. Wanniski, that Mr. Laffer first drew the now-famous "Laffer curve" on a napkin to illustrate his theory. Mr. Wanniski, the only one who remembers the incident, says it sticks in his mind because the curve "hit me as a propaganda device." (The dome-shaped curve shows that as tax rates rise, government revenue climbs until a "prohibitive range" is reached; then, any additional tax increases discourage economic activity and cause tax revenues to fall. Mr. Laffer argued—contrary to much of the economics profession—that the U.S. income tax was operating in the "prohibitive range.")

Over dinner with Messrs. Laffer and Mundell, Mr. Wanniski decided on a political strategy. "I said, 'We can't talk about fixed exchange rates and gold, because no one's listening. We've got to talk tax cuts first,' " Mr. Wanniski recalls.

Back at the Journal, the other writers for the editorial page (which is run separately from the news pages) initially reacted coolly to Mr. Wanniski's push for editorials endorsing the tax-cut idea. But Mr. Wanniski wrote some signed "op-ed" features on the subject and tried to persuade various Washington policy makers to take up the cause.

Kristol's Hunch

One of Mr. Wanniski's most important early efforts was an article, extolling Messrs. Laffer and Mundell, that he wrote in 1975 for the influential journal Public Interest. "We aren't economists," says Irving Kristol, Public Interest's editor, so when an article on the subject is submitted, "we'll usually ask one or two economists to read it for us." Of those reading the Wanniski piece, "No one thought well of it. But I had the feeling that conventional economic analysis was in trouble, and something new was needed." Mr. Kristol, a frequent contributor to the Journal's editorial page, later became one of supply-side economics' biggest boosters.

The Public Interest article intrigued Jeffrey Bell, a young former staffer for the American Conservative Union. He excitedly presented the tax-cut idea to his boss, Ronald Reagan, who was then looking for an issue to use in his race against President Ford for the 1976 Republican nomination. As a result, Mr. Laffer was invited to explain his theories to Mr. Reagan. Mr. Laffer recalls that the future President was most receptive to supply-side notions, although Mr. Reagan didn't formally endorse tax cuts in his 1976 campaign.

At the Journal, meanwhile, Mr. Wanniski was receiving letters from the office of a little-known Buffalo Congressman named Jack Kemp; the letters touted a bill, introduced in the House by the former quarterback for the Buffalo Bills, to cut some business taxes. But the Kemp bill didn't appeal much to Mr. Wanniski because it didn't involve a reduction in individual tax rates. So Mr. Wanniski threw out the letters. "I thought, 'Who cares about this right-wing football player?' " he says.

To help develop tax-cut ideas, Rep. Kemp in 1975 hired Paul Craig Roberts, who had earned his doctorate at the University of

Virginia, as his staff economist. Mr. Roberts, in turn, retained Mr. Ture, then a respected economic consultant in Washington. Mr. Roberts, who now is the assistant secretary of the Treasury for economic policy, knew that Mr. Ture has done research in an area that Mr. Roberts had long considered important.

"Ture emphasized over and over again how the tax system is biased against savings and investment," says David Meiselman, an economics professor at Virginia Polytechnic Institute. "He became a big pain in Washington and was really the first to hammer away at this."

In 1976, Mr. Wanniski finally did meet Rep. Kemp, and the two hit it off immediately. Before long, Rep. Kemp also became an ardent supporter of Mr. Laffer's theories. In a speech to the 1976 Republican convention, he declared: "We have to realize that we can no longer make a political career of just opposing what the Democrats are for."

On Aug. 4 of that year, a Journal editorial endorsed Rep. Kemp's business tax-cut bill. After arguing that a deficit needn't be inflationary unless monetized by the Federal Reserve, the editorial stated: "In any event, it is far from clear that a tax cut will always cause a deficit. It depends on whether it succeeds in stimulating the economy enough that the lower rates yield a larger net revenue."

"Converting" an Editor

The "conversion" of Robert Bartley, the editor of the Journal's editorial page, had been a gradual process. Mr. Bartley, who says most of his economics training came "on the job," had listened to the Wanniski-Laffer arguments and then to the orthodox economists' counterarguments.

"In college," Mr. Bartley says, "I had a bacteriology teacher who gave me a great insight into life. He said that if you were transported back into time and met (Louis) Pasteur or Koch (Robert Koch, the German discoverer of the tuberculosis germ), you'd probably think they were just like a lot of other nuts—except they were right."

Meanwhile, a push for tax cuts was starting in Congress. Mr. Roberts left Rep. Kemp's staff in late 1976 to join the House Budget Committee, where he drafted legislative proposals to cut personal tax rates. Rep. Kemp soon changed his bill toward the individual tax-cut approach, and in 1977 the Congressman introduced a bill calling for a 30% across-the-board reduction in marginal income-tax rates. Sen. William Roth of Delaware, who introduced the legislation in the Senate, insisted that the cuts be phased in over three years, so that was written into the bill.

The Kemp-Roth bill was endorsed by the Republican National Committee, but it was still regarded as economic heresy by many conservatives. Even within the supply-side camp, there were some uneasy alliances.

Some Misgivings

Messrs. Roberts and Ture never were comfortable with the idea that tax cuts would pay for themselves through expanded production. Mr. Ture, who forecast that the Kemp-Roth personal tax cuts would substantially reduce federal revenues, says the Laffer curve created difficulties for his moderate brand of supply-side economics because it set up an easy target for opponents. Mr. Roberts, writing on the Journal's editorial page (which he joined in 1978), called the Laffer curve a "caricature" of the arguments for cutting taxes.

Supply-side theory, according to Mr. Ture—who is fond of citing precedents in the writings of classical economists such as Adam Smith—holds that "changes in marginal tax rates will change the extent to which people are willing to offer labor and capital." A tax cut will pay for itself "only under the most extraordinary circumstances," he adds. Nevertheless, Mr. Ture supported the Kemp-Roth proposal on the ground that the resulting deficit could be financed out of a vastly increased pool of savings—itself a questionable assumption to many economists, but less extreme than the Laffer-curve argument. "The cocktail napkin," Mr. Ture says, "has nothing to do with supply-side economics."

Mr. Laffer isn't fazed by such criticism. "I call them as I see them," he says philosophically. But if one sect of the supply-side movement got the most publicity, it undoubtedly was Mr. Laffer and his "radical" followers. The radicals continued to advocate a gold standard but stuck by the original plan to give tax cuts top billing.

Mr. Wanniski, for example, was quoted in the Village Voice as saying: "One of the first insights I had was when I asked Laffer, How can these (tax-cut) incentives be instantaneous? Won't we have to wait three years for them to occur? Laffer said, How long does it take you to reach over and pick up a $50 bill in a crowd? Aah! That's how quick it is. If the incentive is there, the production is there." (Mr. Laffer says that he meant that the incentive would begin to act instantly but that the tax cuts would pay for themselves within two to four years.)

First Political Victory

In 1978, Mr. Wanniski resigned from the Journal after some of its executives complained that they had spotted him handing out campaign leaflets for Jeffrey Bell; the former Reagan aide was challenging Sen. Clifford Case in the New Jersey Republican Senate primary on a supply-side platform. "I figured that if Bell didn't win, there was no way supply-side would go anywhere, and there would be no way to avoid global depression and war," says Mr. Wanniski, now a private consultant. Although Mr. Bell upset Sen. Case in the primary—the first solid political victory for the supply-siders—he lost the election to Bill Bradley.

Also in 1978, Congress was considering a change in capital-gains taxes and heard an analysis from a distinguished Harvard economist, Martin Feldstein, who said a reduction in the capital-gains tax rate would increase revenues. His work and a few other academic studies "gave an air of respectability to the whole movement" to cut taxes, says the American Enterprise Institute's Mr. Penner. In addition, Milton Friedman, the Nobel Prize-winning economist, endorsed the Kemp-Roth bill as a way to force a reduction in government spending.

As the 1980 election year neared, Rep. Kemp considered a race for the presidency on a supply-side platform—a prospect that worried the Reagan strategists. So, at a luncheon in Los Angeles for Rep. Kemp, Mr. Reagan and their wives, the former California governor assured the young Congressman that he favored the tax-cut religion. Accordingly, Rep. Kemp gained an important position in the Reagan campaign.

At the campaign's outset, Mr. Reagan sounded like a supply-side purist. In one early television commercial, he noted that the Kennedy administration's tax cut had been an economic success. "Even the government gained $54 billion in unexpected revenue," Mr. Reagan declared. "If I become President, we're going to try that again."

The radical supply-siders had misgivings about the depth of Mr. Reagan's commitment, however, especially when he began to get most of his economic counsel from some establishment economists who had served in the Nixon and Ford administrations. "We carried on guerrilla warfare," Mr. Wanniski recalls. When a Reagan speech hinted of backsliding into old-time Republican economics, Mr. Wanniski says, "We would call Kemp and scream, 'Deviation! Deviation!' And he would call people and scream, 'Deviation!' " Also beating the drums were Rowland Evans and Robert Novak, the syndicated Washington columnists.

The rest, as they say, is history. Mr. Reagan stuck by his campaign promise to support the Kemp-Roth tax cuts, although he appointed nonradical supply-siders — Messrs. Ture and Roberts and OMB Director David Stockman—who favor simultaneous cuts in spending.

Mr. Ture says Mr. Reagan should be judged by what he has said about his tax program since taking office. "The President never promised the public a rose garden," Mr. Ture says. And the radicals, while still agitating for a gold standard, say things could be a lot worse. "If we had not cut taxes," Mr. Wanniski says, "we would have the Dow Jones (industrial average) at 500, 15% unemployment and riots in the cities."

Policy for Power

After 7 Years' Debate, U.S. Finally Is Nearing Broad Energy Program

Aim Is a Sharp Move Away From Petroleum Imports; High Price Is a Weapon

One Critic: 'Pure Politics'

By Rich Jaroslovsky
Staff Reporter of The Wall Street Journal

WASHINGTON—For better or worse, the U.S. is finally about to get a national energy policy.

The policy may well fall short of the high hopes of its sponsors and proponents. Critics say it avoids making tough choices and goes off in too many directions at once. And time is working against it: The threats to the nation's economic health and national security from rising oil imports are immediate. But it will be several years before the U.S. knows whether its program will work.

Nonetheless, after seven years of debate, dispute and compromise, a comprehensive program is emerging. It combines a broad range of efforts to reduce energy use—with modest production incentives for existing energy sources and the development of new technologies.

Over the next few weeks, Congress is likely to pass a $227 billion "windfall-profits" tax on oil-company revenues, create a huge program to increase production of synthetic fuels and set up an Energy Mobilization Board to speed the construction of major energy plants. President Carter already is gradually decontrolling domestic crude-oil prices, and the other steps that he and Congress have taken since the 1973 Arab oil embargo are starting to be felt.

A "Point of View"

"I'd say I think we will have something that we can call a national energy policy fairly soon," says Edward Mitchell, a University of Michigan professor and the director of energy studies for the conservative American Enterprise Institute. While he has strong reservations about the program,

Prof. Mitchell says, "There is a sort of point of view, a philosophy underlying the various elements." That philosophy: "Reduce demand and divorce ourselves from the oil cartel."

The energy program as originally proposed by the President aimed to halve U.S. oil imports by 1980 from the 8.5 million to 9.5 million barrels a day that it's estimated will be coming into the country by that date. While Congress has softened some of Mr. Carter's targets a bit, the plan still represents a sharp move away from foreign oil, which is currently being imported at a rate of about 8.4 million barrels a day.

To meet the targets, the strategy will emphasize conserving energy, mostly through higher prices but also through fuel-efficiency standards in autos, buildings, equipment and the like, and through economic incentives such as tax credits. Other details:

—Holding domestic crude-oil production steady or slowing its rate of decline that is expected as the U.S. runs out of easily exploited reserves.

—Increasing the use of other energy sources, including coal and, despite its many problems, nuclear power.

— Establishing important new energy sources, including synthetic fuels and, later, solar power and nuclear fusion.

No Exclusive Credit

Although much of the program was put together in the last three years, the Carter administration isn't claiming exclusive credit. Charles Duncan, the Secretary of Energy, talks of an emerging "broad consensus" in the nation on what needs to be done. Cynics, though, say such statements seek to share the blame should the program fail to meet its ambitious goals.

The program's broad approach invites broad criticism. Critics dislike its effect on consumers and on the environment. Many believe that more drastic moves are needed, such as a stiff gasoline tax or rationing. Others, such as William Simon, the former Treasury Secretary and energy chief under President Nixon, say the program increases government interference in the energy area when it should be stripping regulations away.

The energy program as it is taking shape is "pure politics," fumes Mr. Simon, now a consultant to the securities firm of Blyth Eastman Dillon. "It's pandering to the public to buy votes," he says, by giving a false impression of doing something meaningful.

Phasing Out Controls

But Eliot Cutler, a Washington lawyer and until recently the White House's en-

ergy-policy coordinator, disagrees. "This isn't to say it's perfect, but we have made great strides," he says. "We are far better prepared to deal with a world of growing energy uncertainty than we were before." He defends the policy's wide-ranging approach on the basis that "this isn't the time to choose one path. We just don't know enough about the future."

High prices, officials argue, are the best way to hold down energy use. By phasing out price controls on domestically produced oil over the next 19 months, President Carter is allowing its price to rise to the already astronomical levels set by the Organization of Petroleum Exporting Countries. Administration officials estimate that decontrol will add an extra 7½ cents to 22½ cents to the price of a gallon gasoline by October 1981. And under the Natural Gas Policy Act of 1978, newly discovered natural gas is to be decontrolled by 1985; by late this decade, the Energy Department figures, gas may become nearly as expensive to use as oil.

Officials say there already is evidence that their strategy will hold down demand. They point to 1979 when world oil prices doubled, and they say it isn't a coincidence that U.S. oil consumption declined for the first time in four years. The only way to wean the country from its foreign-oil dependence, Mr. Duncan says, is to price energy at its "true cost"—the cost of developing new energy to replace the energy being consumed.

Decontrol, especially of oil, "was a courageous step" by President Carter, says Charles DiBona, president of the American Petroleum Institute, the group whose members stand to profit from the move. "No politician likes the consequences of the actions that have to be taken for a rational energy policy," he says.

Many liberals argue, though, that decontrol is unfair to the consumers who must pay higher energy bills. "The next administration should recontrol the price of oil," says Sen. Edward Kennedy of Massachusetts. Controls, he says, are "necessary to protect the poor and average-income consumer until the energy economy reaches the point of sufficient supply and genuine competition."

The energy policy sidesteps the major non-price weapon it could use: mandatory gasoline rationing. Although President Carter isn't happy with the tightly limited rationing powers Congress has given him, administration officials believe rationing is more useful for handling an immediate shortage than for long-term conservation.

But political pressures could force a coupon-rationing system if other steps fail. A recent Conference Board public-opinion poll showed "surprising support" for rationing, and Sen. Kennedy has made it a major theme of his bid for the Democratic presidential nomination.

Energy planners have also shelved, for the time being at least, another potentially potent weapon: a stiff tax on gasoline. Administration officials floated the notion last year, then withdrew it as being politically unacceptable. But President Carter has said he may impose oil-import fees if the nation doesn't save enough fuel this year. And that could be designed to have the same effect as a gasoline tax.

Less noticed in the furor over decontrol and rationing, the government has in the last few years also adopted a wide range of non-price measures to curb energy use. The measures, many of which haven't yet fully taken effect, cover everything from gas-guzzling autos to home insulation. By 1985, for example, each auto maker's new-car production will be required to average 27.5 miles a gallon, up from the present standard of 20. The Energy Department is writing rules to set mandatory energy-efficiency standards for every new building in the country. Heating and cooling levels in public buildings have been set by presidential declaration, and the government is giving tax credits and other assistance to insulate homes and other buildings.

In contrast to the sweeping efforts to reduce demand, the energy program is restrained in its attempts to stimulate production of domestic oil and gas from existing sources. The "windfall-profits" tax would claim up to 50% of the oil companies' additional profits resulting from decontrol. This, says Prof. Mitchell of the University of Michigan, shows that the program "doesn't seem to believe in using the price mechanism to increase supply."

Mr. DiBona of the petroleum institute is more blunt: "On the production side, we still have it all screwed up." The "windfall" tax, he says, will "discourage two million barrels a day of production" by depriving the oil industry of money to find and produce more oil.

Administration officials concede that the tax will indeed hold down some oil production. At best, they say, decontrol and the tax will keep domestic output for the next several years more or less steady. The proceeds for the tax, they contend, are needed to redirect efforts away from finite energy sources like oil and gas toward synthetic fuels—oil and gas from coal and oil from shale, for example—and renewable energy sources such as solar and wind power. "You contol the reinvestment decision so that you ensure meeting national needs," the White House's Mr. Cutler says.

$20 Billion in Guarantees

The energy program makes synthetic fuels the chief beneficiary of that investment. The legislation now in Congress would establish a government-chartered corporation that could spend up to $20 billion of the "windfall-tax" money for loan guarantees on synthetic-fuel projects and for price guarantees on the fuel itself. But with oil and gas prices rising sharply, some observers say the $20 billion may never be needed. By 1990 energy officials see production of 1.75 million barrels a day of synthetic fuel.

The energy program also is counting on increased direct use of coal. The Energy Department already has ordered some power plants to burn coal instead of oil, and the administration is proposing a $12 billion aid plan to encourage further switching by utilities.

But big problems remain. For one, there are the environmental consequences of the increased mining and burning of coal. Environmentalists argue that with proper safeguards the country can exploit its vast coal reserves without gutting existing pollution rules. As the price of energy rises, says David Masselli, an official of Friends of the Earth, "the cost of pollution control is peanuts." But Ralph Bailey, chairman of Conoco Inc., which owns Consolidation Coal Co., maintains that the clean-air rules must be relaxed to make the use of coal more practical and economical.

Nuclear Power's Problems

Even basic logistics can create problems. Just now, for instance, the Department of Energy and Transportation are trying to find a remedy for a shortage of coal-carrying railroad cars.

Nuclear power's problems are even more grave. Administration officials are privately pressing to speed up licensing of plants now under construction, and one aide says that "we have to rehabilitate the nuclear option." But rising costs, sluggish electricity demand and the Three Mile island accident have made utilities increasingly wary of investing the billions of dollars needed for more plants. The industry ordered only two reactors in 1978 and none since then, compared with a peak of 41 orders in 1973.

"It will be a while before orders for new plants pick up," says John Sawhill, the deputy energy secretary. "The utility industry isn't going to be willing to commit itself until the nation decides" how much nuclear power it wants, he says.

Meanwhile, the government will pour billions of dollars into developing longer-term solutions. For the first time, the federal government is proposing to spend more money on developing solar power and other renewable energy sources than on nuclear fission. Scientists are also continuing their efforts to harness nuclear fusion, although a breakthrough is said to be many years away.

Time could be the energy program's biggest obstacle. As the Iranian situation has shown, events in the politically unstable Middle East can move swiftly, while the energy program will take several years to produce results.

"We just keep lurching from crisis to crisis," says Mr. Simon, the former energy chief. In the meantime, he says, the nation's energy situation gets worse and worse: "The President's program is a joke. If I had tried to fool the people like that, I would have been torn apart."

Secretary Duncan argues, however, that slow but steady progress is the only answer. "Through the decade of the 1980s we will still be dependent on foreign oil," he says. "But we are setting a target and moving toward it. We will have done a hell of a disservice" to future generations, he says, "if we do again what we did in 1973—which was nothing."

Clean-Air Fight

Plain Dust Is the Key To Pollution 'Bubble' At Armco Steelworks

Ohio Program Provides Test For EPA's New Policy; Is a Rust Trade-Off Fair?

How to Breach a Brick Wall

By Margaret Yao

Staff Reporter of The Wall Street Journal

MIDDLETOWN, Ohio — Revolutionary, yet mundane-looking, air pollution controls are at work at Armco Inc.'s sprawling steelworks here.

Mounted spray systems regularly wet down 11 acres of coal piles. Roads are periodically sprayed or swept. New grass lines the side of an open hearth. A former school bus carries workers to job sites from perimeter parking lots because plant traffic is restricted.

All this is part of a carefully orchestrated program to control what is mainly ordinary open dust. Armco is the first steel company to try open-dust controls.

The company is in the vanguard of about 100 firms that have embraced, with formal proposals, the Environmental Protection Agency's so-called bubble policy adopted last December. None of the proposals have yet been approved. The policy treats an industrial plant as if it were in an imaginary bubble that has a single stack emitting pollutants. It allows companies to limit emissions on a plantwide basis rather than forcing them to meet specific limits for every pollution source at the plant.

Technology and Politics

The history of Armco's bubble proposal points up the ever-increasing intertwining of economics, technology and politics. It also shows how dealings between bureaucrats and businessmen can lead to major regulatory changes affecting the public at large.

The bubble policy, proponents say, can lower pollution-control costs without sacrificing air quality. Many environmentalists call the policy too easy on industry. They say that it will be hard to enforce and that it won't save the companies much money anyway.

Under the policy, only pollutants of the same type can be offset against one another. Armco is applying the concept to nontoxic particulates, hence can trade off one nontoxic particulate against another. There are three kinds of nontoxic particulates: some smokestack emissions; some process emissions such as rust; and open dust, or windblown dust, which arises outside the production process and which has largely been ignored in the past as a pollution source.

Armco, which is already controlling smokestack emissions, proposes in effect, to trade dust for rust. The company can reduce airborne dust more cheaply than it can reduce the particles that escape from plant doors, windows and vents.

John E. Barker, Armco's director of environmental engineering, likes to sum up the program which got fully under way on Aug. 1, this way: "We can control six times as much (pollution) for one-third the cost in half the time and at a tiny fraction of the energy consumption."

Huge Saving Foreseen

Armco is spending $4 million on the dust controls instead of $11.5 million on conventional hoods and on the bag filters that act like giant vacuum cleaners inside a plant. It estimates that if it duplicates the dust-control program at its other major steel plants, it will save $42 million more in pollution-abatement costs.

Such estimating, though, may be jumping the gun. The EPA still hasn't given final approval to the Middletown project, and it won't until it sees proof of improved air quality.

From the first six weeks of raw data, Mr. Barker says, the measurements appear "mighty close" to meeting national air-pollution standards. Armco plans to submit data to the EPA in the next few weeks, he says.

He acknowledges that control of the dust particles probably won't make the air better to breathe. "The quality of life is going to improve, but it won't necessarily be more healthful," he says. "If we had 1,000 acres of ragweed, we could plow it up and plant grass. That would reduce the particulates."

Bruce Steiner, supervising engineer for the Armco project, says that Armco is simply complying with current regulations permitting such a trade-off as dust for rust. "There are certain rules of the game that we have to live with," he says. "and that's the game we're playing." Actually the bubble rules first proposed by the EPA didn't envision open-dust trade-offs, because of measurement problems, but Armco got the agency to change its mind.

"Great Ideas Take Time"

Some companies, particularly in the steel industry, complain the EPA bubble regulations are too restrictive to do the companies much good. Many others are waiting to see how the pioneers, mostly chemical companies, fare.

The concept, says William Drayton, the EPA's assistant administrator for planning and management, eventually will get more acceptance. "Great and simple ideas take time," he says. "It took American farmers 15 years to accept hybrid corn."

Even now, industry generally favors the bubble idea but complains that state environmental agencies and the EPA have been slow to approve individual bubble proposals. Those complaining the loudest are companies—including Armco—that, under federal law, must clear up operations in dirty-air areas by the end of 1982. Minnesota Mining & Manufacturing Co. and others say they are worried that if they don't get bubble approval in the next few months, they might not have enough time to install more expensive controls and will end up paying hefty fines for being late.

EPA officials are well aware of the complaints about bureaucracy, but they don't want to risk approving bad bubbles by rushing. "You only need one or two cases of disasters about how a bubble made the environment worse to blow the whole thing up." says Deborah Taylor, acting branch chief for air economics at EPA headquarters.

Armco's proposal, Mr. Drayton says, is "a typical example of something taking time." Armco will certainly vouch for that. It has been more than two years since the blunt-spoken Mr. Barker first went around "selling the concept on the roast-beef-and-green-pea circuit," as he calls it.

Armco, the seventh-largest steelmaker, has been something of a trend-setter in pollution controls in the steel industry. Applying the mid-1970s work of a joint steel-industry and government task force to its own operations, Armco determined that more than 61% of its Middletown works' emissions were from open-dust sources.

Armed with that knowledge and believing that the EPA would approve, Armco developed its program to keep dust from flying. Noting that snow-cover improved air-quality measurements, Armco sought to duplicate nature's effects. By its calculations, its program can control 4,000 tons a year, or 83% of the open dust at the Middletown plant.

A Brick Wall

Then Armco had to make the idea politically acceptable. But it ran into a brick wall when, in January 1979, the EPA's draft bubble policy left out the open-dust trade-off. "I was almost ready to throw in the sponge," the usually battle-spirited Mr. Barker recalls. However, he persuaded some EPA officials to visit the Middletown mill.

When a visitor arrives in Middletown, a community of 47,000 tucked away in the farm country between Cincinnati and Dayton, the smokestacks of the works signal the first greeting. Middletown seems very much a company town. Dominated by Armco for decades, its major thoroughfare is named Verity Highway, after George Verity, who founded Armco and whose grandson C. William Verity Jr. is chairman of the company today.

The 2,600-acre Middletown works annually produce about 3.2 million tons of steel when operating at full capacity, or about one-third of Armco's production. It is Armco's largest operation. It is the oldest, too, but improvements over the years have made it the most modern as well.

The visiting regulators came away impressed. "We would be very uncomfortable about a plant that was billowing out heavy metals and all kinds of nasties and then wanted to solve the problem by watering the roads," Mr. Drayton says. "But Armco's facility is well run. They've cleaned up their act on most of their basic processes. Management is acting in good faith. They have done a conscientious and good job. That's another reason to look at this very closely."

Revision Granted

When the EPA came out with the official bubble policy, one of the many revisions was a major section on open-dust trades—rewritten "specifically with Armco in mind," Mr. Drayton says.

"The only way to get intelligent regulations is to work with the agency," Mr. Barker says. "We may think there are a bunch of pigheaded nuts over there, but we tell it to their faces. We've always had a dialogue."

Armco's dust-for-rust trade-off raises a number of technical questions for regulators. "A little bit of heavy metal, especially when it has had some chemical interactions, is different in its impact on the body than the salt of the earth is," Mr. Drayton says. He adds, though, that undoubtedly many of the open-dust particles Armco is trying to control are chemically tainted.

Environmentalists such as Frances Dubrowski, senior attorney at the private, non-profit Natural Resources Defense Council in Washington, wonder whether the trade is equal. Miss Dubrowski asks, "Are we trading fine particles for particles that may be less harmful?"

Such questions have prompted the EPA to begin developing stricter standards—due next May — to govern particle size in trade-offs. The uppermost limit now is 30 micrograms; particles that size are just large enough to be seen by the naked eye. Smaller particles can fly farther, and those under three micrograms can be ingested into the lungs, traits that make smaller particles likely to be more hazardous. Generally, open-dust particles are larger than those resulting from the production process. But Armco contends that it is reducing the amount of dust to such an extent that air quality is benefiting more than it would without the trade-off.

For all the excitement, the bubble's approval essentially rests with instruments whose reflection of air quality isn't always very clear. When Armco in 1977 was forced to shut off scrubbers on the stacks of its six open-hearth shops for 10 weeks to conserve energy during a coal strike, "you could see the red cloud in the sky," Mr. Barker recalls. But two of the instruments didn't even notice; the third did notice, but by an insignificant amount.

There is one other catch. Before its bubble proposal can be approved. Armco must reach a consent agreement with the EPA concerning coke-plant emissions here that the EPA says violate a separate pollution standard.

EPA officials are rooting for Armco. "It's hard when somebody's so sincere and a good partner for you," Mr. Drayton says. "I'll be as happy as Armco if it works."

The big fear is that observers may misinterpret a turndown of Armco's bubble as an indication that the EPA isn't serious about the whole concept. "The significance of Armco lies in its symbolism," says Mrs. Taylor of the EPA. "To the extent that Armco has received a lot of publicity, it could be a big damper on other people's efforts if Armco runs into trouble with EPA."

92*October 20, 1980*

Review & Outlook

Toxic Science

Love Canal has already gone into the language as the most potent symbol of the danger of toxic chemical disposal. So it comes as a bit of a surprise to discover that upon review of the evidence, a distinguished medical panel has concluded that so far there is no scientific basis for concluding that it has damaged public health.

In a report to Governor Hugh Carey of New York, five respected physicians led by Dr. Lewis Thomas, chancellor of the Memorial Sloan-Kettering Cancer Center, have sharply criticized the existing "scientific" literature on the subject, as well as the role of government officials in aggra-vating the fears and anxieties of Love Canal residents.

The panel argues, for example, that there was no scientific justification for the New York State Health Department to declare that Love Canal was an "environmental nightmare," a "great and imminent peril" capable of causing "profound and devastating effects"—as it did in a September 1978 brochure entitled "Love Canal—Public Health Time Bomb."

Health Department investigators had found an abnormally high number of miscarriages and infants with low birth weight in the Love Canal area—a discovery which led to the evacuation of 236 families in August 1978. But in the absence of suitable control groups, the Thomas panel argues that these "data cannot be taken as more than suggestive."

The panel dismisses as "literally impossible to interpret" a 1979 study by Dr. Beverly Paigen, which claimed to show increased nervous disorders and birth defects in the areas of greatest chemical seepage. Dr. Paigen, according to the panel, failed to include adequate control groups, to validate medically the illnesses she cited or to distinguish between different age groups in her study. Her work, says the panel, "cannot be taken seriously as a piece of sound epidemiological research."

And the panel is especially critical of the chromosome study sponsored by the Environmental Protection Agency and released last May. This study, which claimed to find chromosome breakdowns in 11 of 36 Love Canal residents, led to an understandable wave of new fear among local homeowners and prompted the evacuation of 710 more families, even though the study contained no simultaneous controls and was therefore scientifically meaningless.

Shortly after the evacuation, moreover, suspicions about the EPA study mounted when its director, Dr. Dante Picciano, refused to show his slides to a review panel from the Department of Health and Human Services. And when an EPA panel headed by Dr. Roy Albert of New York University got a chance to look at photocopies of the Picciano slides, it saw no evidence for any chromosome breakdown observations. An article in Science magazine declared the study to be "botched."

Dr. Picciano never tried to pretend that this was in any sense a full-fledged scientific study. It was rather a pilot study, designed to help the Justice Department in its Love Canal lawsuit against Hooker Chemical Co. But in the words of the Thomas panel, "such a poorly designed investigation as this one should not have been launched in the first place. With so much at stake for the residents involved, to have set up experiments that lead to public conclusions of such magnitude, without prior review of the protocol by qualified uninvolved peer scientists, and without any after-the-fact, independent review by competent scientists before release of the results, was a disservice to the citizens most intimately concerned."

The Thomas panel doesn't rule out any public health dangers from Love Canal. It argues instead that those dangers—past, present and future—are still unknown. Nor does the panel try to argue that Love Canal residents shouldn't have been evacuated. Indeed, Dr. Thomas has been quoted as saying he personally believes that the anguish caused by the presence of noxious chemicals underneath homes was reason enough to leave the area.

But the Thomas panel does suggest that poorly conducted scientific studies can threaten people's well-being just as much as improperly disposed of toxic wastes can. The residents of Love Canal, according to the panel, "have been subjected to more than two years of the most intense anxiety and fear. [Many] have come to believe that their health is in fact irreversibly damaged, that they are at future risk of cancer, congenital malformations in their offspring, and an increased incidence of miscarriages and abortions." In the future, one hopes that both scientists and public authorities will treat scientific findings more circumspectly, and not try to encourage fears that may be unjustified.

In the meantime, it may be best to remain a little skeptical of the more alarming pronouncements in our debates about toxic wastes. Toxic waste dumps do pose public health threats, and it is important both to clean them up and to monitor them carefully. But not every waste dump is a festering Love Canal. And even Love Canal, when subject to the careful scrutiny of distinguished scientists, may not be as dangerous as we have been led to imagine.

Health and Welfare Issues

93   *February 15, 1980*

Health Care and the Poor

By HARRY SCHWARTZ

Nothing stirs the ire of supporters of national health insurance more than what they see as the difference in access to medical care by the poor and the rich. As usual it is Senator Edward M. Kennedy to whom we can turn for the most typical rhetoric.

"Nowhere are the inequalities of our society more obvious than in the sickness of our poor. We know that our affluent few can buy the world's best medical care," the Senator has declared, adding, "In the United States today—the wealthiest nation in the history of man—millions of our citizens are sick. And they are sick because they are poor . . . . The difference in health care between the rich and the poor is measured by the stunted bodies, shortened lives, and physical handicaps of those who live in poverty."

Such words, of course, always bring to mind old and venerable stereotypes. There are no doctors in the slums and inner cities, we have been taught to believe, while on the Park Avenues of America physicians fall all over themselves, they are so densely packed. From this it is but a short step to the conviction that the poor have little or no medical care from physicians or hospitals because they cannot afford the price.

The persistence of such stereotypes is particularly curious since it is now 15 years since the enactment of Medicare and Medicaid, which provided for comprehensive and largely free (to the recipient) medical care for the old (many of whom are poor) and for the non-old poor.

Hard Statistics

By now, moreover, there are hard statistics showing that the nation's poor get on the average as much as or more medical care from physicians and hospitals than those in more affluent income groups. But somehow these data rarely get the attention they deserve.

Take the number of physicians' visits received by individuals in different groups on the average. Even in 1963, the best data available show, there was almost no differences among Americans by broad income category. In that year low-income individuals averaged 4.4 physician visits a year, middle income 4.3 and high income 4.6. By 1970, there was already apparent an inverse relation between income and average number of physician visits per individual. Low-income individuals had 4.9 physician visits a year, middle income 3.9 and high income 3.6 visits that year.

The data for 1972 and 1977 show little change from this earlier picture. In 1977, for example, in families earning less than $5,000 annually, individuals had on the average about 5.8 physician contacts a year. Persons in families with incomes from $5,000 to $9,999 a year had about 4.9 physician contacts a year, and persons in families with $10,000 or more income had only 4.7 physician contacts a year. Thus the government's own data completely demolish the usual stereotypes.

What about hospital care? Well, in 1963, even before Medicare and Medicaid, the poorest Americans—those with annual incomes under $2,000—had the highest number of hospital admissions—16 per hundred people, while the higher income groups had only 10 to 14 admissions annually per hundred people.

By 1977 the evidence was overwhelming that poor people get on the average much more hospital care than middle or upper class Americans.

In 1977, for example, those earning less than $5,000 annually accounted for 158.3 hospital discharges per thousand persons that year. From that figure the corresponding number of hospital discharges per thousand people goes down steadily with rising income until for families earning $25,000 or more the number is 93.4, 40% less.

The figures showing that poor people get more hospital care than anybody else are even more stark when we look at number of days of hospital care in 1977 per thousand people in each income group. In families earning less than $5,000 that year, there were 1,541 days of hospital care per thousand individuals. This went down steadily with rising income, until the most affluent — families earning $25,000 or more—had only 678.8 days per thousand population, well under half the figure for the poorest group.

The statistical data show convincingly to anybody with an open mind that the stereotype of the poor being denied medical care in the United States is completely

---

By now there are hard statistics showing that the nation's poor get on the average as much or more medical care from physicians and hospitals than those in more affluent income groups.

---

without foundation. The poor in this country get more care from physicians and hospitals than any other group of Americans, a result that is not surprising since many people are poor because they are sick and because this country has a very expensive system for providing the poor with medical care that costs them little or nothing directly.

Why then does the stereotype persist? One reason, of course, is ignorance. The United States government has never trumpeted these figures, while investigative reporters tend to find them boring. Another reason is the fact that those interested in painting the worst possible picture of American health care often deliberately confuse the issue of the amount of health care with the environment in which people receive health care.

'The Endless Lines'

Thus Senator Kennedy has written, "For too many of the poor, the only 'doctor' they know is the cold and impersonal emergency ward of the municipal or county hospital. For too many of our citizens, the family physician has disappeared, to be replaced by the endless lines and depressing waiting rooms of hospitals built at the turn of the century."

In other words, a physician visit doesn't count unless in the ambience of a physician's office building in Scarsdale or Marin County. But in 1977, the data show, only 20% of the poorest citizens' physician contacts were in hospital outpatient departments, while the richest Americans had 10% of their physician contacts there. Even this factor, in short, does not radically alter the overall picture that the poorest Americans get the most medical care.

And finally, of course, there is the ultimate irony. Senator Kennedy and many who agree with him want all Americans to join Health Maintenance Organizations (HMOs) where the old-style family doctor is replaced by a bureaucratic organization. And in some of the largest and oldest HMOs in this country, non-poor patients wait in conditions resembling those the Senator cited above for the poor. Anyone who doubts that need only visit the Kaiser Permanente doctors' building on Geary Boulevard in San Francisco or the HIP office building on Broadway in Washington Heights, Manhattan.

Mr. Schwartz is a researcher affiliated with the Department of Surgery at Columbia University College of Physicians and Surgeons.

Welfare for Radicals

Tom Hayden and Jane Fonda are too rich to need federal money, but some of their friends apparently do. Thereby hangs a tale in the unending saga of CETA abuses. CETA, you will recall, is the federal Comprehensive Employment and Training Act, which has ballooned into a $9 billion budget item; the bulk of the money goes for "public service" jobs in public or nonprofit agencies. Now the Inspector-General's office of the U.S. Department of Labor has found "prosecutive merit" in charges that some of these funds have helped subsidize political activities of the Hayden-Fonda network.

Focus of the charge is a group called the Center for New Corporate Priorities run by Santa Monica City Councilman Ruth Yannatta Goldway. Ms. Goldway, a consumer issues activist, was the first local candidate to be elected with support of Hayden-Fonda's "populist" Campaign for Economic Democracy; her husband, Derek Shearer, is an old Students for a Democratic Society colleague of Mr. Hayden. Ms. Goldway's Center for New Corporate Priorities makes no secret of its hostility to big business. In 1978, the Center received a $126,000 CETA grant for job training. More than half of Ms. Goldway's own salary at the center came from CETA money.

During the 18 months before Ms. Goldway voluntarily renounced the grant, according to a detailed report in the Santa Monica Evening Outlook, the Center placed 57 CETA trainees with 29 different community organizations. These "work-sites," in CETA jargon, ranged from the Coalition for Economic Survival, active in rent control and tenant issues, to the Interfaith Hunger Coalition, active in the Nestle boycott over infant formula marketing, to the Southwest Working Women's Coalition, to the La Raza Center for Alternative Education, and so on. Two of the recipients, the California Public Policy Center and the California Housing Research Foundation, are said to be closely aligned with Hayden-Fonda's CED, and the others would appear to be in sympathy with that brand of politics.

But the Labor Department (and its intermediary, the Los Angeles County Department of Community Development) didn't seem to mind parcelling out money to this web of activist groups. But the government sponsors professed shock at the revelation that some of these CETA workers might be involved in politics. Federal regulations bar CETA contracts from supporting political campaigns or legislative lobbying. A former CETA worker under the Center's contract has charged that fellow trainees were campaigning for Santa Monica's rent control initiative and for Ms. Goldway's own election to the City Council.

"It's all very gray," Mike Fonte, co-director of the Interfaith Hunger Coalition told the Evening Outlook. "Defining what a CETA worker can and cannot do is a real problem because the lines are not always clear."

In one sense, the charges against Ms. Goldway's group pale in comparison to other CETA abuses. A congressional committee recently heard that one CETA contractor, the Washington, D.C. Institute for Careers in Tourism, devoted more than $100,000 to such things as "Happy Hour Training" at D.C.'s Red Lion and Black Tahiti restaurants. Another contractor used CETA money for a $2,850 wedding and reception on the Queen Mary.

Ms. Goldway has also been criticized for hiring many white, well-educated CETA workers in their 20s and 30s, and that may be unfair. The program is meant to give skilled jobs to the long-term unemployed with a history of low incomes, and the people who best match that profile are graduate school drop-outs. CETA workers nationally are by far the best educated group ever to go on the government dole.

But the Santa Monica case can't simply be dismissed as a teapot tempest blown up by the far right. As one Los Angeles County official did timidly wonder, "community advocacy" doesn't seem like the kind of job training CETA was supposed to provide. In fact, the "advocacy" practiced by the Haydens, Fondas and Goldways of the world looks pretty much like undiluted politics. Federal poverty programs have been notorious for financing a whole new breed of political machines. Now CETA is making its contribution, in ways that are just now coming to light.

---

95 *January 29, 1981*

Equal Access

Colleges Spend Millions To Modify Buildings For Disabled Students

---

Ramps, Wide Doors Installed Under Federal Pressure, But Some Schools Resist

---

Ben Mattlin's Mean Machine

BY JONATHAN KAUFMAN
Special to THE WALL STREET JOURNAL

CAMBRIDGE, Mass.—In the past three years, Harvard University has spent $680,000 so Ben Mattlin can major in social studies.

It has widened doorways and installed special ramps, lowered drinking fountains and rebuilt bathrooms. Taking into account similar changes begun or planned, Harvard's total bill for such improvements will run to more than $2 million.

Mr. Mattlin, who is 18 and a freshman, is a quadriplegic. Since birth he has been confined to a wheelchair, limited in the use of his arms and hands. "I never wanted to be a hockey player," he says between bites of a salad at a restaurant near Harvard's campus. "And, socially, if I go to a dance I'm not going to do as well as some disco king." He shrugs. "But that's not me anyway. I guess you could say I'm something of a square."

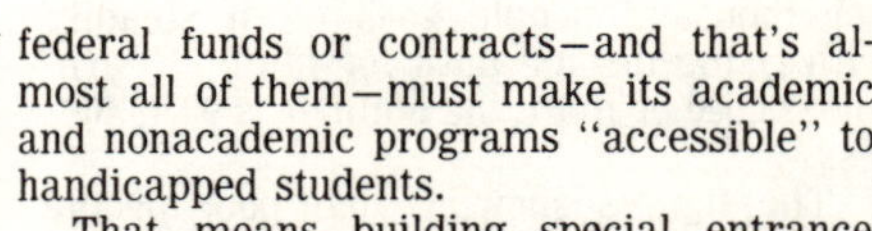

Along with 150,000 other disabled students at colleges and universities across the country, Mr. Mattlin belongs to what could be called the nation's first "accessibility" class. Under federal regulations that took effect last summer, any college that receives federal funds or contracts—and that's almost all of them—must make its academic and nonacademic programs "accessible" to handicapped students.

That means building special entrance ramps and installing elevators for students like Mr. Mattlin who are confined to wheelchairs; providing tape recorders for blind students so they can record class lectures, and making sure professors don't mumble into the blackboard when deaf students who can read lips are in the class.

And because many of these special services cost money, "accessibility" has also meant resistance, and a rash of lawsuits by the colleges.

"We've spent $2.2 million on physical modifications to make this campus accessible, and that's $2.2 million we didn't spend on buying books for the library," says Ronald Brown, vice president for student affairs at the University of Texas at Austin. The University of Texas is embroiled in a legal fight over whether it must pay for a sign-language translator for a deaf student.

"When you have the federal government requiring all sorts of physical changes and requiring all sorts of special services without providing a cent of help, you have a situation that warrants some real concern," says Sheldon Steinbach, general counsel for the American Council on Education, a university-sponsored group that is backing the University of Texas challenge.

Equal Tuition, Equal Opportunity

Supporters of making colleges more accessible to handicapped students argue, as supporters of special efforts to help blacks and Hispanics have argued before them, that providing special services simply equalizes opportunity. "A handicapped student pays the same tuition as a non-handicapped student," says Alfred DeGraff, director of disabled-student services at Boston University. "He or she has as much right to take chemistry or go hear a speech by Bella Abzug as an able-bodied person." (When Bella Abzug or anyone else speaks on Boston University's campus, Mr. DeGraff's office provides deaf students with a sign-language interpreter.)

Backers of the accessibility rule also say that university administrators exaggerate when they cry poverty at a $3,000 bill for a sign-language interpreter or a $20,000 bill for a ramp leading to the chemistry building. "The University of Texas subsidizes its football team heavily," says Chester Avery, director of the office of handicapped concerns at the Department of Education. "And like most colleges, it receives a lot of federal money. With some creativity and a little imagination, colleges can find ways to fund all these changes."

When F.D.R. Revisited Harvard

Both Mr. Avery—a Carter appointee—and Mr. Steinbach believe the Reagan administration is likely to ease the pressure on colleges to quickly make all their buildings and programs accessible. In the meantime, however, many schools have already moved to accommodate the handicapped. Harvard's new ramps and other modifications are used by more than a dozen "mobility-impaired" students, including one besides Mr. Mattlin who uses a wheelchair.

"Back when I went to Harvard in the 1950s, they accepted one blind guy a year—for diversity," says Mr. Avery, who is blind. When President Franklin Roosevelt, Harvard '04, went back to visit his alma mater in the 1930s, notes Mr. Avery, he had trouble getting around campus because he wore leg braces and used a wheelchair. "Today," says Mr. Avery, "F.D.R. would have a much easier time of it."

Indeed, he could easily stay with Mr. Mattlin.

"Come in, come in," says Mr. Mattlin, as he swings open the door to his room, flicks a switch on his motorized wheelchair and rolls backward. The room looks much the same as other rooms in Harvard's freshman dormitories. A stereo system dominates one wall; shelves of books and papers another. Only a long work table in the middle of the living room looks out of place.

"I couldn't get my legs and the front of my wheelchair under the standard-issue Harvard desk," Mr. Mattlin explains. "A day or so after I got here, I saw this table and mentioned to someone that it would be perfect. The next day some workmen arrived and brought it in."

Harvard has been similarly accommodating on other issues. When Mr. Mattlin said he wanted to take a popular freshman course that met on the second floor of a building that had no elevator, the university moved the class—displacing another class in the process.

"I was also placed in an expository writing class that was up two or three stairs," Mr. Mattlin says. "They offered to switch me to a different class that met in a more accessible classroom. But it would have met at nine in the morning. I told them I'd handle the stairs."

Mr. Mattlin needs some help for that and for a few other tasks. Before coming to Harvard, he attended a regular private school in New York. "I've always been in a normalized environment, among ambulatory people," he says. "I went to a special camp for handicapped people once, and I didn't like it."

Here, however, Mr. Mattlin shares his room with a full-time attendant paid for by his parents. The attendant gets Mr. Mattlin ready in the morning and takes him to his first class. After that the attendant or a student volunteer accompanies Mr. Mattlin from class to class. "This is a pretty mean machine," says Mr. Mattlin, gesturing at his motorized wheelchair, "but I still need someone to help me get a coat on or to give me a push if I get caught on a bump. I don't strive to prove that I can function independently. OK, I can't."

Mr. Mattlin figures that his "mean machine," the attendant and other special needs that Harvard doesn't pay for probably add $10,000 to $20,000 a year to the annual $10,000 tuition bill his parents must pay. "That's one of the reasons I'm considering going to law school," he says. "I'm going to have to make a lot of money to pay for an attendant, for special transportation, things like that."

Still, as Mr. Mattlin and other handicapped students say, having enough money to remove the obstacles in the way of a handicapped person doesn't remove the handicap itself—or the way people respond to it.

"I find that very often people will assume that because I walk with crutches, I don't want to be included in certain activities, like going out at night for pizza," says Rani Kronick, a Harvard freshman. "They'll plan things when I'm not around because they don't want to 'embarrass' me."

Raymond Wayne, a Harvard senior who is blind, complains that too often "I'm known just because I'm blind. There are other things I'd like to be known for."

Mr. Mattlin shares many of these frustrations. "Sure, first encounters are difficult," he says. "Every time I enter a class I wonder what's going through people's minds."

Mr. Mattlin has even divided some of the responses he gets into categories. There are the "God-bless-yous," the people who think Mr. Mattlin is a "poor suffering soul." Then there are those who speak to Mr. Mattlin in baby talk, or speak only to his attendant.

"But you can't worry about that," he says. "Most people feel uncomfortable around handicapped people. That's their problem. You have to hope that by showing the breadth of your personality they'll see you for the person you are."

"You start out being 'that guy in the wheelchair,'" he goes on. "Then you become 'that guy in the wheelchair with a sense of humor,' and the process continues until the handicap isn't so prominent." It is, Mr. Mattlin says, almost a game one plays. "Soon after I got here, I wrote an article for one of the student newspapers about what it was like to have a handicap. After that people kept coming up to me saying, 'So you're the guy who wrote that article.'"

"You know," he says, pushing aside his salad, "I don't want to sound like those people who say you learn through suffering. But having a handicap has taught me things I wouldn't have known if I hadn't had it. It has given me an education."

Then Ben Mattlin says something startling. "I'm happy with the person I am," he says. "So I'm happy with the handicap that made me this person."

Kids, Buses, Judges and Public Schools

By Chester E. Finn Jr .

NASHVILLE—Impressions to the contrary notwithstanding, the Reagan revolution in social policy has not put an end to complex social engineering schemes designed by judges or a preoccupation with numerically determined educational "equity" that largely ignores school quality. Congress and the administration may be deregulating, reordering and reforming as if there were no tomorrow, but the third branch of government continues to bear fruits of an earlier era.

Nowhere is that sense of design more palpable than in central Tennessee, where the public schools of Nashville-Davidson County opened yesterday, three weeks late, due to a heated desegregation dispute within the federal judiciary.

Like many Southern communities, Nashville had dithered and dawdled in dismantling its old dual school system. Not until 1971, when large-scale busing was imposed on most of the county, were the schools significantly desegregated. In numerical terms, that arrangement was a success. Whereas 79 of the 101 schools affected by it had been either almost-all-white or almost-all-black, by 1976 this was true of just one school, while 67 of them had black enrollments between 25% and 50%.

But little else was gained. The pupil assignment scheme, crafted by HEW and ordered into effect by federal Judge L. Clure Morton was clumsy and unpopular. It featured disruptive yearly changes in who was sent to which buildings; frequent alterations in the character of individual schools; long bus rides for many youngsters, a burden disproportionately borne by black families; practically every child attending at least four different schools between kindergarten and twelfth grade, and most blacks going to five or more schools.

Objections All Round

Though some urged even more busing, most people found the 1971 plan too single-minded and dislocating. Black leaders lamented the loss of community control and the implicit racism that required nearly every youngster to attend a majority-white school.

Parents of every color objected to long bus rides for six-year-olds, the lack of parent-teacher contact and the difficulty of re-trieving a child who took sick at mid-day. Though a handful of schools retained distinctive identities and traditions, and many fine teachers did commendable work, any attention paid to educational quality was in spite of the court-ordered desegregation plan, not a result of it.

In 1980, at the behest of both the NAACP Legal Defense Fund and the school board, federal Judge Thomas A. Wiseman reviewed the consequences of his predecessor's actions and found a community haunted by the "specter" of "a public school system populated by the poor and black, and a private school system serving the affluent and white."

He concluded that the "osmosis effect" —the proposition that black children would learn better in the presence of white classmates—"appears not to have had the desired effect" and saw a necessity to introduce what he termed "educational components" into the desegregation plan.

Their dollar cost, he observed, could be offset by spending less on busing. Finally, he insisted, "It is not undemocratic, nor does it violate equal protection of the laws to have a system that allows for recognition of and respect for differences in our society. A rigid adherence to racial ratios premised upon the social goal of assimilation . . . is not only constitutionally unrequired, but socially undesirable."

Judge Wiseman then sketched an altogether different approach to desegregating —and improving—public education in Davidson County. The school board turned this into a detailed plan modeled on the judge's design, and on April 17, 1981, he ordered it put into effect when the 68,000-student system opened on Aug. 21.

From kindergarten through grade four, all children would attend neighborhood schools, but with attendance zones enlarged to maximize integration. Grades five through eight would have some busing, but less than before, and there would be a countywide "magnet" school for educationally gifted youngsters of every race. The high schools would be regrouped to ring the metropolitan area, with each drawing students from a wedge-shaped zone reaching from the inner city to the outer suburbs.

The thrust of the entire plan was greater emphasis on educational quality: intensive teacher training, new curricula (including a heavy dose of multi-cultural studies), smaller classes, more parent involvement and fewer resources siphoned into busing.

Most of the community responded with enthusiasm, and teachers and administrators spent a busy summer preparing for the new plan. Parents of talented children eagerly sought admission to the magnet school. Morale was generally high, and so were expectations.

Not everyone was content, to be sure.

The thrust of the judge's plan was emphasis on educational quality: more teacher training, smaller classes and fewer resources siphoned into busing.

But the most consequential protest came from the NAACP attorneys, who charged that the return to neighborhood schools in the early grades was tantamount to re-segregation, and who appealed to the Sixth Circuit in May to reverse Judge Wiseman's order. That court, which had approved the 1971 busing plan and which now includes former NAACP General Counsel Nathaniel Jones and former HEW Secretary Anthony Celebrezze, agreed to take up the matter in October.

But two days before the schools were to open, NAACP attorneys urged the Sixth Circuit to stay the new plan—thereby reimposing the old one—until the appellate review was finished. The appeals court agreed to this, and hinted strongly that its review of the substance of Judge Wiseman's plan would likely result in permanent rejection.

The Supreme Court Justices sought out by the school board's attorneys declined to overrule the Sixth Circuit's "stay."

So the schools stayed closed until yesterday, and though a dedicated board of education and its able staff did their utmost to minimize chaos and keep tempers cool, it cannot be entirely coincidental that on Sept. 3 Davidson County voters overwhelmingly defeated a referendum that would have slightly raised property taxes to offset recent cuts in the school budget.

The old busing plan, seemingly still favored by the Court of Appeals, embodies just one value: racial balance, numerically determined. Its "success" is easily measured. Its "costs" are harder to gauge, but involve such potent if intangible considerations as reduced support for schools generally, the exodus of families with alternatives and subtle degradation of community and ethnic pride. Above all, they involve who decides which youngsters should attend what schools and how much compulsion-by-government should be built into those decisions.

But Judge Wiseman did not shy away from such choices, either, and in its way the plan he crafted was as manipulative an exercise in social engineering from the federal bench as that which it was meant to replace. It included less compulsion, but it also included a hefty dose of "educational components" the desirability of which ought not obscure the question of a judge's competence to make such decisions.

Judge Wiseman's Concern

Still, Judge Wiseman's scheme embodied many of the social and educational values of the Reagan revolution: voluntarism, quality, parental involvement, choice and neighborhood institutions. Overall, it manifested a greater concern for the content of a child's education than for the color ratio in the classroom.

Judge Wiseman's order would also have been, to my knowledge, the first instance of a federal court *undoing* an extant busing plan, an event in its own right, and a complement to the actions of a few other judges who have recently declined to order additional busing, the administration's efforts to negotiate voluntary desegregation plans and the decisions by several communities to scrap self-imposed pupil assignment schemes.

The Sixth Court of Appeals, by contrast, appears likely to remain content with the familiar single standard of numerical integration, to be achieved with buses and compulsion if other means do not produce the right ratios. If this view persists, and to the extent that it is shared by other appellate courts and carried into other policy domains, it will not augur well for the Reagan revolution, either. One recalls the 1930s, when for several years the courts all but crippled the New Deal.

Yet the Nashville situation also raises perplexing questions for those who share Judge Wiseman's priorities, but are skeptical of the ability of jurists to direct the affairs of complex social institutions. For here we have two very different ideas, each in the hands of an unabashedly activist judiciary that displays no doubt as to its competence to handle such matters and the propriety of its doing so. That we may strongly favor one approach is almost beside the point. The real tragedy is that, after more than a decade of litigation, the public schools of Nashville today are first a battleground for lawyers and judges, and only second a place for children to learn.

Mr. Finn is a professor of education and public policy, Vanderbilt University.

In Defense of Court-Ordered School Busing

By Michael Meyers

The federal government's recent proposals to give financial inducements to students who aid the desegregation process are no effective substitute for judicially mandated busing. But most important, they are part of the drive to stall rather than accelerate the transition to democratic, racially integrated public schools.

Twenty-seven years ago the Supreme Court ruled in *Brown vs. Board of Education* that intentionally segregated schools are unconstitutional. The 1954 decision urged "all deliberate speed" to achieve compliance with the Constitution, but state education and public officials massively resisted the *Brown* mandate.

Faced with continuing, flagrant violations of the law and of the constitutional rights of black children, the NAACP and the federal government returned to the courts repeatedly to stop school officials from segregating children on the basis of their race. In every case, there had to be proof of *intentional, purposeful* segregation on the part of state agencies in order for the courts to have power under the Constitution to order any remedy at all.

As the pattern of violations grew more pervasive and sophisticated, the remedies also had to be more exact and tailored. Thus, courts in some cases had to redraw school district lines, alter school locations, scrutinize transfer policies and reassign pupils to overcome the illegal segregation. Busing, too, has been a tool available to the courts to cure exceptionally extensive racial segregation.

Defiance of the Law

Those who interpret the Constitution not to require affirmative integration have misread the 1954 decision and ignored the history of defiance of the law by local governments. The courts' role has not been to foster a social theology but always to cure purposeful segregation. In every case since the 1954 ruling, the courts have intervened only to disestablish a dual school system when state authorities were proven to have intentionally separated students because of their race.

Occasionally, the school bus is used to accelerate desegregation. The function of busing is to implement an affirmative plan that promises to work now to eliminate widescale segregation brought on by illegal actions. Busing per se was not designed either to raise academic standards or to be the express to quality education.

Academic achievement is not, of course, unrelated to or unaffected by racism. The 1954 decision found conclusive evidence that "separate educational facilities are inherently unequal" and cited the psychological studies that underscored the relationship between segregated education and injury to minority children. Achievement, in any event, is not a substitute for desegregation. Nor is it an impossible dream in a desegregated school.

The evidence is that minority students' academic achievement has improved in desegregated schools and that whites' scores have not declined. The task of raising academic achievement in the public schools is one deserving the attention and commitment of a united vanguard of educators, parents and students.

Attempts to talk about an alleged decline in academic achievement by white students in a desegregated setting reflect a principal concern for giving whites priority over the constitutional rights of blacks to equal educational opportunity. Such logic is a recycled version of the *Plessy vs. Ferguson* "separate but equal" doctrine.

It is also illusory to assail the use of buses in the desegregation process because the 1954 ruling and 1964 Civil Rights Act had *color-blind* dicta. As a matter of public

their most basic citizenship rights. And racism stirs whites to guard the privileges and deceptive status they have gained illegitimately from previous racially discriminatory practices.

It is no wonder that in communities throughout the country attempts to carry out policies or court orders promoting desegregated schools have met with widespread opposition. The point of desegregation has been adopted by the segregationists as their line-of-no-further retreat be-

polls do not decide complaints of discrimination. These polls will probably continue to reflect the ambiguity and divisions on racial questions felt by many Americans until the real issues are addressed and faced up to. The real issue is not "forced busing" but forced segregation and the remedies for it.

Social Chaos Could Result

A democratic society cannot continue to tolerate the miseducation of its children in segregated schools. Political maneuvering to get the Justice Department to go slow in pressing for school desegregation, to abandon the busing remedy and to remove courts from "educational matters" belittle the moral and legal imperatives to eliminate racial discrimination "root and branch" in our school systems. If the courts pull back from their constitutional duty of assuring due process and equal protection for all, social chaos of disastrous proportions could result.

In communities where whites and blacks have joined together, where politicians and public officials implement creative, affirmative programs to foster integration, desegregation is working.

---

policy, no one should be assigned seats in a school or privileges on the basis of his color. But to raise the rule against "assignment of students to public schools and within such schools without regard to their race" in the context of a desegregation plan is Orwellian doublespeak.

A desegregation plan recognizes that there has already, in fact, been an impermissible assignment on the basis of race, which has led to racial segregation in the school, and the courts must act whenever students are deprived of their public rights to be free of such discrimination.

Had the proscriptions of the 1964 Civil Rights Act been heeded early; had America not had a history of deliberate segregation; had blacks, in fact, been accorded equal opportunities free of racism, *then* an easy desegregation might have occurred in American institutions. The problem is that we are living in a country where racism has shortchanged blacks and denied them

cause it signals an end to white supremacy. That is why the desegregated school, caught in the crossfire between those challenging and seeking to uphold the racial status quo, has not always been the most congenial place for nurturing positive attitudes between the races. But this is no fault of busing. Opponents of desegregation use busing as the pretext to argue that "desegregation does not work."

But the real question is: Why don't people join forces to promote desegregation? In those communities where whites and blacks have joined together, where politicians and public officials implement creative, affirmative programs to foster integration, desegregation *is working* to break down racial stereotypes and the system of racial caste.

No doubt the majority of Americans are confused about the objectives of desegregation. Fortunately for the Bill of Rights and the Fourteenth Amendment, public opinion

The emotional outcry about "busing" diverts attention from the festering racism in the schools and body politic. Since 1919, busing has been commonplace in the United States. Today, on any day of the school year, some 43% of all students are bused to school. Only 3% are bused for purposes of desegregation. Busing as a "problem" for many parents and politicians seems to dissipate if white children on the bus ride end up at lily-white schools.

No, it's not the bus or the courts to which so many object. Stripped bare, the passionate objections to busing are thinly disguised arguments against the sensible mandates of justice.

Mr. Meyers is assistant director of the National Association for the Advancement of Colored People and director of its office of research, policy and plans.

Day in Court

Government-Paid Legal Services for the Poor Stir Local Contention and a Growing National Debate

By STEPHEN WERMIEL
Staff Reporter of THE WALL STREET JOURNAL
WAYCROSS, Ga.—The Legal Services Corporation has left its mark on this rural town alongside the Okefenokee Swamp.

Hugh Allen, a justice of the peace, says the LSC's federally financed lawyers are "aiding the deadbeats." He is so mad that he is circulating a petition among merchants and others who want to either "cut

back on them and give them new guidelines, or abolish them."

Elavene Peacock, a 59-year-old widow who supports a retarded son and daughter on Social Security payments, won't sign Mr.

Allen's petition. Without Legal Services, she would be out $635 for a roof treatment that washed off in the first rain. "I'd be in a real fix if they weren't here," she says.

The LSC, created in 1974 to provide free legal help for poor people in noncriminal cases, currently employs a total of 6,000 lawyers in all 50 states. In some ways, the fight here in southeastern Georgia is typical of the growing national debate over legal aid for the poor.

Financial Aspect

In Washington, the issue ostensibly is a financial one. President Reagan, backed by budget-slashing conservatives, wants to eliminate the $321 million-a-year Legal Services Corp. He proposes to allow states to decide whether they want to provide lawyers for the poor out of general federal block grants.

But the fight doesn't stop there. "To call this a budget issue is absurd," says John Cromartie, the director of the Georgia Legal Services program. "It's ideological." There is evidence on both sides that he is right.

As governor of California, Ronald Reagan in 1970 tried, without success, to stop federal financing of lawyers for the poor in his state. And the dislike for such legal aid voiced by Mr. Reagan and others has increased since the LSC was created. Michael Horowitz, the budget-office lawyer who is coordinating President Reagan's efforts against the LSC, says, "What we dislike is the use of clients as a means of furthering broad political strategies in court . . . that political, public-interest-type lawyering."

"The Legal Services Corp. has festered into a gaggle of political activists run amok," charges Sen. Jesse Helms, the conservative North Carolina Republican. Critics say the young lawyers spend their time lobbying for "social change" or suing federal and local officials instead of representing the poor.

Liberals strongly defend the legal services. "The program is based upon the very simple, fundamental premise that the poor—no less than the wealthy—are entitled to legal representation to redress grievances and defend their interests," says Democratic Sen. Alan Cranston of California.

LSC officials contend that the attack on the program is largely political. "We always feared we might be the one bone thrown to the far right," says F. William McAlpin, a St. Louis attorney who is the LSC's chairman. Mr. McAlpin also is secretary of the American Bar Association, which itself is actively supporting continuation of the program.

Much of the debate is over what the LSC's role should be. "This is the program of America's liberal elite," charges Howard Phillips, the director of the Conservative Caucus. He has a list of "atrocities" financed by Legal Services: a case to force Connecticut to pay for a sex-change operation; forced school-board redistricting in

Hereford, Texas; suing in behalf of Indian tribes for two-thirds of the land in Maine; fighting a University of California program to develop new farm machinery that would use less labor; and suing to protest county and state jail conditions.

Admitted Aberrations

Legal Services, Mr. Phillips says, "is the glue that holds together a lot of liberal causes."

Some cases cited by critics are, Mr. McAlpin says, aberrations that shouldn't have been given priority by Legal Services lawyers. Others he defends, noting that the corporation is run largely on the state and local level. Lawsuits aren't centrally approved, he says, a feature that should appeal to the Reagan administration. The program's supporters contend that making value judgments about which suits to handle and which to turn away denies effective representation to poor people.

The LSC's defenders also argue that private lawyers won't pick up indigents' cases if the corporation is killed. "You go to a major firm and they know tax laws; you come to Legal Services and they know food stamps, Medicaid and Social Security," says Mr. Cromartie, Georgia's program director. Adds Gloria Einstein, a legal-aid lawyer in Waycross, "They don't want our clients in their offices."

In the Legal Services office in Waycross, the agency's four lawyers have aggressively represented their indigent clients as if they were paying customers. Sometimes that has involved suing city housing authorities, state agencies and local business people and even Justice of the Peace Allen.

Such aggressiveness can disturb the tranquillity of Waycross, a town of 22,000 people surrounded by pine trees as far as the eye can see, and its environs. "It's harassment more than anything else," says Wilfred Smith about the suit filed against him as manager of 200 units of public housing in nearby Alma. "We don't appreciate that, no, sir."

Mr. Smith doesn't have to appreciate it; but he does have to abide by the court-ordered agreement governing the way he runs the housing units.

Lockouts Charged

"As a routine collection practice, they would change the locks on apartments" of tenants who hadn't paid their rent on time, says Miss Einstein, the legal-aid lawyer who handled the class-action case. The lockouts were made without required advance notices, she says. "There are pretty decent government regulations about what rights public-housing tenants have, but in Alma, they didn't have any."

The case of Ozell Johnson in nearby Willacoochee is still in court. The 46-year-old Mr. Johnson, a truck driver with a fourth-grade education and three children to support, thought a new exterior for his 20-year-old wood-frame house on an unpaved street

sounded attractive. According to a suit filed against a contractor by Robert Rosenblum, a Legal Services lawyer, Mr. Johnson signed a $4,840 contract for which he received Styrofoam insulation thinner than the Styrofoam in a cooler and vinyl-plastic siding like a Frisbee.

That isn't all Mr. Johnson signed. The suit charges that unwittingly and without the disclosure required by law, he also signed a deed to his house, in case he failed to pay, and an unspecified interest clause that made the actual cost $11,603 over 14 years. The contractor has denied the charges in court papers.

"You find thousands of people around the state who have had the same kind of problem and end up losing their homes," says Willacoochee Mayor Lace Futch. Without Legal Services, he says, "It's going to be hell on our poor people."

Protecting the Poor

In another local town, Homerville, Susan Kenney, who runs a nutrition program for the elderly, says some businesses often take advantage of the uneducated poor. "Grocery stores don't have prices on the food and charge more to food-stamp recipients," she says. "Insurance agents sell them hospitalization policies they don't need because they have Medicaid."

"A lot of this is stopping because they have legal aid to help," Mrs. Kenney says, but without that aid "it will go right back." When Mary Wrasman, a Legal Services lawyer, "stands up here and tells people the electric company can't just cut the power off," Mrs. Kenney says, "their eyes open wide."

Much Legal Services work is tedious. Three paralegals in the Waycross office spend hours at administrative hearings trying to prove that residents are eligible for Social Security and disability benefits. Some clients can't prove their age except with the family Bible and don't have medical records. Divorces, child-custody disputes and personal bankruptcies are also common fare.

To qualify for legal assistance, clients must fall below the LSC's annual income guidelines, set most recently at $5,388 for one person, $7,113 for a couple and $10,563 for a family of four. Critics question whether poor people should get free legal aid when many lower-middle-income people can't afford lawyers, either. The program's defenders say that's a reason to expand the program, not kill it.

The greatest clash in Waycross has been with Hugh Allen. In Georgia, the justice of the peace isn't a typical judge and often, like Mr. Allen, isn't even a lawyer. He is a local arbiter of disputes with power to issue a summons and to garnishee property to settle a debt.

Mr. Rosenblum calls it an "archaic" system in which the justice of the peace acts as "a collection agency" for merchants. A summons is served by a uniformed constable, and it frightens some people into thinking that they can be jailed for a debt. This is ironic because one goal in the founding of Georgia in 1733 was to provide a haven for debtors.

Mr. Allen says legal-aid lawyers advise clients "not to agree to pay honest and just debts. They've gotten so they won't come to court at all. They just appeal."

The lawyers say they are simply exercising the automatic right to appeal any debt over $50 to superior court for a fresh trial. That right is lost if the person agrees to pay the justice of the peace.

Officials Sued

In another case, the lawyer in charge of the office, Mark Gorman, recently sued to force state officials to notify a welfare recipient if the state rejects a Medicaid claim submitted by his doctor. Existing procedures require the state to notify only the doctor. The case arose when a collection agency demanded $90 from the grandmother of a young boy for an examination of his eyes. The grandmother, the suit says, assumed that the bill had long since been paid by Medicaid.

Miss Einstein won a consent decree last summer forcing Georgia to set guidelines for the amount of unemployment compensation that can be denied to a worker if his own conduct contributed to the firing. State law allows penalties of five to 12 weeks but doesn't specify how the number should be determined from case to case.

It was just those kinds of lawsuits that prompted Georgia Gov. George Busbee and the state legislature to cut off state aid to Legal Services in 1976. It isn't known whether the state might consider restoring funds to Legal Services if federal financing is ended. But the propriety of using government funds to sue government is one of several issues raised against Legal Services nationally. Democratic Sen. Russell Long of Louisiana said recently, "The most insane thing I could think of was to hire a lawyer to sue yourself. . . . Nobody but an idiot would do that."

Mr. McAlpin, the LSC chairman, responds, "The real, critical problems of poor people, more often than not, involve government on the other side." He says it would be "devastating" to have Congress finance the program on the condition that lawyers don't sue government.

It is too early to tell whether the Legal Services Corp. will survive and in what form. Few states are likely to use federal block-grant funds for legal aid. House and Senate committees have both suggested some federal financing for Legal Services groups, although on a curtailed basis. Legislation to authorize continuation of the program will be debated soon on the House floor. White House aides say they will urge the President to veto such legislation as it now stands.

Both sides in the fight over Legal Services say the outcome will have long-run implications. If Legal Services persists, Mr. Phillips warns, "thwarting the popular will through the courts is going to become the thing to do." Without Legal Services, says Mavis Trowell, who runs a community center near Waycross, "poor people are going to have to suffer for what the country voted for."

---

99 *July 2, 1981*

Healthy Ambivalence

We have never been able to address the subject of abortion in any tone except profound ambivalence, an attitude guaranteed to make you unpopular with both sides of a moral and cultural dispute.

We are unimpressed by the scholasticism with which the moral question is settled by the Roman Catholic Church (and formerly by other theologians as well). The ordinary moral instincts of mankind do not equate early abortion with outright murder; that conclusion came only from the attempt to push morality through the sieve of Aristotelian logic. The same scholasticism, of course, also brands contraception a sin, a position increasing numbers of the Church's followers find impossible to accept. We have no doubt that when this theology was written into law, it caused needless suffering and agony.

At the same time, we are repelled by the attitude of much of our upper-middle class elite, which seems to endow abortion with some kind of intrinsic virtue—not as exalted as mother, perhaps, but clearly more wholesome than flag or country. Surely abortion is something more than merely another medical procedure carrying no more moral implications than an appendectomy.

To take the limiting case—which has in fact occasionally happened—what do you do if the fetus survives the operation? Do you strangle it on the operating table? Do you plug it into the same life-support systems you would naturally employ if it had been born naturally but prematurely? Can it be said the society and the law have no interest in the answer to these questions? And is the moral equation really different five minutes after the operation than it was five minutes before?

Even in the far more common case of early-term abortion, we have trouble imagining that many women walk away without a twinge of guilt over a potential son or daughter. And it is not necessarily second-guessing the woman's decision to say this is a morally healthy human reaction.

From these musings we carry away a feeling that the morality of abortion will always be ambivalent, that hard-and-fast lines cannot be drawn, except perhaps in an arbitrarily pragmatic way. And given this ambivalence, we worry about any attempt to impose one judgment on those who have come to a different one. Our only firm conclusion is that in a pluralistic society, the abortion issue should not become the ground for socio-political aggression.

In the case of Harris v. McRae, which the Supreme Court decided Monday, it is not easy to decide which side is the aggressor. The issue is not whether anyone can have an abortion, but whether the state is going to pay for it under its medical care programs. Justice Stewart, writing for the majority, made the common-sense point that nothing in the Constitution requires such a subsidy. Against this, Justice Stevens argued in dissent that if the woman has a constitutional right to decide, her decision should not be used to deny her a benefit for which she otherwise qualifies.

For our own part, we have no strenuous objection to using tax money to subsidize abortions. We would rather have it spent for that purpose than for building microwave systems for Cesar Chavez or bailing out Chrysler. But the fact remains that a substantial minority of the pop-ulation does believe abortion to be murder, and naturally objects to being taxed to support it. We further doubt that, given the resources of this society, any substantial number of women who really want abortions will fail to find some way to finance them without public funds.

Courts, which pretend to deal in legal and constitutional absolutes, are not very good at drawing the uneasy compromises on which a pluralistic society depends. Legislatures are gen-erally better at registering and ba-lancing the distribution and intensity of opinion. Between the courts and the legislature, we seem to have arrived at a tolerable compromise, that abor-tions will be allowed but, except in ex-traordinary cases, not paid for out of tax funds. We suspect the court ma-jority was wise in not interfering fur-ther.

---

100   *August 5, 1981*

Speaking Up on Affirmative Action

By WALTER BERNS

Not so long ago, in a seminar room at the Federal Executive Institute in Charlot-tesville, Va., (a sort of "think tank" for high-level civil servants), a number of fed-eral government career executives, mostly strangers to one another, were chatting in-formally about their management prob-lems. At a certain point, one of them blurt-ed out, no doubt inadvertently, that in his experience the greatest obstacle to intelli-gent and efficient management was the go-verment's own affirmative action pro-gram. At which point the conversation came to an abrupt end, just as if he had said. "Well, my broker is E.F. Hutton, and E.F. hutton says. . . ."

I have never had occasion to learn what it is that E.F. Hutton has to say, nor was I present in Charlottesville on the reported occasion—the episode is recounted in a re-cent issue of the Washington Monthly—but I have no reason to doubt its authenticity; it has the ring of truth about it.

Every federal executive knows, or ought to know, that the equal employment opportunity program has been corrupted beyond recognition, but it is the rare exec-utive who is willing or, as we shall see, is permitted, to talk about this. I mean talk about it publicly; there are many who are willing to say much if they can say it pri-vately or, better yet, anonymously.

I learned this immediately after pub-lishing my first article on this subject in these pages ("The Carter Agreement That Creates Racial Quotas," Feb. 5, 1981). That piece, and a subsequent article in the May issue of Commentary ("Let Me Call You Quota, Sweetheart"), brought me a flood of letters and phone calls from federal offi-cials (most of them anonymous) assuring me that the situation was even worse than I had depicted.

I had written critically of the consent decree "negotiated" by the Justice De-partment on behalf of the Office of Person-nel Management, according to which the OPM was required to phase out its prac-tice of hiring by competitive examination and to replace it with a system of hiring by racial quotas. In the course of reciting the details of this devious business, (I called it a sweetheart deal, coming out of a sweet-heart suit, because the Justice Depart-ment, asking nothing in return, actually gave the plaintiffs more than they publicly

---

Every federal executive knows, or ought to, that the equal employment opportu-nity program has been cor-rupted beyond recognition, but it is the rare executive who is willing or is permitted to talk about this.

---

dared to ask for) I pointed out that the Justice Department had signed the agree-ment without informing the agencies that would be most affected by it, and had signed it over the objections of the OPM, the agency principally concerned with Ex-ecutive Branch hiring.

The Name of the Game

The mail brought me a mountain of ma-terials—in-house journals, memoranda and the like—demonstrating that the name of the game now being played in many if not most major federal agencies is not equal employment opportunity, but unequal em-ployment opportunity, otherwise known as affirmative action.

Almost every one of these agencies has its own Office of Civil Rights, staffed, as these ancillary operations usually are, by misfits and discards from offices where real work has to be done, and they stand ready and eager to hear complaints of dis-criminatory treatment (on the basis of race, sex, national origin and even age).

Of discrimination there is, I am as-sured, very little; but of complaints there is a growing avalanche. Some employes apparently do little but file com-plaints—eight in six months is the individu-al record in one agency, and 30 in just over a year in another—and supervisors can do nothing about it (except, of course, to rec-ommend the transfer of the complainer to the agency's Office of Civil Rights).

To threaten to discharge someone be-cause he spends his time filing complaints is itself a ground for formal complaint. The point has been reached where time spent filing and otherwise working on com-plaints is considered time spent on the job, the job for which one is being paid, and to be asked to forgo the former in favor of the latter justifies the filing of still another complaint.

It takes a lot of time to pursue a com-plaint. If the complainant is not satisfied with the judgment rendered within his own agency, he is entitled to a hearing before an examiner in the Equal Employment Op-portunity Commission, the agency that be-came notorious under the recently retired Eleanor Holmes Norton. After that, to skip over a few of the stages in this almost infi-nite process, he can always go to court.

Many do and, in one way or another, they all win because the accused supervi-sor can only lose. For even if the supervi-sor manages to escape dismissal or reprimand, in the climate now prevailing he cannot escape the suspicion of deserving dismissal or reprimand. Besides, he can be made the object of a personal damage suit, a prospect made much more likely by a recent Supreme Court decision. Having personally to meet the cost of defending such actions, to say nothing of the damages if the plaintiffs prevail, is enough to persuade most federal supervisors to tread carefully and keep their mouths shut.

They will want to avoid the fate of—let us call him—Mr. Jones, who, after reviewing the resumes of many applicants and interviewing some of them, offered a position to—let us call her—Ms. Smith, who, after being "cleared," as they say (for this was a sensitive agency), came back to Mr. Jones and informed him that she was expecting a child and could work only on a part-time basis, at which point Mr. Jones made the mistake of saying that he was sorry but it was a a full-time position.

What happened after this can be summed up as follows: (1) she sued him and the agency; (2) the agency, ever eager to avoid the charge of being soft on sex discrimination (and, besides, it was the taxpayers' money), settled with *her* and joined in the suit against *him*; (3) he was formally reprimanded, which, being made a part of his official record, will preclude his ever again being promoted; and (4) he was left to pay some $1,800 in legal expenses out of his own pocket.

The mail also brought me copies of what might be called Eleanor Holmes Norton's legacy to the federal civil service; a test to end all tests by discrediting testing.

When she was still "chair" of the EEOC, Eleanor Norton said that "tests do not tell us very much about who is qualified to do the job," and while this was not true of the former test, the one scrapped by the Justice Department as part of that sweetheart deal, it is emphatically true of the test that replaced it.

The old one, the Professional and Administrative Career Examination (the PACE), was a real test, one that most applicants failed: white as well as black and Hispanic, male as well as female. It is difficult to imagine anyone failing the new one.

On one form, applicants are asked to give their names, addresses and Social Security numbers; on another "supplemental form," to be completed at home and returned "in the enclosed envelope within 15 days," they are asked merely to describe what they "consider to be (their) major accomplishments." (Those without accomplishment or the ability to compose a narrative describing them are free to rely on their friends for assistance, or perhaps some friendly commercial resume-writing service.) One would like to think there is someone in the new administration with the courage to blow the whistle on this business.

Leave it to Hillsdale

Unfortunately (and here I am no longer relying on my mail), federal executives are not the only ones to hold their public tongues on affirmative action. So do university presidents—the major universities appoint "vice presidents for compliance" and leave it to little Hillsdale College to take the government to court—and, most surprisingly, so do the executives of major private corporations.

If they think what is going on within the federal workforce won't eventually affect them, or, if it has already begun to affect them, that they have seen the worst of it, or, even, that the Reagan administration will be able to put an end to it, they should wake up.

The administration is not going to be able to defeat the powerful affirmative action lobby outside as well as inside the government—I'm thinking primarily of the EEOC, the Civil Rights Division in Justice, and the Labor Department's Office of Federal Contract Compliance Programs—unless it acquires more vocal public support than it now has.

And that support will not be forthcoming so long as the persons who ought to be leaders of that public can be cowed into silence or gulled into thinking that the equal employment opportunity law is being used only, or nowadays even primarily, to eliminate discrimination.

That was Congress's intention when it enacted Title VII; indeed, Title VII *forbids* what has come to be called affirmative action or reverse discrimination, to say nothing of quotas, but the government now uses it to promote affirmative action as well as quotas.

It would be interesting to know how many private corporation executives—the CEOs, not personnel managers — even know of the existence of the Uniform Guidelines on Employee Selection Procedures. They ought to know about them; these guidelines were adopted in 1978 and are avowedly designed to require affirmative action hiring on the part of private and public employers alike.

If the Justice Department has its way—which is to say, if that consent decree is given final approval by the federal judge with jurisdiction in the case—the guidelines will be used to impose a quota hiring system, on the federal government immediately and on private employers eventually. Fortunately, it is formally within the power of the new administration to modify or even abolish those guidelines, but to do this it will need more support than it seems to be getting.

____

Review & Outlook

Pandora's Worth

When the nine-day strike by municipal workers in San Jose, Calif., was settled Tuesday, the lid was removed from a Pandora's box, and a new approach for setting pay for women has made its escape. Under the innocuous name of "comparable worth," it would abolish the labor market and have everyone's pay set by bureaucrats.

The comparable worth doctrine was the rallying cry in the San Jose strike. The notion is that women working in female-dominated jobs such as secretaries, nurses and elementary school teachers suffer sex discrimination because these jobs do not draw as much pay as those traditionally held by men. Thus, feminists argue, a secretary who isn't paid as much as an air-conditioner repairer perhaps should be and the employer brought to court and forced to do so. Preposterous? Maybe, but this issue has the support of the AFL-CIO, whose members persuaded San Jose to spend $1.5 million to raise pay for jobs such as those held by librarians and secretaries. San Jose, whose Mayor Janet Hayes calls it the "feminist capital of the world,'' was easy game, having early on agreed to the principle of the thing.

Buoyed by this success, supporters of the comparable worth approach have raised their sights to replacing the equal pay for equal work doctrine made law by the 1963 Equal Pay Act by equal pay for comparable work. They are counting on convincing the courts that pay determined by the market is unacceptable. Instead, employers should adopt what they call a point-factor test, which includes variables as easy to define as the ''skill, responsibility and effort'' required in a job, so that jobs in different areas can be compared and wages assigned. The National Academy of Sciences will release a report later this summer on how feasible such a policy would be, but it seems that even after a two-year study, the potential costs to employers cannot even be estimated.

The notion that there ought to be equal pay for work of comparable value is a can chock-full of worms. Value, we have always thought, is what the market says it is, not some notion that one job is as ''important'' as another. If supply and demand leaves telephone operators who are mostly women paid less than truck drivers, then their jobs simply aren't of comparable worth. What we would

expect to see, and do see, are more women driving trucks.

Further, who would decide that the market is somehow being unfair or sexist with regard to various jobs? Clearly, the feminists will say, the government. We shudder at the thought. And how much would it cost a year to force a rise in women's wages in these areas? Estimates are in the billions of dollars. The real point, though, is that this isn't Communist China; men and women are meant to be paid in relation to what we produce, not what a government agency or a court thinks is ''fair.''

The Supreme Court may have given some support to proponents of this scheme. The Justices last month ruled that jail matrons in Oregon who performed work similar to but not identical with the work of male jailers could still sue for equal pay. That was a case, though, of *intentional* discrimination against women, which is clearly outlawed by the 1964 Civil Rights Act. Four Justices dissented, mortified by the comparable worth gloss the majority opinion seemingly put on the law. Noting that the Kennedy administration had unsuccessfully urged a doctrine of comparable worth rather than the equal pay for equal work doctrine, Justice Rehnquist concluded in a dissent that

''Congress realized that the adoption of the comparable worth doctrine would ignore the economic relations of supply and demand and would involve both governmental agencies and courts in the impossible task of ascertaining the worth of comparable work, an area in which they have little expertise.''

The only case that has so far been argued solely on the comparable worth question puts a bit of sanity back into sex discrimination law. The high court refused last year to hear an appeal by nurses employed by Denver who had sought more pay based on a comparison of the worth of their jobs with totally different city jobs, such as tree-trimming. The trial judge rejected their case and noted that the comparable worth claim was ''pregnant with the possibility of disrupting the entire economic system.''

If the taxpayers of San Jose choose to hoist themselves with this petard, then so be it. But the Supreme Court will some day have to tackle directly this issue of whether equal pay for essentially different jobs can be construed as the intent of Congress. We can only hope that the Court, as Congress intended, will fear to tread in so deep a conceptual mire.

---

102 *July 20, 1980*

Why the Equal Rights Amendment Is Stalled

By Diane Ravitch

With less than a year to go before the deadline for consideration by the states, the Equal Rights Amendment is stalled. Among the 15 states that have not ratified it, none appears to be close to approving it. Of the 35 that ratified it, five (Idaho, Nebraska, Tennessee, Kentucky and South Dakota) have tried to rescind or nullify their earlier action. Not since January 1977 has a state endorsed it.

If the amendment fails, as appears possible, its supporters are likely to claim that it lost because of sex discrimination or because of the inflammatory tactics of ERA's opponents. While there is merit in both explanations, there are others that must be

seriously considered if anything is to be learned from the ERA experience.

The amendment had some unusual advantages. It directly appealed to half the population; it received favorable treatment in the mass media; it had the support of a dedicated and tireless cadre of workers; and, when it failed to win the necessary number of states within the seven years provided in the Constitution, the deadline for ratification was extended for three years by Congress. Yet the campaign bogged down after Indiana ratified ERA in January 1977; even the support of President Carter and his wife failed to produce a single new state during his four years in office.

Future historians might consider some of the following as causes to the plight of ERA:

Leadership Style. Although the overwhelming majority of ERA supporters are women and men from every walk of life, during a crucial period the leaders of the campaign projected an image of association with Lesbian and radical causes. So long as this was true, many potential supporters backed away. Only last December, Gloria Steinem told a meeting of the Socialist International that women could achieve equality only under socialism, an opinion scarcely calculated to gain new adherents in the states where ERA remains in limbo.

Tactics. In their eagerness, supporters of ERA resorted to undemocratic tactics to coerce individuals and groups to go along. ERA partisans have made the secondary boycott a principal weapon in their campaign, urging organizations to refuse to meet in states where ERA has not been ratified. For years, civil libertarians have rejected the secondary boycott as an unfair tactic, when used for example by the Arab states to isolate Israel from commercial contacts. Similarly, the insistence that the Democratic Party platform specifically disavow any candidate who did not support ERA was a coercive tactic to force dissenters into line by submitting to a single-issue, ideological test. It did not help either ERA or the Democratic candidates.

Attacks on Traditional Roles. Polls show that substantial numbers of women oppose ERA. Much of this opposition is founded on the belief that its supporters deride the traditional activities of women as mothers, wives and volunteers. ERA partisans, who customarily tie their own cause to issues like abortion and day care, appear to believe that no woman would actually WANT to be with her children, whatever their age, or to forgo a "career" or to work in an unpaid job. To the extent that these attitudes were conveyed as hostility to the traditional family, potential supporters were alienated.

Confusion About Goals. It never became clear whether the supporters of ERA wanted to achieve absolutely equal, gender-blind treatment for women or to win special preferences for them as a historically oppressed group. Sometimes, as in discussion about the draft, gender-blind treatment seemed to be the goal, but when affirmative action was at issue, the same people were quick to seek special treatment for women. Similarly, the surge of "consciousness-raising," which led to women's caucuses, to special facilities for women, and to something akin to separatism within institutions and organizations, contradicted the appeals to gender neutrality. This occasionally reached absurd proportions, as in professional women's meetings where men were barred or in the decision of a New England women's college to create a "women's center" in the middle of its all-female campus.

In the end, if the amendment fails, it will be because, in the eyes of both its supporters and opponents, it came to symbolize an effort to impose a new lifestyle on men and women. Those who did not want a new lifestyle felt threatened in a way that aroused unexpected passion. No amendment other than the one that outlawed alcoholic beverages tried comparably to change social mores; that it not only failed but was repealed suggests the futility of using the constitutional amendments to rearrange social patterns. The very nature of amending the Constitution requires that any change must be practically noncontroversial in order to be adopted, since approval is required by overwhelming majorities in individual states and in the nation as a whole. If we are to keep the Constitution free of amendments intended to impose solutions on difficult social issues, like abortion and busing, then women would do well to rest their case for equal rights on the Fourteenth Amendment, like other citizens, rather than on the ERA.

Whatever happens to ERA, the social and legal position of women has changed in significant ways. As David Riesman has often pointed out, there have been multiple women's movements, not just one. These will survive regardless of the fate of ERA.

Diane Ravitch is associate professor of history and education at Teacher's College, Columbia University.

Foreign Policy and National Defense

January 18, 1980

Is This Journey Necessary?

By ARTHUR SCHLESINGER JR.

"The superpowers often behave like two heavily armed blind men feeling their way around a room, each believing himself in mortal peril from the other whom he assumes to have perfect vision. . . . Each tends to ascribe to the other side a consistency, foresight and coherence that its own experience belies. Of course, over time even two blind men can do enormous damage to each other, not to speak of the room."

This fine passage—from Henry Kissinger's fascinating memoirs—is worth recalling these days when we stand on the verge of being swept away on one of those Soviet-master-plan waves of national panic. Jimmy Carter, in an astonishing confession of presidential naivete, tells us that the scales have fallen from his eyes and he doesn't think the Russians are good guys any more. Where in the world has he been for the last half century? Having had too enraptured a view of the U.S.S.R. in the past, he now appears ready to swing to the opposite extreme. A Carter Doctrine to contain the Soviet Union in Southwest Asia is reportedly in the offing: our master plan to counter their master plan.

'Hawks' and 'Doves'

So we are back to playing "hawks" and "doves" again. This has never seemed to me a very useful game. Like most people, I am a hawk when I think the security of the United States is threatened, and I am less hawkish when I think that we are getting unduly excited over developments that do not threaten our security and are beyond our power to control anyway. I was therefore a hawk in 1941 and an anti-hawk in 1966. If the Soviet Union were to charge into Yugoslavia after the death of Tito, I would regard this as a *casus belli.* When the Soviet Union charges into Afghanistan, it is an outrageous act calling for condemnation by the international community. But does it justify the current national panic? Does it demand American military intervention in Southwest Asia?

The panic-mongers cry—and Jimmy Carter, judging by his January 4 speech, seems to agree—that Afghanistan is the first step in the unfolding of a giant Soviet scheme to encircle Iran, dominate Pakistan, establish bases on the Arabian Sea and begin the conquest of the oil fields. Maybe there is such a master plan. Maybe, while our side gropes around blindly, those superhuman Russians have perfect vision. Still, before drastic conclusions rush on to drastic counteractions, leading to more drastic counteractions from the other side, let us hold our horses. Maybe there are other conceivable interpretations of the Soviet motive in invading Afghanistan.

One can imagine a meeting in the Kremlin some weeks back. A comrade says gloomily, "Look, fellows, everything is going against us these days. The Chinese are getting into bed with the Americans. I don't know whom you can count on in Eastern Europe any more. The Americans are bringing their new nukes into Western Europe. SALT II is down the drain. We're getting nowhere in Africa, and Lord Carrington has dished us in Rhodesia, and Somalia is offering bases to the Americans. We can't feed our own people or get them consumer goods. We're in trouble all over. And now that mess in Afghanistan! We can't trust that fellow we have in Kabul, Amin. He won't take orders. He may not even beat the guerrillas.

"Fellows, we've got to have a success somewhere. And we certainly can't accept the humiliation of a defeat in a country right on our own frontier. Afghanistan is slipping away. If we don't do something, we will lose all credibility everywhere. When the Americans were in trouble in Vietnam, they threw out Diem and put in a new government. Let's do that. Then they made their big mistake and didn't follow up with their own combat units for another fifteen months. Let's learn from that. Incrementalism is hell. Let's put in a big force at once and get it over with."

Our hard-liners like to think that the Soviet Union is a dynamic and purposeful state following a policy laid down with consistency, foresight and coherence. But it may as well be that the Soviet Union is a weary, drab country, led by sick old men, beset by insuperable problems at home and abroad and living from crisis to crisis. It may well have invaded Afghanistan out of weakness, not out of strength, for reasons that are essentially defensive rather than aggressive, local rather than global, despairing rather than joyously premediated.

Of course the Soviet Union enters any situation with minimum and maximum objectives. It expands by targets of opportunity. If the noncommunist world does not handle the problem intelligently, the Russians may conceivably try to move on toward the Persian Gulf and the oil fields. But this will not be so simple as it sounds; even Afghanistan is not going to be all that simple. A Soviet invasion of the Persian Gulf area would estrange the Moslem world, including some of the 40 million Moslems in the Soviet Union. Moreover, little is easier to sabotage than oil fields and pipe lines—and little is harder to extinguish than Arab nationalism and Moslem fanaticism.

The problem now is to deter the Soviet Union from exploiting targets of opportunity. International condemnation, especially from Third World countries, is essential. As for President Carter's roster of symbolic gestures, I am in favor of cancelling our participation in the Olympic Games—and in the Winter Olympics too, Senator Moynihan. The cancellation of the grain sales is one of those spurious "decisive" actions

Board of Contributors

Before drastic conclusions rush on to drastic counteractions, leading to more drastic counteractions from the other side, let us hold our horses.

that imposes a disproportionate sacrifice on a single group, the farmers, and gives the rest of us the pleasurable feeling that we can be tough without personal discomfort to ourselves. It will have no great impact on the Russians. They are used to eating poorly.

If we want real sacrifices that would have real impact, let us sharply reduce our dependence on Middle East oil by cutting down on our oil consumption—and the way to do that quickly, visibly and equitably is through a system of gasoline rationing.

But instead of seizing the opportunity to appeal to an aroused nation to conserve energy, the administration talks of a Carter Doctrine for Southwest Asia. A Carter Doctrine doubtless has a good ring for domestic politics in a presidential year. But it will raise a host of expectations and imply a multitude of commitments on the international scene; or else it will be worse than useless. What kind of *action* does the President intend under his Doctrine?

The idea of a rapid deployment force makes me nervous. Such a force would have been of no use in Iran or in Afghanistan. Suppose we create such a force now, send it to the Persian Gulf and it gets into trouble. Then what? By this time our national prestige will have been engaged. We will be told that we can't accept the humiliation of a defeat. We will send in conventional units to save the rapid deployment force. Then, with our troops committed to the Persian Gulf, Tito might die, and the Red Army might think it safe in such circumstances to go into Yugoslavia—as it went into Hungary in 1956 when England and France were preoccupied with Suez.

Sending arms into the area in any serious quantity is problematic too. Such arms are all too likely to be used against us at the next spin of the dial. Consider what has happened to all the arms we shipped into Iran. I would, though, keep American naval and air power in the area to discourage the Russians from trying something fancy.

Tough Talk and Flag Waving

The presidential campaign confuses our reactions. Tough talk and flag waving bring cheers from the crowd and improvement in the polls. But let's keep Afghanistan in proportion. We have been through crises with the Soviet Union before, and we will go through them again. The Cuban missile crisis was an infinitely graver threat to American security than Afghanistan. Yet 10 months later the test ban treaty was negotiated in Moscow.

And let us also resist the demagoguery that invokes patriotism in order to suppress debate. The Iran blackout of the presidential campaign was just starting to wear thin when Afghanistan came along to give President Carter a free ride for another few weeks. The administration will try to convert every primary into a referendum on backing the President in a time of national emergency.

The blackout of debate endangers us all. Unless the American people insist on discussing the issues that will truly decide their future, they will in effect hand over the choice of our next President to the Aytollah Khomeini and brezhnev. And unless voices of realism and reason speak out, the two blind men are going to do enormous damage to each other—and to the room.

Mr. Schlesinger is Albert Schweitzer Professor of the Humanities at the City University of New York, winner of Pulitzer Prizes in history and biography and a member of the Journal's Board of Contributors.

Our Foreign Policy Illusions

By Irving Kristol

Just because you have ceased to see reality through the distorting lens of a particular ideology, it doesn't mean that you are now able to see it clearly. You may simply be substituting a weak and wavering vision for a clear if false one.

I am, in this connection, thinking of President Carter's new approach to foreign policy. Though it is obviously superior to the old, in that it is not based on patently false ideological assumptions, it may nevertheless be a dangerously inadequate approach. There is an air of improvisation about it, a desperate reaching for the *ad hoc* response to the exigencies of the immediate situation.

The myths of "detente," of a "North-South dialogue," of an American-led crusade for universal "human rights"—all these are in tatters. But bits and pieces of this ideology still float freely and visibly, if semi-submerged, in the thinking of the White House, the State Department and the National Security Council. They have now been oddly coupled, however, with other bits and pieces of ideological wreckage that the administration has grabbed onto—remnants of the Acheson-Dulles approach of "containing" Communist aggression by means of a complex patchwork of alliances with highly unstable nations.

Yet this older approach gradually crumbled before *its* moments of truth—in Vietnam above all. (Of what use was SEATO then?) It is hard to see how it can be truly revived. We seem to be in the process of wedding yesterday's dead illusions to yesteryear's. Only strange and barren fruit can issue from such a union.

Republican Instinct

I do not say this in any partisan or captious spirit. If we had had a Republican administration in office this past year, I do think we might have managed our affairs somewhat better—but only "might have," and only somewhat and only temporarily. Republicans don't really *think* much about foreign policy. They tend to be guided more by nationalist instinct, and such instinct is generally less treacherous than false preconceptions.

Still, instinct is not enough, as the record reveals. As for John Foster Dulles' record, the less said the better. He, more than anyone else, may be held responsible for the Middle East chaos of the past two decades.

The trouble with instinct, aside from the fact that it might propel you to an inappropriate or downright wrong response,

is that it has no staying power. Even the right decision, if based solely on instinct, will gradually fade into a diminishing series of random, ineffectual decisions. Doing the right thing, whether it be for the wrong reason or for no reason at all, is surely to be preferred over doing the wrong thing for the wrong reasons. But in the end a foreign policy, if it is to be successful, has to be coherent—it has to consist, more often than not, of doing the right thing for the right reason. And, with the possible exception of the administrations of Theodore Roosevelt, the United States hasn't had such a foreign policy since the days of the Founding Fathers.

One does not wish to exaggerate the importance of ideas in the realm of foreign policy. To a very large degree, makers of

---

Board of Contributors

We have responded to the Soviet aggression in Afghanistan by economic and cultural reactions that are signs of weakness, not strength. Our diplomacy is reverting to the defensive 'pactomania' of the 1950s.

---

foreign policy are constantly being made captive to unexpected events, and the notion that Presidents or Secretaries of State should somehow be able to anticipate all crises, and are to be blamed for failing to do so, is preposterous. Professors or Congressmen or journalists who talk this way ought to be sentenced to investing all of their capital in commodity futures. They would quickly learn how important a role luck plays in the world's affairs, and how even the most sophisticated analyses collapse before the onrush of events over which *no one* has any control. In foreign affairs, most of the time, you are flying blind, in the sense that no one can possibly figure out all the consequences of everyone else's actions—or even of one's own.

Nevertheless, some pilots are better than others when it comes to flying blind. It is a matter of experience, character and a whole set of general principles and ideas—which, in turn, form attitudes and instincts—about the relation of one thing to another. It goes without saying that a skill-

ful pilot must have no sentimental illusions about the nature of the elements he is coping with, or a naive faith in the instruments he employs to cope with them. Above all, he must remember what country he is in, and what the likely terrain is.

The conduct of American foreign policy has long been plagued by all of the attitudes, underlying ideas and preconceptions which one would *not* want to find in the pilot of such a plane. We are naive; we are sentimental; we are legalistic; we are impulsive; our memories are short; and, above all, we have the greatest difficulty keeping in mind what world we are in.

It is a world ordered by military force and by the willingness to use that force when circumstances require. Whoever does not have such force, or is overly reluctant to use it, ends up living in a world that has been ordered by someone else. The advent of nuclear armaments has not really changed the nature of this world. Those armaments have the purpose of deterring one's enemies from using such weapons in the first place. This deterrence having been achieved, we are back to conventional power politics, with conventional arms.

But Americans are taught to believe that power politics is un-American, because immoral, and that the use of force in international affairs ought to be, and can be, replaced by the rule of law—or even by the rule of love, if some official statements are to be believed. It is this naive utopianism that has plagued American foreign policy for three-quarters of a century now. We believe that, in the end, the nations of the world must admire us for what we are, and for the nice things we are always ready to do for them. But the world is full of nations that detest us precisely for what we are—free, democratic, capitalist—and are much more interested in what they might do to us than in what we can do for them. And even those who have no hostile feelings toward us will not be reliable allies unless they also respect us—perhaps even fear us a little. The "hearts and minds" of the world go out to winners, not to nice guys who finish second.

One frequently gets the impression that American statesmen regard other nations the way sentimental criminologists regard a juvenile delinquent — someone to be "rehabilitated" by patient, compassionate therapy. That was the idea behind "detente": As the Soviets "matured" by virtue of closer association with us, they would be more like us, less like themselves. That was the idea, too, behind our foreign-aid programs, and our support of the United Nations. Well, it hasn't worked with our juvenile delinquents, and it won't work in the case of nations who do not for a moment think of themselves as in any sense "delinquent.

The foreign policy of the United States ought to have as its central purpose a world order that has been shaped, to the largest degree possible, in accord with our national interests as a great power that is free, democratic and capitalist. To be sure, this might mean living in an uneasy truce, and for an indefinite period of time, with the Soviet Union and other nations that are in principle hostile to freedom, democracy or capitalism. But we should use our power, as they use their power, to see that the terms of this truce, which are always in flux, are as consistently to our net advantage as circumstances permit.

I do not see that the Carter administration—or even its critics, for that matter—have moved toward any such clear conception of our national interest, or of the role of power politics in expressing that interest. Instead, we have responded to the Soviet aggression in Afghanistan by economic and cultural reactions that are signs of weakness, not strength. Simultaneously, our diplomacy is reverting, as if by automatic reflex, to the defensive "pacto-

mania" of the 1950s—a jumble of defensive alliances with highly unreliable allies.

Thus, we are sending arms to Pakistan—a shaky regime incapable of using those arms effectively. It is also a regime that praises the Ayatollah Khomeini and is engaged in creating an "Islamic nuclear bomb" financed by the lunatic ruler of Libya, Colonel Khadafy, who will presumably take delivery. At the same time, we are going around the Indian Ocean with a begging bowl, humbly asking for permission to establish naval and air bases in the area. How pathetic! Why aren't we *demanding* bases in Pakistan (or South Yemen or Saudi Arabia) as a condition of support? Indeed, why aren't we demanding bases on pain of our hostility?

We don't need any more "paper allies," for whose inept regimes we then take responsibility. Just think how much better off we would be in Iran if, as a condition for selling the Shah all those arms, we had insisted on bases in the Straits of Hormuz, instead of trying to build *him* up as the defender of *our* interests in that region.

Cuban Contempt

Meanwhile, in our very own backyard, Cuba blithely supports insurrectionary movements throughout Latin America, sends troops to Africa and the Middle East and generally behaves as if it holds our interests and our power in utter contempt.

Are we helpless before such belligerency by Castro's Cuba? And if we are, how on earth can we be strong in Pakistan?

It will be said that any such American behavior would mar our image (and self-image) as a peace-loving nation. But the way things are heading, we shall awaken one of these days and discover that we can no longer afford to be such a peace-loving nation. As the late G. F. Hudson wrote:

"There is perhaps no factor which drives a state into war so inexorably as a steady loss of relative power. Sooner or later a desperate now-or-never mood overcomes the calculations of prudence . . . ."

It would be ironic—but an irony that history is only too familiar with—if our very reluctance to use our power while we have it resulted in a holocaust that might have been avoided had we been less "peace-loving." As a matter of fact, wasn't it something like this that happened to Britain and France in the 1930s?

Mr. Kristol is Professor of Social Thought at the NYU Graduate School of Business, a Senior Fellow of the American Enterprise Institute and a member of the Journal's Board of Contributors.

Spectacle of Impotence

The collapse of the UN Commission in Iran leaves the U.S. with no policy whatever for freeing the hostages in the American embassy, starkly revealing that in its current posture the Carter administration has absolutely no leverage over the situation. Our countrymen have been held captive now for four months, and we are reduced to hoping for the best from the whim of an aged zealot.

Eventually, perhaps, it will suit the Ayatollah's pleasure to send the hostages home. Some quirk of mood or twist of Iranian domestic politics may yet provide a way out. But while we wait for such a stroke of luck, 50 Americans remain held—perhaps still bound day and night. From what we last heard, some are in severe mental distress. Seven of them, including those most specifically accused of

spying by their captors, have not been seen since the seizure. Three American diplomats are held hostage not by militants but by the Iranian foreign ministry itself.

Meanwhile a diplomatic game is played, the purpose of which is to teach the United States and its President to jump through hoops. The no use of force hoop. The Ramsey Clark hoop. The clergymen's visit hoop. The kick out the shah hoop. The forget economic sanctions after all hoop. But while the circus dog at least gets a tasty morsel after each jump, Mr. Carter's reward is some fresh task and fresh humiliation.

The UN Commission is only the latest example. Mr. Carter originally opposed the whole idea, but then agreed to it just in time to provoke a burst of optimism about the hostages

before the New Hampshire primary. By this week the initiative ended precisely in the dead end we predicted in these columns at the time: "The next step probably will be a demand to open the commission first and release the hostages on its completion."

So the U.S. has agreed to the principle that an international tribunal, including representatives of such paragons of human rights as Syria and Algeria, is competent to pass judgment on the rule of the shah, our ally for 37 years. As quid pro quo, we are told to wait the decision of an Iranian legislature to be elected over the next two months. Even now, the UN panel is not disbanded but only suspended; to judge by the record in a few weeks we will be edging toward accepting the conditions we now reject.

Down in his Panamanian exile, the shah now needs another operation for a grotesquely enlarged spleen. It would be a dangerous procedure even in a great medical school, but apparently will have to be carried out in a Panamanian hospital. The U.S. government does not seem to care. The shah's death might further unsettle the kings among our present allies, but would no doubt lead to another two weeks of hope for release of the hostages.

By now, though, we ought to be doubting whether the hostages would in fact be released even if we kidnaped the shah from his hospital and delivered him in shackles to Tehran. The point of the hoop-jumping game is not retrieving the shah, but humiliating the United States. The exercise shows that the U.S. is not a reliable protector of its own citizens, let alone its allies. It shows that even if the United States is treated with repeated contempt, we will do nothing about it.

In the early days of the crisis, this image might have been avoided, and the hostage problem resolved, through stronger rhetorical and diplomatic reaction. But by now the situation has been so badly bungled that the only answer is military force, or at least the credible threat of it. At the very least, President Carter should seize the collapse of the UN mission as the occasion to heat up the crisis so such a threat is again possible.

At the same time, we should start to take note of a few facts. The American embassy in Tehran is a compound of 27 acres. Elite American paratroopers are trained to open their chutes at 200 feet. In 1967, two Jolly Green Giant helicopters flew the Atlantic to visit the Paris air show, with nine air-to-air refuelings. During the Vietnam war, seven of the same helicopters flew some 500 miles, with in-flight refueling at night, to land undetected in the Son Tay prisoner of war camp (which unfortunately had recently been vacated). A raid to rescue the hostages would obviously carry risks, but it cannot be ruled out as militarily infeasible.

Military action, whether in a raid, a blockade or punitive bombing, would of course carry a risk to the lives of the hostages. But their lives have been at risk for four months now, and despite our entreaties and compromises there is no end in sight. The immobility of the U.S. in the face of this provocation has already helped embolden the Soviets in Afghanistan and a new batch of embassy terrorists in Colombia. This is but a taste of what is to come if this spectacle of American impotence is allowed to continue indefinitely.

Southern Strategy

U.S. Tries to Influence Central America Unrest But Finds Task Tricky

---

Policy Is an Anti-Left Blend Of Cash, Human Rights, Help for a Bloody Junta

---

'The Domino Theory Lives'

By Karen Elliott House
and Beth Nissen
Staff Reporters of The Wall Street Journal

In the not-so-distant past, nations like Nicaragua, El Salvador and Guatemala didn't figure much in Washington's diplomacy. U.S. policy toward Latin America consisted largely of election-year homilies on hemispheric friendship.

But events are forcing the U.S. government to take a more active role. Revolutionary ferment threatens Central America and the Caribbean, raising the possibility for Cuban intervention, not in faraway Africa this time but in America's back yard. Nicaragua has installed the first revolutionary government in the hemisphere since Fidel Castro's, and neighboring El Salvador is slipping into civil war. Guatemala's military regime is viciously repressing leftist dissent, but revolution there, too, is probably just a matter of time.

For the moment, these developments primarily are one more political embarrassment for Jimmy Carter. On the defensive for failing to free the hostages in Iran and to influence events in Iran and Afghanistan, the President also appears unable to mold change nearer to home. The turn of events in Central America is particularly discomfiting for Mr. Carter because he argued two years ago that relinquishing U.S. control over the Panama Canal would open a new era of cooperation between this country and its southern neighbors.

Panama Canal, Mexican Gas

Potentially, much is at stake in the region. In themselves, none of the countries of Central America are of great importance to the U.S. But growing Soviet or Cuban influence in the region could threaten vital American interests.

Creation of another Soviet satellite such as Cuba is a big concern. But short of that, growing unrest and radicalism could undermine the governments of Mexico and Panama. Continuing access to the Panama Canal remains of economic and military significance to the U.S. And Mexico's oil and gas and its population and proximity make it the most important country in the region to the U.S.

"We recognize the extreme strategic importance of the region," President Carter said recently at a White House ceremony unveiling the Caribbean-Central American Action Group, a new private organization created to improve hemispheric relations.

To many in Central America, that recognition is long overdue. "We 'banana republics' haven't had the attention of the busy U.S. for a long time," says a high-ranking Guatemalan official scornfully. "You have been preoccupied—in Vietnam, in the Middle East, in Iran and Afghanistan. Now you wake up to find that the gardens of Eden next door are being tempted by your darkest foes."

Trying to Mold Change

Some U.S. officials believe that temptation will be reduced by the Central Americans' awareness that several thousand Cubans are swarming into this country to escape Castro's communism. "Psychologically," says a senior official, "it has to have an effect on those to whom Castro is trying to export revolution."

Nonetheless, recent political upheavals in Central America have forced a change in U.S. policy there. Instead of trying to maintain the status quo, the U.S. is trying to guide change that seems inevitable. "The U.S. has learned that repressive dictatorships do not forward U.S. interests," says Ambler Moss, U.S. ambassador to Panama.

But so far, America's more pragmatic policy hasn't proved all that effective either. The State Department's first try at influencing the transition from dictatorship to populist rule in Nicaragua did nothing to strengthen America's hand in the region. "The U.S. couldn't decide whether Anastasio Somoza or the Sandinists were more harmful to its interests, so we simply went limp with despair," says an embarrassed American diplomat. "We recognized Somoza's weaknesses too late and the Sandinists' strengths even later. As a result, I fear it may be too late for democracy in Nicaragua."

The same fear is growing in neighboring El Salvador, where political violence has killed more than 1,000 people so far this year. With the lesson of Nicaragua still fresh, the U.S. appears determined to act more promptly — and more forcefully — to achieve what Assistant Secretary of State William Bowdler calls a "peaceful solution to the country's political and economic crisis."

To the dismay of conservatives in Congress and throughout Central America, the U.S. is supporting the military-civilian junta that seized power from right-wing President Carlos Humberto Romero last October. Even when the junta expropriated 60% of the tiny country's richest private farm land and nationalized the Salvadoran banking system in March, the U.S. support didn't waver. In fact, the Carter administration helped thwart a planned rightist overthrow of the junta—which is despised by both the extreme left and right—by threatening to cut off a proposed $49.8 million in economic aid plus $5.7 million in military credits if a rightist regime took over.

Administration officials defend U.S. support for an undemocratic junta engaged in bloody crackdowns on its foes. And they insist American diplomats in Salvador are urging the junta to stop the killing and broaden its base. "There are problems with the junta," says an administration official in Washington. "But we're supporting it because we're committed to change, because we want to end repression by a handful of wealthy families in Salvador, and because it is the only hope for avoiding a leftist government."

"Behavior Modification"

In a region being swept by change, the U.S. suddenly finds former levers of power no longer available. Unable now to rely on moderate regimes in the region and unwilling to intervene militarily as it did in the Dominican Republic in 1965, Washington is increasingly relying on American aid for leverage. "Our use of aid is pure behavior modification," says one U.S. career diplomat in Central America. "U.S. dollars are rewarded like lumps of sugar to good little countries and withheld for shock value from stubborn, naughty countries, especially those accused of human-rights violations."

The largest U.S. aid contribution being newly offered is a proposed $75 million for Nicaragua, but the money is tied up in the new U.S. budget squeeze. American officials hope the money, if forthcoming, will encourage cooperation from the increasingly radical junta. Aid to Salvador has a similar purpose.

In neighboring Honduras, a pro-American military government has just received $3.9 million in U.S. military aid, including helicopters and advisers, to brace itself against surrounding political turbulence and potential internal problems. It is widely reported that Honduras is the Cubans' favorite conduit for smuggling arms to Salvador's leftist guerrillas, although the Honduran government says it has no proof of this.

The amounts of American aid, however, are minuscule compared with the billions in economic and military assistance the U.S. provides Middle Eastern nations, particularly Egypt and Israel. Still, Congress is reluctant to assist Central American governments; finite U.S. resources shouldn't be gambled in such unstable areas, many lawmakers argue.

"Giving money to these countries is a terrible risk," says a U.S. Senator who says he reluctantly voted for aid to Nicaragua. "It's like giving a dollar to a wino and trusting he'll really spend it on coffee. Even if he does, he's still a wino."

Regardless, the Carter administration has been successful in drawing money from Congress by dwelling on both the fear of Communist expansion and the desire to protect human rights.

The administration has managed to summon congressional support with details of increasing Cuban involvement and influence in Central America, first in Nicaragua and now in Salvador and Guatemala. Despite fears that the proposed aid for Nicaragua would be used for the "Sovietization" of that country, Congress went along when the administration stressed that Cuban influence there could only grow if U.S. assistance wasn't forthcoming. Officials also argued that Nicaragua's radicalization would fan revolution in Salvador and eventually Guatemala, which shares a border with Mexico.

"The domino theory lives," says Lawrence Pezzullo, U.S. ambassador to Nicaragua, "and Carter is using it to advantage. No President wants to lose something to communism during his watch."

Isolated Cornerstone

Less effective than that approach is Mr. Carter's human-rights campaign, which one Nicaraguan leader derides as "the lonely cornerstone of U.S. foreign policy that has never been further constructed."

Reproachable records on human rights are grounds for the strongest U.S. action—denial of aid or cuts in aid. The U.S. has shut off all military and most economic aid to Guatemala to protest increasing repression there and has made recently approved aid to Nicaragua conditional on respect of human rights by the Sandinist government. "It's a simple policy," says Mr. Pezzullo. "We reward the ones who don't abuse their people."

Critics of the "simple policy" say it undermines traditional U.S. friends like Guatemala without any appreciable easing of repression. Even U.S. diplomats acknowledge that the effects are less than hoped for. "I don't think our policy has actually affected the body count," concedes Frank Ortiz, U.S. ambassador to Guatemala. "We haven't always been skillful at enforcing human rights. But I can't think of anything we've done lately that's been more right."

However moral the policy is, working diplomats say it is difficult to apply fairly. "People want to know why we're so het up over a relatively few deaths in Guatemala when we didn't speak up in Nicaragua until thousands were in their graves," says one U.S. diplomat. "Frankly, I don't know how to answer them."

Undeniably, Washington's human-rights emphasis has helped give U.S. diplomacy in Central America a reputation for inconsistency. But there are other reasons for confusion. Businessmen throughout the region are baffled by U.S. protection of Nicaraguan businessmen as "vital guarantors of democracy" and the simultaneous condemnation of Salvadoran businessmen as secret backers of terrorism. Nor do most Central Americans understand why the U.S. insisted that 60% of its aid to Nicaragua be used to support private enterprise while at the same time the administration is backing expropriation of private property in El Salvador. President Carter recently praised the junta in El Salvador for undertaking "the most sweeping land reform efforts that I have ever witnessed."

Officials in Washington explain the divergent positions by saying each country must be dealt with differently. "In Nicaragua we're trying to preserve the private sector; in Salvador we're trying to broaden the government's base," one administration official says.

Another bluntly concedes, "We're still working our way toward a strategy for Latin America. We don't know how to reinforce moderation but we'd better learn quickly."

107

Flight to Freedom

American Hostages Are Released by Iran Minutes After End of Carter's Presidency

By Gerald F. Seib

Staff Reporter of The Wall Street Journal

WASHINGTON—The 52 American hostages flew to freedom from Iran yesterday, their long ordeal ending just minutes after Jimmy Carter's presidency.

Mr. Carter's successor, President Ronald Reagan, was the one who announced that the hostages were free after 444 days in captivity. In one of his first statements in office, Mr. Reagan told reporters that "just following" his inauguration he learned that two planes carrying the captives had left Iran.

Iran's official Pars news agency said that the Algerian planes left Tehran's airport at 12:25 p.m. EST, about half an hour after Mr. Reagan took the oath of office. During the process of boarding the plane, the hostages were subjected to one final humiliation: A crowd at the airport shouted in English, "down with America" and "down with Reagan," Pars reported.

Mr. Carter spent his final minutes in the White House monitoring reports that the hostages were being prepared to leave Iran, in hopes that he could announce their freedom before turning over his office. According to aides who were with Mr. Carter, he speculated that Iran was delaying the hostages' departure until after the change of office to give him one more embarrassment.

Frenzied Negotiations

The hostages were freed only after the Carter administration endured one final night of frenzied negotiations to clear up a misunderstanding of an agreement that had been struck to end the crisis. After resolving the snag, a dispute over the meaning of an appendix to the agreement, the administration transferred Iran's frozen assets into an escrow account early yesterday morning.

After their takeoff from Tehran, the planes carrying the hostages flew for an hour and a half before leaving Iranian air space and crossing into Turkish space. Later they made a refueling stop in Athens.

The planes continued to Algiers, where the former hostages were transferred to U.S. planes for the next leg of their journey, to Wiesbaden, West Germany. "I'm so glad to be here," one freed woman said in Algiers. Witnesses said some of the Americans looked dazed, but none appeared ill.

The Americans will be reunited with their families in the U.S. after several days at the U.S. military hospital in Wiesbaden, adjusting to freedom and undergoing medical checks.

Mr. Carter accepted an invitation from the Reagan administration to greet the hostages in Wiesbaden. Delays in carrying out the complex agreement robbed Mr. Carter of a chance to greet the hostages while he was still President. The agreement was signed early Monday morning.

To free the hostages, the U.S. sent about $8 billion of frozen Iranian funds to the Bank of England, for transfer to Iran upon release of the hostages. The money consisted of $4.7 billion in Iranian deposits in overseas branches in U.S. banks; $800 million in interest on those deposits; $2.4 billion in gold and securities that Iran had deposited at the Federal Reserve Bank in New York, and $40 million in a trust fund established to pay for arms purchases.

About $3.7 billion of the money will be returned to the U.S. Federal Reserve Bank to pay off Iran's loans with major American banks. Another $1.4 billion of the money will be used to establish an escrow account to pay off other U.S. bank loans and resolve a dispute over the amount of interest the major banks owed Iran. Iran's interest payment was computed at about 17%, although some banks thought that was too high, U.S. officials said. The banks will try to settle the interest dispute through their own negotiations, but can turn to an international claims commission if that fails.

A further $2.2 billion in Iranian assets deposited in the U.S. won't be returned to Iran immediately because claims have been made against those funds in U.S. courts. Mr. Carter ordered the claims transferred to an international claims commission, and the assets will be returned to Iran if the government's authority to make such a transfer is upheld. Iran will establish a $1 billion escrow account to pay for claims settled by the commission.

The U.S. also agreed to lift trade sanctions against Iran and to identify and freeze U.S. assets of the late Shah Mohammed Reza Pahlavi. Iran will seek control of the shah's assets, although U.S. officials are skeptical that any of his major holdings remain in this country.

The freeze of assets and trade sanctions were the principal levers used by Mr. Carter in his efforts to win freedom for the hostages. U.S. allies joined in the trade sanctions, isolating Iran from much of the world community.

Initially, 66 Were Seized

But the pain inflicted by the U.S. steps didn't become severe enough to prod Iran into serious negotiations until last fall, when it began fighting with Iraq. The war has cut Iran's oil production and sapped government revenues. U.S. officials believe that costs of the fighting helped force Iran into settling the hostage crisis so that it could reacquire its assets and resume normal trade.

In addition, Iran seemed to want to avoid the delays and uncertainty involved in opening negotiations with a new administration in Washington—particularly the administration of Mr. Reagan, who once referred to the Iranians as "barbarians."

The hostages had been in captivity since Nov. 4, 1979, when radical students stormed the U.S. embassy in Tehran. The students were protesting admission of the shah to a New York hospital for treatment of cancer. The Iranian government supported the takeover.

Initially, 66 Americans were seized, including three who were held at Iran's foreign ministry. Shortly after the seizure, Iran's religious leader, Ayatollah Ruhollah Khomeini, threatened to try the hostages for espionage. He warned that they would have to "submit to the verdict of the Islamic court."

Twice during the ordeal, hostages were released. Early in the crisis, Ayatollah Khomeini and the students released 13 black and female hostages. Then, last July, they released Richard Queen, a consular officer who was ill.

Both times, U.S. officials hoped the release of some hostages signaled a break in the crisis, but they were wrong. Similarly, the shah's death in Egypt last August failed to break the hostage impasse.

Military Rescue Failed

Frustrated that patience hadn't paid off, President Carter last April ordered a military attempt to rescue the hostages. The attempt failed, and eight American soldiers died in a collision of aircraft used in the mission.

After that, the U.S. turned to quiet diplomacy to settle the issue. Last September, Ayatollah Khomeini finally set the basic conditions for release of the hostages, clearing the way for serious negotiations.

One side benefit of the negotiations may be an improvement in relations between the U.S. and Algeria, which acted as an intermediary between Tehran and Washington. U.S.-Algerian relations have been cool, but American officials are grateful for the patient negotiating of Algerian diplomats. "We're in Algeria's debt," said outgoing Secretary of State Edmund Muskie. "Their assistance will be long remembered."

U.S. officials said that Mr. Carter signed all the executive orders needed to carry out the agreement with Iran, but some tasks will have to be handled by the Reagan ad-

ministration. For example, the federal government has promised to help holders of small claims combine and press their cases before the international claims commission. And the new administration will have to deal with any challenge to the government's authority to transfer claims to the international commission.

In New York, H. David Willey, a vice president for foreign affairs at the New York Federal Reserve Bank, described the mechanics of transferring the Iranian assets held by U.S. banks.

Yesterday, at about 4 a.m. EST, Mr. Willey told a press conference, the Treasury ordered the Fed to contact banks holding Ira-

nian assets. Using special codes, the banks authorized the Fed by telephone and wire to transfer the assets to a special account that had been set up at the Bank of England last Friday.

By 6:43 a.m. EST, the Bank of England received a wire from the Fed which said: "For value today, transfer all funds in our dollar deposit account, as fiscal agent of the United States government, to the account on your books for" the Algerian central bank. The wire repeated the order for the gold and securities to be transferred.

---

108 *January 21, 1981*

The Troubled Atlantic Partnership

Every recent President of the United States, following his inauguration, has included strengthened alliances, especially with the North Atlantic Pact, in his list of priorities. Ronald Reagan will follow the example of his predecessors and attempt to resolve the differences between Europe and America that he is inheriting from Jimmy Carter. What are his chances of success?

After some hesitation, Western Europe's leaders decided to welcome the arrival of a determined and unified team in the White House. They will not have to worry about repetitions of incidents such as the issue of the neutron bomb: Chancellor Schmidt personally committed himself to the weapon at the suggestion of President Carter who, at the last moment, postponed implementation of the program. The majority of Europeans, whether ordinary

Europe

by Raymond Aron

citizens or statesmen, are expecting a reestablishment of American policy, an effort to rearm and an end to America's low profile—steps which they are pleased with, at least in the abstract. It remains to be seen whether Europeans will readily follow Ronald Reagan the day he abandons the language of detente and reverts to a policy of vigorous containment.

European reactions to the Soviet invasion of Afghanistan should be remembered. Neither Bonn, Paris nor London reduced trade with the Soviet bloc nor imposed tougher financial conditions. The entry of Soviet troops into Kabul provoked a sudden

shift, if not an actual change, in United States diplomacy, but there was no such response in Europe.

President Giscard d'Estaing and Chancellor Schmidt seem more concerned with preserving detente than deterring the Kremlin from new acts of aggression by making it pay for that action as dearly as possible. They are likely to find themselves even further apart from Mr. Reagan than they previously were from Mr. Carter.

Do Europeans and Americans view the present international situation differently? I am not entirely certain. Mr. Schmidt and Mr. Giscard cannot disregard the fact that their gasoline comes through the Strait of Hormuz and that the producer states do not have the means to defend themselves. Nor can they disregard the overarmament of the Soviet Union in terms of both nuclear and conventional weapons. They do recognize the danger but they are pretending to disregard it because they are doubtful of the present strength of the United States.

After all, the American press continues to publish highly critical reports about the worth of America's volunteer army; and U.S. experts are citing the "window of opportunity," the vulnerability of the Minutemen to the Soviet SS-18s and the vulnerability of NATO's vital centers to the SS-20s. The hesitation of certain European countries to accept American Pershing or cruise missiles on their territory is explained by the assessment of the current ratio of forces. Will Euromissiles deter attack or make it more likely? The fact that this question is raised at all reveals the European mind-set.

The enormous gap between America's prosperity and Europe's poverty, obvious a quarter of a century ago, has long since disappeared. The major countries of conti-

nental Europe enjoy a standard of living generally—to within 10% or 20%—comparable to that in the United States.

The reconstruction of a more or less unified Western Europe, which Washington sought, encouraged and helped, takes a form least propitious to the national interest of the United States. The economic unity of the ten members of the European Community tends rather to intensify competition between businesses on opposite sides of the Atlantic; it does not help to lighten the military burden borne by the United States for the defense of the free world. Europeans could allocate to their military budget a percentage of the GNP comparable to what the United States allocates.

Relations between Bonn and Washington have deteriorated. The Bonn-Washington alliance has ensured the survival and vitality of NATO from the time France left the organization. Bonn is not planning to quit NATO but it no longer follows a diplomacy hinged exclusively on the alliance with Washington. With its *Ostpolitik* and the agreements signed with Moscow and Warsaw, the Federal Republic has developed national interests of its own that do not necessarily coincide with those of the United States or the Atlantic Pact.

West Germany considers the preservation of detente a matter of national interest; in concrete terms, it seeks as good relations as possible with Moscow. Bonn is faithful to the Atlantic Alliance but it is careful not to clash head on with the Kremlin, not out of friendship for the Soviets but out of fear of reprisals.

The Germans have already paid politically for the humanitarian concessions they obtained—the repatriation of Germans from the East, the easing of restrictions of visits to East Germany by West

Germans and security for West Berlin. But they have no illusions about the value of the agreements. Moscow has the means to respond to any Bonn policy that displeases it, and East Germans would be the victims in any reprisals. Chancellor Schmidt's expression that the Soviets hold hostage not 52 Americans but millions of Germans has to be interpreted in this light.

Ostpolitik is being accompanied by increased trade. Bonn and Paris are signing pacts that have the effect of curtailing West Europeans' freedom of action more than they do that of East Europeans. When

Messrs. Schmidt and Giscard preach that detente must be preserved, they are mindful of this network of agreements that were intended to tame the Soviet bear but actually paralyze the would-be tamer.

Not a very optimistic analysis of facts that are hardly contestable. No wave of the magic wand will instantly bring Mr. Reagan's advisers closer to those of the German chancellor and the French president. However, in the Atlantic Alliance much still depends on the team in the White House. The less confidence the Germans and French have in the strength and com-

mitment of the United States, the less they resist the attractions of *Ostpolitik*. The new Secretary of State, who has lived in Europe for many years, is fully aware of the crisis of confidence and maybe knows how to overcome it.

———

Mr. Aron, the French social philosopher, is a professor at the University of Paris and a columnist for L'Express magazine.

———

The Case for Military Reform

By Gary Hart

Both major candidates in the presidential campaign put heavy stress on the need for a stronger defense. President Reagan is committed to increasing the defense budget, possibly by as much as $25 billion to $35 billion annually. But will increased spending really strengthen America's defenses?

The answer is: not necessarily. If the Reagan administration is serious about efforts to strengthen the military, it will have to look beyond the size of the budget. It will have to embrace a cause that has quietly been growing among defense academics and writers, officers in the field and a few elected officials: the cause of military reform.

Military reform means three basic changes:

It means spending more, selectively, for defense.

It means allocating funds to innovative weapons and programs.

And it means addressing a number of non-budgetary problems which, although not related to defense spending, relate directly to winning or losing wars. This includes re-examination of basic defense doctrine and concepts.

Underfunded Defense

First, we do need to increase the defense budget. Major elements in our defense establishment have been underfunded for some time. These include shipbuilding, military pay, operations and maintenance and strategic forces.

Second, we must direct our spending toward innovative weapons and programs. Just spending more will not solve our problems. We risk being like the French in the 1930s, debating how much to spend each year on the Maginot Line.

If *what* we are buying will not work on

the battlefield, then it does not matter how much of it we have.

Perhaps the Navy provides the best example of the need to spend our money for innovation. In an era when new weapons have made every surface ship significantly more vulnerable than it was 20 or even 10 years ago, the Navy has become dependent

———

Unless we re-examine our entire concept of land warfare, it won't do much good merely to spend more money to buy more hardware.

———

on just 13 ships—the 13 large aircraft carriers. Most other types of surface ships—cruisers and destroyers—are not only wedded to the aircraft carrier, they are themselves more vulnerable and increasingly less able to carry out their escort mission.

New concepts and technologies could free the Navy from many of its current problems. Vertical/short take-off and landing (V/STOL) aircraft could permit us to build smaller, less expensive carriers in much larger numbers. Modern diesel-electric submarines could complement our extremely expensive nuclear attack subs, enabling us to afford a much larger submarine force. Hydrofoils and surface effect ships could provide the high speeds—up to 80 knots—needed for truly effective anti-submarine ships. But this means spending our naval dollars in innovative ways, which we haven't been doing.

The third basic component of military reform, the need to attack some non-bud-

getary defense problems, is seldom addressed in our national defense debate. But these problems may be the most serious of all.

Our concept of land warfare is a good example. The doctrine of the Army still reflects the post-World War I French concept of a war of attrition dominated by massive firepower. Its object is to destroy the enemy physically, tank by tank and man by man.

The Germans demonstrated in World War II that a concept based on maneuver is more effective, especially for the side with fewer men and less equipment. The Russians learned maneuver warfare the hard way, from the Germans in World War II. We still haven't learned it. One can place the U.S. Army's field manuals side-by-side with those of the French in 1940 and find remarkable parallels. Unless we re-examine our entire concept of land warfare, it won't do much good merely to spend more money to buy more hardware.

The military education and promotion system is another example of a serious non-budgetary weakness. The military education system—the service academies, the command and staff schools, the war colleges—gives little attention to *ideas* about warfare. It emphasizes the study of management and lower-level leadership, not military history.

Promotion reinforces the effects of poor education. The services value the manager, tolerate the troop leader, but have virtually no place for the theorist.

We must give our officers a chance to think about warfare, both in our service schools and while on regular duty assignments. This means changes in the schools' curricula, including much greater emphasis on military history and theory, and possibly lengthening the school terms. It means upgrading and revitalizing our military journals. It means reducing the administrative load on the officer in the field, to give him time to think. And we should consider providing a formal career path for those officers who excel in military theory, to parallel those already existing for the troop leader and the manager.

Why have there not been stronger efforts from within the armed forces to create a place for the military theorist? This brings up what is perhaps our most fundamental military weakness: The armed services have in large part become bureaucracies.

Traditionally, the forces were organized on a "corporative" model. Each officer was inculcated with, and worked in every way to advance, the overall goals and purposes of his service. Today, only the Marine Corps adheres to this model.

Narrow Outlook

The Army, Navy and Air Force have instead adopted the bureaucratic model, in which the officer specializes in one or several narrow functions, and the overall goals of the institutions are supposedly attained by linking the "boxes" which define each individual's job. Unfortunately the narrow outlook this produces often causes those overall goals to be forgotten, while decisions are based on what the institutions find comfortable—which is to say, what they have done in the past.

If we are to avoid the military dangers this trend toward bureaucratization could cause, we must reform the very basis of our armed services—the way they make decisions—while we also reform specific military concepts and force structures, military education and the promotion system. Otherwise, the other reforms will only be temporary, for the ongoing process of change and adaptation which must characterize an effective military will not develop. This may be the single most challenging defense task we face.

Military reform presents a difficult challenge to the new administration. But it also offers an enormous opportunity. It offers a new basis for something we lost in Vietnam—a genuine national consensus on defense. There is nothing ideological about the issue. It is a task in which liberals and conservatives can join. It will indeed require a joining of those who have differed in the past. But if we are willing to think new thoughts, and see today's problems in the light of present realities, not as reflections of debates long past, it can be done.

Mr. Hart, a Democrat, is U.S. Senator from Colorado.

Review & Outlook

Casey's Challenge

Central Intelligence Agency Director William Casey is striving hard to restore the agency's woefully depleted intelligence capabilities, which were immeasurably sapped by the congressional witch-hunts of the 1970s and by the subsequent actions of the Carter administration. As a part of this task, Mr. Casey must decide what to do about a tangle of legal restrictions on the agency's activities—specifically, President Carter's Executive Order No. 12036. The administration's decision on the fate of that order will likely as much determine the success of the CIA's rebuilding efforts as any amount of new funding and additional personnel.

Mr. Casey's task has been made no less challenging by the considerable flak he has encountered since being named CIA director by his close friend, President Reagan. At his confirmation hearings, Senate Democrats accused Mr. Casey of planning to "gut" the legal prohibitions and to "unleash" the agency. These criticisms reached a crescendo following press "leaks" that the administration planned to permit "domestic spying" by the CIA — charges that were strongly denied by the administration. On the other hand, some conservatives were miffed by some of Mr. Casey's appointments, mainly his decision to retain and even to promote some holdovers from the previous administration.

We hope that this political dust-kicking will not inhibit Mr. Casey and President Reagan in deciding the fate of Mr. Carter's Executive Order. The current choices are between a "warmed-over" version of the existing order, trimming some of the more confusing legal prohibitions and writing an entirely new order, detailing the agency's mission and responsibilities and reducing the legal restrictions. In the interests of upgrading our intelligence operations, we hope the administration chooses the latter course.

E.O. 12036 is a hangover from the Church committee investigation into alleged CIA "abuses," many of which turned out to be either non-existent or minuscule. It is long on ill-defined legal restraints and short on definitions of responsibilities and purpose. It severely curtails the agency's ability to gather information, particularly in the difficult area of counterintelligence, which aims at uncovering and neutralizing operations hostile to U.S. interests. It is so rife with confusing legalisms—and this is said to be especially true of the classified sections of the order—that it has become a straitjacket on the CIA and, in some cases, an excuse for doing nothing at all.

The Carter Executive Order reflects a fundamental confusion between law enforcement and the CIA's inherently extra-legal activities. Previous administrations had little trouble drawing that distinction ever since George Washington admonished his generals in 1776 to "leave no stone unturned" in gathering intelligence on the British.

The CIA is not a law enforcement agency. In many important respects, its role is the exact opposite—to conduct a defined set of activities that cannot be carried out through normal law-enforcement channels. The agency's function is to scout out potential international flashpoints and foreign intrigues and, when directed by the

President, to try to counter these threats. It is the agency's mission to preclude the need for overt, legally sanctioned intervention by the U.S., which carries all the risks of an escalation in international tensions or even outright war.

But a recent Senate committee report concludes: "The U.S. intelligence system is not able to deal with the multiple crises as we have experienced recently, without diverting resources from other high priority missions. Moreover, in many areas of the Third World, coverage by the U.S. intelligence system is either marginal or nonexistent."

In short, the CIA has been weakened as an instrument of the President's highest responsibility, to protect the security of the United States and its people. The exaggerated claims of the past about the agency's alleged infringements on the constitutional rights of Americans must be weighed against the need for an intelligence agency that can function effectively. Part of the job of a President is to make such judgments and defend them against attack. We hope that Mr. Casey and Mr. Reagan will not be timid as they face up to this one.

111

Tarnished Report?

Apparent Errors Cloud U.S. 'White Paper' On Reds in El Salvador

State Department Aide Says Parts May Be Misleading But Defends Conclusions

A Raid on an Art Gallery

By Jonathan Kwitny
Staff Reporter of The Wall Street Journal

WASHINGTON—The State Department's now-famous white paper "Communist Interference in El Salvador," which was issued on Feb. 23, has served the Reagan administration well as the launching pad for its anti-Soviet foreign policy.

The anonymous authors of the eight-page document displayed no false modesty in declaring in its preamble: "This special report presents definitive evidence of the clandestine military support given by the Soviet Union, Cuba and their Communist allies to Marxist-Leninist guerrillas now fighting to overthrow the established government of El Salvador."

Bearing copies of the report, State Department emissaries visited the principal capitals of Western Europe and elicited statements of support from most of them. Domestically, too, the white paper, said to be based on 19 captured guerrilla documents, was accepted as fact by most of the nation's press, and there were numerous follow-up stories quoting administration spokesmen on their plans for countering the allegedly growing military power of the Salvadoran guerrillas. Within days, the National Security Council announced it had approved plans to provide the tiny country with $25 million of additional military aid and $40 million of economic assistance.

Admissions of "Mistakes"

With this kind of track record for the white paper, it is surprising, therefore, to hear Jon D. Glassman, who is given the major credit for its existence, describe parts of it as possibly "misleading" and "over-embellished." In a three-hour interview in his new office just one floor below Secretary Alexander Haig's at State Department headquarters, policy planner Glassman freely acknowledges that there were "mistakes" and "guessing" by the government's intelligence analysts who translated and explained the guerrilla documents, which were written in Spanish with code names.

The white paper says that the 19 documents prove El Salvador is a "textbook case of indirect armed aggression by Communist powers." But a close examination of the documents the State Department has brought forward indicates that, if anything, Mr. Glassman may be understating the case in his concession that the white paper contains mistakes and guessing.

Several of the most important documents, it's obvious, were attributed to guerrilla leaders who didn't write them. And it's unknown who did. Statistics of armament shipments into El Salvador, supposedly drawn directly from the documents, were extrapolated, Mr. Glassman concedes. And in questionable ways, it seems. Much information in the white paper can't be found in the documents at all. This information now is attributed by the State Department to other, still-secret sources.

A Loss of Credibility?

The shortcomings of the white paper don't necessarily invalidate the Reagan administration's policy of providing more support for El Salvador's ruling regime—a policy that apparently had been decided upon well before the white paper was issued. A close reading of the white paper indicates, instead, that its authors probably were making a determined effort to create a "selling" document, no matter how slim the background material.

Few deny that Marxists are active in the El Salvador rebellion or that they have received at least some training and supplies from Communist countries overseas. But the month-by-month arms buildup, of almost blitzkrieg proportions, described in the white paper with such emphatic detail and precision, may lose credibility with Mr. Glassman's admissions that he doesn't know who wrote some of the allegedly captured documents on which the white paper is based.

In fact, the dire circumstances described in the white paper seem to have little bearing on what has subsequently happened in El Salvador this year. Far from being overwhelmed by the power of imported Soviet arms, the Salvadoran government put down a desperate rebel offensive in January; reporters on the scene say the guerrillas still are able to operate freely in large parts of the country, but that there haven't been successful large-scale attacks indicating big new arms supplies.

Conclusions Defended

Mr. Glassman, then deputy chief of the political section of the American embassy in Mexico City, was sent to El Salvador last January on a special mission to find and analyze guerrilla documents. He says he sent back to Washington some 80 pieces of material, comprising about 200 pages. Although only 19 of the documents were cited as background in the Feb. 23 white paper, the rest of the papers, plus other material, are expected to provide background for another State Department white paper, which officials say will be released shortly. (See story on page 10).

Mr. Glassman and other State Department officials strongly defend the conclusions that were reached in the original white paper. "We possibly never again will have such an intimate insight into the development of guerrilla movement and its gathering of financial and military support," Mr. Glassman says.

But the 37-year-old career diplomat, who was promoted after his success in finding the documents, concedes that problems arose almost immediately after the white paper and its documents had been distributed by the State Department. A message came from the El Salvador government, he says, declaring, in effect, "You guys have made some mistakes." Among them, he says, was the misidentification of an alleged guerrilla leader whose code name Mr. Glassman thought he had broken.

"We completely screwed it up," he now says, referring to the attribution of the document. A list of weapons and other equipment supposedly going to El Salvador from Vietnam, Ethiopia, Bulgaria, Czechoslovakia, Hungary and East Germany was compiled by alleged guerrilla leader Ana Guadalupe Martinez, the white paper analysis says. But apparently she had nothing to do with it. The document itself—the most prominently featured document in the white paper—bears the name "Ana Maria." The Salvadorans say the list was really drawn up by Ana Maria Gonzalez, who belongs to another group, according to Mr. Glassman. But he adds, "This was the Salvadorans guessing. They don't know either. I could be right."

The white paper was more certainly wrong, Mr. Glassman indicates, in attributing to Shafik Handal the authorship of an account of an arms-soliciting trip last summer to the Soviet Union and six other Communist countries. Mr. Handal is secretary general of the Salvadoran Communist Party and is also identified as the emissary who made the trip. (The trip report itself refers to the emissary simply as "the comrade.") Mr. Glassman acknowledges that the report couldn't have been written by Mr. Handal, because from the context the author clearly wrote from Cuba after Mr. Handal himself had left.

Mr. Glassman says that he doesn't know who wrote this report, which is central to the white paper. He concedes that the wording precludes authorship of the document by a known Salvadoran Communist representative in Cuba.

No such uncertainty was evident in a Feb. 6 story that ran at the top of page one of the New York Times, which quoted from the trip report as a first-hand account and said that the emissary was "believed to be" Mr. Handal. The leak, more than two weeks before the white paper was issued, didn't come from the State Department, Mr. Glassman says, but probably came from one of the friendly Latin American governments that had seen an advance copy. In fact, Mr. Glassman adds, the leak caused government officials to rewrite parts of the white paper "to make it different from Juan de Onis (the Times reporter who wrote the story). It caused the government a lot of hard work," he says.

Who Wrote Document C?

The white paper also says Mr. Handal wrote another document — two pages of handwritten notes called Document C. The notes don't contain Mr. Handal's name or any date or identification, but the white paper says that they are notes "taken during an April 28, 1980, meeting of the Salvadoran Communist Party." The notes, however, appear to be written in at least two different handwritings, making them difficult to ascribe to one author. Mr. Glassman says the handwriting looks different to him, too, and adds, "They change people writing on them. At a lot of the meeting things (notes of meetings), different people are writing it." Nevertheless, in four places the white paper quotes the words as Mr. Handal's own.

Also in question is the most widely publicized statistic in the white paper — the amount of arms that it said were proved to have been delivered to the insurgents. The second paragraph of the white paper says, "From the documents it is possible to reconstruct chronologically the key stages in the growth of the Communist involvement." It then lists as the fourth such stage "the covert delivery to El Salvador of nearly 200 tons of . . . arms, mostly through Cuba and Nicaragua." But nowhere in the documents is there any mention of 200 tons.

Mr. Glassman says, "That (200 tons) comes from intelligence based on the air traffic, based on the truck traffic. In other words, it doesn't come from the documents."

A Bit of Extrapolation

He says that secret intelligence observation showed increased air traffic between Cuba and Nicaragua late last year. This was presumed to be arms shipments for El Salvador, he adds, because new arms cropped up in an unsuccessful rebel offensive in mid-January of 1981. He says that part of the estimate of the truck shipments into El Salvador was based on extrapolating the cargo-hauling potential of several trucks that were listed in "Document N," attached to the white paper. This document, an undated, unsigned and barely legible hand-scrawled sheet, lists four trucks, three of which apparently are still to be bought or built, along with the initials of four guerrilla groups and some purported tonnage numbers, totaling 21, under the headings "sea," "air" and "land."

Another frequently quoted statistic in the white paper is that "the series of contacts between Salvadoran Communist leaders and key officials of several Communist states . . . resulted in commitments to supply the insurgents nearly 800 tons of the most modern weapons and equipment."

The 800-ton figure also represents an extrapolation, Mr. Glassman says. He says he multiplied 130 (the tonnage of arms one document says are stored in Nicaragua) by six to arrive at "nearly 800."

Expanding on Arafat

Oddly enough, "Document I," which provides the rationale for this extrapolation, seems largely given over to complaints by the unidentified author about the ineptitude of guerrilla leaders in even finding a meeting place, and the *slowness* of arms deliveries from outside El Salvador. The document purports to be the minutes of a meeting of three men, said to be the "Guerrilla Joint General Staff." The State Department translation of the minutes includes a date at the top, Sept. 26, 1980, which isn't on the document, and only the first page of an unknown number of pages was distributed. The key paragraph follows:

"It contradicts military reality to discuss percentages of arms when barely four tons of the 130 warehoused in Lagos (believed to be a code word for Nicaragua) have been brought into the country. These four tons have been in intermittent supply and the material now in Lagos is only equivalent to one-sixth of all the material obtained that the DRU (the Unified Revolutionary Directorate, a group of leftist organizations) will have eventually concentrated in Lagos."

Other major assertions in the white paper seem questionable. One is that on July 22, 1980, Yasir Arafat, the Palestine Liberation Organization leader, met Salvadoran guerrilla leaders in Managua, Nicaragua, and gave "promises (of) military equipment, including arms and aircraft."

Mr. Glassman acknowledges that the only mention of Mr. Arafat in the documents is an aside in parentheses, which says, ". . . on the 22nd there was a meeting with Arafat."

This reference is contained in an unsigned report, "Document G," in the context of much complaining that a delegation of Salvadoran leftists was cold-shouldered and otherwise insulted on a visit to Nicaragua for the anniversary celebration of that country's revolution. Mr. Glassman says that the white paper's report of Mr. Arafat's promises to the Salvadorans came from other, secret intelligence.

As another example, the white paper quotes a report allegedly prepared by Mr. Handal as saying, "In reference to a unification of the armed movement, he (Mr. Handal) asserts that 'the idea of involving everyone in the area has already been suggested to Fidel himself.' " An obvious reference to Cuban Premier Fidel Castro.

Soviet Aid: A Plane Ticket

"I think that could be a misleading statement," Mr. Glassman concedes, noting that in the context of the document, the idea that had been suggested to "Fidel" was getting various Communist parties in Central America to cooperate. The discussion, however, appears to be about labor unions.

At another point, the white paper says that Salvadoran guerrilla leaders formed a unified front "as a precondition for large-scale Cuban aid." Mr. Glassman acknowledges that there is nothing to that effect in the documents, but he says, "This comes from the Nicaraguan situation where they (the Salvadorans) saw that the Cubans wanted that (a unified front)."

The only concrete instance of Soviet aid delivered to the Salvadoran rebels reported in the 19 documents was an airplane ticket from Moscow to Vietnam for one guerrilla, presumably Mr. Handal. Whoever was writing the documents complained frequently that various countries, particularly the Soviet Union, were footdragging in procuring and transporting arms.

Mr. Glassman, however, contends that recent captures of arms in El Salvador indicate that the Soviets made good on promises of deliveries. He says that American-made arms, found in an El Salvador-bound truck intercepted in Honduras in late January, have been traced by their serial numbers to a shipment delivered to Vietnam during the American presence there. He says that this was the first known appearance of such weapons outside Vietnam and that this proves that weapons, said to be promised in the documents, were actually delivered.

Raiding an Art Gallery

"In my mind, the Russians cooperated fully," he says, and the guerrillas' complaints were "ill-founded."

How Mr. Glassman came upon the documents makes a tangled tale itself, with several versions extant. Mr. Glassman says that William Bowdler, then assistant secretary of state for Latin American affairs, called him on Jan. 14 from Washington and told him that because of the guerrilla offensive that had begun Jan. 10, the department thought that there might be some captured documents to account for where the arms were coming from. Some 15 or 20 documents had been discovered the previous November and had been turned over by the Salvadoran ministry of defense. Mr. Glassman was to be temporarily assigned from Mexico City to the job, according to the State Department, because then-Ambassador Robert White, in El Salvador, had said he was too short-handed to handle the assignment.

The November documents were said to have been captured in a raid on an art gallery owned by Mr. Handal's brother. They had already been sent to Washington, analyzed and their contents reported to various U.S. embassies, including Mr. Glassman's in Mexico City, Mr. Glassman says. Among these documents was the report on the arms-soliciting trip believed to have been taken by Mr. Handal, and one other document of the 19 that were later released on Feb. 23, he says.

Mr. Glassman says he flew to El Salvador within a couple of days of getting Mr. Bowdler's instructions. He says that he went straight to the Salvadoran minister of defense but was told that the only documents available were the ones already delivered in November. Says Mr. Glassman, "I know

from our own bureaucracy and other bureaucracies that what is found down below doesn't always get passed up the chain of command." So he says he went to several other agencies—the national guard, the treasury police and, finally, the national police, where he was shown a new pile of documents.

"Fortunately for us," Mr. Glassman says, "just a few days earlier, they had captured a Venezuelan correspondent, a journalist, who was bringing in money for ERP (a guerrilla group) and by following him were able to capture the ERP propaganda commission as a whole, meeting in a house." The owner of the house denied involvement but was persuaded to tell police of other locations mentioned by people on the propaganda commission, Mr. Glassman says.

One such location was a grocery store owned by a known leftist. There, police found a false wall, behind which were a mortar, some shells, and more documents in a plastic bag and a suitcase, according to what Mr. Glassman says the police told him. He says he thinks the documents were kept there because the guerrilla coalition consists of four groups, "none of which fully trusts the others," so that records must be maintained.

News for an Ambassador

About 15 of the 19 documents released on Feb. 23 came from the grocery store, Mr. Glassman says. After receiving them, he says, he went to Col. Jaime Abdul Gutierrez, the vice president of El Salvador, and asked for a further search. Other documents were turned up, and two or three of them were included in the batch released on Feb. 23, he says.

Mr. White, the former U.S. ambassador to El Salvador, takes issue with Mr. Glassman on several points. He denies that he asked for outside aid from Washington to help with the documents. "Captured documents were not uppermost in my mind. We were dealing with a final offensive and a general strike situation," Mr. White says.

He expresses incredulity at Mr. Glassman's story of the discovery of the second batch of documents. "All of this is news to me," he says. "It strikes me as unlikely that I would not have heard this story before—this business about following a Venezuelan and finding this wall and breaking it down."

He also says that Mr. Glassman was pointed to the documents by Col. Eldon Cummings, American military group commander at the embassy, who already knew

they existed and where. Col. Cummings, in a separate interview, agrees. Mr. Bowdler and Luigi Einaudi, the State Department official who supervised the analysis of the documents, also say they were aware of the new documents well before Mr. Glassman's trip.

Mr. White was removed as ambassador in late January after policy differences with the Reagan administration and has since become a senior fellow at the Carnegie Endowment for International Peace. So it is perhaps understandable that he has a poor opinion of the Feb. 23 white paper—"bizarre, tendentious, tries to prove more than the evidence warrants."

A Feeling of Skepticism

His feeling about the documents is almost equally harsh. "The only thing that ever made me think that these documents were genuine was that they proved so little," he says. He concedes that he is a great skeptic when it comes to captured documents, adding, "It was unthinkable that the documents on the Handal raid would have been sort of lying around the national police station for several weeks. It would have been normal procedure for the authorities of El Salvador to share with us any intelligence discovery that took place."

Nevertheless, Mr. White believes that it's possible, as the white paper says, that Mr. Handal did visit Moscow and other Communist capitals, that some "semi-outlaw governments," such as Vietnam, Ethiopia and Libya gave support to the Salvadoran rebels, and that the leaders of Cuba and Nicaragua did "sit down with" the Salvadoran insurgents and "talk strategy and tactics."

Mr. Glassman says that once the documents were in his hands, one of the first things he did was to satisfy himself that they were genuine. There was the possibility that the Salvadoran military might have fabricated them or that they had been planted by the Central Intelligence Agency.

Says Mr. Glassman, "I submitted all of the documents to them (the CIA), and I asked, 'Did you fabricate any of the documents, or is there any indication they were fabricated by anyone else?' And the answer was no to both."

In defending the white paper's documentation, Mr. Glassman even expresses an opinion very close to that of Mr. White—that the shortcomings of the documents indicate that they are genuine "and disprove the fabrication argument."

Arm's Length

Soviets Grow Certain Of America's Hostility But Not of Its Will

---

Mixed Signals From U.S. Set Stage for Gromyko Talks With Haig Next Week

---

Playing to European Gallery

By Karen Elliott House
And Gerald F. Seib
Staff Reporters of The Wall Street Journal

WASHINGTON — For the last nine months, the White House and the Kremlin have viewed each other through a thick fog of bellicose rhetoric. But the Soviets now have seen enough to draw some tentative conclusions.

First, that the American mood has undergone a fundamental hardening that transcends the personalities of Jimmy Carter or Ronald Reagan. Second, that the mask of detente has been shredded, revealing the reality of protracted rivalry.

But most important, the Soviets believe President Reagan may not be the formidable rival they earlier feared he would be; his recent decision to trim defense-budget increases, his slowness in making important strategic-weapons decisions and his problems winning allied support for defense plans all make the Kremlin doubt the Reagan administration's ability to back up its tougher talk with decisive action.

In capsule form, that is how American Kremlinologists describe the U.S.-Soviet relationship as Secretary of State Alexander Haig and Soviet Foreign Minister Andrei Gromyko prepare to meet next week in New York.

Mainly Exploratory

The talks are the first high-level dialogue between the two major powers in 16 months. Unlike similar meetings in recent years, the two sides aren't coming together to negotiate strategic-arms limitation or anything else. So frayed is the relationship that these talks will be largely exploratory; the only immediate tangible result is expected to be agreement on a date in November to open previously scheduled talks on limiting Soviet and American nuclear armaments in Eastern and Western Europe.

Still, the talks are important for other reasons. Mr. Gromyko will be probing to discern whether the Reagan administration has formulated clear strategic priorities. The Soviets now aren't sure which parts of the Reagan rhetoric can or will be backed up with action. Mr. Gromyko's assessment of which objectives the U.S. is genuinely serious about will be critical in shaping future Soviet behavior around the globe, because he is a veteran and valued member of the ruling Soviet Politburo.

"The Soviets are confused about us," says a senior State Department official. "And unfortunately, it's not the result of some careful design by the administration."

Mr. Haig, for his part, will be trying to convince the Soviets that the U.S. is resolved to be a stronger adversary, despite recent mixed signals. He wants to underscore the administration's position that relations can improve, but only when the Soviets cease meddling in places like Southeast Asia, Africa and Central America.

An Eye on Europe

The talks also have important implications for U.S.-European relations. Because each foreign minister expects to make little headway with the other on narrowing the deep differences that divide the super-powers, both will be playing primarily to the European gallery. Moscow, has tried, with some success, to loosen the European-American alliance by striking the pose of peacemaker and portraying the U.S. as the irresponsible superpower seeking confrontation. U.S. officials hope the talks with Mr. Gromyko will help reassure Europe that isn't so.

While the prospects for a reduction in U.S.-Soviet tension remain dim, the potential for confrontation looms larger than at any other time since the early 1960s. The turmoil in Iran, which appears beyond the influence of either major power, could nonetheless become a flash point for both. Poland, too, could explode, sending East-West tension to dangerous new highs. Soviet surrogates in Central America and southern Africa also pose problems.

Against this tense backdrop, Mr. Haig must face a Soviet leadership that seems convinced of American hostility but uncertain of American willpower. The Soviets believe that "the basic trend in U.S.-Soviet relations will be regulated rivalry," says Dimitri Simes, a Soviet emigrant who is at Johns Hopkins University's School of Advanced International Studies. "What they haven't decided is whether this administration will be a very effective rival," he adds.

End of Detente?

The Soviets have seen enough of Ronald Reagan to decide that he sincerely believes the harsh anti-Soviet talk that marked his campaign and early days in office, analysts say. Moreover, the Soviets are becoming convinced that this hostility is part of a long-term American trend that started before the Reagan administration and will linger well after it.

Previously, the Soviets seemed unsure whether the chill in relations at the end of the Carter administration and Mr. Reagan's blustery talk were mere aberrations. Now, experts believe, the Soviet leadership has concluded that a broad decline in relations has finally killed chances of salvaging detente, the Nixon-era effort to reduce superpower tensions.

At the same time, though, the Soviets have seen signs that are more reassuring to them. Most significantly, the Reagan administration has wavered on tough defense decisions, raising Soviet doubts about its ability to produce on the promise to "rearm America." The most recent was the decision to scale back defense-budget increases; though slight, the decreases signaled that the defense budget won't be sacrosanct in the Reagan administration.

But the budget trimming is only one of a series of signals raising questions about Washington's ability to back up its words with deeds. Wary of domestic political problems, the administration hasn't decided how to base the new MX missile. It hasn't decided whether to renew development of the B1 bomber. And it staunchly resists a return to the military draft, which some Soviets consider a litmus test of U.S. resolve to muscle up its defenses. And now, because of delays in preparations by allies, the U.S. may have to delay slightly the stationing of a new generation of nuclear missiles in Europe.

The administration also has wavered from its tough anti-Soviet line in some non-defense decisions. Under pressure from the American farm belt, the Reagan administration lifted the grain embargo. Under pressure from Senate Foreign Relations Committee Chairman Charles Percy and other influential members of Congress, it allowed export of pipe-laying equipment, made in Sen. Percy's home state of Illinois, to the Soviet Union.

A Bark or a Whine

As a result, analysts say, the Soviets may be thinking they are confronted largely with rhetoric. "It's much worse to have a big bark and then reduce it to a whine," says Zbigniew Brzezinski, the national security adviser in the Carter administration. "That's what we're going to be doing—whining about the Soviets."

Such actions also could reinforce a broader Soviet suspicion that political realities will limit the actions of even the toughest U.S. administration. "Although the Politburo is quite wary of the possibility of a new U.S. assertiveness, it is by no means yet convinced that the U.S. will ever again satisfy either the political or the military prerequisites for effective opposition to the gradual further expansion of the Soviet position," concludes a recent study prepared by the Rand Corp. for the Defense Department.

Administration officials contend that the Soviets still know they will be facing sizable U.S. defense-spending increases, even if the increases will be somewhat less than at first proposed. Even now, these officials say, the Soviets have to be pondering whether they must increase their own defense spending.

And analysts both in and out of government think that the President's concessions on some issues recently could actually prove beneficial in dealing with the Soviets. The concessions demonstrate that Mr. Reagan is a reasonable and flexible man, the analysts reason, and show that the administration hopes to have some kind of relationship with the Soviets. "They probably see it as a sign we want to do-business," one administration aide says.

Talks Still Possible

Indeed, some analysts believe the most striking aspect of Soviet policy is that, despite its own recent tough talk and propa-

ganda, the Kremlin hasn't closed the door to negotiations with the U.S. To a large degree, Moscow professes willingness to talk merely as part of its drive to convince European politicians that Russia is the more reasonable superpower. "If there's going to be a break between the Soviets and the U.S., they want Europe to believe it is precipitated by America," not by Soviet misbehavior in Afghanistan or elsewhere, one analyst says.

But the willingness to negotiate also reflects a belief that negotiations could be in the Soviets' own interests as well. Though it can easily gear up defense spending, the Soviet Union would like an arms-control agreement so it can divert resources to a sluggish economy, analysts say. The Soviets find it difficult to make technological advances while devoting a large share of their resources to defense production.

The Soviets, then, might want to head off part of the Reagan defense buildup at the negotiating table. The Kremlin already has a plateful of security problems. Soviet relations with Japan have grown more rancorous recently. To the south, the Soviets must worry about their continued occupation of

Afghanistan and the blossoming friendship between China and the U.S. Poland remains a large worry. To handle it all, the Soviets must rely on an aged leadership slow to change its ways.

"They're hemmed in on East and West," says former Secretary of State Cyrus Vance. "They've got problems on the south and they've got problems internally."

For the Reagan administration, Soviet professions of willingness to negotiate strategic and European arms control present a delicate problem. On the one hand, Washington wants to show Europe that it is willing to talk to the Soviets in order to blunt the Kremlin's propaganda campaign painting Washington as unreasonable. But on the other hand, it doesn't want to yield to the Soviets on arms matters.

The administration also wants to make sure the Soviets are convinced the U.S. intends to negotiate from a position of greater strength. Currently, "there has got to be a question in their minds if we're serious for the long haul," concedes one U.S. official.

113

Arms and the Man

Reagan Campaign Plan For Rearming America Hits Budget Realities

---

Narrower Increase in Outlays Projected to Ease Deficit; Weinberger vs. Stockman

---

What About the MX and B1?

By Walter S. Mossberg
Staff Reporter of The Wall Street Journal

WASHINGTON—The expansive military rhetoric that helped install Ronald Reagan in the White House last January has run smack into a stone wall of reality.

After only seven months in control of the Pentagon, the new administration is still struggling to deliver on the sweeping campaign promise Mr. Reagan made last year to "rearm America." Promised improvements in some areas, such as increased military compensation, have been delayed. A detailed defense strategy has yet to be published. And a messy fight has erupted over the MX missile and B1 bomber.

And now, just as its critics predicted, the administration is being forced to weigh a painful retreat on its only specific defense proposal—a five-year plan unveiled last March to more than double the annual Pentagon budget to $368 billion by 1986, even while taxes are being drastically slashed.

White House aides now predict Mr. Reagan will be forced to cut as much as $30 billion from planned increases in Pentagon outlays for fiscal 1983 and 1984, in order to balance the budget by 1984 as he has promised. The military services have been told to prepare to narrow the ambitious spending increases they were encouraged to project just a few months ago. Even the Pentagon's budget authority for fiscal 1982, which starts Oct. 1, may have to be lowered, although Congress has already approved most of it.

At White House meetings scheduled to begin today, Defense Secretary Caspar Weinberger and Budget Director David Stockman are expected to square off over the spending issue. The Pentagon chief will battle to avoid the reductions, contending that they could impede top-priority efforts to rebuild combat-readiness, could cut into planned expansions of the Army and the Navy, and could force the early retirement of some existing Army units, Navy ships and Air Force planes.

Self Delusion?

"They had a defense policy that was totally inconsistent with their fiscal policy," asserts James Schlesinger, former Republican Defense Secretary. "They were just kidding themselves."

Democrats have long made the same charge. But the White House has argued that its tax cuts would stimulate the economy and produce new revenue. This, coupled with cuts in nondefense spending, the argument went, would pay for the big Pentagon-budget increases the President considered essential without requiring budget deficits.

Pentagon officials still believe fervently in that reasoning. Mr. Weinberger, a former White House budget director and longtime foe of federal deficits, contends the defense-budget figures presented in March "aren't excessive in any way." He has described them as the minimum needed to restore U.S. military competitiveness with the Soviet Union, a task he calls the most important his administration was elected to carry out.

What's more, the Defense Secretary argues that "we're making very good progress" on carrying out the campaign pledges.

Evidence of "Progress"

As evidence, he cites management revisions at the Pentagon and the $25.6 billion increase (now jeopardized) from President Carter's proposed 1982 Pentagon budget, which allowed him to commit more money to combat readiness, training, spare parts and new weapons. In addition, he says, the administration is "close to announcing an absolutely massive increase in the strength of our strategic forces," as a result of its six-month study of the MX missile and the B1 bomber programs.

"We've only been here six months," Mr. Weinberger says, "and we don't have any large, shiny objects to show you yet. But we have, I think, pursued a clear, straightforward, easily perceived policy."

By proposing fatter defense budgets, Mr. Weinberger says, the U.S. has sent "a strong signal" to the Soviet Union and to America's allies "that President Reagan's election and his actions constitute a really watershed change in American policy, and that it's no longer safe for the Soviets or anyone to regard America as weak, irresolute or divided."

Comparisons With Carter

Nonetheless, the Weinberger defense policy is under attack in the White House, particularly at the Office of Management and Budget, where Mr. Stockman has focused his attention on another Reagan campaign promise: cutting federal spending.

"Getting onto our track to a balanced budget without cutting defense is so difficult as to verge on the impossible," one Stockman aide declares.

Budget officials contend that the defense-spending increases proposed in March are so huge that the President can afford to trim them and still argue that he has increased the Pentagon's budget more than President Carter planned to do—a major campaign pledge last year.

To defend this approach, some Stockman aides even echo arguments used by the Carter Pentagon. One budget official says, "We started with a false perception that defense spending was flat under Carter. Actually, Carter raised it a lot in his last year."

The Secretary's vigorous fight against smaller spending increases angers some White House aides. They contend that as a longtime political associate of Mr. Reagan and as a former budget chief who earned the name "Cap the Knife," Mr. Weinberger should realize that the defense plan is politically unavoidable. "The trouble with Cap is that he thinks you can cut Aid to Dependent Children and always spare the military," says one presidential adviser.

One former Carter administration official says, "We knew that, sooner or later, they'd run into this conflict between budget-cutting and defense spending. But it's amazing it's happened so fast."

The budget impasse, however, isn't the only roadblock that has cropped up in the path of Mr. Reagan's effort to "rearm America." Though the President's campaign made much of the urgency of the new military buildup, the elements of the program are emerging slowly.

The five-year budget plan was issued March 4, but there still hasn't been any detailed explanation of what the added funds would be used to buy after 1982. Mr. Weinberger has given several speeches and interviews on defense strategy, but he has limited his remarks to broad generalities, saying the U.S. must be prepared to fight several long, conventional conflicts simultaneously in different places.

The administration has formally called for increasing the size of the Navy to 600 ships from 450, but it hasn't released a shipbuilding plan and hasn't said where the ships would be used or how.

A new G.I.-benefits bill promised during the campaign has been deferred until next year. And a 5.3% military-pay raise promised for last June was blocked in Congress and won't take effect until the fall, if ever.

But the delay that has caused the most confusion and controversy has been on an issue Reagan defense advisers stressed heavily in last year's campaign: how to revamp America's three-part nuclear-weapons force to overcome recent Soviet advances in the number and accuracy of atomic warheads.

During the campaign, and since, the President and Mr. Weinberger have charged that the Soviets now possess enough highly accurate warheads to wipe out U.S. land-based missiles in a sneak attack. In addition, they said, U.S. B52 bombers are so old that they can't be counted on to penetrate Soviet air defenses past the mid-1980s.

Mr. Reagan promised to "close" this "window of vulnerability" faster than President Carter would have. He suggested building a new bomber such as the B1 aircraft that Mr. Carter canceled in 1977. And he proposed finding a substitute for Mr. Carter's idea of shuttling a new missile, the MX, among 4,600 barn-sized shelters in Utah and Nevada to fool Soviet strategists.

Delayed Decision

At first, Mr. Weinberger promised Congress he would announce decisions on the bomber and MX plans by June (even though a law required a bomber ruling by March). Later, Pentagon aides promised decisions by July or August. But none has emerged. Now a final decision is promised for later this month.

The delay has been compounded by a widespread impression of confusion and uncertainty in the decision-making process. Mr. Weinberger at first publicly suggested putting MX missiles on ships, then the idea disappeared. Later, administration sources say, he backed a plan for putting the missiles on aircraft, and another idea that would delay an MX basing decision for several years. Each was opposed by other Reagan advisers.

A fierce battle has been waged over the decisions. Top Air Force officers, who back the B1 bomber and the Carter MX plan, have complained privately to reporters and friendly Congressmen that the Air Force has been cut out of the decision process. Conservatives from Utah and Nevada have argued, along with the Mormon Church, against putting the missiles in their area.

John Tower of Texas, chairman of the Senate Armed Services Committee, and other key Congressmen have been privately critical of the process and have complained directly to the President. Even some White House aides accuse Mr. Weinberger and presidential counselor Edwin Meese of delaying the decision too long.

But Mr. Weinberger vigorously defends the MX and B1 deliberations. "There may very well be a problem of perception," he says, "but most of it stems from the fact that there is an inordinate amount of (press) comment on things that aren't finished or decided." He insists he hasn't made any final decisions or backed away from any.

Defending the Delays

It's perfectly proper, he says, to have taken six months to study such momentous strategic decisions, adding, "None of this will cause us any delay whatever" in actually fielding the new weapons. "I would do exactly the same again," he says.

But the biggest crisis by far for the administration's young defense program is the current battle over cutting the Pentagon budget. Under the March spending plan, Pentagon budget authority would have climbed 14.6% in 1982, after accounting for inflation, to $222.2 billion from $178 billion in the current fiscal year.

After that, authority would have increased about 7% annually, to $254.8 billion in 1983 and $289.2 billion in 1984, reaching $367.5 billion in 1986. The Carter plan called for a 5.3% rise in 1982, and 5% a year thereafter.

The actual spending of money wouldn't climb as rapidly at first because it takes a while for the Pentagon to dole out the budgeted funds for long-range projects such as big weapons. But the March plan projected a two-year inflation-adjusted jump of 17.4% in outlays during fiscal 1983 and 1984, just when the President promised to balance the budget.

Mr. Stockman has argued that the increase in budget authority for 1982 should be pared back well below 14.6% in order to cut as much as $30 billion in outlays that would result in 1983 and 1984.

Stockman's Approach

To make the spending retreat more palatable politically, Mr. Stockman is urging the President to announce that he still intends to raise the Pentagon budget 7% a year, on average, but has decided to use a different base for the increase. The new base would be the 1981 budget, rather than the much fatter 1982 budget based in the March plan.

In addition, OMB officials are suggesting that much of the cut can be achieved by reducing funds available for fuel, training, ammunition, spare parts, maintenance and benefits. These cuts show up much more quickly in actual outlays because funds for these items are spent rapidly. Further, such reductions have historically been preferred because they are less visible and more politically digestible.

If the OMB plan is adopted over Mr. Weinberger's vigorous objections, the President will still probably be able to claim his defense budgets are higher than Mr. Carter's would have been, though by a much smaller margin. And the lower figures can be arranged so that Pentagon spending increases will march steadily upward at 7% a year, after inflation.

But the administration will find it may have to swallow some of its bold defense rhetoric. Even the huge budget increases laid out in March weren't generous enough to accommodate all the proposals the services have given Mr. Weinberger in recent weeks for carrying out his general plan to build forces that can fight long wars around the globe.

Sending Out Signals

Mr. Weinberger and Secretary of State Alexander Haig could find it actually embarrassing to confront their counterparts from allied nations in the aftermath of defense cuts. Both have privately lectured the allies to emulate Mr. Reagan's policy of increasing defense spending while cutting taxes and social spending. Some Pentagon officials also fear that the Soviets will interpret any cuts as weakness.

Domestically, defense cuts would also send some signals that could hurt in the future. "The President can pass a reduced defense budget if he wants," says one congressional expert on defense matters. "But the long-term political damage will be done. It'll be clear that they've decided defense is second in importance to balancing the budget, and that will hurt with the national security forces, on issues such as the MX missiles, or arms sales to the Saudis."

Sen. Tower has already been angered by the proposals for reductions, contending they would leave the Pentagon with "less in the way of defense capability than even Jimmy Carter projected."

Congressional hawks also fear that, if the President seems to signal a retreat on defense spending, it will encourage those liberals who have already been planning to fight hard on some parts of the 1983 defense budget.

"There could be a hell of a fight on the 1983 budget up here if Reagan offers people something to sink their teeth into," says Democratic Sen. Carl Levin of Michigan, an Armed Services Committee member who has been critical of some of the plans for bigger spending.

Justices Uphold Limiting Draft Register to Men

Ruling, 6-3, Holds Congress Wasn't Biased as Law Bars Women in Combat

By STEPHEN WERMIEL
Staff Reporter of THE WALL STREET JOURNAL

WASHINGTON — The Supreme Court ruled that Congress was "well within its constitutional authority" when it revived draft registration for men but excluded women.

In a six-to-three ruling, the high court offered two reasons for upholding the decision by Congress in 1980 to revive registration limited to men.

Writing for the majority, Justice William Rehnquist said, first, that actions by Congress in the area of national defense must be shown great deference by the high court. Second, he concluded that the sole purpose of registration is to identify citizens for combat duty. As women are excluded from combat by law, it isn't discrimination to exclude them from registration, he said.

Assumptions Are Challenged

But, in dissent, Justices Byron White, Thurgood Marshall and William Brennan challenged the assumptions about the purpose of registration. "The scenario appears to exist only in the court's imagination," said Justice Marshall, noting that even the Pentagon recognizes the need for women in noncombat roles.

Defense Secretary Caspar Weinberger, who like President Reagan is opposed to the draft, said in a speech Monday to the American Stock Exchange: "We hope to use more women in noncombat jobs," to free up men for increased combat-related duties.

The most direct effect of the ruling is to remove any cloud from the law requiring men born during or after 1960 to sign up after they reach 18 years of age. "Our comment," said Selective Service spokesman Brayton Harris, "is that, if you're a male about to turn 18, don't forget to register within 30 days of your birthday."

Other Effects Are Cited

There are other effects, too. Although the ruling didn't appear to break any new ground in sex-discrimination law, it may take its toll on women just the same. The National Organization for Women had said in a friend-of-the-court brief that "exclusion reinforces the sex-role stereotypes harmful to women that have proven so resistant to change." Justice Marshall said the law "categorically excludes women from a fundamental civic obligation."

David Landau, a lawyer for the American Civil Liberties Union, said the decision could undermine the Constitution's protection against discrimination, the guarantee of "equal protection of the laws." The ruling creates "a national defense exception to equal protection that may affect other cases," Mr. Landau said.

In Los Angeles, deputy White House press secretary Larry Speakes said, "generally, we are pleased." He said the decision is "generally in line with the President's view." In Alton, Ill., Phyllis Schlafly, leader of forces opposing the proposed Equal Rights Amendment, thanked the court "for recognizing that our national security demands different roles for men and women."

Draft registration was reviewed by Congress at President Carter's request. Since July 21, 1980, when it began, 5.6 million men have registered, according to the Selective Service. Almost 500,000 have failed to sign up, and last Friday, the Selective Service began sending letters to a handful of those, telling them they are in violation of the law. The service has difficulty identifying the individuals who didn't sign up because a federal appeals court ruled it couldn't use Social Security data to locate 18-year-olds.

Support for Volunteer Army

The ruling yesterday isn't likely to affect the volunteer Army, which began in 1973 and which has the continued support of the Reagan administration. The President has said he will even consider scrapping draft registration, again.

In his ruling yesterday, Justice Rehnquist relied heavily on the role of Congress in national defense and military affairs. "Perhaps in no other area has the court accorded Congress greater deference," he said.

His ruling cast aside the decision last July of a special three-judge federal court in Philadelphia that found registration only of men unconstitutional. That July decision focused on how closely the court should examine the draft law to see if it violated the "equal protection" guarantee. The Supreme Court has, over the years, outlined three levels of "scrutiny" to be used by judges to see if the equal protection clause has been violated. Racial discrimination receives "strict scrutiny" while sex bias is accorded somewhat less examination. Other types of discrimination get the lowest level of scrutiny.

Service to Country Shouldn't Depend on Class

Sacrifice is not a word that can be easily found in this administration's lexicon, particularly as it might apply to those who make over $20,000 a year. Since, as the new team in Washington is fond of reminding us, you can't get anything for nothing, someone must pay for the grand New Beginning of tax breaks for the affluent. The collective someone in this case is the largely invisible (and non-voting) poor,

---

Viewpoint
by Hodding Carter III

---

who are not among the President's enthusiastic supporters in any case.

But if everyone is well aware of this particular reality behind the Reaganite domestic programs, too few appreciate how basic it is to current defense policy as well. The President is determined to make the rich richer, which is to say the major industrial concerns that will benefit from the massive defense expenditures for shiny big-buck strategic toys. He is equally determined to protect the vast majority of middle- and upper-class Americans from the contamination of military service. That leaves the burden of protecting a nation that has already shortchanged them upon (surprise) the poor of all races and on minorities in particular.

As in so many other matters, the President can plead the dubious virtue of consistency. He has said repeatedly that he does not favor a return to the draft. He can also correctly note that the tattered remnants of the liberal left are almost as one in opposing any form of universal national service, let alone renewal of the old Selective Service system.

Can so many of the nation's ostensible leaders be wrong? Absolutely. So long as the United States has over two million people under arms, it is inherently dangerous to this country's long-term stability that so large a Praetorian Guard has so little emotional, economic or political investment in the nation it defends. Further, as one military leader after another has said with increasing public and private emotion, the fighting ability of the armed forces is adversely affected by the severely limited pool from which the forces are able to draw personnel.

Anyone who cares about this country knows that it is inherently wrong and morally offensive that our most favored youngsters are exempted from defending it. The late President Harold Dodd of Princeton wrote an article for the Atlantic Monthly shortly before I entered college in 1953 in which he made the case for the ROTC. It led directly to my own service in the Marines, by way of the Navy ROTC, and to a lifelong conviction that he was right. In brief, he argued that those to whom society had given the most in education and privilege should repay that gift in part by participating in its military defense. In that way the military services, the society and the individual would all benefit. If all Americans shared the obligation of service, all might also share in a sense of community.

Such notions went out the window with the anti-war movement, which tied opposition to the Vietnam war to opposition to the draft. Among Richard Nixon's many bad ideas, repeal of the draft was probably the worst, but he was vociferously abetted by everyone from peaceniks to hawks. His success in the endeavor effectively collapsed the anti-war effort as a mass movement overnight, which says something about the principles that sent so many to the streets in those days. The nation then entered on its ignoble experiment with what is euphemistically called the All Volunteer Force.

The experiment has begun to get long in the tooth, which means that most households such as my own have never had to wrestle with the anguish of seeing a child go off to possible war. It's amazing how much more lustily some Americans find they can cheer for armed confrontation hither and yon when they know their children won't have to do any of the confronting. We can now buy our mercenaries, which means we can buy our patriotism with other people's lives. The new motto of those who agree with the President is, "Billions for defense, but not one of my kids." What that does to the attitudes about duty to country of those so favored does not require much imagination to guess.

And what of the kids who respond out of economic necessity to the financial incentives of the military, incentives which cannot and should not compete with private industry's inducements to trained young men and women. The lesson they learn is as clear as the one learned by their better-off contemporaries: The only thing your nation believes you are fit or entitled to do is serve as cannon fodder.

The people are far ahead of the politicians on this one. The latest Gallup Poll showed that 71% of those surveyed said they favored "requiring all young men to give one year of service to the nation—either in the military forces or in nonmilitary work here or abroad." Another 24% were opposed. It was not a question on the draft per se. It also left out women, who should not be excluded from national service of some kind, and that, too, may have skewed the results.

Nevertheless, a sizeable majority has the healthy belief that service to country should not depend on class and that those about whom society has demonstrated its indifference should not have the sole responsibility for its defense. The President should take note, but he won't. He knows on what side of this issue his real constituency's bread is buttered.

Mr. Carter was assistant secretary for public affairs at the State Department in the Carter administration.

State Issues

Exhausting States' Rights

Can a federal administrative agency coerce a state legislature into enacting a law? You might think not, given the long-standing American tradition of federalism and states' rights.

But don't be too sure. The Environmental Protection Agency, armed with its wide-ranging mandate from Congress, is conducting such an assault on the California legislature as part of its efforts to require 29 states to set up special auto emissions inspection stations in certain areas. If California doesn't give in to its demands the EPA has undertaken to have $700 million in federal funding for highways and sewers withheld. It also is threatening to hold up environmental impact approvals for further industrial expansion in the state.

The California legislature is to be congratulated for standing up to this exercise of brute force from Washington, but it is by no means assured of winning in the courts. Indeed, the progress of a related court case in Colorado does not bode well for its chances. The Clean Air Act of 1970 seemingly gives the EPA the power to use this form of coercion. And if that doesn't work, it can, at the risk of further outrage, try out a direct mandate to the states.

Obviously, the EPA would prefer the legislatures to roll over and do as they are told. The inspection plan the EPA has worked out will not be popular with motorists or taxpayers. It requires that in areas of the states

where ambient air quality falls below the standards set for 1982, the states establish auto testing stations. Motorists would be charged $20 to be told, quite possibly, that their cars had flunked the test. Most motorists think cars are clean enough as they are right now, and they are right.

The California legislators refuse to take the rap for the EPA's program. Ironically, California has had a successful auto emission inspection program of its own since 1965. Thirteen state legislators have sued the EPA, charging that coercion of states into passing laws in order not to lose funding and industrial construction permits is an unconstitutional violation of states' rights under the Tenth Amendment. Their case, now before the 9th Circuit Court, could do much to define just where, if anywhere, the feds must stop meddling in the affairs of the states.

A 1976 Supreme Court decision in *National League of Cities v. Usery* held that Washington could not force upon the states its choice as to how "essential decisions regarding the conduct of integral government functions are to be made." But the ruling opened a Tenth Amendment can of worms: What are essential state decisions? What are integral government functions? Moreover, the court held that the sovereign rights of the states could be balanced against the needs of federal policy. The Californians make the reasonable argument that since the EPA is in effect ordering

them to enact EPA doctrine into law, the agency is taking away the ability of the state to perform an integral government function, making law.

Colorado was cowed by the EPA into giving up its right to make its own law in May when the EPA withheld $300 million from the state. Twenty-seven state legislators had sued the EPA, but a Colorado court refused to rule on the states' rights issue. Leaders of the Colorado legislature still are pressing the case, complaining that the EPA "utilized brute force and blackmail to obtain our compliance." Colorado Senate President Fred Anderson recently told the National Conference of State Legislatures: "What we've got here is a federal bureaucracy actually filling the function of elected state legislators."

There will be a serious question of accountability if the EPA is allowed to get away with muscling the states into enacting legislation that the legislators cannot defend. The EPA would have neatly eluded responsibility for its costly program and the electorate would be left to wonder just to whom to complain about a program of which its state legislators disapproved, but were forced to accept. To the states, which have seen their sovereignty nibbled away by court and congressional mandates, the EPA cases may be a rare chance to recapture the once respected tradition of local control.

117

Massachusetts Cities, Towns Begin to Face Growing Fiscal Crisis

* * *

Moody's Says State Must Find Funds or Municipalities' Bond Ratings Will Suffer

By MITCHELL C. LYNCH

Staff Reporter of THE WALL STREET JOURNAL

BOSTON—The Massachusetts fiscal crisis deepened as the troubled cities and towns got some unusual help in their bid to pressure the state legislature for bailout money.

In a strange turn of events, Moody's Investors Service Inc. suspended its debt rating on 37 municipalities and seven regional school districts. The bond-rating company indicated that if the state doesn't relent and provide the money by the time the fiscal year begins July 1, Moody's would downgrade those ratings so that municipal borrowing would be prohibitively high.

State officials figure that all 351 cities and towns borrow more than $2 billion annually, much of it this time of year for cash needed as they await the inflow of new tax receipts. The state, itself, they emphasized, doesn't face any inordinate fiscal problems, and its role in the municipalities' crisis involves the amount of money it channels back to the cities and towns.

The crisis is caused by Proposition 2½, a referendum approved by voters last fall that puts a tight limit on the amount of money a municipality can raise through property and excise taxes. It also would limit spending increases to 2½% a year.

Authorities figure the measure would cost municipalities $500 million in tax money in the coming fiscal year. Gov. Edward King showed he wasn't going to nullify the effects of the tax and spending lids when he asked the legislature to increase funds to the municipalities by only $37 million.

Faced with the $463 million shortage, towns and cities already are closing some schools, firing teachers and public-works employes and threatening to reduce the number of police and firemen. The city of Quincy, for example, is releasing more than 250 teachers and closing four schools. Boston, reeling from the effects of a current fiscal crisis, may have to close its schools in April and Mayor Kevin White is talking about "bankruptcy."

The measure is called Proposition 2½ because eventually it would limit the amount raised by property taxes to 2½% of the fair market value of real estate in the municipalities. Spending is to be cut 15% a year until it reaches that level and then property tax increases would be held to 2½% a year.

Many municipalities were relieved that Moody's decided to suspend the ratings rather than lower them. Many officials said they would delay borrowing rather than to pay higher amounts for borrowing money in the market. The lower a rating, the higher the price municipalities must pay buyers of the debt.

The Proposition 2½ spending limit includes debt costs as well as operational costs.

In central Massachusetts, Worcester, the state's second biggest city, is committed to borrowing $4 million as its share of a federal matching grant for sewage-treatment facilities, said Francis McGrath, city manager. "We'll hold off for as long as we can," meaning at least until Moody's would give a rating on the issue, he said.

Cambridge, which already has plans to lay off 800 city employes, including 350 teachers, faces the prospect of "paying an arm and a leg" for borrowing $15 million until its tax receipts come in, said George E. O'Brien, assistant city manager. He said Cambridge's work force would be slashed 20% and its $144 million budget would be cut $14 million because of lower property and excise taxes. Mr. O'Brien said the city mightn't be able to delay the $15 million tax-anticipation borrowing.

Proposition 2½ reduces automobile excise taxes about 40%.

In western Massachusetts, Springfield will delay borrowing $5 million in the market for public-works projects, that city said.

At the State House, Robert McLain, secretary for administration and finance, termed Moody's action "logical." He said a cabinet committee met with Moody's executives and as a result "Wall Street felt better."

Boston said it may be forced to close its schools because of a severe cash shortage and the fact that the school committee is spending far beyond its budget. For the first time, Mayor White is talking of "bankruptcy" unless the state legislature decides to appropriate far more money to Boston.

Born Again?

Big Old Cities of East, Midwest Are Reviving After Years of Decline

Population Drain Is Halting; Culture, Cheap Housing Lure Middle Class Back

But Federal Aid May Shrink

By Frederick C. Klein
Staff Reporter of The Wall Street Journal

Not long ago a visitor from Europe looked out over Chicago from the 94th-floor observatory of the John Hancock building and remarked that it resembled an ancient Oriental rug: bright and busy in some places, worn and bare in others.

The bare spots on the face of Chicago and other older American cities began to develop in the middle 1950s, when people and firms started to leave the crowded metropolises in search of the space and greenery of the suburbs then abuilding. By the early 1970s, mounting urban racial strife and crime had turned the exodus into a rout, leaving behind vast areas of abandoned houses, apartment buildings and factories.

Between 1960 and 1976, the combined populations of the dozen largest cities of the U.S. East and Midwest—New York, Chicago, Philadelphia, Detroit, Baltimore, Washington, Milwaukee, Cleveland, Boston, St. Louis, Kansas City and Pittsburgh—dropped by 11.5%, with more than two-thirds of that loss coming in the last six years of the period.

Vanishing Cities?

St. Louis, Cleveland, Pittsburgh and Detroit each suffered population declines of 13% or more from 1970 through 1976, and analysts note somewhat wryly that if their losses continued at that rate, they would be virtually uninhabited by the beginning of the 21st Century.

But now, as the federal government tabulates the 1980 census, many city officials and students of urban affairs believe that the big-city population drain has slowed markedly and perhaps even been reversed in a few places, including Washington and Boston. Interestingly, many of the experts credit the losses of the 1960s and 1970s with setting the stage for the turnaround.

"Conditions seem more fruitful for a genuine urban resurgence than they have in the last 20 years," asserts Norman Krumholz, head of the Center for Neighborhood Development at Cleveland State University. He is the former director of the planning commission in that city, where the population has fallen to below 600,000 from 876,000 in 1980.

Mr. Krumholz says that until recently he was a "consistent naysayer" on big-city prospects, but he says it is "possible now to see the end of the population hemorrhage and the reintroduction of stability into many aspects of urban life."

More Per Person

Martin Murray, acting commissioner of planning in Chicago, agrees. He notes that building abandonments in Chicago over the last two decades have allowed the accumulation of land parcels "that permit serious, large-scale new developments, some of which already are under way." He adds, "The basic facilities that supported a population of 3.5 million here in 1960 are still in place to support our three million people. Companies and individuals are beginning to realize the advantages of that."

This, of course, isn't to say that an urban millennium is at hand. All the problems of the 1960s and '70s still plague the cities to some extent, and their solution has been hampered by the loss of municipal tax dollars caused by the flight of the white middle class; only partially replaced by lower-income minority-group members. Most of the back-to-the-city movement that has occurred consists of young adults without children and older couples whose children are grown, reflecting the low estate of public education in many older cities.

But observers see several trends that could stimulate a broader new interest in city living in the years just ahead. One of these is a decline in urban crime. According to the Federal Bureau of Investigation, which compiles national crime statistics, the crime in cities of 250,000 or more residents fell by 6.1% between 1975 and 1978, the last year for which detailed figures are available, after rising steadily through the 1960s and '70s. An FBI spokesman attributes the drop at least partly to lower urban populations. (However, tentative FBI figures for 1979 show a slight increase in urban crime.)

New Funds Set

Big cities also have fared well in official Washington in recent years—at least until budget-cutting fever struck President Carter and Congress in the last few months. Federal spending for urban mass-transit systems has been generous, and the Carter administration began a program to rehabilitate older city buildings instead of tearing them down and erecting new ones, a process that had destroyed many inner-city neighborhoods.

Federal mass-transit spending jumped from $984 million in 1974 to $3.6 billion during the current fiscal year, and more new funds are earmarked for that purpose in the "windfall profits" tax on oil companies. In the fiscal year ended June 30 last year, 38,027 housing units were rehabilitated with federal help, up from 2,359 units five years earlier.

Perhaps most important, though, has been the fact that increases in big-city rents and home and land prices didn't nearly match those of most suburbs during the 1970s, making city living a relative bargain. (There are exceptions. Rents in Manhattan are sky-high. But there is no shortage of apartment seekers there.)

During the 1970s, the rent component of the U.S. Labor Department's Consumer Price Index rose by about 60%, far narrower than the greater-than-90% increase in home purchase prices and the cost of living as a whole. U.S. median family income about doubled in the decade.

The city-suburban gap in home prices can be even wider. In parts of just about every large city of the East and Midwest, three-bedroom brick homes can be had for between $40,000 and $50,000, against a typical range of $60,000 to $80,000 in nearby suburbs. "The point seems to be arriving where those differences will lure families back to the city," notes Anthony Downs, a senior fellow at the Brookings Institution in Washington who specializes in analyzing real-estate trends. "When you throw in the rising cost of auto fuel, the attraction becomes even stronger."

In some cities, the housing reversal already is under way; Boston, for instance, gained housing units during the 1970s, after losing them in the previous decade. In others, such as Chicago, Cleveland and St. Louis, the rate of abandonment is down sharply from the early 1970s.

Changes in urban land-use patterns have opened new areas to housing in some cities; the widespread conversion of warehouse loft buildings to apartments in New York is one example. In Chicago, a large tract of land just south of the central "Loop," once used as a railroad marshaling yard, is being turned into an apartment and townhouse complex that builders hope will house some 30,000 people by 1990. Almost 1,000 housing units have been completed on the site, and most are sold or rented.

Cozier Commuting

Observers further assert that the decrease in big-city population has improved the quality of urban life in some respects. An obvious one is a reduction in commuting time in a few places. Cleveland's Mr. Krumholz says a 10-mile trip to downtown Cleveland from almost any direction takes about 20 minutes at rush hour now, quite a bit less than it did when the city had 200,000 more residents. "And that's on city streets—not on any new expressway," he says.

A good part of the drop in urban population has stemmed from a general reduction in the size of the American family over the last two decades, and this has brought a welcome lower population density to many city areas. In Baltimore, about 50,000 persons now occupy 18,000 public-housing units, or fewer than three persons a unit; 10 years ago the average was more than four persons a unit.

"There's less noise in public housing buildings, crime is down, and the parks and playgrounds are less crowded," says Jay Brodie, Baltimore's commissioner of housing and community development. "Public housing here is more livable than it used to be."

Old Battleground

The decrease in population density has had another important effect: a general easing of the pressure for racial change—and an increase in stability—in many older urban neighborhoods. This is reflected in general ways, such as the increase in the membership of the six-year-old National Association of Neighborhood Organizations, a Washington-based lobbying group, to 350 local units from about 200 at the beginning of 1979. "Stability helps breed organization, and we're seeing organizations in neighborhoods that never had them before," notes Milton Kotler, the group's executive secretary.

It also is reflected in particular areas, such as the southwest side of Chicago. This was a battleground of racial change in the middle and late 1960s, when blacks marched to protest housing discrimination and whites first angrily massed against them, then moved out in droves.

Now the scene has cooled appreciably, and the area is making something of a comeback. At 63rd Street and Western Avenue, in the heart of the area, merchants have just spent some $4.5 million to renovate their offices and stores. The neighborhood to the east of that intersection has changed from all-white to mostly black in the last 10 years, but it has retained its middle-class character. Housing demand by whites lately has perked up in the western section of the area after a long decline.

"A lot of things went into the change, including legal moves that halted panic peddling by real-estate salesmen; but the relaxation of sheer population pressure certainly helped," says James Caprano, head of a local community-development group there.

Finally, cultural and night life have brightened considerably in the downtowns of several large, older cities as a result of the recent influx of the young single people and couples who demand such services. Washington, Boston and Pittsburgh are among the cities in this category.

This aspect of the back-to-the-city movement has been greeted skeptically by some observers who believe that the young adults will follow earlier patterns and leave for the suburbs once they begin their families. But others see in it the opportunity for a more thoroughgoing upgrading of city life.

"All indications are that the young people who've moved near the downtowns like it there and would like to stay when they start having children," says George Grier, a population researcher and analyst who has followed closely the back-to-the-city movement in Washington.

"The present trend has maybe 10 more years to run. If city governments can get their acts together in that time and provide the schools and other things that will enable the newcomers to stay, we'll see a real city renaissance."

---

119 *March 19, 1981*

Balancing Act

New York's Finances Improve—but at Cost Of a Decline in Services

Budget Surplus Seen, but City Must Find Funds to Stem Crime, Slide in Subways

Moody's Mood Remains Sour

By Daniel Hertzberg

Staff Reporter of The Wall Street Journal

NEW YORK—Back in 1975, many Americans figured this city had taken the A Train straight for bankruptcy court.

The nation's biggest, brashest metropolis —ever the bellwether—was the first of the large Northern cities to crumble under the weight of urban decay and fiscal irresponsibility. After decades of living beyond its means, New York's *annual* deficit was approaching $2 billion. Middle-class taxpayers were fleeing in droves: The city had lost 600,000 jobs in six years, or more than the population of Buffalo, the state's second-largest city. To repay city debts and stay afloat, New York officials had to slink to Washington for a bailout in the form of short-term loans and federal guarantees for city bonds.

The intervening years saw an austere retrenchment, and lately the dark clouds that have hung so long over the famed Manhattan skyline have begun to lift. The city's budget—now that the tangled bookkeeping has been unraveled—is balanced for the first time in recent memory. New York should finish the current fiscal year with a budget surplus exceeding $200 million.

Moreover, the local economy, which nose-dived in the early 1970s, has rebounded briskly. Employment is on the rise, retail sales surged 16% last year, and the Manhattan real-estate market is booming. This recovery, together with galloping inflation, has swollen city tax coffers, further easing the fiscal crunch.

"Relative" Stability

"The worst of the pain is behind us," declares New York's flamboyant Mayor Edward I. Koch, adding that he believes the city is entering a "period of relative fiscal stability."

But even the ebullient Mayor Koch concedes that the stability is a precarious one, accomplished at a huge price. Basic city services, once the model for urban areas across the nation, have been slashed to the point of breakdown. About a quarter of the 300,000 jobs on the city's bloated payroll were eliminated, including 20% of its police force, 19,000 teachers and 2,000 of its 2,500 street sweepers. Evidence of the cutbacks is everywhere: The streets are blanketed with garbage. Robberies, to name but one crime, are at an all-time high. The subway system is near collapse, plagued by aging equipment, vandalism, and frequent breakdowns and derailments.

"The fiscal crisis has become a service crisis," says the Citizens Budget Commission, a private watchdog group.

Nor does the brightening fiscal and economic picture portend a speedy return to the halcyon—if ruinous—days of abundant services. "It doesn't mean the city is going to return to service levels of the early 1970s," warns George Roniger, a Citibank economist.

A Decade of Neglect

For one thing, in the aftermath of a decade of neglect, New York is in critical need of refurbishment. Repairing the lamentable transit system—as well as rusting bridges, pothole-pocked roads and a water-supply system that now leaks 100 million gallons a day—will cost $40 billion over the next decade, the city comptroller's office estimates. (Current plans call for spending $30 billion in city, state and federal funds over that period for capital improvements, $15 billion of which is to come from public bond offerings by the city.)

If the repairs aren't made, it could undermine all the progress made thus far. Mass transit is a case in point: Though New York's Gov. Hugh L. Carey has proposed spending $5 billion in state and other funds to repair New York's bus and subway system—and though a fare increase this summer is a virtual certainty—the system's salvation isn't ensured. Subway ridership has been declining steadily, and the combined bus and subway system faces a $150 million deficit in the coming fiscal year. "If the subway goes down the flue, it will sink the city," observes David H. Troob, a senior vice president of Shearson Loeb Rhoades Inc., a large New York securities firm.

Moody Blues

Comer S. Coppie, executive director of the Financial Control Board, the state agency that has overseen the city's finances since 1975, cautions that New York's current rebound must be viewed in perspective. Its problems may no longer be "extraordinary," he says, but now New York is joining the ranks of Chicago, Detroit, Cleveland "and other older cities that have difficulties in maintaining recurring budget balance." Already, he says, $733 million in spending increases written into the fiscal 1982 budget —mainly to hire more police and sanitation workers—is outpacing revenue increases. And, he adds, proposed Reagan administration cuts in the federal budget—particularly those affecting mass transit—"complicate the situation even more." Mayor Koch says those cuts would cost the city $353 million in federal aid next year.

Moreover, New York is still saddled with a financing crisis. Later this month, it plans to reenter the long-term credit market for the first time since 1975, with a proposed sale of $75 million of long-term bonds. Prospects for this sale were bolstered when Standard & Poor's Corp., a major credit-rating agency, recently raised the city's securities to a triple-B rating, thus deeming them a moderately good risk. However, Moody's Investor Service, the other major rating agency, is less sanguine about the city's credit-worthiness. On Tuesday it announced it would stick with its single-B rating of city bonds, a speculative rating equivalent to a corporate "junk bond." Moody's cited New York's "underlying economic weakness, costly service demands and revenue inadequacies" in explaining its decision.

Even a successful bond sale this month won't come close to meeting New York's mammoth long-term financing needs, estimated at $1 billion annually. The city hopes for a gradual reentry into the bond market, with full access by 1985. But the process could take much longer, underwriters say. In the meantime, New York is staying solvent through sales of federally guaranteed bonds and borrowings by the state's Municipal Assistance Corp.

Other cities will be watching closely to see whether New York surmounts these obstacles. The city's fiscal crisis reverberated through the municipal bond market, and ever since, investors have demanded more detailed financial disclosure from state and local governments.

The New York debacle also "called into question all the postulates of blind social welfarism," according to George Sternlieb, director of Rutgers University's Center for Urban Policy Research. It "was a first signal of the whole process that has culminated in Mr. Reagan's budget cuts," he adds.

Though undeniable hurdles remain, New York has made huge strides toward long-term solvency. With spending and revenues in better balance, the fiscal outlook "is more promising than it has been in a long time," says Sidney Schwartz, the deputy state comptroller who monitors the city's financial performance.

Few would argue that Mayor Koch deserves part of the credit for the turnaround. Elected in 1977, he has held New York's spending increases below the general inflation rate and has balanced the $14.8 billion municipal budget a year ahead of schedule. Mr. Koch, who doesn't hesitate to label his detractors "dummies," says his policies are simply "common sense." He is ebulliently running for reelection in a race that so far has produced no opposition candidates.

A Tax Windfall

The mayor also has had a lot of help, as is evident from figures supplied by Mr. Schwartz, the state watchdog. For one thing, New York has been the beneficiary of a vast, inflation-generated tax windfall. During Mr. Koch's four years in office, the city has experienced nearly 50% growth—equal to an additional $1 billion annually—in inflation-sensitive sales, income and business-tax revenues. (Expenses, too, have risen, but not as sharply. Municipal labor costs, which together with pensions, account for 50% of the current budget, have lagged behind inflation. Contracts are up for negotiation again next year, however, and officials fear that salary demands may wipe out some revenue gains.)

In addition, the bustling real-estate market in Manhattan—where property values have risen some 40% in two years—will net the city treasury an extra $125 million in real-estate taxes next year, according to Mr. Schwartz.

And at the same time that the city has been reaping extra revenues, the state has relieved it of some of its more burdensome costs, including court administration and higher education. If the legislature approves Gov. Carey's recent offer to have the state gradually assume the city's share of Medicaid costs, the combined savings for the city should total $1.5 billion annually by 1985.

Unlike other U.S. cities, New York pays 25% of its Medicaid costs, a $750 million annual bill that, in Mayor Koch's words, was "breaking our back." A state takeover of Medicaid, together with continued strength in the city economy, "would ensure the stability of the city from a financial point of view," asserts Felix G. Rohatyn, head of the state's Municipal Assistance Corp.

Finally, the city budget was made easier to balance by a restructuring and "stretch-out" of the city's debt, which has lowered annual debt-service payments by $600 million from the 1977 level.

Economic Resurgence

New York's newfound fiscal health is inextricably linked to the resurgence of its local economy. During the early 1970s, the profligate spending mood at City Hall was matched in the private sector, observes Citibank's Mr. Roniger. Skyscrapers had been erected with little thought to future demand, and some 30 million square feet of office space languished vacant. The financial industry vastly overexpanded during the flush of the late-1960s bull market. Wages soared to new heights, way out of kilter with the rest of the nation. New York was "pricing itself out of the market," Mr. Roniger says. The city lost more than 100,000 jobs during the 1969 recession and another 200,000 in the 1973-1975 downturn.

In the past three years however, New York has gained 110,000 new jobs. More than half of the gain came in service-related businesses—such as advertising, consulting, law, and data processing—that are less vulnerable to recession than manufacturing. Foreign firms have also flocked to Manhattan in recent years.

New York weathered the brief 1980 recession better than most large cities, gaining 20,000 jobs. The total employment gain of about 3% in three years still is trifling compared with booming Sun Belt cities. But, Mr. Roniger says, it represents a "very dramatic" departure from the job losses of the recent past.

Rising employment helped ignite the real-estate market in midtown Manhattan. The office vacancy rate, a woeful 15% in 1972, has declined to about 3%, according to a Chase Manhattan Bank survey. (The reduction was accomplished despite the addition of some 15 million square feet of office space in the interim.) Moreover, an acute housing shortage has pushed rents on the fashionable East Side to well over $1,000 monthly for a two-bedroom apartment.

The Outer Boroughs

Keeping this economy stoked will be a herculean task for city officials. Even now, the revival is largely confined to Manhattan. "The city of the outer boroughs is falling apart," says Rutgers' Mr. Sternlieb. And New York is still seen by many big corporations as inhospitable; its wages, rents, and taxes remain high relative to the rest of the nation. The much-publicized departure of companies based here continues: 19 major concerns, including Singer Co. and American Airlines, left between 1976 and 1979, according to a Chase Manhattan Bank study. To help curb the exodus, New York State in the past few years has enacted tax cuts on corporate and individual income amounting to $2.3 billion a year.

And so the delicate juggling act continues: To sustain economic growth, city services must be upgraded—without, of course, veering back into deficit financing. May or Koch insists his overriding priority is maintaining strict fiscal discipline. Indeed, New York officials say they have little choice in the matter, given the slew of controls written into law since 1975. A truly balanced budget, for example, now is required under law. And the Financial Control Board will retain its oversight powers until New York returns fully to the long-term credit market and manages the refunding of all outstanding federally guaranteed bonds.

If a chastened New York has done much to polish its tarnished reputation, it has only begun to regain the confidence of the financial community, upon which its future finally rests. To obtain stable, long-term financing, New York must show that it can consistently maintain a balanced budget, says Jac Friedgut, a Citibank vice president who follows city finances. "And backsliding," he warns, "will be interpreted by the market as a possible return to . . . fiscal irresponsibility."

Bad Times Are Here For Good Old Boys Caught in a Dragnet

* * *

Kickback Inquiry Threatens Two-Thirds of Oklahoma's 231 County Commissioners

By Roger Thurow

Staff Reporter of The Wall Street Journal

GEARY, Okla.—Robert Petticrew shoves a wad of chewing tobacco into his mouth as he ponders the mess he's in. After admitting to taking kickbacks from road-material suppliers while serving as Blaine County commissioner for the past nine years, he's facing the possibility of jail and a big fine.

"It's a hell of a way for an old boy to end his life," he says with a sigh, punctuating his disgust by spitting into a tobacco-stained tin can. Sixty-nine years old and scarred by the corruption scandal, Mr. Petticrew realizes that there isn't much left he can do with his life, "except dying, I guess." He spits again.

Halfway across the state in the little town of Farris, Dorothy Griffin faces an equally grim future. "I'm just a dumb old country woman standing out here in my bare feet," she says, "but I do know that you don't do wrong and get by." For years she did do wrong: writing more than $1 million of phony invoices for nonexistent transactions between suppliers and county commissioners, stashing them in garbage bags and hiding them in her lumber barn.

Rather Talk Football

Neither did she, along with many others, get by. A three-year investigation by a trio of federal agencies has revealed that for decades county commissioners have been routinely taking kickbacks from suppliers—10% when materials were delivered and 50% on fake deals when no goods were delivered. At last count, about 100 people had signed (as did Mr. Petticrew and Mrs. Griffin) agreements to plead guilty and to cooperate with the investigation, or had been convicted. By the time they are through, investigators expect to round up about 250 people in all. That includes about two-thirds of the state's 231 county commissioners, who administer courthouse budgets and spend the county tax revenue, most of which goes to maintaining roads. "The totals change almost hourly," says assistant U.S. Attorney William Price, whose office is cluttered with files on everyone ensnarled in the case.

For Oklahoma the episode is an "embarrassing and shameful situation," scolds Democratic Gov. George Nigh. "Right now it's a black eye on Oklahoma," he says. "I'd rather talk about football."

But by no means is county corruption confined to Oklahoma. The investigation here has already seeped across the Red River into northeast Texas, where two commissioners have pleaded guilty and nine others have been indicted. Also, separate investigations have recently uncovered courthouse corruption in Tennessee, Alabama and Arkansas, where 17 of the state's 75 county judges (similar to Oklahoma's commissioners) have been convicted of being on the take.

Grassroots Crisis

These widespread exposures of corruption are shaking the traditional grassroots foundation of county government and may give momentum to a reform movement that has been sabotaged since the turn of the century by the politically mighty commissioners. "This could cause a real crisis of government, since the commissioners are the closest elected officials to the people," says Oklahoma state Sen. John Clifton. "After all, there's something to be said for the citizen living on an unpaved road to have some access to the guy who gets him in and out of the mud." That's what government is all about in many rural parts of the country, as about 2,300 of the 3,105 counties in the U.S. still cling to some form of the age-old commissioner system.

Over the years, county commissioners have parlayed these sturdy grass-roots ties to the voters into considerable political power. Individually, a commissioner who knows all his constituents by their first names can be a powerful vote-deliverer for state office seekers, and, as a group, the commissioners line up as a formidable lobbying force, stifling most attempts to diminish their influence.

James Howard Edmondson, Oklahoma's reform-minded governor of two decades ago, tried to take away much of the commissioners' road-building power and put it in state hands. Commissioners swarmed the state capitol in Oklahoma City, and his legislation never had a chance. Neither did his further political ambitions in the state. "It caused his total administration to go down the tubes," says Gov. Nigh, who was the lieutenant governor at the time.

It may be 20 years too late, but in the wake of the corruption scandal, some change seems inevitable. The clamor for reform intensifies each time another commissioner resigns, worrying those who are comfortable with the chummy way of life the commissioner setup fosters.

"If the state takes things over, we'll never get anything done in little rural places like this," frets Oren Kennedy, a farmer who lives in Calumet along with 385 other people.

The offices of many Oklahoma commissioners have evolved into tiny replicas of the old big-city machines. The counties are divided into three districts, and each commissioner has his own patronage plums to dispense, usually with little interference from his colleagues. It's commonplace, for instance, for a commissioner to order that county machinery, on the way to repair a county bridge, also be used to patch up a pothole in a farmer's driveway or to blacktop a church parking lot. Or, if someone can't find a job, the commissioner can dole out a spot on the county road crew. It all pays off on election day.

The pattern that evolved in Oklahoma is staggering in its scope. Mrs. Griffin's invoices for nonexistent material have been traced to items sold to 57 commissioners, representing 29 counties. Guy Moore, who operated a company supplying road and bridge material, has testified that in the 28 years he dealt with Oklahoma commissioners, only three refused his kickbacks, which, during that time, added up to more than $1 million.

Many Oklahomans had an inkling of some under-the-table dealing in their courthouses, but, generally, as long as their roads were in good shape, whatever the old boys did was fine with them. "It's something that's been winked at a long time," says Jackie W. Parker, a barber in El Reno, the seat of Canadian County, where all three commissioners have been forced to resign. "Some of those guys would go into the job flat broke, and you could watch them progress economically." Betty Eisenhour, the Canadian County clerk, says sometimes that progress was amazing, considering the commissioners in the county were drawing a salary of $991 a month (they just got a raise to about $1,500 a month). "They'd come into office with nothing," she says, "and leave with everything: Lincolns, Cadillacs, farms, businesses, land, racehorses."

Even now, though upset that their tax dollars were being wasted all these years, many of the people living alongside country roads aren't laying heavy blame on their commissioners. "It's the old case of 'well, he may be a son of a bitch, but at least he's our son of a bitch,'" says an aide to the governor.

In Madill, the seat of Marshall County, Ed Benton was admired by his constituents throughout his 28 years as a commissioner, and his resignation and agreement to plead guilty in the kickback scandal haven't changed a thing. "I didn't know Ed had his hand out, but he's still my friend," says Willie Morgan, a veteran oil-field hand. "Hell, you don't knock a guy down for doing something like this. Anytime I needed something done, I'd call Ed and he'd come do it."

Mr. Petticrew has done some good, too. For instance, there are those two river bridges he built so the farmers' machinery wouldn't have to slosh through the water anymore. "That machinery's too expensive to be driving it through water," he says. "Not to be bragging on myself, but I've served the people well. This district is in the best financial shape it's ever been in."

Mr. Petticrew is a typical good-old-boy commissioner. He has lived around Blaine County all his life. He knows all 1,500 voters in his district by their first names, and they call him Shorty. He's in charge of maintaining 514 miles of road, and he's familiar with every curve and dip on them. Driving his dusty pickup truck down one of those dirt roads, he's trying to understand where the system went wrong.

Mr. Petticrew admits that taking kickbacks was wrong, but he finds it easy to rationalize the practice. "It's the supplier sharing his profits," he says. "If the old boy wants to share some of his profit with you and you don't take it, then he keeps it all.

"It's just too bad I'm the one who has to be in office now," he adds, "when all this has been going on for 50 or 75 years."

He can blame the timing on Mrs. Griffin. Investigators didn't have much to go on until the Internal Revenue Service checked out discrepancies in her tax returns about two years ago. Under questioning from the agents, she laid out the details of how suppliers like herself and county commissioners had been rigging phony deals for years. The Federal Bureau of Investigation wired her up and sent her out to try to implicate those she dealt with. She made 110 tapes. Since then the case has snowballed.

"I hope people understand," she says. "Something needed to be done."

Mrs. Griffin, a squat, pleasant woman, hardly looks like someone who could get wrapped up in a million-dollar fraud. She started selling lumber supplies from the back of an old hay wagon in 1963, and when her husband later started having heart problems, she began working the deals with the commissioners to make more money. "All these bills were stacking up," she says. "We're just poor country folks. We didn't know what we were getting into. But ignorance is no excuse."

These days, Mrs. Griffin keeps a sharp lookout for any traffic on the dirt road in front of her house. So do her two dogs. The FBI and the IRS have been frequent visitors, and she says she never knows whom to expect next. "Some of my friends haven't stopped by in a long time," she says, "because they're afraid some FBI people might be around."